York

1900 t

A. J. Peacock

YORK SETTLEMENT TRUST

York

1900 to 1914

A. J. Peacock

YORK SETTLEMENT TRUST

YORK 1900 TO 1914

VOLUME ONE OF A
TWO VOLUME
HISTORY OF YORK
FROM 1900 TO 1918

Keyed in by   PIP STEVENS

Cover design and
illustrations by   BRIAN KESTEVEN

ISBN 0 9519229 0 4

Published by   The York Settlement Trust,
126 Holgate Road,
YORK YO2 4DL.

Printed by   G. H. Smith & Son,
The Printers,
Easingwold,
YORK YO6 3AB.

FOREWORD

This book is the first of two volumes on York from 1900 to the end of the Great War and it is published by the York Settlement Trust. This is an educational charity set up with the residue of the estate of the York Educational Settlement, an adult education centre established during the period covered in this volume and dealt with at some length in these pages. The Trust hope to publish more volumes on York history (and other subjects perhaps) in the future. I am very grateful to the Trustees for their help and encouragement.

My primary source materials for this work are the newspapers published in York and I am everlastingly in the debt of the staff of the York Reference Library who have been extraordinarily helpful in allowing me access to their archives and helping with innumerable queries. I have chosen to give references primarily to the two most important of the York papers for two reasons: the first is that they are the most easily accessible to readers; the second is that they (dailies) are simply the best papers (the *Gazette* is a weekly).

Finally, I must thank Brian Kesteven for designing the cover for this volume and the drawings of York politicians, and Pip Stevens for preparing the text. I hope they like the finished project (at least a little).

A.J. PEACOCK

ILLUSTRATIONS

J. G. Butcher

J. M. Hogge

J. R. Inglis

Fred Morley

William Bentley

Henry Rhodes Brown

Oscar Rowntree

S. W. M. Meyer

W. Boddy

All redrawn from contemporary illustrations by
Brian Kesteven

CONTENTS

VOLUME 1
YORK 1900 TO 1914

VOLUME 2
YORK IN THE GREAT WAR: 1914-18

CONTENTS

CHAPTER 1

THE TURN OF THE CENTURY

At the beginning of the 19th century York had been a small, depressed place with seemingly no future; at the beginning of the 20th century it was, of course, much larger, was a major rail centre and was famous for its manufacturing industries. The newspapers began the year with predictable, seasonal greetings, but without those in-depth surveys of the preceeding century which one might have expected. Why was this? One reason may have been because there 'was a war on', and it is a fact that the reader of the press of the early months of 1900, who is also interested in the Great War of 1914-18, will experience an uncanny feeling of *deja vu*. The papers were filled with accounts of troops leaving for the front and returning wounded; of community efforts to get comforts for them like balaclavas; of letters from men at the front telling of the storming of Boer trenches; and atrocity stories intended to discredit the country's enemies. At that stage of the war the conflict was popular and the jingoism of 1900 (well into the struggle) was very like that of August 1914 and the popularity of the war was about to be argued over and tested in York, because there was an election pending.

York was a two-Member parliamentary constituency and had been throughout the 19th century - though its representation had seemed to be threatened on occasion. (1) Usually, in the early years of the century, the city had split, returning one Liberal and one Tory and this had been the case even during the time when York was under the Tory 'thraldom' of George Hudson's time. In the 1880s, however, two Gladstonian Liberals were returned, but a decade later representation was again split between the two major parties. The Liberal was the extremely popular Frank Lockwood, QC, (2) and he died while in office in 1898. At the ensuing by election the Tories achieved a remarkable victory when Lord Charles Beresford beat Christopher Furness, by a margin of only eleven votes (5,559:5,648).

Beresford (1846-1919) was a sailor who in March 1861 'was appointed to the *Marlborough* flagship in the Mediterranean and one of the finest of the old battleships.' In 1863 he was transferred to the *Defence*, an ironclad, and subsequently served on a number of famous ships including the royal yacht *Victoria and Albert*. In 1882 he was in command of the gunboat that bombarded Alexandria, (3) and returned home and went on half-pay shortly afterwards. Beresford was then appointed to the staff of Lord Wolseley during the expedition to relieve Khartoum and commanded the naval brigade which took part in the battle of Abu Klea in January 1885.

Beresford had been MP for Waterford between 1874 and 1880 and in July 1885 (and in 1886) he was elected as a Tory for East Marylebone. Beresford was an intimate friend of the Prince of Wales who had urged Lord Salisbury, the Prime Minister, to give

1

him high political office.   Salisbury had 'preferred' to appoint him as fourth naval lord of the Admiralty under Lord George Hamilton - a wise decision, it seems, as Beresford, in the words of the *Dictionary of National Biography*, 'proved a difficult colleague and ... hostile to the policy of the Board' of Admiralty and an objector to the 'supreme authority of the first lord in naval administration.' In January 1888 Beresford resigned office and 'For the next two years was a constant and outspoken critic of naval affairs in the ... Commons.' In late 1889 Beresford was appointed to command the *Undaunted* cruiser in the Mediterranean, and he resigned his seat in Parliament - something he did no less than four times during his career. (4)

Beresford returned to Britain in mid 1893 to take charge of the Medway dockyard reserve and four years later he was appointed aide-de-camp to Queen Victoria. In 1898 (not in 1887 as the *DNB* said) (5) Beresford won York for the Tories at that remarkable by election. In January 1890 he ('to the general public the best-known sailor of his day') resigned his seat when sent again to the Mediterranean as second in command to Sir John Fisher, someone with whom he had a celebrated, prolonged and acrimonious relationship. (6)

By New Year's day the York Tories had chosen their candidate to replace Beresford. On 1 January the *Evening Press* announced that the two wings of the party - the York Conservative Association and the York Liberal Unionist Association - had decided to recommend George Denison Faber to a selection conference. Who was he ? He was 'one of the great Denison clan, of which Lord Grimthorpe must ... be regarded as the present chief.' (7) He was under 50 years of age; had been Registrar of Privy Councils from 1887-96; was married to a Netherby Graham; and had inherited a large fortune from Andrew Montagu of Ingmanthorpe Hall near Wetherby. (8) Faber was adopted and addressed the selection conference dealing, mainly, with the war but mentioning also the issue of trades disputes (urging conciliation instead of striking) and the need for technical education. ('That is where the Germans beat us'.) (9)

Things never went as easy for the Liberals as they did for the Tories and to begin with they tried to get their candidate of 1898 again, but Furness had promised the Liberals of Hartlepool that he would stand there at a general election. He dithered and wrote to Henry Tennant, who had presided over the conference which decided to invite him, saying that as the Tories had snatched the 'Liberal' seat when Lockwood died, moves should be made to get a Liberal candidate 'acceptable' to the Conservatives, then he should be let in without a contest, and a 'proper contest should take place at the next general election. What he meant by an acceptable Liberal is difficult to understand as (as always) that party was split, with, at this time, the major cause of the rifts being the war. Furness probably meant the party should choose a supporter of the war effort, but had it done this dissidents would almost certainly have found and probably run a 'pro-Boer', and in any case the Tories would never have agreed to give up the first chance they had in the 20th century of registering support for the government when success must have looked certain. The *Evening Press* nicely indicated Liberal problems and splits among them and the current dilemma of people like Furness. That person was dithering, the *Press* reported on 5 January, and what he denounced in 1898 as jingoism now found some favour in his eyes. ('He now blesses that which he previously anathematised'.) This was enough to bring him into disfavour with a section of the Liberal party in York, it went on, though another section would applaud the course he was in fact advising - 'support for the Government in the conduct of the war in South Africa.'

Furness was held to his promise by the Liberals of Hartlepool, and following his refusal to stand it was reported that some York Liberals favoured allowing the Tories a walk-over, while others spoke of the 'candidature of Mr. Lever of Sunlight soap fame.' Eventually, however, a candidate was found. He was 30 year old Alexander Murray, the Master of Elibank. He was to have the services of K.E.T. Wilkinson, a solicitor, as his agent, and the night before his adoption conference stayed at Studley Royal with Lord Ripon, his former chief at the Colonial Office. On 23 January 1900 the *Press* reported that Murray had been adopted at a meeting at which from those present it chose to mention J. Bowes Morrell and Arnold Rowntree. (The paper that reported that Murray was at Studley Royal also told its readers that Beresford was in York as the guest of a formidable lady called Edith Harriet Milner, at Heworth. Much more will be heard of Edith.)

Murray (10) gave his views on political matters to Rowntree and the rest of the audience, and his speech shows that he intended to conduct his campaign dealing with a comprehensive series of issues - something his opponents had no intention of letting him do. Murray told his party that he wanted the registration law reformed, contending that the present system effectively disenfranchised many working men. He also wanted the powers of the House of Lords curtailed and was for taxing unearned land values. Asked about vivisection Murray said he supported it, and, inevitably, he was questioned about his attitude to the licensed trade. Was he in favour of licensing clubs, he was asked, and did he favour 16 or 18 as the age at which one could legally drink? To this the Master of Elibank replied that he would abide by the findings of and support legislation based on the recommendations of Lord Peel's committee - but he had not yet read them! On the war Murray said it was 'unnecessary' and could have been avoided and he dealt at some length with what he said were its causes. One, he said, 'was that we left our old traditional policy of governing South Africa through the majority of the population there, that was the Dutch and Afrikaner population.' Later Murray enlarged on some of these topics saying, for example, that he favoured one man one vote for parliamentary elections with a three month residence qualification. In addition he advocated disestablishment, was for a system of old age pensions, home rule and an eight hour day for miners. On the eight hour day he revealed during his campaign that he was not for statutory regulation of the working day in general ('he was very averse to State interference in labour'), but favoured the government, as employers,

3

setting the pattern as the Liberal government of 1892-5 had done in the arsenals and dockyards. Murray also attacked the working of the Workmen's Compensation Act, contending that the Tories had not kept their undertakings of the last general election when Arthur Balfour had promised a comprehensive compensation act but had produced one which covered only six out of 13 million workers, leaving groups like the agricultural labourers and seamen completely outside its provisions.

Murray wanted to fight the campaign on a traditional Liberal programme stressing the need for urgent social reform at home, while dealing with the war as only one issue among many, and on the war he declared himself for it, while criticising the events that had led up to it and the state of preparedness the nation had found itself in, and agreeing that the rights of British subjects in the Transvaal had to be protected. The Tories, however, he said, dealt with the war and the war only. '... he had been taken to task because he had talked about nothing but the war', said the Tory Faber. Of course he had talked about nothing but the war. There was no other topic that anybody in 'York ... cared to talk about. ... He was a war man, he might as well tell them that, out and out.'

Faber was not quite right. There were others in York interested in political issues other than the justness of the war and its objectives, but they hardly got a hearing. Faber was forced to concern himself with other topics, and he did so - but only cursorily. He was, he revealed: against the payment of MPs; he favoured a six months residence qualification for voters; believed voting rights should be on property; and was against all the polls being held on the same day ('"No ... I am not in favour of that, for it is only one man one vote in another shape."'). Faber was also continually questioned about the 'need' to extend the Workmen's Compensation Act, but was able to concentrate on the war. 'Don't rock the boat' was the essence of his message. 'The storm was raging high,' he told a gathering in Walmgate, 'The man at the wheel was the Prime Minister, Lord Salisbury ... trust the man at the wheel.' Replying to the charge from Murray that the government had been ill prepared when the war started Faber attacked a future Liberal Prime Minister. Henry Campbell-Bannerman, he said, 'was turned out of office for not providing sufficient for the army.' Earlier he had traced the train of events which had ended in conflict back to a former Liberal leader. The war was about whether the British or the Afrikaners 'should be supreme in South Africa,' he said, and the policy started by Gladstone after Majuba had been bound to end the war.

Faber, naturally, was helped by prominent Tories in his campaign, amongst whom was John George Butcher, (11) York's sitting Member. He spelled out what he thought the war was about, contending that the British Empire was at risk. Murray had said that 'the surrender that followed Majuba Hill' was 'the greatest act this country had done.' (12) That was nonsense, Butcher said, it was 'a disgraceful surrender'; it was 'one of the greatest stains ... ever placed on the British.' And 'What were [we] fighting about'? In the first place we were fighting to repel an insolent invasion of our territory by the subjects of two corrupt oligarchies in South Africa, and for British supremacy there.

We were fighting to prevent the oppression of British subjects who wanted the same rights as the Boers and to make sure that no such invasion as had occurred should happen again. But basically we were fighting to maintain 'the interests of our Empire as a whole' - if we lost the Cape, Butcher said, we should lose 'our road to India ... our road to Australia, and ... the most important coaling station for our fleet and merchant navy that we had in the world.'

Murray, inevitably labelled a pro-Boer, was forced to adopt an attitude during the election which was one of supporting the war, demanding a 'just' peace, and criticising the government for diplomatic boobs prior to the outbreak of hostilities, while desperately trying to fight on domestic issues. The Tories had no trouble whatsoever in stopping the attempt to move the debate away from international affairs, and Ralph Creyke correctly summed up the situation in York when, during the campaign, he said that 'The present was one of the most remarkable elections ... as there was no question of politics, but only the question ... of the war.' (13) Were there no dissentient voices from outside the ranks of the Tory and Liberal parties ? Did not the city's powerful Quaker community come out as opponents of the war in South Africa ? It seems not; it seems that people like Seebohm and Arnold Rowntree were content to make whatever protests they made within their party. However, there was one brief interlude during which an organisation surfaced; it aired its views - and extremely radical, almost Marxist, they were - but it got nowhere. This was the York Bye Election Peace Committee. (14)

The York Bye Election Peace Committee issued a manifesto on 16 January. 'Our national honour' it said, ' is being be-smirched, righteousness outraged, our sons slain, and our treasure wasted, to serve the sordid, money-grabbing interests of unscrupulous millionaires, mostly foreign, and gratify the ambition of an apostate Radical.' Earl Grey, the manifesto went on, had boasted that he would allow the South African mines to be worked by 'black and yellow labour', and the 'millionaires' had said that if the Transvaal Republic was defeated they would 'reduce wages 40 per cent. and add £2,000,000 yearly to their dividends.' Murray had contrasted the situation in the Transvaal with the situation at home when attempting to get a debate on electoral qualifications going, and so did the Bye Election Committee. Settlers in the Transvaal got the vote after being there for four years, it said, and then they could also vote for the equivalent of the House of Lords. ('Have the citizens of York a vote for the election of the House of Lords in England ?'). The government of the erring republic, moreover, ' keeps up wages, shortens hours to eight per day, puts taxes on the rich, and generally protects the poor, which is the real reason why we are at war with them.'

The York Bye Election Peace Committee made no impact and Murray, in the words of the Tory MP Grant Lawson, went into the election with a task like that of 'the character ... in Pilgrim's Progress, ... Mr Facing-both-ways.' Towards the end of the campaign an element of nastiness appeared in a contest which the *Evening Press* had earlier called 'one of the flattest and most devoid of incident the city had seen' when, first of all, the Tories said the Liberals were gloating over the fact that many soldiers and reservists who were at the front would be stopped from voting for Murray, and then when Henry Broadhurst said from a Liberal platform that the government (which had a majority of nearly 130) intended to issue bogus telegrams on polling day announcing the fall of Ladysmith.

Polling in York took place in the first week of February between the hours of 8 a.m. and 8 p.m. at 28 booths distributed throughout 18 districts in the city. There were 12,582 voters on the register, made up of 1,406 freemen, 10,701 occupiers and 475 lodgers. The number who polled was 11,066, with 6,248 doing so for Faber and 4,818 for Murray. News of the Tory victory arrived at the Commons while Campbell-Bannerman was putting forward his views on the war and speaking on Lord Edmund Fitzmaurice's 'amendment to the address'. It was greeted with great enthusiasm from the government benches (and the government won that vote by 352 to 139).

What was York like when Faber was returned to parliament ? During his campaign he had said that while representing a 'great patriotic sentiment' he saw 'at home a prosperous Britain, a sober Britain, a religious Britain, a simple-minded and simple-lived Britain ..., a Britain not intent on tearing up old institutions ...' Was York like that? How was it governed ?

The system of local government in York in 1900 was basically that established in 1835 by the Municipal Corporations Reform Act, introduced as a part of a package of reform measures by the Whig governments that followed the Reform Act of 1832. The boundaries had been extended since 1835, (15) but York was still divided, for municipal purposes, into six wards - Bootham, Castlegate, Monk, Walmgate, Micklegate and Guildhall. In George Hudson's time (just after the reform of 1835) municipal politics had been hectic and corrupt, but by the turn of the century, while local government had much more power than before, all the steam (and excitement) seemed to have gone out of them. Nevertheless, there were still party issues as the elections that gave York its first municipal corporation of the 20th century were held showed. The Conservatives or Independents had a healthy majority.

Municipal elections took place in November and before those of 1899 were held the city council tried to persuade the sitting Lord Mayor - Alderman S. Border - to continue in office, but that invitation was refused (16) and in his stead they chose Alderman J. Sykes Rymer, the Tory leader. (17) Party groupings on the council were loose - in the case of Liberals sometimes acrimonious as the general election showed - but in October the various organisations clicked into gear and chose (or re-selected) their candidates. The contest was to be fought over the issue of 'municipalisation' of essential services, with the Tories for leaving things as they were. The Conservatives of Walmgate met to re-select Joseph Peters, and at their meeting he summed up their prevailing attitudes.

The subject of the compulsory substitution of water-closets for privies was discussed, the *Press* reported. 'and Mr Peters' declaration of his opposition to that principle was well received.' (18)

The people putting forward the ideas of what is sometimes described as 'municipal socialism' were variously described as Progressive, Independent Labour or Cooperative candidates and one of these was Thomas Anderson, clearly a member of the Independent Labour party, chosen to stand in Monk against the Tory William Robie Robinson who described himself as a gentleman (and 'Independent') and William Banks, a Liberal standing for the first time who was a provision merchant. Two seats were up for grabs and Anderson demanded better housing to be provided through the provisions of the Workmen's Dwelling Act. 'They were in a backward condition in this respect', he told electors, 'because so many members of the Corporation were property owners, house jobbers, rent collectors or deputy landlords.' (19) Another Progressive to stand was George Price, the Cooperative Society's general manager. He put up in Castlegate against Councillors J.A. Shaftoe (Independent) and J. Lumb (Liberal) in a fight for two seats. Price gave the most comprehensive account of 'Progressive' policies to be reported in the newspapers at a meeting at the Cooperative Hall. He was in favour of municipalising all public monopolies, (20) and said that, like Anderson, he thought (knew) York was behind in municipal affairs. The electricity supply industry, locally, despite its Tory complexion, was about to become the property of the Corporation; Price wanted its product to be made widely available. He also wanted: the trams to run earlier and later for the benefit of working men; gas and water to be taken over; the establishment of a public slaughterhouse; more open spaces and open air gymnasiums; better sanitation; a cemetery on the south side of the Ouse; and an extensive slum clearance programme. George Briggs, the Cooperative Society's general secretary, was a third Progressive candidate (for Bootham) and he spent a great deal of time speaking of conditions in the poor areas of York like Bootham Row, and his descriptions of that area with its dreadful drains and ash pits could almost have been scripted by Edwin Chadwick. (21)

People like Briggs and Anderson made a lot of noise - and surely a lot of sense - but all three Progressives came bottom of the poll. In Bootham it was a close-run thing with Briggs only 27 votes behind the second successful candidate (Jones - 839; Atkinson - 817; Briggs - 790). The situation on the Council was as it had been, with the electors seemingly preferring the Peters to the Briggs; and privies to water closets. What happened in 1900 ?

The York papers reported that preparations for the annual municipal elections of 1900 were delayed and overshadowed by more serious political matters, but they began early in October. Over half the retiring councillors were not seeking re-election, the *Yorkshire Herald* reported, (22) and these retirements led to the candidacies of at least two men who were to become well-known in the city - James Birch, a plumber, who stood in Micklegate, and W.A. Forster Todd an 'Independent' who stood in Guildhall. On this occasion 'the Progressives' ran a candidate whose campaign highlighted the state of the city as it really was. This was William Henry Shaw who was nominated by the York Cooperative Society (of which he was a director) and actively supported by the York Trades Council, the York Central Branch of the Amalgamated Society of Railway Servants (23) and other bodies sympathetic to labour.

W.H. Shaw's campaign was similar to those fought by George Price and Thomas Anderson a year earlier. Shaw wanted: a municipal cemetery; the streets levelled; better working class housing; a fair wage clause inserted into every corporation contract; the extension of the tramway system; and electricity made more widely available. Shaw also drew attention to the cost of emptying the foetid ash pits of York. In one street, he said, the cost of cleaning these things amounted to 10d., 1s.0d, and 1s.4d. Whenever the job was done owners had to go and make the the necessary arrangements. Shaw wanted the pits cleaned regularly 'without the ratepayers having the annoyance of making pilgrimages to the Guildhall every time their pits wanted emptying.' (24)

Thomas Anderson reappeared as a candidate in 1900 with the same programme he had had 12 months earlier (and the same as Shaw). He stood, the papers said, as a candidate representing the Independent Labour Party but he denied this. (25) He criticised York for dithering and not taking over the local electricity supply industry when it could have, (26) and pointed to the profits municipally owned tramways made in places like Glasgow, Halifax and Leeds. Anderson said the York Corporation should have taken over the water supply company five years before 'When it was offered to the Corporation on fairly reasonable terms,' and demanded a municipal cemetery. ('Private enterprise in the disposal of the dead constituted a traffic in human bodies that ought not to be allowed to continue.') Like his colleagues he was well briefed and indeed eloquent when describing the conditions people like he had to live in in the area he was contesting. Walmgate, he said, was a slum, and he produced statistics of what that meant. The death rate in England and Wales, Anderson said, (27) was 148 per thousand born; while in York (in 1897) it was 200 per thousand. In the Bootham registration district deaths of children under five (in 1898) equalled 4.8 per thousand; in Micklegate 5.8 per thousand; and in Walmgate a staggering 9.8 per thousand. 'That meant', Anderson said, 'that with the class of property existing in Walmgate ten children out of every thousand under five died there as against five children out of every thousand in the Bootham district.' Yet while these appalling conditions (and their consequence in terms of crime and drunkenness) were there for all to see, the Corporation had done nothing to improve them, while, like all similar authorities, having the power to do so. The 1890 Housing Act had been ignored. '... in York for ten years the measure had been treated as though it had never been passed', Anderson said, 'and the city authorities seemed to be as far as ever from utilising it.'

One of the other candidates of November 1900 was Alfred Proctor, a sitting councillor for 15 years, and one supported by the Liberals of York, whatever label Proctor chose. He held election meetings in the Leeman Road area of the city - where conditions were particularly bad at the time. Among his prominent supporters was Arnold Rowntree and Proctor spoke of the evils that prevailed in the city and must have been all- too- evident to his listeners - the dreadful sewers, the annual typhoid outbreak and so on. (28) Proctor's speeches and his demands, in fact, were not very different from those of Anderson and Shaw. Why then did the latter put up against the Proctors and their colleagues? Because, it is almost certain, they thought that their protestations and demands were at the worst insincere, and at the best ineffective. For years people like Proctor had been members of the York Corporation and still conditions like those in Leeman Road prevailed. Labour, as the needs got greater, began to organise itself and demand representation and reform. Anderson and others were among the Labour pioneers. The process of squeezing out the Liberals had begun, a fact the *Yorkshire Herald* seemed to sense in its issue of 1 November. There has been more interest in the local elections than usual this year, it said. Hitherto they had been 'languid'. Why? Because in the past, since the time of George Hudson and George Leeman, there had been a 'gradual elimination' of the political element on the council, 'both in the deliberations of the Council and the attitudes taken by the candidates themselves, and partly' also, the *Herald* went on, in an extraordinary passage, due 'to the absence of anything that could really be described as a burning question awaiting solution.' Anderson's (and Proctor's) speeches would seem to give the lie to this amazing contention (as would a book that was shortly to appear). (29) It is true that the population of York had grown from 69,584 to 74,250 in Proctor's stint on the council, as he told electors, and it must be true that this had worsened matters. Public health, with all its implications, was a burning question, at least for people like Anderson if not for those the *Herald* seemed to be speaking for. That many others thought so too might be inferred from the election results of November 1900, when Proctor's tenure of office was brought to an end. There was more interest in the contest than before, the *Herald* said, not because of any burning issue, but because candidates had appeared 'in two ... wards who not only claim to be independent but seek the support of ratepayers on the ground that they are bona-fide working men, and that this class of the community should have a share in the representation of the Council.' It did not mention that point about them being clearly fed up with people like Proctor who had failed to tackle the problems which were obvious to them, if not to the leader writers in the *Herald*.

The campaigns of Anderson and Shaw forced the municipal candidates of 1900 to address themselves to 'real' issues, a fact the press drew attention to just after the declaration. 'In other years', the *Herald* said, on 2 November, 'the candidates have for the most part stated their views on general lines, without pledging themselves to any extent, concerning specific measures. The gentlemen who have on this occasion sought "election" have, however, been compelled to face certain pertinent queries which could not well be evaded, as it was evident that considerable feeling existed among the citizens concerning them.' This was from the paper which had suggested only a day earlier that there had been no 'burning issues' for the councillors to concern themselves with. What had happened ? Well clearly the speeches of Anderson and Shaw had concentrated minds, but in addition to this, candidates in the three wards where there were to be elections, had had questionnaires sent to them by the York Trades Council (of which W.H. Shaw was president) asking for their views and pledges on such questions as what would later be called 'council housing', a municipal cemetery and 'the need for an improved system of sewer ventilation, and the systematic cleansing of ashpits at the expense of the city instead of the inequitable method now prevailing by which the citizens are allowed to treasure [sic] up their refuse to the detriment of their own and their neighbour's health, until they can afford or feel inclined to pay the Corporation for taking it away.' (30) Taking a leaf out of the Trades Council's book the York Amateur Swimming Club and Humane Society questioned candidates about whether or not they were in favour of direct Corporation control over the St George's swimming bath - 'at present on lease.'

The results of the electioneering and lobbying ended with Anderson topping the poll in Walmgate, where there were 2,820 voters, nearly 200 ahead of his nearest rival. (Anderson 1,046; George Moss, builder, Conservative, 859). In Micklegate Shaw came second behind James Birch, Conservative, who got 946 votes, and ahead of Proctor who got 813. Shaw polled 844 and the analysis of the votes was impressive. The number of voters on the register was 2,688 and the plumpers (those who used only one of their two votes) polled as follows: Birch 465; Shaw 538; Proctor 218. The split votes were: Birch and Shaw 96; Birch and Proctor 385; Proctor and Shaw 210.

Labour had made impressive gains and new techniques had been introduced into local politics in York, and a welcome reform was made almost immediately. The emptying of those ash pits was taken over by the corporation. Of course not everyone was pleased with the way things went, and perhaps E. Smith of 26 Layerthorpe was representative of them. It is difficult not to feel some sympathy for him. He complained that now that the council had taken over the work the men chosen for that essential task started earlier. Last night, he said in a letter to the *Evening Press*, they 'commenced operations in Bilton-street very soon after ten o'clock, to the great discomfort and annoyance of everybody in their immediate vicinity. The smells given off were of such an obnoxious, pungent and disgusting character, as to be a positive danger to the public health. Several persons complained that they had been much upset by these smells, and made to feel seriously unwell.' (31) Clearly Smith was what commentators somewhat earlier would have called a miasmist, and one hopes he did not suffer frequently.

The labour successes of 1900, small though they were, look just that little more impressive when what happened at the general election of that year is borne in mind. It seems certain that the York by election of February, when Faber was returned, had more than a little to do with the timing of the general election later in the year. Faber had got in with an unexpectedly large majority and, according to a Tory speaker, 'the news of the ... York election was awaited in Cape Town' with great 'anxiety' and the result 'was welcomed as an indication of the strength of Imperialistic opinion in England.' If that is true then the government surely took heart and considered a dissolution in September sensible - and they were right. 'Lord Salisbury had chosen exactly the right time for the dissolution', Butcher said, 'The war having come practically to an end, the question of the settlement came to the front, and it was essential that the verdict of the country should be taken upon that as soon as possible.' (32) The following day he told a meeting in York that 'Great Britain was unanimous in deciding that the Boer Republics must henceforth form part of the Queen's dominions, and that never again could their independence be restored.' (33)

The York Liberal party was demoralised (and as usual split) and it was decided to allow the Tories to have a walk-over. On Saturday 29 September the Sheriff presided over a gathering at the Guildhall to receive nominations and Butcher and Faber were duly put in. An hour was given for objections; there were none; and at mid-day J.G. Butcher of Riccall Hall, and George D. Faber of Townshend House, the Mount, York, were declared elected. Faber reminded his followers of his by election when, he said, 'York gave birth ... to a patriotism which rang through the country, which had never been forgotten, and never would be.' (34)

R.C.K. Ensor wrote that the 'Khaki' election of October 1900 'was quite frankly an attempt to capitalise the emotions of military victory in terms of votes for the government', and that 'High-minded students of politics, irrespective of party, were inclined at the time to regret it, as derogating from the best traditions of fair play in the English political game.' (35) It deviated from the rules of fair play in another way - that is if some critics are to be believed. The election was called as the parties were preparing for the revision of the voters' lists and at a meeting in York J.H. Hartley maintained that it would have been fairer to the workers had the election been delayed until the new register was in force. He was probably right. Hartley was to become a considerable force in York politics in the not too distant future.

Faber, it will be recalled, was asked in the by election if he favoured 'all the Polls being held on the same day' - and said he was not. The system he defended meant, at the 1900 general election, that the polls were spread over an enormous period. The York results, for example, were declared on 29 September, and the very last results were declared in the York papers of 31 October. In between these dates the press regularly printed 'barometers' of the polls. When the results were all in the government had increased its majority by six (134 to 128). Results overall were: Unionists, 402; Liberals, Nationalists and others 268. It was a remarkable result; normally Faber would have been expected to lose, but had been helped by tactics which, as Ensor also said, were to be used again in 1918. They still rankled with the Liberals years later.

At times York would have seemed to have been in a perpetual round of electioneering, canvassing and voting, because, in addition to the parliamentary contests and the annual council elections, there were others. The Board of Guardians, for example, were due to be re-elected in March 1901. The York Poor Law Union was the creation of the Poor Law Act of 1837 and 'was an area of 103 square miles embracing 32 city parishes, 7 parishes in the West Riding, 16 in the East Riding, and 25 in the North Riding.' (36) The history of the guardians had been somewhat fraught, with disputes frequently taking the form of town versus county. There had been changes since the Union was set up, and, when nominations for 1901 were in, it was seen that 17 wards were to return members unopposed.

A feature of the York Board of Guardians that is of some interest is that it contained several lady members, (and women had a municipal vote if they qualified) and among those to be returned unopposed were Mrs Leetham, a member of a well-known local family of corn millers, and a Miss H.M. Bower. Both these ladies were already members of the Board and joining them, also unopposed, was a Mrs May Carett. (37) When the elections were over there were others - a Mrs Gray, a Mrs Dodds and Miss M.O. Kitching. An interesting candidate (also successful) at the same time, for District No 26, was Henry Gladin Cuss who put up as a working men's candidate, and was supported by, among other bodies, the York Typographical Association, other trades unionists, the Liberals and the Castlegate Conservative Association! Cuss, as has been said, got in and so he should have with that support. (38) If ever there was a 'popular' candidate it was Henry Gladin.

Cuss's candidacy is difficult to understand; not so those of four other candidates. These represented the burgeoning labour movement and were Thomas Anderson and W.H. Shaw, both of whom have been mentioned before, Andrew Moody, and that J.H. Hartley who had questioned the ethics of Lord Salisbury calling the general election in September 1900. They were all returned and Anderson rapidly established himself as an energetic, outspoken critic of things as they were. He had a prolonged dispute with the chairman of the Board, an ambitious lawyer called R.H. Vernon Wragge, over rate assessments during which threats of writs were made. That entertaining dispute can be followed in the reports and verbose letters that appeared regularly in the *York Herald*, (39) and later Anderson laid about him in fine style over meat contracts for the workhouse. (40) In January 1902 Matthew Rymer said that he thought Anderson should be gaoled for his activities, (41) and in June 1902 he caused a right furore in his other capacity as a councillor. When peace was declared Anderson refused to stand and sing the National Anthem in the Council chamber. What Matthew Rymer thought of this is unknown, though it seems reasonable to assume that it did not lessen his belief in Anderson's suitability for a spell in the nick. (42) Edith Milner and the Milner Habitation of the Primrose League did not comment. Perhaps they were speechless. The *Press* said Anderson was guilty 'of a deplorable exhibition of bad manners.'

The labour members of the York Board of Guardians started work with all the energy of newly appointed politicians angry at what they saw as the slackness and unfairness that had prevailed for well over half a century. Their remarks and attacks seem justified and they may well have been aware that their performances might well bring credit and success to their infant movement. They broke into other bodies - again in a small way - at about the same time. They got representatives onto the School Board at a time when education was beginning to be one of the major issues in British politics.

The York School Board was incorporated in 1889 and since then the 'voluntary' party had been in a majority - people who believed that educational provision was not primarily the concern of the state. Several famous commissions had reported towards the end of the century, and it was clear that a major reform of some kind would be produced that would have the objective of rationalising the 'system' under which secondary education 'was being developed partly by the councils of counties and county boroughs under the Technical Instruction Act' and partly 'by the school boards under the Elementary Education Acts.' (43) Such a measure would in all probability abolish school boards and Butcher, for example, spent some time discussing the government's attitude to education during his election meetings.

Like the Board of Guardians, the York School Board had some women members. In the last election of the 19th century Miss Anna Maria Wilkinson, a Congregationalist, was returned, getting 9,334 votes from an electorate that numbered between 13 and 14,000. Edith Harriet Milner, she of the Primrose League (Milner Habitation), had then stood as a Church candidate, naturally, and had not been returned, though she polled a very respectable 6,073 votes. (44)

Miss Wilkinson was a candidate again in 1901, when six of the eleven old members sought re-election, and she got in. But the real interest of the election was that, once again labour flexed its muscles. 'A new element is imported into the contest', reported the *Evening Press*, 'in that for the first time in the history of the city a direct representative of Labour interests is nominated.' (45) This is not quite true, unless the *Press* meant someone officially put up by a labour organisation, as the redoubtable Thomas Anderson had stood before then.

Because there were things to be done; because labour was under attack, seemingly by a hostile government; (46) because, maybe, of the cynicism shown at the general election; the 'threats' to education; and lastly because there were candidates available, labour decided to fight the School Board elections in York in a modest, but organised way. In the early days of January 1901 a conference of delegates from the York Trades Council, the city's socialists and the Cooperative Society was held to discuss the forthcoming contests. At that gathering a letter was read from 'the Priory-street Socialist and Political Questions Guild' saying it was not interested, but it was decided to send a deputation to a group of prominent 'unsectarian' candidates (Arnold and

Joseph Rowntree, J.W. Proctor and K.E.T. Wilkinson) to try to get concerted action. A.P. Mawson was chosen as a candidate and it is not reported whether or not the unsectarians allowed him to go unchallenged (by them). Probably they did, and by the end of January there was in existence a United Workers Committee with W.H. Shaw as chairman and G.P. Anderson, a Cooperative Society director, as election agent. (47)

There are few reports of Mawson's campaign for membership of the York School Board, but Shaw was active helping him - maintaining that labour had a right to be represented - and the few reports there are of Mawson's public pronouncements suggest that he spent much time speaking of the inadequacies of British technical education which had been shown up for the world to see at international exhibitions. (Mawson said that part of the trouble was the alienation felt by British workers - working men knew, he said, 'that the Continentals and the people of the United States had made such vast progress in commerce because of the interest felt in the welfare of their countries by the masses of the people.') (48) At one stage in the campaign a Mr Chrichton of the West Ham School Board had been brought in by the United Committee to help Mawson.

Other candidates for the School Board elections came from rather higher up the social scale than did Mawson. Henry Tennant, the leader of the city's Liberals was one, an unsectarian who was a Quaker, and another was the corn miller, H.E. Leetham, another unsectarian who was a Wesleyan! Robert Kay was an unsectarian yet also a very energetic Methodist and Miss Wilkinson was unsectarian/Congregationalist. At the time of the contest there was a considerable dispute about where exactly a new school for the unsavoury Leeman Road area should be built, and Miss Wilkinson came out strongly for it to be sited in Leeman Road itself, as against Poppleton Road where it was eventually built. (49) The Rev G.H Hewison (the current chairman) stood as a voluntaryist (or church candidate) and he went on record as saying that if voluntary schools were abolished each new Board school would cost £1,000 a year. Edward Sardison Dashwood Carter, a candidate also for municipal honours and a solicitor, had said that 'If he was elected' - and he was - 'he would go on to the Board as a Churchman to carry out the views of the Voluntary party', (50) and later said he thought the voluntary schools were efficient. (51) The Voluntaryists' platform was, in the last resort, simply an intention to keep Board schools away if possible and to retain the reins of education in the hands of the religious bodies.

J.W. Proctor, during his election campaign for the council, had boasted about the educational and other advances that had been made during his career as a councillor. A public library and technical schools had been established, he said, an asylum was to be built (at Naburn) and he had personally been deeply involved in unifying the parishes of York and establishing a uniform rate, which was then 5s.8d. and had varied from 4s.9d. to 8s.9d. (52) That old system had also meant that there were in York parishes which varied from that which had 'a population of eight, all told', to another

14

W. Boddy.

of 8,000. (53) This had necessitated an order from the Local Government Board to take account of the new arrangement.

When the York School Board contest was over the board consisted of: five churchmen; one Quaker (Henry Tennant); one Roman Catholic, the Rev Provost Dawson; one Congregationalist, Miss Wilkinson; one Wesleyan, Robert Kay; one Primitive Methodist, R.G. Heys, the Headmaster of Elmfield College; and A.P. Mawson.

Both Mawson and Miss Wilkinson (54) had expressed their concern about the provision of technical instruction and they, and members of school boards everywhere, were concerned at this time about the consequences of what were known as the Cockerton judgements. Cockerton was a District auditor in London who had succeeded Lloyd Roberts, a man who had, seemingly, been sympathetic to the way education had been developing under the London School Board - and, by implication, everywhere. The government was clearly anti-school boards and over the years the boards had provided more and more so-called Higher Grade Schools and more and more evening continuation classes dealing with adults and offering work varying from recreational to 'advanced work to a high standard.' (55) This had happened on a modest scale in York. (56) But was it legal ?

A Royal Commission (the Bryce) had seemingly wanted to have the higher grade schools absorbed into a coherent system and controlled by committees of either the county councils or county boroughs (of which York was one) (57) and in the aftermath of its report a famous civil servant began an intrigue to abolish the school boards. (58) This was Robert Morant, and as a part of his intrigue Cockerton challenged the London School Board's accounts. 'The legal point' under contention was quite simple: 'were the School Boards allowed to subsidize advanced education' - the higher schools and the continuation classes - 'out of the rates' ? Although the case went to appeal the answer was equally simple. It was no; and Justice Wills put the matter succinctly, and in reactionary language that was slightly unfair, because the value of the higher grade schools and the evening classes was *not* universally condemned. What was at issue really, was how they should be provided. But Wills clearly thought they would be no great loss. (It would have been interesting to hear his explanation of why Britain had fallen behind her industrial competitors.) Anyway he said that to teach adults and children 'indiscriminately ... higher mathematics, advanced chemistry ... political economy, art ... French, German, [and] history ... appears to me to be the *ne plus ultra* of extravagance.' (59)

Following the Cockerton judgement the York School Board's evening programme was immediately at risk, and the board itself equally so. Quite obviously there would have to be some temporary legislation, and some was duly produced enabling a board to carry on its programme for 12 months, if application was made to the local council.

(And a second Act allowed the same for 1902-3.) (60) At the end of July the York School Board applied to the city council to be allowed to carry on their evening work, (61) and permission was eventually given. The press report announcing the decision revealed that the number enrolled was a very respectable 668, with each student costing the city 6s.7d. (as against 7s.0d. a year earlier.) (62)

The long-awaited - and feared - Education Bill was introduced by Sir John Gorst on 7 May 1901. It was an unsatisfactory and inadequate measure and was eventually abandoned. The education issue was to revitalise the Liberal party to a great extent and a protest meeting was held in York at which the Rev J. Hirst Hollowell was the main speaker. He attacked the new measure on many grounds saying that it was anti-feminist, and that it destroyed local control. '... we had reached one more phase of that eternal conflict between priest and people, as to whether a nation had the right to educate itself or to leave education to ecclesiastical caretakers', Hollowell said, 'The Education Bill which the Government had just withdrawn violated all the principles of the Act of 1870. County councils were not the best authority to administer education. Poor men could not afford to sit on County Councils, women were excluded from them, and effective local management was impossible for them.' (63) (Women could not only sit on the school boards, but could vote for them too.) (64)

Voting at parliamentary, school board, guardians and municipal elections did not exhaust the list of contests in the early years of the 20th century. Since the Reform Act of 1835 there had been York city auditors, but there never had been a contest for them. In March 1901 there was, with the Cooperative Society and the Trades Council putting forward a candidate. He was George Richard Anderson, an insurance superintendent, and he challenged the serving auditors Henry Scott, china merchant, and John Seller (or Sellers) railway dues collector. Voters had only one vote and the voting was on the municipal list. Anderson lost (65), but his candidacy is one more piece of evidence of labour beginning to challenge for a place in government.

The Trades Council, which was a party to setting up the United Workers Committee to fight the school board elections of 1901 was the best-known labour organisation in York at the turn of the century, and the forum in which people like W.H. Shaw and Andrew Moody gained some local prominence. Its reports give some indication of what other modest labour organisations there were locally at the time. Shaw was a signalman on the North Eastern Railway and there was an active York branch of the Amalgamated Society of Railway Servants of which Moody was secretary. It had been created in the late 1870s and at the end of 1900 it had 430 members, and funds of some £300. At the time of their annual meeting of 1901 the Railway Servants were in dispute with their employers (who were reporting lower profits) and were demanding wage increases of ten percent with time and a quarter for night duty and time and a half for Sundays. What were their wages then? According to the ASRS assistant general secretary engine drivers were receiving 8d. an hour, signalmen 'less than 6d., and firemen less than 4d., wages that a bricklayer would scorn.' (66) A little later, in March 1901, the railwaymen's demands went in to the NER for 'improved conditions of service'. Despite protestations of slack trade dividends were then some seven per cent, but the company's reply to the union mentioned possible reductions in wages! This reply was regarded as 'most injudicious and unwarrantable, and calculated to invite men to extreme action.' (67) (It was the Amalgamated Society of Railway Servants who were in dispute with the Taff Vale Railway Company, and the legal case which was to be of monumental significance in labour history, started in the courts just after it was announced that the railwaymen had been given a pension scheme from the NER.) (68)

The railwaymen's earnings compared unfavourably with the bricklayers. They had a trade union in York, and in May 1901 the Operative Bricklayers' Society was engaged in a strike over working rules and 'walking time', a strike which they seem to have won. (69) The bricklayers seem to have been amongst the most militant of York's workers and they had been since the early years of the 19th century. There were two unions catering for builder's labourers in the city, and in June 1901 Mawson spoke at a public meeting and urged them all to join the city's branch of the Federated Builders' Labourers' Association of Great Britain and Ireland - an organisation which had recently held its national conference in York. (70)

In addition to the railwaymen and the builders, there were other groups in York which had organised themselves into unions. In 1901, for example, a branch of the National Amalgamated Union of Shop Assistants, Warehousemen and Clerks, was formed, (71) and there was then in existence a branch of the United Kingdom Society of Amalgamated Smiths and Strikers. (72) The annual report of the York Trades Council for 1901 recorded that it had 18 societies affiliated to it, with 2,506 members, who sent 60 delegates to the Council's meetings. (73) B.S. Rowntree, in a famous book that was noticed in the press in October 1901, published an Appendix H in which he described 'TRADE UNIONS IN YORK'. It contains some organisations which were clearly not affiliated to the Trades Council and shows the branches of the ASRS as having 480 members. This was by far the largest union, though the various organisations in the building trade were strong by York standards. Most of the unions provided sick pay - and that must have been a prime reason for many joining - and strike pay. Weekly membership contributions ranged from 2s. (the Flint Glassmakers) to 2d. (the Glass Workers and General Labourers). Several organisations claimed to have enrolled 'practically all the possible members in the city' and the following table was compiled about union membership as a proportion of the population. (It was estimated 'that 67 per cent of the total population of York belong to the working classes.') A comparison is made with the United Kingdom as a whole:

	Population in 1899	Ascertained Trade Unionists in 1899	No of Trade Unionists per hundred of population
York	75,812	2,539	3.3
United Kingdom	40,630,247	1,804,768	4.4

As has already been mentioned the York Trades Council was - as it was intended to be - a forum for working class opinion. There people like Andrew Moody discussed the great issues of the day and both highlighted them and attracted attention to them. It was a most important body, and its debates, as reported in the press, were seemingly of a high level. In May 1902, for example, it discussed the Education Bill (of course) and the Taff Vale judgement wherein the House of Lords decided that a trade union could 'be sued and mulcted in damages for wrongs done by its agents'. (74) On that occasion the Trades Council asked the city's two MPs to support a Commons' motion protesting against workmen being placed by judge made law in 'a position inferior to that intended by Parliament in 1875.' (75) The Trades Council had an interest in getting Labour representatives on the school boards and earlier it had discussed and supported such things as old age pensions, Sir Charles Dilke's Shops Bill, and the minimum wage then being demanded by Keir Hardie and Captain Cecil Norton in the Commons. (76) (Twenty-four shillings for a 48 hour week.) It was inevitable that eventually the Trades Council would take the logical step and consider the possibility of a Labour MP for York. It did so in April 1902 when J.R. Woodall, its secretary, presented to it a paper titled 'Direct Labour Representation in Parliament; is it possible for the City of York?' The meeting decided it was possible, and announced there would be such an attempt made to achieve that objective at the first favourable opportunity. (77)

An organisation specifically designed to achieve the objects outlined by Woodall was eventually set up in 1903, but until then the United Labour Committee remained in being and in February 1902 it discussed (78) an issue which it certainly would have regarded as embodying many of the featues of municipal socialism - even though it emanated from York's Tory controlled corporation. This was the York Parliamentary Bill which the Committee urged citizens to support. It had been discussed in council and in effect contained six provisions. These had to be put before a public meeting by statute and this was done in January 1902, just before the United Committee made its recommendations. The results of the meeting demonstrated that the possibility of increased rates (as always) weighed more heavily with some than the obvious benefits that action based on the bill would bring. Senior council members put the six provisions before the meeting without much success. The resolution proposing that the corporation should purchase the tramways was put - and defeated; a second outlining new tram routes was put - and defeated; a third on street improvements was heavily defeated; a proposal to license and register pleasure boats using the Ouse was approved; as were proposals to license sites for advertisements; and a last 'omnibus' proposal referring to minor improvements. In March there had to be a poll on the same issues and, with over 30 per cent of the voting papers being spoilt, the results were exactly the same as those described above. (79)

Much has been said about labour demands, and something has been said about wage rates (to railwaymen). What was the general picture in York in this respect in the early years of the 20th century? Again that famous survey by B.S. Rowntree is an invaluable authority, and much of what he revealed in 1901 in *Poverty, a Study of Town Life* had been criticised and highlighted by those participants in the municipal elections who have been mentioned. *Poverty*, however, reached an enormous audience.

Benjamin Seebohm Rowntree (1871-1954) was a member of the famous family of confectioners who employed some 600 workers at its large factory on Haxby Road, about a mile from the city. It moved there in 1890, a year after Seebohm began working for the firm. Influenced by the work of Charles Booth and alarmed by the conditions he saw in areas like Leeman Road, Rowntree began a survey of the conditions in which the York working class lived. He was criticised for his methods, particularly by those who thought poverty was self imposed and its alleviation no concern of the state, but what he showed was horrendous. (80) The conclusions he and his researchers came to are well-known, and they have been mentioned repeatedly. (81) Setting his definitions of poverty high and using workhouse dietaries as guide lines Rowntree showed that 1,465 families in York - over 15 per cent of the working population and almost ten per cent of the whole population - lived in what he called 'primary poverty'; poverty which they could do nothing to avoid. In addition to this there were many suffering from 'secondary poverty' - poverty caused by unwise spending, by having too many children, by unemployment or old age. These were families which had a large enough income to keep them 'strong and healthy', but who, according to a *Times* correspondent's report, through drinking or betting or being 'careless in housekeeping', found themselves in dreadful straits. How many were there like this in York? Rowntree quantified. (82)

> it was found that families comprising 20,302 *persons, equal to 43.4 per cent of the wage-earning class, and to 27.84 per cent of the total population of the city, were living in poverty*. If the 7,230 persons found to be living in "primary" poverty are deducted, it is found that 13,072 *persons, or 17.93 per cent of the population, were living in "secondary" poverty* ... That nearly 30 per cent of the population are found to be living in poverty is a fact of the gravest significance.

The *Times* correspondent, quoted above, was grossly unfair to many of those identified by Rowntree as being in his second category of sufferers. Of course there must have been many who found the pub an attractive escape from a hard life, and who caused trouble to their families by spending their money on booze, but there were others who did not, yet who still only just managed to supply those basic needs. Rowntree, in an oft-quoted and moving passage, described what this meant. If they were to survive and provide food for the family that was needed they could never spend anything 'on railway fare or omnibus', on newspapers or concerts, or letters to absent children. They could never give to their chapel collection, join a sick club or a union, smoke, drink or buy pretty clothes. 'Should a child fall ill,' he went on, 'it must be attended by the parish doctor; should it die, it must be buried by the parish.' Finally, the wage earner must never be absent from work for a single day.

Perhaps Rowntree did not stress this last part enough. People like those who were fairly well-paid in the building trades and who had joined the unions mentioned above, could be thrown out of work at any time, (83) and if that happened were immediately in trouble. They had no protection and this must have meant, surely, they would take a decision to strike only very reluctantly or in extreme circumstances. This knowledge, that things could all go appallingly wrong in no more than a day, must have meant that working class families lived in constant fear of short time working or the sack. (Strike pay was miniscule.)

What were the solutions to the problems of poverty, bad health and housing that Rowntree so graphically highlighted ? Clearly, as people like W.H. Shaw saw, state intervention in the form of old age pensions, social security and municipal housing were needed to alleviate its effects. But people like Rowntree were devoted Liberals wedded to the doctrines of free trade and private enterprise. How could they support what in retrospect seems to have been so obviously necessary and sensible ? With great difficulty is one answer. Reluctantly is another. By treating these things as 'special cases' to which the traditional Liberal dogmas did not apply was a third. Frequently in the years that remained before the outbreak of the Great War, the Liberals made the same demands for reform in York as did the representatives of labour. Those demands, however, sounded more genuine when they were made by Anderson or Shaw, than when they were made by the likes of Seebohm Rowntree who, when all was said and done, was one of the city's leading employers.

Rowntree's book dealt with education, housing and, and this was inevitable, the drink trade. What did he say about it ? In the second edition of *Poverty* he revealed that there were '338 premises licensed for the sale of intoxicating liquor in the city' - 199 fully licensed houses; 37 beer houses; 27 'off licenses' selling wines and spirits; and 75 'off licenses' selling beer only. 'The population of York being 77,793', he went on, 'there is therefore one "on" license for every 330 persons. If we take all licenses into account ... that is one licensed house for every 230 persons.' (84) How did this compare with other towns and cities ? Northampton, with a population of just over 87,000, had 519 outlets - a ratio of one to every 167 persons; Birmingham had one to every 240; Leeds, with a population of nearly 429,000, had 1,182 outlets, making a ratio of one to 362.

Drink was readily available to those who could afford it (and to many of those who could not according to the commentators on Rowntree's work). What of the pubs themselves ? Rowntree recognised their attractions (there was 'an absence of irksome restraint' in them which, he said, 'must prove very attractive after a day's confinement in factory or shop') and described them - or some of them - as places of entertainment, and places where, just occasionally, a landlord organised a 'treat' for his customers. But who frequented them ? Certainly those who spent money which needed to go on the family, but in addition to these there must have been those who were going through one of those rare periods in their life when there really was enough to go round and a little to spare. (85) Those and others in classes which did not concern Rowntree. (A factor which he did not take into account was that many working class families might just have had some illegal supplement to their income, maybe taken in the form of a 'perk' that might have made things just a little easier than he thought for some of them. It is inconceivable, for example, that labourers working in the fields outside the city did not bring home the odd vegetable. Perhaps others were able to get other items. This 'black economy' surely existed and any supplement to a wage of 18s. or so a week must have made a difference.) (86)

Seebohm Rowntree, as a Quaker, was a temperance advocate, and he gave it as his opinion that 'something equally [as] attractive' as the pubs should be established 'on temperance lines', but he did not press his views on drink in *Poverty*. His concern was the effect money spent on drink had on the family. The Brewster Sessions which regulated the trade were splendid affairs in those days, and that of September 1900 is a good example. (87) The Lord Mayor, presiding, announced that the justices had met that morning and decided that in the ensuing year 'an inspection' of 'all the licensed property' would be made to ascertain their 'suitability' and the necessity 'for the renewal of any of the licenses for the next year'. He was pleased, he said, that nothing had been said in reports to him of 'any licensed victualler unduly, or in any way, supplying children with liquor nor to any of the license holders having given sweets or any other inducements to go to their houses. He trusted that there was no such thing going on in' York (if there was Rowntree did not mention it), 'but if there was ... the magistrates ... would view it with great displeasure.' The Lord Mayor reminded his listeners that 'some year [sic] ago the justices [had] passed a resolution that in their opinion there were more licensed premises in the city than the population required for ordinary legislative purposes.'

Despite the foregoing there were four new applications for licenses in 1901. (88) A Mr J.H. Turner, solicitor, appeared on behalf of the Rev Canon Argles, an Anglican member of the York School Board. Argles and some colleagues, Turner said, had not objected to the renewal of any licenses because of the bench's stated policy to visit and look at all the properties in their jurisdiction. Clearly Turner and Argles were simply flag flying, and indicating that temperance advocates had every intention of attempting to cut down the number of pubs, beer houses and off licenses in the future. They also opposed some of the new applications. (89) The first of them is indicative of many things about York in 1901. (It had been been submitted in 1900 and refused then, with an 'eminent barrister ... from London' conducting 'the opposition'.)

Frank Reynolds applied for a full license for 105 Nunnery Lane, premises which then were licensed only for the sale of beer. A Mr Warren said the property had been licensed as a beer house since 1863, and within the last six years had been 'considerably improved, about £1,000 having been spent upon it in making it more adaptable for the purposes of the licence and in the installation of electric light.' The population of the area had grown in the last two decades and although 'no full license had been granted for over 20 years, ... there now existed an undoubted necessity for the granting of one.' The area was a working class one, where people 'had to confine their purchases to small quantities, and the granting of the suggested facilities would be an undoubted boon to the neighbourhood.' But was the extension a necessity? Turner questioned Reynolds (who had his application turned down). It was his (Reynolds') third application.

Is the Victoria Inn within 215 yards of your place? - About 300 yards.
And the Slip Inn - About the same distance.
And the Wheatsheaf? That is only a beer house.
How far is the Britannia off? About 240 yards.
So that within a radius of 500 yards there are five other houses, four fully licensed? - Yes.

Also at the Brewster Sessions of 1901 a Mr David Bellerby applied for 'an "off" beer license for the premises ... at the corner of Kitchener-street and Huntington Road.' He was represented by two of the local Tory lawyer politicians who have already been mentioned as candidates for membership of the York School Board, the guardians and the council. These were R.H. Vernon Wragge, the barrister, who was instructed by Dashwood Carter, a solicitor. Wragge, perhaps put on the *qui vive* by the drubbing Reynolds had got, drew attention to the house building going on in the area and said the nearest pubs were the Punch Bowl and the Bowling Green Hotel, both a half mile away, as was the nearest off license in Fountayne Street. Thomas Oliver and Henry Lyon, both nearby householders, supported the applications, saying that 'an off-license was required as beer got flat in carrying it such a distance from the nearest licensed houses.' That seems a good point, but the application, which was also opposed by the York Licensed Victuallers Association, was refused.

22

The last new application of 1901 also involved Wragge, and yet more of the lawyer politicians of York, and it also drew attention to the way the city was growing. John J. Hunt, Ltd, brewers of York who operated from Aldwark, applied for a pub to be built on the Bishopthorpe Road estate, 'at the junction of Nunthorpe Avenue and South Bank Avenue.' The application was opposed by Turner acting on behalf of Argles, the Rev C. Pates and that J.W. Proctor who was so well beaten by labour in the 1900 election for Micklegate. K.E.T. Wilkinson appeared on behalf of another objector - 'the holder of an "off" beer license on the South Bank estate.' Wragge told the bench the application 'was the most important that had been brought' before them 'for a considerable time.' The Bishopthorpe Road estate had an area of 35 acres and there were on it 320 completed and 69 uncompleted houses already. During the next year 100 more would be built and before the John J. Hunt pub was completed (if permission was granted) 'there would be 300 more than at present.' Land worth £30,000 had been sold for building and it was estimated that in four to five years there would be 1,600 houses with a population of 8,000. 'It would be practically a little town', Wragge said. Nearby was the Nunthorpe estate, some eleven acres in extent, and Hunt's 'had the liquor rights on those two estates entiely [sic]: no one [else] could sell drink on them at a public house, a club, a shop, or anyway whatever.' There was another estate 'near the South Bank district' and the number of houses occupied or being built on the three estates was 611 with the population computed at 3,055. Where could they drink ? The nearest off license was in Adelaide Street, and the nearest pubs (the Mount Hotel and the Grand Stand) were each a mile away from the proposed pub. 'It was unreasonable that the people on the estate ... should have to go so far' for a drink Wragge said, though they could go to a working men's club in South Bank.

Wragge said he was 'sorry' that the South Bank Working Men's Club had been established (well he would be). The absence of pubs would induce men to join such places, he went on, and they were springing up 'rapidly all over the country.' They did not benefit the working man, they made proper police supervision difficult, they were unsupervised, they were assessed for the rates at a lower rate than pubs, 'and there were no restrictions. For a nominal sum the people of the district could become members, and the club was nothing more or less than an evasion of the law.' Wragge ended his harangue by saying that 'There were three thousand people on the estates, there would be ten thousand, and if their worships thought the time had not arrived for a licence, Messrs. Hunt would have to do something and not stand any longer in their own light.' At an adjourned meeting (90) Wragge heard that his application was turned down, the bench objecting to the proposed site, and contending that the new pub, if it was to be built, 'ought to be on the main road.'

Prior to listening to the new applications the Brewster Sessions of 1901 had heard the Chief Constable's report for the year. He gave the bench the figures for the number of outlets that had been used by Rowntree and revealed that during the year 415 people had been proceeeded against for drunkeness, and of them 366 had been convicted. The average for the number of people prosecuted for being under the influence was 401 over the last five years. Who was responsible (apart from the tipplers themselves) ? Not only the licensees, 'as in addition to the premises licensed within the city, a number of clubs have of late sprung up, in several of which I have reason to believe large quantities of intoxicating liquors are sold. These clubs,' the Chief Constable went on, 'remain open until long after licensed premises are required to be closed.' How did York compare with other places for drunkenness ? Regularly a league table of a dozen towns was produced including statistics of people proceeded against per 1,000 of the population, and York always scored well. In 1901 it came second to Stockport. In the *Press* of 22 August 1901 there appeared a report from the Huddersfield Brewster Sessions when the Chief Constable there compared figures for drink related offences in Yorkshire and Lancashire towns. This showed that Bradford, Halifax, Huddersfield and Leeds were 'passably sober', while Wakefield occupied 'an unenviable position.' York's entry was: 'convicted 281 males, 85 females; dismissed, 26 males, 23 females; total, 415; population 78,041; percentage, 5.31.'

York, then, had an impressive record for drunkenness, and the Chief Constable and Vernon Wragge clearly implied that working men's clubs were not forces for good in this respect. But were there many, and did they really present the threat to the pubs that the barrister implied ? Well Wragge was certainly correct in saying that many clubs had appeared in York in the few years before he made his impassioned speech on behalf of J.J. Hunt and Company. The oldest of these establishments seems to have been the Irish National League Club which sent a delegate to that meeting which created the York United Workers' Committee. The INL grew out of a Fenian Club, and dates its existence from July 1884. (91) In 1900 a Burton Stone Working Men's Club had been created and two years before that the Clarence Club had started its existence. What eventually became the Groves Working Men's Club opened in 1899 and in the dreadful area that so concerned the municipal reformers, a Leeman Road WMC came into being in 1895. This place was established in Salisbury Terrace until it moved, many years later, with what looks like corny logic, to Balfour Street - street names which are indicative of their dates surely. The Promenade Club was opened in 1902, the St Lawrence Club was in existence by the end of 1899, and the Acomb Club was in existence and affiliated to the Club and Institute Union by the same year. This latter organisation demonstrated once again York's penchant for naming streets after politicians, and cynics of the time might just have thought that its omens were not good as its secretary was named after the city's most famous scoundrel. The Acomb Club was sited in Beaconsfield Street and its secretary was one George Hudson. Before the Great War began other Working Men's Clubs were established in York. (92)

What were these places like ? Very little remains to give a detailed picture of their early days, but there are a few details about South Bank. It seems that it may have owed a lot to the initiative of three brothers - C.W., J.E. and A.C. Chapman - who seem to have devoted a great deal of time and energy to the club movement, but who do not appear to crop up in any other political or quasi-political movements. The Chapmans helped create South Bank (and St Lawrence and Clarence) which was located in what had been six cottages in Argyle Street. Butcher and Faber, York's two MPs, were said to have been frequent visitors there (if not members) and members were allowed to run up debts on a slate of 2s.6d. a week - a considerable attraction presumably. The club was said to have done great business when Buffalo Bill's Wild West Circus visited the Knavesmire in 1904, and in 1910 membership was some 450. The Burton Stone Club advertised mild beer at 2d. a pint earlier in its history, and Leeman Road's first secretary (Cooper Harling) served it for no less than 19 years.

The working men's clubs in York and elsewhere are examples of that 'self help' which was so venerated by Victorians. Seebohm Rowntree would have undoubtedly applauded the initiative of people like the Chapmans, though regretted, in this instance, the outcome. People like W.H. Shaw probably deplored the fact that working class organising ability and energy was channelled into other than political ventures. Vernon Wragge, as has been shown, also regretted the fact that working men had set about creating places where they felt more at home and got cheaper beer than they could get in the pubs. Why ? Well one reason was that he was instructed to criticise them by his clients. But what did he mean when he said there were 'no restrictions' at the clubs, and that this gave them an unfair advantage in the market place ?

It will be recalled that the Master of Elibank was asked during his election campaign whether he was in favour of licensing clubs. The questioner clearly meant working men's clubs, and it is a fact that they were indeed outside the law to all intents and purposes. Not until the passing of the Licensing Act of 1921 did the clubs become 'the subject of general legislation.' (93) That act reduced the number of hours for the supply, sale and consumption of intoxicating drink in both pubs and clubs, but at the turn of the century things were very different. Seebohm Rowntree said there were nine 'drinking clubs' in York and gave a graphic description of those two situated 'in a very poor part of the city.' These, he said, were often frequented by Irish labourers and entrance to them was 'jealously guarded.' No wonder; but in spite of the security drunken men had been seen in them plastered beyond recall and 'lying on the wooden forms, but', Rowntree went on, members were 'careful not to allow any one to leave ... until he is sober enough to escape the risk' of being prosecuted 'for being drunk in the streets. Often', he concluded, members remained in these places 'through the night, and even from Saturday until Monday.' The other clubs were situated in the newer working class districts - like South Bank - and were frequented by skilled workers, labourers and 'to a small extent by clerks.' There was 'heavy drinking' in them, 'but very little actual drunkeness or disorder.' The bars closed, generally, at 11 pm. A little later (1906) Seebohm's father published a large book and drew on his son's work, reproducing in part the impressive balance sheet of an unnamed York club for 1899. Profits would have been higher than they were, he said, 'were it not for the fact that the prices paid for drink by the members are lower by about 33 per cent than those ordinarily charged in public-houses.' He summed up their privileged position thus: 'At present the only payment made by the clubs for the privilege of selling alcoholic liquors to members and their guests is a small registration fee of five shillings.' (94) Both Mr Gladstone and Lord Randolph Churchill recognised the anomalous and privileged position enjoyed by clubs and the latter had unsuccessfully introduced a bill to register them. The Yorkshire Branch of the Licensed Victuallers' Defence League meeting at Goole in 1901 'expressed' a hope 'that before long there would be some legislation to protect' their members from what it called 'illegitimate competition when' they had 'to pay such heavy taxation.' There cannot have been many occasions when the LVA agreed with the Rowntrees, but they did over the licensing of clubs.

Despite the fact that working men's clubs had a privileged position in society (some would say) there had been legislation at the turn of the century which imposed conditions on 'the trade.' In 1830 it had been deemed 'expedient ... to give greater facilities for the sale of' beer than had hitherto been afforded, and the Beerhouse Act of that year enabled any householder assessed to the poor rate to obtain 'from the Excise' - not from the justices - a license enabling him to sell ale from his dwelling house for consumption off the premises. 'Great evil' was reckoned to have arisen from the passing of this measure (in an incredibly short space of time) and an alteration in the law was made by an act of 1834 (also called The Beerhouse Act). This made a distinction between 'on' and 'off' retail beer licenses, making different charges for the two and making the production of a certificate of good character a necessary part of an initial application for one. This remained the situation until 1869. In the same period the Refreshment Houses Act of 1860 made provision 'for the licensing of refreshment houses not already licensed as alehouses or beerhouses.'

The Wine and Beerhouses Act of 1869 provided that none of the existing licenses should be renewed or granted without a justice's certificate. A subsequent act of three years later introduced a uniform mode of application to the justices and authorised the granting of those 'six-day licenses' which have bemused many of later generations. The benefit of this provision was obvious and logical - a lower rate of duty would be paid if the premises were closed on Sundays. The next important piece of legislation was in the process of going through its parliamentary stages when Vernon Wragge and Dashwood Carter were preparing their submissions for a pub in the Bishopthorpe Road area and their attack on the working men's clubs of York. This was 1 Edw 7, chap 27, An Act to prevent the Sale of Intoxicating Liquors to Children, a measure which was known from its inception as 'The Child Messenger Bill.'

The Child Messenger Act repealed the Intoxicating Liquors (Sale to Children) Act, 1886, a short measure which simply prohibited the sale of 'any description of intoxicating liquors to any person under the age of 13 for consumption on' licensed premises. There followed a considerable agitation for what the *Annual Register* called *'Bit-by-Bit Temperance Reform'*, and in 1901, the temperance advocates, being then convinced that during the war they stood little or no chance of obtaining any root and branch legislation, introduced a number of measures into parliament, some of which attempted to incorporate the recommendations of that Peel report to which one of York's candidates had made reference. The Bishop of Winchester, for example, supported a Habitual Drunkards Bill, which would certainly have taken account of some of York's great drinkers of the past (like Screampoke) (95) by which artists (96) who had been convicted three times in one year of certain offences specified in the Inebriates Act of 1898 could 'be placed by the court upon a black list, when penalties would fall alike upon anybody serving him with intoxicating liquor and upon the man himself if he endeavoured to obtain it.' This kind of proposal has been made in more modern times, and it had the sympathy (he said) of Lord Salisbury who, however, said he 'wished to draw as strong a distinction as he could between the legislation which punished only the intemperate and that which sought to reach them by restricting the natural liberty of temperate consumers.' Winchester's bill made no progress, but on 20 March the Member for Kincardineshire introduced the Child Messenger Bill in the Commons. (97) This originally made it an offence to sell intoxicants to children under 16, for consumption either on or off the premises. It got overwhelming support (372 votes to 54 on second reading) and eventually became law 'in a reduced form, the age limit being fixed at 14, and permission given for children to fetch sealed bottles of liquor from public-houses.'

What attitude did York's leaders and organisations take to the Children's Bill ? The government took a neutral stance on the measure, so the two MPs had a free hand, but they were urged to support it as indeed they did - as indeed they should have. The very first 'ordinary' meeting of the York School Board after the elections urged Butcher and Faber to vote for the second reading (98) and the same issue of the *Press* that recorded the court appearance of 'Ginger Wright, the York pigeon eater' reported that the city council publicly supported the bill after being petitioned to do so by the York and District Band of Hope Union. (99) It seems reprehensible that the voting was 20: 21! A little later in the year the Rev J.J. Davies, the rector of Bulmer, presided over a meeting calling for support (100) but the Yorkshire LVA at their meeting at Goole, where they declared themselves for club registration, opposed raising the age for drinking. (101) Mr Webster, the secretary, revealed that there had been petitions 'against the Child's Messenger Bill' sent in to their parent body amounting 'to 107, representing 244,865 signatures.' It would be interesting to be able to read their contents. Delegates at Goole regretted that an attempt to get the bill referred to a Select Committee had failed, 'but it was stated an effort would be made to bring about a considerable reduction in the age limit, in addition to other alterations, before the report stage ... was reached.' At the annual dinner of the York LVA in October those present were addressed by Mr H.H. Riley-Smith of Tadcaster, (102) who seemed to engage in a rather transparent piece of dissembling. They were 'threatened men' he told the Victuallers, 'but he did not regard their trade at all in the nature of a creaking gate ... it rested on a firmer, a safer, and a more solid foundation than at any period during which he had been connected with it. Speaking of the Child's Messenger Bill [it was an act by then], he remarked' that it had been 'received by various people from different stand points', but what he thought was 'the most sensible section of the community ... regarded it as a not unsatisfactory measure.' He agreed with them, and their presumption 'that the State should step in and make laws and enactments for the regulation of those parents ... who had neither the moral nor physical welfare of their children at heart.' What 'After all ... were the provisions of the bill', the speaker concluded, they were not of a prohibitive, but only of 'a precautionary nature.' In the years since Riley-Smith gave his address it has become the practise for the York LVA to invite the Lord Mayor of York as its speaker at their annual dinners and, it must be admitted, their speeches are rarely as exciting as that of Riley-Smith. They seem, however, to be usually better informed (but not always). Had that denizen of Tadcaster read the Act closely, (and it only ran to seven paragraphs) he would have seen that it was rather more than a 'precautionary measure.'

During the Child Messenger Bill's progress through parliament, as has been noted, amendments were made to it. The word 'knowingly' was inserted to make the offence of selling to under 14s read 'knowingly sells' and later penalties were imposed on persons who 'knowingly' sent under 14s to purchase hard drink. A great deal was made of this during the debates (hence the name Child Messengers) and an exception was made for 'intoxicating liquors as are sold or delivered in corked and sealed vessels in quantities of not less than one reputed pint.' The last amendment was that which reduced the age of legal drinking from 16 to 14. The bill was a private measure and during the earliest debate on it Sir William Houldsworthy revealed that there had been 5,627 petitions supporting it. Some Members revealed that magistrates in some places (like Chester) had already imposed a limit of 14 years and Marshall Hall (Southport) was one of the first to suggest that as an amendment. Sir J. Ferguson played the role of a latter day Colonel Sibthorpe and said he regarded the measure as 'an invasion of the liberties of the working classes of this country.' Fergie revealed that he had been drinking beer since he was twelve - and he was now almost 70. (103) Whether he had ever been a 'Child Messenger' who swiped his parents beer on the way home from the pub (a matter of grave concern) was not revealed.

Earlier on it was said that a person interested in 1914-18 would get a strange feeling of *deja vu* reading the press reports of 1900-02. That feeling would have been strengthened by the reports of prominent soldiers speaking of the dangers of the public 'treating' servicemen; it would also have been strengthened by the numerous reports about 'conscientious objectors.' Who were they ? They took up a great deal of the time of magistrates courts and provoked almost as many bad-tempered rebukes from the bench as did their successors in 1916-18. The conscientious objectors of 1900-02 were anti vaccination protestors. The Vaccination Act of 1867 (30 and 31 Vic cap 84) ordered that children had to be taken to a public vaccinator, treated for small pox, and then taken back for an inspection. An act of 1898 established the right of objection, and a court case (Regina v Welby) led to many queries in the law journals. (104) How could an objection be made ? A parent had to go before the magistrates and 'satisfy' the justices that he believed that 'vaccination would be prejudicial to the child's health.' (105) Many did this, and were held up to ridicule. John E. Thompson, of Borrowby, for example went before the Northallerton bench and applied for an exemption certificate for his one month old daughter. The following exchange took place: 'The Chairman: We have no choice. You say you have a conscientious objection. Applicant: Yes. The Chairman: Well, you would not get it if we had a choice.' (106) In Scarborough, a little earlier, Christopher Swales Jackson, a farmer, was fined £1 for 'having neglected to have his infant daughter vaccinated.' (107)

In York the vaccination officer was a Mr W. Wrigglesworth, the vaccination authority was the Board of Guardians, and in August 1902 he gave that body a report on the period July to December 1901. In that period, Wrigglesworth said, there had been 1,364 births and 'of these 1,109 were successfully vaccinated, four unsusceptible, 18 adjourned, 150 died, 16 were postponed by the medical officer, one removed to a district unknown, and 27 were unaccounted for.' (108) Later in the month Wrigglesworth complained that some parents were not getting their children treated and this led Thomas Anderson to lecture him on the law, and complain that one JP had called an applicant an idiot. (109) This might well have been Alderman Purnell (the Lord Mayor in 1901) who had refused to sign a certificate that his colleague, Joseph Rowntree, was quite willing to sanction. Rowntree had complained and this led the clerk of the court (F.J. Munby) to lament that 'I cannot control the magistrates.' (110) People like Purnell were undoubtedly influenced by the fact that small pox had broken out in London, leading medical officers to urge revaccination. (111) By March 1902 it was established at Leeds, and a year later it was causing grave concern in the West Riding. (112) In January 1902 Henry Broadhurst, MP, announced that he was going to try and amend the parts of the law which said that any justice's court 'or other authority' could compel parents to have their children treated. Broadhurst was one of the Lib-Lab Members, and he would have been influenced by stories of the behaviour of people like Purnell and G.S. Pollard, a magistrate for the West Riding. The latter had been the scourge of the local objectors, it seems, and his activities had led to a note in the *Wharfedale and Airedale Standard* complaining about 'the humbugging treatment received by applicants for exemption under the Vaccination Act from the Otley Bench.' Whenever Pollard 'happens to be in the chair', it went on, 'the poor conscientious objector is subjected to endless conceited humbug', and his behaviour was an argument for the 'appointment of capable stipendiaries.' (Arguments for a York stipendiary were made at the same time.) Pollard applied for a rule of criminal information against the publisher of the *Wharfedale*, and the case was heard in the King's Bench in August 1901. While regretting the tone of the newspaper's report, Justices Wells and Kennedy refused the rule.

The protestors against vaccination (and innoculation) continued to be active and caused considerable problems for the Army when the Great War broke out, (113) but the courts had other things to deal with (of course) than the successors of Screampoke and conscientious objectors. In 1900-02 the police and the magistrates were waging a 'CRUSADE AGAINST MOTOR CARS', and many successful prosecutions for what the papers called 'MOTOR SCORCHING' were brought. In September 1902, for example, William J. Robson, a JP from Pontefract was fined, (114) and a little earlier one J. Suggitt was done for driving above the legal limit of 12 miles per hour. (115) In July Thomas Coupland was fined for racing a motor car on his bike, (116) and at the end of the year a lady, perhaps the first in the area, struck a blow for women's liberation when she was fined for speeding. (117)   Ernest Jennings was done for a second offence of speeding, fined £10 and got his name in the *Evening Press* of 28 September 1901.

It does not seem that erring motorists ever got the verbals that the conscientious objectors got from the magistrates, who were conducting other crusades than those already mentioned. Street betting and Sunday gaming (pitch and toss on the commons and wastes) were of concern to the beaks and were being campaigned against; the campaign, perhaps, heightened by the appearance in 1902 of a report from the House of Lords Betting Committee. Just before the appearance of that, raids were carried out in York under Section 1 of the Betting Act of 1863, (118) and one of those nicked (Thomas Horner, a 40 year old) got a month in prison with hard labour for his troubles. (119) People playing pitch and toss was not the only form of Sabbath breaking that concerned the justices. In 1902 a campaign against Sunday trading began (120) which grew in intensity in the years that followed. The *Press* of 24 February that year mentioned that the corporation had decided to emulate places like Darlington and Hull (where there had been an enormous number of convictions) and had instructed the Watch Committee to clamp down on Sunday traders. Some proceedings in York were started, but the campaign was not pursued with any vigour by the Tories. It was by the Liberals a few years later - with disastrous consequences for them.

Tom Horner's punishment looks a little harsh by modern standards, but Ernest Skeldrake, a 15 year old, perhaps escaped an equally unpleasant experience. By 'ancient custom' it was then the practice to let off the first person who appeared for trial at the city's magistrates court on the first occasion that the new Lord Mayor (an ex-officio JP) sat. In November 1901 this was Alderman L. Foster and after giving an applicant for a certificate of exemption for vaccination a right roasting he let off young Ernie who had allegedly stolen a shilling 'as a bailee.' (121)   What might have happened to that young man ?   Well presumably that would have depended on his record, but the courts were not averse to handing out punishments collectively referred to as 'whipping' in the magistrates' reference works and administered under the provisions of the Summary Jurisdiction Act of 1879. (122)   In August 1902 Ernest Cooper, 12 years, of 44 Jackson Street, York, was given six strokes of the birch for stealing five shillings, (123) and eight months later William Ware got a similar

Oscar F. Rowntree

sentence for stealing a handkerchief. (124) In October 1902 Samuel Walker, Mark Herbert Smith and Arthur and George Knight were all flogged at Tadcaster for scrumping plums. (125) Were there no critics of such punishments ? Of course there were, and in May 1901 Joseph Collinson of the Humanitarian League wrote to the York papers criticising the Recorder of Scarborough who had gone on record saying that he thought whipping should be resorted to more often. Collinson criticised the current Youthful Offenders (Whipping) Bill which, perhaps, prompted the Recorder's remark, (126) but it was many years before the likes of him were effectively listened to. During the Great War the Humanitarian League came out as arch critics of the army punishment of 'crucifixion' (Field Punishment Number One). (127) They were ignored.

It is perhaps strange to read about the whippings that were ordered by the York bench and neighbouring justices, then to realise that they were being criticised both locally and nationally - in *Truth*, the leading satirical journal of the day - (128) for being too lenient. Just after Ernie Cooper was ordered to be birched, the Watch Committee of the city council publicly criticised the magistrates for imposing only a very small fine on a man who had assaulted a police officer, and in the discussion leading up to the decision to attack their worships Alderman Coning revealed that there had once been in York the crook's equivalent of a friendly society. Twenty five years ago, Coning told the council, 'the ruffian element in the city had a club to which they contributed, and when they were fined for assaulting the police they went to the club, and the money was paid.' (129) This was taking the doctrines of Samuel Smiles to perhaps unreasonable lengths. Coning said the Watch Committee hoped 'that in future more severe sentences would be' imposed upon offenders, in order to protect police officers in carrying out their duty.

The Lord Mayor had sat on the bench the day the assault on the police had been dealt with, and he said that although they could have sent the man to prison they took into account the fact that the assailant 'had been very much provoked for a long time, and had been a very forbearing man'. Not only that, but he and his colleagues 'thought the police themselves had punished the man sufficiently even if the Bench had not punished him at all.' Purnell did not elaborate on what he meant by that last remark, but Coning said the convicted man had been bound over to keep the peace three times since 1897, and that the assault 'was one of the most savage and the most outrageous which had been committed on the police in his time.' The policeman assaulted had still not recovered and furthermore his attacker had not paid a penny of his fine. That old organisation of a quarter of a century earlier may have gone, but there was a community spirit which could be tapped. There had been a whip round, with the money for the fine 'being raised by those living in the district.' The man treated so generously by his neighbours (and the magistrates) was a 28 year old labourer called Thomas Foster, who lived in Garden-place.

Foster was prosecuted by the Chief Constable and a report of his case appears in the *Press* of 26 August. Foster had assaulted his wife in a pub called the Wheatsheaf and she had had to go to hospital in a cab (but not until after the cabbie had been assaulted). After treatment she was escorted home by Inspector Blackburn and P.C. Hebden and on arriving home was assaulted again. Foster then set about the policemen in the full view of 'hundreds of people', and was eventually subdued. Dashwood Carter had a nice line in mitigation and told the bench that Foster was a reservist who had returned from the front in March, and that 'Whatever happened in this case he was prepared to sign the pledge.' He was fined 5s. and costs for assaulting his wife; £1 for the assault on Inspector Blackburn; and 5s. for the attack on P.C. Hebden; a total of £2.12s.6d. which was paid forthwith. Why was he treated so leniently asked *Truth* ? Was it because it had been said on his behalf that his wife provoked him ? Or was the York bench influenced by the statement that Foster was a reservist ? Whatever the reasons that lead to Foster's 'escape on these ridiculously easy terms', *Truth* went on, 'As to the prisoner's promise to take the pledge, the magistrates must be exceptionally muddy-minded if they accept that as any extenuation for such an outbreak of ruffianism.' Foster's treatment does seem extremely lenient, but a promise to sign the pledge was a fairly common ploy used in those days when temperance movements were vocal and active. Thomas Hudson, in a case reported in the *Press* of 22 August, was another reservist who had served 16 months in South Africa. He returned home in July and on Saturday 17 August got 'very drunk' and was refused any more drink by the landlord of the Garden Gate in Hungate. Tom thereafter refused to leave the pub; the police were sent for; and he was summonsed. In court he said he was 'very sorry'. He had been in the Militia Reserve, but his time had expired. He had not tasted drink for 16 months. 'The magistrates' clerk: "Good reason, you could not get any." Defendant, on promising to sign the pledge, was bound over to be of good behaviour for six months, and to pay the costs.'

An interesting example of the way in which the magistrates' powers were gradually being increased in licensing matters in the early years of the 20th century might be illustrated by mentioning a submission made to the licensing bench in 1902. A new road - Deangate - was being built, and the owners of the Cross Keys, Goodramgate, wanted to alter that establishment. Plans were submitted for the approval of the bench as was the custom, the legal representative of the applicants said. He made considerable play on the fact that he and those he represented did not have to do so, but conceded that from 1 January 1903 such a submission would be a statutory necessity. (130) Thereafter benches would have to 'approve' plans for alterations, except and unless those alterations were of a minor nature. They still do.

The problem of drunkeness in York and the attitudes of people like Canon Argles have been mentioned, and they would certainly have been members of one or other of the city's temperance organisations. These abounded, allied to churches, chapels and workshops. In 1901, among other organisations there were in existence: the York and

District Band of Hope Union; the North Eastern Railway Temperance Union; the York White Cross Temperance Society; the York Temperance Society; the York Adult School Temperance Society; and the Army Temperance Society. (131) All these kept up a continuous criticism of 'the trade' and the effects of hard liquor, even although the turn of the century was clearly not a propitious period for the movement. Robert Kay, a Wesleyan member of the York School Board, was a particularly active temperance reformer and was the presiding teacher at the Priory Street Wesleyan's Young Men's class. In September 1900 he persuaded that body to lobby the York licensing bench with a resolution saying they were 'of opinion ... that the time has arrived when the ... Magistrates ... should refuse to renew licenses to houses which, ... are not now needed for public convenience' and that no new ones should be granted 'because there are enough already.' The young men also said that licenses tended 'to degrade the neighbourhood in which they are placed, cause adjoining property to depreciate in value, and act detrimentally to the moral and physical well-being of the citizens.' (132) The Rowntrees were also active in the temperance cause and so were Henry Tennant and Morrell. These two were present at a Temperance Bazaar when J. Ankers demanded Sunday closing and the raising of the minimum age for drinking to 21. (133) People like Ankers had plenty of evidence to support their cause, but just occasionally they shot themselves in the foot. In September 1901, just a year after the Welsleyan young men had lobbied the bench, another Robert Kay, a reformed artist who affected total abstinence beliefs, was prosecuted for neglecting his children by the NSPCC and gaoled. (134) The cause of his downfall ? The answer was a reversion to using what W.C. Fields once called Old Nick's Brew.

Who were the temperance advocates in York ? Some have been mentioned. The Quakers were prominent among them, as were many nonconformist clergymen, and the adult schools that abounded in the city at that time were definitely intended by their friends (the Quakers) to be a part of the temperance movement. (135) Many ladies found an outlet in these organisations for their energies.

There were women members of the temperance organisations, the York School Board and the guardians. Where else - if anywhere - were they able to play a significant role in society ? Both political parties, one of which certainly (in York) did not even pay lip service to women's rights arguments, used the enthusiasm and ability of female sympathisers and gave one of them a platform from which to draw attention to herself. She was the aforementioned Edith Milner of Heworth House.

The Conservative party in York was organised into ward organisations with a central governing body which can be seen at work in the accounts of the elections of 1900. Also in existence in York were two 'Habitations' of the Primrose League. Their aims were fairly predictable but readers of the local press were reminded of them by R.H.V. Wragge in April 1901. They were, he said, 'the upholding of religion, the maintenance of the Constitution, and the maintenance of the British Empire.'

Wragge was speaking at the annual meeting of the Ebor Habitation of the League No 2366, an organisation which had 1,335 members, and along with its other branch, was, Wragge said, 'a terror to the Radicals of York.' The second branch of the League was Edith's, and it was the Milner Habitation No 646, and a very active branch it was too, organising cycle clubs, trips to the continent and (non political) lectures like Edith's on 'The Miracle of Ober-Ammergau'. (136) Edith was the 'ruling Councillor' of Habitation 646, and a dab hand at the kind of patriotic recitation Nosmo King gave to later generations. There was a political element in the League's programme, naturally, the tone of which might be gauged by an event of March 1902 when Edith chaired a meeting at which her brother lectured on the state of the Liberal party. It was an unbelievably jingoistic speech he gave which, given the stage the war had reached at that time, and given the way York had been disturbed about it somewhat earlier is, perhaps, not surprising. It will have been noted from the stated aims of the Primrose League that Edith and her like were not exactly aching to get a parliamentary vote. The 'maintenance of the constitution' was as unambiguous a statement of aims as one could get. Did the League have a wide membership ? Were there representatives of the working class among the 2,000 or so members in York ? It seems unlikely - and if there were they may well have felt ill at ease (maybe as ill at ease as those people in the adult schools who were supposed to meet on Sundays as equals in a spirit of 'fellowship' with the people who may well have been their employers). Edith revealed that among her 590 members in 1902 there were '14 knights and 34 dames.' (137)

The Liberals, who were also organised down to a ward basis, also welcomed women as workers and helpers. In 1901 there was in existence a York Women's Liberal Association which discussed such issues as education, (138) and that Miss Wilkinson who was on the School Board was a committee member of the York Liberal Club. (139) In 1902 Miss E.T. Wilkinson was made president of the Women's Association (140). All these ladies were almost certainly believers in the need for women's suffrage and they probably pinned their hopes for success on a future Liberal government. If they did they were to be bitterly disappointed.

There was in existence a York Women's Suffrage Society. Edith Milner was not a member, but those that were met in March 1901 and gave as their opinion 'That ... the continued exclusion of women from the exercise of the Parliamentary franchise is unconstitutional and injurious' and they recommended that Butcher and Faber in the Commons support a resolution in their favour to be moved by Mr T. Taylor on 19 March. (141) Butcher and Faber did not do as they wished. When the York Women's Suffrage Society (142) was first formed is unknown, but by the time the first issue of the *Women's Suffrage Record* appeared Miss Wilkinson was prominent enough to be on the 'Sessional Committee' of the National Union of Women's Suffrage Societies and was reported meeting with a groups of MPs at the Commons to discuss Colonel Penny's Representation of the People Amendment Bill. (143) This was in February 1903 and just a month later the York Society held its annual general meeting. Its secretary then was Mrs Denis Taylor, Standcliffe, the Mount, and one of its main speakers - who had also addressed them earlier - was the Lady Mayoress. She was the wife of Alderman Edwin Gray who had been elevated to that position in 1898 and who had also been appointed Lord Mayor a year earlier - when he was not on the council. (144) He was the head of the firm of Gray and Dodsworth, solicitors, and his wife's speech shows that she was no mean performer on a political platform, and her remarks seem - at this remove of time - to have been so unanswerable that it seems incredible that she and her ladies had to wait until after the Great War before they got the vote. The logic of her (their) case was overpowering and Mrs Gray drew attention to the anomalous fact that although they could not vote for Members of Parliament they could vote - if they qualified (and exactly who qualified for a vote in York was succinctly summarised by the *Evening Press* on 1 August 1902) - for county councillors, for guardians and for parish councils. There was even a little enclave in the United Kingdom - the Isle of Man - Mrs Gray went on, where they had a parliamentary vote. Women could not sit on a county council, she said, but could sit on a parish council. She pointed to the example of New Zealand where giving the vote to women had not brought chaos to society, and told her hearers that there were in the country 270 female members of school boards; 1,000 guardians; and 160 rural district councillors.

Mrs Gray was a Liberal who was very prominent in some other radical reform organisations - notably one set up to draw attention to (and do something about) the appalling working class housing that existed in York. It has been mentioned that the York corporation resolutely refused to use the powers that it could have had by adopting the Housing of the Working Classes Act of 1890, and in 1901 a York Health and Housing Reform Association was brought into existence to highlight the evils of slum dwellings and to pressurise local government into action. Rowntree's *Poverty* (it was announced as about to appear in October) and the research work undertaken for it must have heightened attention and the Housing Association began to hold propaganda meetings which got considerable press coverage. Early in the summer of 1901, for example, an open air meeting was held on St George's Fields where lantern slides contrasting the poor areas of York and Leeds were contrasted with conditions in places like Bournville, Aintree and Port Sunlight. (145) In February 1902 the Association forced the York corporation to make a public pronouncement about better housing - which was negative. The Health Committee announced in reply to resolutions which had been sent in that the councillors could not see their way to using the 1890 Housing Act 'in view of the heavy calls which are [already] being made upon the ratepayers,' an announcement which would not have surprised the housing reformers, perhaps, but which would have hardened their resolve without doubt. (146)

Mrs Edwin Gray took her messages (better housing was only one of them) out and into other organisations. In December 1901 she addressed the York branch of the Charity Organisation Society, the Girl's Friendly Society, and the Mother's Union. In February she spoke to the York Cooperative Women's Guild (147) on the need for better working class dwellings (this at a time when there was a major small pox scare) and continually raised the question at political meetings. She and the York Housing Reform Association may well have been largely responsible for making the York corporation take what seems to be its first initiative under the 1890 Act in June 1903. Then R.P. Dale made a successful application (which was appealed) to the York magistrates to close six tenements in Beedham's Court, Skeldergate. It was there that the cholera outbreak of over a half century earlier had broken out. (148)

Sometime after the corporation at last made a start on clearing Skeldergate Mrs Gray led a deputation to the city council from the executive committee of the York section of the National Union of Women Workers. (149) This organisation was not an industrial union, but that such things might have been needed, however, might be inferred from the report of a court case in 1903. The York and County Hygienic Laundries Ltd was taken to court for six offences that contravened section 103 of a Factory Act. This said that the hours worked in any consecutive 24 hours should not exceed 14 for a woman, 12 for a 'young person' and ten for a child, or 60 or 30 hours a week. Evidence was given that five girls at the time of an inspection had in fact worked 67. (150) The six cases were proved. The penalty ? Half a crown in each case plus costs!

What work was there for women in York, apart from being laundresses ? The 1901 census revealed the obvious. York was an unindustrialised city and many of the women workers were either domestics or worked in shops or the confectionery trade. The *Victoria County History of York* drew attention to the difficulty of making precise estimates of the number of people employed in the confectionery trades, but by the turn of the century 'the firms of Terry and Rowntree & Co. Ltd. had developed into large-scale concerns' with the latter expanding rapidly. (It employed 100 workers in 1879; 893 in 1894; and 4,066 in 1909). (151) The following table is compiled from the results of the 1901 census.

Occupations at ages 10 Years and	Ages of Females from 10 years						
	Totals		10-	15-	25-	45-	65+
	Unmarried	Married or Widowed					
Domestic service hotels and eating houses		132	6	1	82	46	9
Domestic service (other)	2,973	151	108	1,868	895	230	23
Charwomen	60	231		13			
Laundry and washing service	247	215	8	158	156	124	16
Teaching	461	20	6	229	195	44	7
Food workers	1,100	59	112	910	132	5	
Milliners, Dressmakers	839	164	26	516	343	97	21
Midwives	166	63	1	57	105	56	10

A similar selective table showing the occupations of men in York at the turn of the century follows. The numbers employed in 'sanitary service' are worthy of note.

Occupations at ages 10 years and upwards	Ages of males 10 years and upwards					
	Total Males	10-	15-	25-	45-	65+
Legal, barristers, solicitors	59			31	19	9
Law clerks	125	6	54	51	11	3
Domestic service indoors, hotels, lodging and eating houses	70	3	33	22	11	1
Other domestic indoor service	77	8	29		27	13

Commercial or business clerks	709	33	354	252	62	8
Conveyance of men, goods, and messages on railways	2,896	10	866	1,380	588	52
Ironfounders	185	1	50	85	41	8
Blacksmiths	495	4	113	252	115	11
Erectors, fitters, turners	673	6	197	321	128	21
Carpenters, joiners	1,106	13	350	408	292	43
Bricklayers and bricklayers' labourers	894	1	278	384	205	26
Printers, lithographers	322	11	104	162	10	5
Food workers	1,330	101	666	417	130	16
Food dealers	1,172	18	384	482	239	49
Gas, water, electricity	180	1	30	82	54	13
Sanitary service	28		6	9	12	1

A summary of the whole population was:

Males	Occupied and unoccupied	Females
38,147	All ages	39,767
8,302	Under 10	8,306
29,845	10 and upwards	31,461

An analysis of the last figures showed:

Males occupied and unoccupied	Total	10-	15-	25-	45-	65+	Unmarried	Married or Widowed
	29,895	3,988	8,207	10,753	5,421	1,476		
Females do		3,888	7,946	11,167	5,982	1,978	14,94	16,520
Retired or unocccupied males	5,018	3,397	476	179	351	615		
do females		3,590	3,412	8,987	4,820	1,726	7,654	14,881
Males engaged in occupations	24,827	591	7,731	10,574	5,070	861		
Females do		298	4,534	2,680	1,162	252	7,287	1,639

It is clear from *Poverty* and from other sources that, unless the workers supplemented their incomes by whatever the equivalent of 'moonlighting' was in the early 1900s, or by some other methods, there was little left over for pleasure - indeed for many there was simply nothing according to Rowntree, whose quote on the subject has been given. What was there especially for them in the city - apart from the working men's clubs that is ? Very little must be the answer, and what there was was frequently sponsored by one or other of the temperance societies or the chapels. The York Temperance Society for example was into lantern slide lectures and put on epics like 'Come Home Mother' while ladies recited and a Mr Nutbrown exhorted. (152) Other temperance organisations regularly put on similar shows and in August 1903 the White Rose Temperance Society announced that it had taken premises in Harper's Yard, Walmgate, which it intended to turn into a club where there would be facilities for billiards, bowls and tennis. It also intended to start a night school there with a library. (153) There were also a number of adult schools in York, (154) and in December 1903, again it seems as an alternative to the pubs, a splendid lady called Miss Knocker started Saturday night penny concerts at the Exhibition Hall where good music and entertainment of an improving kind were to be provided. (155)

What else was there in York that could be enjoyed by the poorer classes on occasion? The local football and rugby clubs attracted support and there were theatres. The Theatre Royal was well established, and in 1902 the York Opera House was opened (156) which, from 1903, began to provide 'varieties' which were, presumably, much more to the liking of the working classes than the fare provided by the Theatre Royal.

Film shows were eventually given there, the *Victoria County History* records, when 'animated pictures' joined variety as a competitor to the Theatre Royal. That new art form seems to have made its first appearance in York in 1901, just a few months after the press reported on the first complete year's working of the municipal electricity supply industry. (157) (When it made a profit of £98.)

Late in November 1901 the *Press* told its readers that there was to be a display of 'animated pictures' at the Exhibition Buildings, (158) and amongst the exciting fare was to be a film of a lion tamer in a den with 40 lions, and a series on the hazards of deep sea fishing called 'Toilers of the Deep'. The show was to be provided by Thomas Edison's Animated Photo Company and its publicity revealed that the fishing film was five miles long and consisted of a quarter of a million pictures (frames). In addition to the aforementioned features the initial programme included an 'Illustrated' account of the life of Joan of Arc and war scenes from China and South Africa. For many years to come cinema shows frequently included local scenes specially shot for particular audiences and the Edison Company had been out in the streets filming for its first shows in York where it offered footage of Clifford's Tower and the local trams, along with shots of a turn out by the city's Fire Brigade (which was shortly to be severely criticised in the House of Commons). Perhaps 'no popular entertainment so strikingly demonstrates the advance of the practical application of scientific discoveries as the cinematograph' wrote the *Press*, and the show was such a success that it was held over and more attractions added to it. These included more local film of the country's favourite soldier - Lord Roberts - distributing war medals in York, and footage of the funeral of President William McKinley and the arrest of his anarchist assassin Goudie. From this point onwards films became a part of popular entertainment in York, though it was sometime before picture palaces devoted entirely to their showing were built. Until then films were part of the entertainment packages put on by various bodies. Perhaps the temperance movement added flicks to the staple fare of songs and recitations with 'connective readings' by people like Mr Nutbrown. Certainly they were part of the bill at the Festival Concert Rooms in January 1903, when Carl Mysto, the Handcuff King, came to York to resist a challenge by one Frank Luty. Mysto did this to the entire satisfaction of the paying public it is certain, and 'The remainder of the programme consisted of the New Century Animated Pictures and two songs by Mrs. Copeland.' An added attraction to the more obvious delights of the animated picture shows in those early days might just have been the fact that there was a considerable element of danger involved in going to see records of Lord Roberts presenting medals or the York Fire brigade turning out. Late in 1902 the Keighley Mechanics' Institute was seriously damaged when film caught fire causing, presumably, the Keighley brigade to turn out with, one hopes, rather more efficiency than had been attributed to that in York. Reports of such incidents are not uncommon. They occurred in Old Ebor.

Without a great deal of industry wages were low in York and, as Rowntree showed, many could just about make ends meet if they were frugal in the extreme. When they became unemployed, however, and there was enough unemployment in the building trade in 1903 to cause anxiety, or when they became old, workers could be in dire trouble. Some, as we have seen, might get some benefit from a trade union - some (like the men of the ASRS who worked on the North Eastern Railway) (159) might get a pension, (160) but many would have to rely on charity, with all that that meant in terms of loss of dignity to people who had been brought up to believe in Victorian values. At just about the time that the papers were reporting that unemployment was rife in the building trades in 1903 they mentioned that the Soup Kitchen had opened once more for business, and York, to its credit, had many other philanthropic organisations set up to help the poor and needy. Edith Milner, for example, was active in the local branch of the Charity Organisation Society, (161) and during the bad weather of January 1903 this body set up 15 district offices in York and distributed help to those in distress. The scale of relief paid was 3s. a week to an adult living alone and 2s.6d. each to two adults living together. (162) There were other worthy organisations of a similar kind. The York Invalid Kitchen, for example, gave dinners to the needy and disabled. (163) The workhouse was there as a dreaded last resort.

York, then, like all Victorian cities, had many worthy charities and to some of these the working class had to resort in times of illness. The York Dispensary set up to offer free medical attention to poor patients in 1788 was sited from 1899 in Duncombe Place, and from 1895 it had provided a maternity service and since 1897 it had taken over the work of the York Lying-In Society. In February 1901 W. Hargrove presided over a particularly interesting annual meeting of the Dispensary at which he revealed they had done slightly less business than in the previous year. Nevertheless there were 614 patients, and: admitted 'with recommendations' had been 4,481 persons; there had been 1,046 'casuals' and 486 'dentals'; a total of 6,627. For the first time in its history, Hargrove went on, the Dispensary was appointing a lady as a house surgeon (a Dr Ford). This would have pleased Mrs Edwin Gray, no doubt, but Hargrove went on to spoil things a little by saying that he and his colleagues had 'undoubtedly been tempted to do so' by the fact that they had been unable to find a suitable male applicant. (164) This nevertheless prompted some York persons to claim a first in this respect, but it was a claim that had no substance. On 18 February the *Evening Press* reported that as long ago as 1896 the Manchester Clinical Hospital for Women and Children had appointed Miss Annie M.S. Anderson as an honorary assistant physician and that last year that same institution had taken on Miss Adeline M. Roberts as a house surgeon.

The York County Hospital, situated in Monkgate, was, like the Dispensary, an 18th century foundation, and in the early years of the 20th century there began a regular fund raising day which became a feature of the city's year. This was York Hospital Saturday, the first of which was held in 1901. (165) Another voluntary body in York whose title is evocative of the conditions that prevailed at the time was a branch of the National Association for the Prevention of Consumption. Mrs Edwin Gray was connected with this body, (166) the secretary of which was Dr William Arthur Evelyn, a person who has a celebrated place in York's history. (167)

In addition to all the above there were worthy York charitable organisations intended to provide 'treats' for the children, and what they did must surely have brought some pleasure in what were just as surely drab little lives - even if the patronising attitudes of some of the organisers may have spoiled the pleasure somewhat. Edith Milner was involved in this kind of work, energetically helping the Children's Order of Chivalry through holding garden parties. The Order was set up to give town children holidays in the country, (168) while the York Cinderella Club provided occasional outings for children of 'the labouring' classes from areas of York like Skeldergate, Layerthorpe and Walmgate. (169)

It is little wonder that the organised working class, and the Liberal party, began to demand old age pensions in these early years of the 20th century. It is little wonder that workers began to organise a political movement of their own to try to achieve these demands - and much more. In the exciting years that remained before the general election of 1906 there was to be much political agitation, and in York, as elsewhere, organised labour emerged as a vital political force.

1. In the 1830s York's election practices were examined by a Select committee of the House of Commons - an investigation which could have had serious consequences.
2. There is a very slight biography of Lockwood by A. Birell
3. The *Condor*
4. In early 1902 he was returned to parliament again - for Woolwich - and resigned in 1903 to take up command of the Channel Squadron. He sat for Portsmouth from 1910-16 - when he was raised to the peerage.
5. The by election was held on 13 January 1898
6. Beresford left a volume of autobiography titled *Memories* (1914). He also wrote *The Betrayal* (1912), a book which arose out of a prolonged dispute with Asquith, the Prime Minister, over naval affairs.
7. The *Evening Press* 1 January 1900 (hereafter *Press*) The references to the *Press* throughout are to the main editions of the day (there were others)
8. *Ibid* 1 January and 3 February 1900
9. The description of the York by election of 1900 is taken from *Ibid* issues to 7 February and *Yorkshire Herald* similar dates. (Hereafter *Herald*)
10. Brief biographical details of Murray in *Press* 17 January 1900
11. First returned in 1893. There is a splendid *Vanity Fair* cartoon of Butcher
12. The British under Sir George Colley were defeated by the Boers on Majuba Hill in February 1881 and the commander killed. After this instead of fighting onand risking a rebellion in the Cape, Gladstone made peace and the Pretoria Convention of 1881 recognized the independence of the Transvaal, subject to British suzerainty
13. *Press* 31 January 1900
14. *Ibid* 19 and 20 January 1900
15. For the extensions see eg the map in C. Feinstein (ed), *York 1831-1981* (York 1981) p 112
16. *Press* 3 October 1899
17. R. Hills, 'The City Council and Electoral Politics, 1901-1971' in Feinstein *op cit fn 5*. *Press* 11 October 1899
18. *Press* 11 October 1899
19. *Ibid* 28 October 1899
20. See the speech in *Ibid* 13 October 1899. See also Brigg's book *Jubilee History of the York Equitable Industrial Society Limited* (Manchester 1909)

21. The great public health reformer of half a century earlier
22. *Herald* 13 October 1900. The number eventually rose to seven out of 12
23. *Ibid* 11 October 1900. He was president of the York Trades Council. See also Briggs op.cit. p 139
24. *Herald* 17 October 1900
25. *Ibid* 23 and 24 October 1900
26. Speech reported in *Ibid* 23 October 1900
27. *Ibid*
28. *Ibid* 24 and 26 October 1900. Proctor wanted to take over the tramways, and the cleaning of the ash pits. He was also for creating a public cemetery
29. This was *Poverty and Progress*. See later
30. *Press* 1 November 1900
31. *Ibid* 6 July 1901
32. *Ibid* 25 and 26 September 1900
33. *Ibid* 26 September 1900
34. *Herald* 1 October 1900
35. R.C.K. Ensor, *England 1870-1914* (Oxford 1936) p 267
36. P.M. Tillott (ed), *The History of Yorkshire. The City of York* (Oxford 1961) p 279. *The Victoria County History,* hereafter *VCH*
37. *Press* 12 March 1901. On the way women got the municipal vote see, eg, R. Fulford, *Votes for Women* (1958)
38. *Press* 25 March 1901
39. See eg issues from 1 January 1902
40. Eg *Press* 3 July 1902
41. *Ibid* 23 January 1902
42. *Ibid* 7 June 1902. Letter from Anderson
43. Ensor *op.cit.* p 355
44. *Press* 9 February 1901
45. *Ibid*
46. Amongst other things that could give this impression was the Taff Vale dispute then going on
47. *Press* 21 January 1901. The conference mentioned earlier reported in *Ibid* 10 January 1901. The deputation of unsectarians was present there
48. *Ibid* 7 February 1901
49. For this dispute see *Ibid* 10 January 1901, where it was said that 85 children were having to go to schools in the city because of overcrowding at that in Bilton Street. Miss Wilkinson also addressed herself to the need for better technical education, making speeches very similar to those of Mawson quoted above. 'She did not believe that our working people were ever beaten out of the markets of the world except by the greater educational advantages enjoyed by other nations', she said at her adoption meeting. *Ibid* 9 January 1901. She had then been on the Board for nine years.
50. *Ibid* 10 January 1901
51. *Ibid* 16 February 1902
52. *Herald* 24 October 1900
53. *Press* 19 January 1901. The unification had been made on 10 April 1899
54. See fn 49 *supra*
55. M. Sturt, *The education of the people* (1969) pp 406-7
56. *VCH* p 288
57. G.A.N. Lowndes, *The Silent Social Revolution* (Oxford 1969) pp 61-2
58. A.M. Kazamias, *Politics, Society and Secondary Education in England* (Philaphelphia 1960)
59. Sturt, *op.cit.* p 411
60. E. Eagleshaw, *From School Board to Local Authority* (1956) Chap 12 *passim*. The detailed background to the Cockerton judgement is given in chapters 10 and 11
61. *Press* 30 July, 8 August 1901
62. *Ibid* 7 September 1901
63. *Ibid* 10 July 1901
64. K. Robbins, *The Eclipse of a Great Power* (1983) p 68
65. *Press* 1 and 2 March 1901. Voting was: Scott, 723; Seller, 425; Anderson, 365.
66. *Ibid* 28 January 1901. See *Ibid* 9 August 1901 for a report of the NER's declining profits - a decline which the company put down to a decrease in mineral traffic

67. *Ibid* 18 March 1901
68. *Ibid* 3 and 8 December 1902
69. *Ibid* 14 and 15 May 1901
70. *Ibid* 29 May and 1 June 1901
71. *Ibid* 1 May and 19 September 1901
72. *Ibid* 18 June 1901
73. *Ibid* 18 January 1902
74. Ensor *op.cit*. p 378. The case against the ASRS went against the union, was reversed by the Court of Appeal, then upheld in the Lords
75. *Press* 16 May 1902. On this occasion the brothers got the date wrong. They were surely referring to the Trade Union Act of 1871 which afforded absolute protection to the union funds
76. *Ibid* 17 May 1901
77. *Ibid* 11 April 1902
78. *Ibid* 20 February 1902. Present at its meetings - and a party to its creation - wererepresentatives of the York branch of the Irish National League
79. *Ibid* 6 March 1902. On the proposals at this stage to take over the city's tram system see H.Murray, *The Horse Tramways of York 1880-1901* (Walsall 1980) Chap 7 *passim*
80. See particularly A. Briggs, *A Study of the Work of Seebohm Rowntree 1871-1954* (1961)
81. See eg D. Rubinstein, 'York: *Poverty and Progress*, 1899-1936', *York History* No 2 (nd)
82. B.S. Rowntree, *Poverty A Study of Town Life* (2nd edition) pp 150-51
83. In *Ibid* there is a list of sick benefits the unions paid to their members
84. *Ibid* p 363
85. Rowntree described a 'cycle' of poverty with five alternating periods of 'wantand comparative plenty.' The periods of 'plenty' were when a child or the children were working and unmarried and contributing to the family income
86. When the Boer War ended, however, severe depression hit York and elsewhere (see later)
87. *Press* 4 September 1900. Also issue of 26 September 1900
88. *Ibid* 3 September 1901
89. An off license application for premises in the Pavement was granted
90. *Press* 27 September 1901
91. *History of Working Men's Clubs in York*, a scrapbook of newspaper articles from the *Herald* in the York City Archives. Reference Y331.83
92. *Ibid*. The Crescent was established in 1909; Fulford Road in 1904; Poppleton Road in 1910. Several of these (and some later ones) were started by groups ofworkers, like the postmen and tramway men. All the clubs had to register under the Licensing Act of 1902 and a list of them, with membership, is given in *Press* 4 February 1903. South Bank then had 226; Clarence 225; Haxby Road 174; and St Lawrence 210. See also A.J. Peacock, 'York's First Working Men's Club', *York History* No 2 (nd)
93. *Paterson's Licensing Acts* (1983) p 13. On the history of Working Men's Clubs (and the CIU) before this date see, eg, the works of the Rev Henry Solly. The clubs approved of by Solly were in the earliest days akin to the latter day adultschools with the emphasis on 'improvement'. Many were founded (like the INL in York) as political clubs, but at the close of the century perhaps most were like those created at that time in York - alternatives to the pub, and places of entertainment. On this period see, eg, J. Taylor, From *Self-Help to Glamour: theWorking Man's Club, 1860-1972* (Ruskin College History Workshop Pamphlet No 7, 1972). Mr Taylor's work relies solidly on various publications and reports of the CIU
94. J. Rowntree and A. Sherwell, *The Taxation of the Liquor Trade* (1906), chap 13. The Goole LVA meeting referred to later is reported in *Press* 5 July 1901
95. On this splendidly named gentleman see *York History* No 3 (no date). The following issue of that same journal rescued from oblivion another York artistcalled Robert Henry 'Genuine' Thompson. Another character nearer the time of this study operated in the Scarborough area, and may well have plagued Old Ebor as well. This was 'Daddy Fra Clayton'. For one of his court appearances see *Press* 15 September 1902
96. A shortened version of a well known name for people like Screampoke. For what it is shortened from see eg E. Partridge, *A Dictionary of Slang and Unconventional English* (1984) p 890 where it is described as a term for 'A habitual drinker: low coll.: since late 1940s.'
97. *Press* 5 July 1901. Details in report of an LVA meeting
98. *Ibid* 2 March 1901

99. *Ibid* 5 March 1901. Ginger got 14 days
100. *Ibid* 6 May 1901
101. *Ibid* 5 July 1901
102. *Ibid* 17 October 1901. Professor R.B. Dobson of Cambridge has a special interest in the family of Riley-Smith, and they will undoubtedly feature prominently in his contemplated work on Tadcaster
103. The progress of the Bill through Parliament can be followed in volumes of *Hansard* for 1901 numbered 91 and 99. For a prosecution (from Scarborough) under the Child Messenger Act see eg *Press* 11 August 1905 when the seller to a child of ten was fined 5s. and costs and the sender 10s. and 8s. costs
104. See eg *The Justice of the Peace* 25 October 1902
105. *Ibid* 23 August 1902
106. *Press* 8 October 1902
107. *Ibid* 17 April 1902
108. *Ibid* 7 August 1902
109. *Ibid* 28 August 1902. In 1903 the Scarborough public vaccinators came under severe criticism and were sacked. See eg *Ibid* 2 April 1903
110. *Ibid* 31 July 1902
111. See the letter from E.H. Smith in *Herald* 7 January 1902
112. *Press* 13 and 14 March 1902. Smallpox appeared in York and, as is mentioned in the text, was still prevalent in 1903. See eg *Ibid* 1 January 1903, reports about Barnsley. See also the report of the York Corporation's deliberations in *Ibid* 7 July 1903. There it was reported that between 28 March and 25 June last there had been 2,929 cases of smallpox reported in the provinces - 794 in the West Riding. See also *Ibid* 2 January 1903 for cases in York
113. See A.J. Peacock, 'Shameful Persecution', *Gun Fire No 1* (nd)
114. Press 17 September 1902
115. *Ibid* 2 June 1902
116. *Ibid* 5 July 1902
117. This was at Thirsk, however. *Ibid* 3 November 1902
118. *Ibid* 3 and 4 July 1902
119. *Ibid* 17 July 1902
120. See letter in *Ibid* 17 February 1902
121. *Ibid* 11 November 1901
122. Eg *Oke's Magisterial Formulist* (1880) produced just after the passing of the Summary Jurisdiction Act
123. *Press* 8 August 1901
124. *Ibid* 13 March 1902
125. *Ibid* 3 October 1902
126. *Ibid* 1 May 1901
127. See eg A.J. Peacock, 'Crucifixion', *Gun Fire* No 2 (nd)
128. *Truth*, quoted *Press* 4 September 1901
129. *Press* 3 September 1901
130. *Ibid* 3 November 1902
131. For meetings of these bodies see, eg, *Ibid* 4 and 25 February, 5 March, 15 May 1901. For a long report of a year's work of the York Band of Hope Union see eg *Ibid* 28 January 1904
132. *Ibid* 3 September 1900
133. *Ibid* 10 October 1902
134. *Ibid* 9 September 1901
135. On the adult schools of York see eg F. J. Gillman, *The Story of the York Adult Schools from the commencement to the Year 1907* (York 1907)
136. On meetings and activities of the Primrose League in York at this time see eg *Ibid* 24 January, 27 March, 11 and 18 April, 16 September 1901, 4 March, 18 April 1902
137. *Ibid* 18 April 1902
138. *Ibid* 25 March 1901, 28 November 1902
139. *Ibid* 16 October 1901
140. *Ibid* 21 January 1902
141. *Ibid* 2 March 1901
142. A York Society for Women's Suffrage
143. *Women's Suffrage Record* June 1903. *Press* 4 March 1903

144. *Press* 23 October 1902
145. *Ibid* 2 May 1901
146. *Ibid* 27 February 1902
147. *Ibid* 5 and 12 December 1901 and 11 February 1903
148. *Ibid* 22 June 1901. On the cholera outbreak of the 19th century see M. Dury, *The First Spasmodic Cholera Epidemic in York, 1832* (York 1974). For a review of this work see eg *York History* No 2 (nd)
149. *Press* 14 November 1903. The deputation went to lobby the new York Education Committee
150. *Ibid* 19 November 1903
151. *VCH op.cit.* p 274
152. *Press* 4 May 1903
153. *Ibid* 18 August 1903
154. See eg F.J. Gillman, *op.cit.* and A.J. Peacock, 'Adult Education in York, 1800-1946', *York History* No 5 (nd)
155. *Press* 14 December 1903
156. *Herald* 18 January 1902
157. *Press* 29 June 1901
158. *Ibid* 23 and 26 November 1901
159. *Ibid* 29 November 1902
160. There is a nice letter in *Ibid* 21 February 1902 complaining that a rural postman had been given notice to quit without a pension. He had had to provide himself with a pony; got under £1 a week; started work at five o'clock; and was 80 years of age
161. *Ibid* 19 February 1902
162. *Ibid* 17 January 1903
163. *Ibid* 27 January 1903. See the same source for the year's work. The kitchen spent £127 on over 4,000 dinners, while income amounted to just over £89
164. *Ibid* 12 February 1901
165. *Ibid* 31 August and 19 September 1901
166. *Ibid* 10 February 1902
167. See H. Murray, *Dr Evelyn's York* (York 1983)
168. *Press* 15 July 1901, 26 June 1902
169. *Ibid* 11 October 1901

g. G. Butcher

CHAPTER 2

POLITICS, EDUCATION, TEMPERANCE, AND R.H. VERNON WRAGGE

The Tories gained sensational victories in York at the 'Khaki Election' of 1900 and the party was securely in power for many years, but in the aftermath of that victory - partly as a result of revelations about the war, partly as a result of new legislation - dissatisfaction with them rapidly began to be shown everywhere, and the resentment that culminated in the great Liberal landslide victory of 1906 set in.

Concern about the causes of the Boer War were expressed during the campaign of 1900, with Joseph Chamberlain urging the nation to stick with the government rather than vote for the Liberals - a 'congeries of disconnected and antagonistic atoms which called itself a party, but was only a conglomerate mixture.' (1) These were ironic words coming from the man who was shortly to split his own party, but in the aftermath of the Khaki Election concern began to be expressed about the *conduct* of the war, rather than its origins. What has been called the 'second phase' of the Boer War had opened in February 1900 and on 27 February - Majuba Day - Lord Roberts forced the surrender of Piet Cronje. Later Roberts captured Bloemfontein, the capital of the Orange Free State, and Pretoria, capital of the Transvaal. The two states were annexed to the British crown and Roberts returned home to become Commander-in-Chief in the United Kingdom, leaving Lord Kitchener in command in South Africa. It must have looked to those at home as if it the war was nearing its end, but in fact it entered a third phase. The Boers split up and engaged in 'commando' raids, one of which ended with the surrender of Lord Methuen with 600 men and six guns. Faced with this situation Kitchener set to work to destroy his difficult enemy and the country was divided up by 3,700 miles of barbed wire and 8,000 blockhouses. Each section so divided was 'driven' and 'to prevent the Boer commandos simply melting back into the farming communities, the farms were burned down and women and children [were] herded into concentration camps.' (2) Conditions in these camps, where some 20,000 inmates died, gave rise to great concern. These concerns were aired in York.

The British got terrible publicity for their activities in the third phase of the Boer War, and the Nazis were still making capital out of them when Emil Jannings made the film *Oom Paul* in 1939. In the summer of 1901 a lady went on the stump exposing the conditions she had found in the camps, and she was invited to York to address the members of two adult schools by J.S. Rowntree. She was Miss Emily Hobhouse.

Miss Hobhouse conducted a campaign of the kind which, now, everyone must realise was perfectly justified, yet which at the time got hardly a hearing. She spoke to her York audience and afterwards the members of the Central Adult School condemned the way hostile crowds had tried to shut her up. They spoke of 'the prevalent spirit abroad, by which freedom of speech is being made impossible', saying it was 'a grave menace to the full and rightful liberty of' the nation's citizens. (3) Emily got the same hostile treatment at Leeds, where she was accompanied by Joshua Rowntree, and on Holbeck Moor a meeting was broken up and a prominent tradesman of pro-Boer sympathies was chased by 'fully 3,000 persons back to his residence'. (4) In Leeds Miss Hobhouse's description of conditions in the concentration camps had been challenged by a Mrs K.H.R. Stuart, a delegate from the Guild of Loyal Women of South Africa, and elsewhere by a Mr Bennett Burleigh. He had been to the camp at Middleburg where, he said, there had been fowls by the thousand, abundant fresh meat and the savoury smell of pastry dishes from frizzling ovens permeated the air. Middleburg, Burleigh said, 'was a paradise of healthy homes, with no work, and an abundance to eat up for old and young , which slum-London would be wild to share'. (5) Eventually a White Paper on the camps was issued which showed that they had 85,410 in them, and from which they appear as rather different from the idyllic places Burleigh had said they were. (6)

The 'campaign' against the concentration camps, if that is what it was, was shortlived, but Emily Hobhouse deserves great credit for her courageous stand against them. So too do the Quakers, and in York they were as prominent among her supporters as they were elsewhere, taking a complete anti-war stand, so making quite sure that they never got invitations to Edith Milner's garden parties. In November 1901 the York Society of Friends passed an anti-war resolution for example. (7) It was by no means the last time they took a stand on such an unpopular issue. They also emerged as major critics of an important piece of reforming legislation in the early years of the new government's life.

Sir John Gorst's Education Bill, which was so savaged in York by the Rev J. Hirst Hollowell, was withdrawn, as has been mentioned, and in March 1902 it was replaced by a root and branch bill which was to end the chaos brought about by the Cockerton judgement. A.J. Balfour, who became Prime Minister during the Bill's progress through parliament, sponsored it, shaking off 'his indolence' in Halévy's words, and 'showing himself the untiring and invincible debater he could be when he pleased'. (8) The Bill abolished the school boards and made county and county borough councils - like York - the local authorities for all secondary and technical education. (Originally, because of the influence of Chamberlain and the Birmingham group of Liberal Unionists, it had been intended that the county councils could take over the school boards at their discretion. In July the cabinet made what had been permissive into a statutory obligation.) Not only were the board schools put under the new authorities, however, but so too were the voluntary schools. 'By an elaborate bargain the managers of the latter, in return for providing the buildings, were to retain the appointment of teachers, while the current expenses of their schools were to be defrayed, like those of the ex-board (or "provided") schools, out of the local rates. Public money was thus made available for the first time to ensure properly paid teachers and a standardized level of efficiency for all children alike.' (9) In the provided schools 'undenominational' teaching was retained 'so that the nonconformists, whom it suited, lost nothing.'

The Education Bill created a tremendous furore. The Anglicans and Roman Catholics welcomed it, 'for it saved their schools, the increasing burden of which ... had reached breaking point. But the nonconformists were furious. Their formal objection was that it would put the cost of sectarian teaching on the rates.' (10) This was a somewhat bogus objection as the voluntary schools, including their own, of course, had long been in receipt of public grants. R.C.K. Ensor has pointed out that, in reality, the real grievances of the nonconformists lay elsewhere, and were twofold. First, in a large number of parishes the only school was a church school and the children of nonconformists had to attend it. The dissenters had seen the church schools running short of cash and had hoped that the church's monopoly in so many places would end as a result. But now the 1902 Bill seemed certain to rescue and prolong that monopoly. They were right, but they were also satisfied with the arrangements in the provided schools. A second reason for their hostility to Balfour's proposals was that the church, in getting its schools saved out of the rates was, again in Ensor's words, having 'it both ways'

The nonconformists of York were as hostile to the Education Bill (and as irrational) as they were elsewhere, but it had its supporters, of course. In April the York Diocesan Board of Education welcomed it, (11) so did the Conservative Association, (12) and so did J.G. Butcher (of course). Butcher told a meeting that 'no attempt had ever been made [before] by any Government to co-ordinate primary and secondary education, and this bill was an endeavour to mould both classes of education into one harmonious whole.' (13) That seems to have been fair comment and the the Convocation of York publicly came out in support of Balfour. Sir Frederick Milner spoke to Edith's branch of the Primrose League and referred to 'hot-headed extremists' who were opposing the reform. '... with absolutely indecent haste, before they could have given any study to the Bill or have mastered its provisions', Fred said, 'a large number of Non-conformists have met and denounced ... [it] in the most furious terms. Nothing more indecent in dealing with the national question had ever came to his knowledge during the whole of his political life.' (14) Faber and Butcher held meetings in the city at which they tried to put the record 'straight' regarding the Education Bill. In August Faber said he thought the government should have bought out all the voluntary schools, while Butcher complained that the Bill did not give 'additional clerical control' and inveighed against the 'campaign of misrepresentation' that was going on. (15) Later he tried again to explain the principles of a Tory bill which owed so much to the Fabian Tract 106, *The Education Muddle and the Way Out*. '...the root principle of the Bill', Butcher said, (16) was that instead of conflicting authorities, attending, some to elementary education, some to secondary, and some to technical education, there should in future be one local authority in each district whose duty it should be to control and be responsible for every grade of education, from the elementary stage upwards. ... that was an absolutely sound principle ... and ... the local authority must be the popularly elected body in the district, namely, the City or Borough Council ... The Council had to pay, and the body that had to pay should have some voice in saying how the money was to be spent ... . It was the old principle of taxation with representation. The people elected the County, or City, or Borough Council as the case might be, and it was only right that they should look to that Council that found the money to spend it.

Just a few days earlier Balfour had addressed a meeting at the St James's Hall and said that (17)

The Bill was an organic whole, which dealt with a great and admitted evil ... on a fixed, an intelligible plan ... He characterised as a shameless and most impudent allegation the statement that the Bill put education under the heel of the clergy. Precisely the reverse was the fact.

Balfour was right, but 'Religion on the Rates' was a splendid catch phrase and in York the people who should have known better took it up. Arnold Rowntree addressed a public meeting from which a telegram of protest was sent saying that 'in the interests of true education we should oppose the new Government Bill,' (18) and Joseph Rowntree, speaking at the York Liberal Club, said he 'trusted at this great crisis [that] ... the friends of religious freedom and of national education would put forth their strength to defeat this dangerous ecclesiastical conspiracy.' (19) This really was dreadful nonsense, and Rowntree knew perfectly well that with the thumping majority the Tories had in Parliament there was no way of defeating the Bill. He would also have known, however, that opposition to it, however irrational it might be, was good for the Liberal party. It had been split over the war (which ended on 2 June, the day the debates on the Education Bill began) and much else, and the Balfour proposals could unite it. Lord Rosebery began to make moves which seemed likely to end his isolation from the party (Sir Frederick Milner said Rosebery was the party's only hope) (20) and Balfour recognised that his proposals 'had given a tonic to the Liberal party. "Well, they wanted it,"' he said, with truth. (21) In July the Liberals had won a North Leeds by election with a candidate (a Baptist) who had fought his campaign solely on the issue of education. 'He was not one of those' who attributed 'excessive importance to bye-elections,' commented Rosebery, 'but he doubted if any single election had caused so great, so deep and wide an impression since Mr Gladstone's first election for Midlothian.' (22) Perhaps it should be recorded that the nonconformists' attitude was perhaps more predictable in York than in many places, because there, out of a total 25 schools existing at the time of the passing of the Balfour Act, only one was nonconformist and the overwhelming majority were run by the church, as the following tables show. (23)

Schools in York			
	staffed for	on register	attendance Sept 1902
Church of England	7,530	6,914	6,155
Roman Catholic	1,475	1,270	1,098
Wesleyan	800	566	513
Corporation	5,950	4,819	4,594
Places in Voluntary Schools 1900			
16 Church of England Schools		7,578	
3 Roman Catholic		1,915	
Priory Street Wesleyan		823	

A correspondent to the press updated the figures immediately above, taking his statistics from the third triennial report of the York School Board. He said that the voluntary sector in York could offer places to 10,300 children, that it was educating 8,754, and that the Board Schools had 4,927 pupils.

The Labour movement, traditionally the home of many nonconformists, and as delighted as the Liberals to have a stick to beat the government with, were as resolute in their opposition to Balfour's bill as were the Quakers and others. A national meeting of trade unionists held in May 1902 summed up its attitude in a resolution which showed that its fears were, perhaps, a little more substantial than some others. They feared that losing the elected school boards would lose them hard fought for representation on public bodies. The resolution condemned 'in the strongest possible terms the Government policy on education, which [it said] would destroy properly constituted bodies on education, expressing the opinion that the abolition of School Boards would have a most destructive effect on the education of the people, and take away the advantages which workers had in direct representation in the management of Board Schools, and calling on the Government to withdraw their Bill.' (24) The York Trades Council agreed. The bill, it said, would 'destroy the present democratic principle of electing the educational authority. In future the people would not have the power of

51

directly electing their representatives, even though it might appear as if this system was still in vogue. The idea of co-opting representatives of various "interests" [on to the Council's statutory education committee] was thoroughly nauseating, and the Council deplored the prospect of working-class representation on educational bodies being abolished.' (25)

Added to the Liberals' condemnation of the Balfour bill, and that of Labour were many from ministers of religion, of course, and education became an issue at the York municipal elections in November. For the first time, the *Press* recorded, a question of national importance was made the 'battle cry of the respective candidates'. There were contests in all six wards and the battle cry was the Education Bill. In September the Castlegate Liberals had chosen Arthur Lawson as their candidate, and he had been chosen for his opposition to the 1902 Bill. (26) In August, just after the Leeds by election the Bootham Liberals had chosen Sebastian Meyer, whose name carried great 'authority in the light railway world.' (27) The Education Bill, Meyer said, was 'a restriction of the freedom which was the watchword of the Liberal party.' Meyer's candidacy was eventually objected to by W.A. Pearson, the Conservative agent, who quoted the case of Middleton v Simpson and showed that Sebastian had not occupied the premises that qualified him to stand for the requisite period, nor had he paid rates on them for some months. (28) The objections failed, however, and Meyer stood, as did A.P. Mawson in Micklegate, a representative of the York United Labour Committee. Mawson was as stringent in his criticisms of Balfour as any. (29)

In the days before the municipal elections the Tories held many meetings and H.V. Scott, a supporter of Balfour's bill, and a retiring councillor for Micklegate, launched a well publicised attack on the York School Board saying it was extravagant, (30) and on the eve of the poll a huge public meeting was held in favour of the bill. On polling day there were some exceptional turn-outs. In Guildhall R.B. Lambert, an Independent (Conservative) supporter of Balfour's measure, topped the poll in an election in which 1,081 out out of the 1,333 on the register voted. In Micklegate Mawson beat Scott into second place, and in Bootham Meyer topped the poll.

In January 1903 the York Corporation announced that it hoped to put the Education Act (31) into operation in March, (32) and in February the press carried announcements that the new education committee would contain two ladies. (33) In November it held its first meeting, not long before the city witnessed the activities of another set of conscientious objectors. These were opponents of the new act, the representatives of large numbers of people in York. They were as irrational in their attitudes to the Act as any, but they were to prolong the hostility that Balfour had provoked to the undoubted benefit of the Liberal party. That they saw more 'religion on the rates' in York than did many has been commented on. York had always been church dominated.

The leader of the 'passive resisters' to the Education Act outside parliament was Dr John Clifford and his activities lost nothing by being supported by David Lloyd George. Followers of Clifford decided to withhold a part of their rate demand - that part which went on education. The 'movement' was strongest in Wales, but the York press carried scores of reports of protests outside the principality. In July distress warrants were executed at Stroud, for example, and in December that Rev Hirst Hollowell, who had addressed meetings in York against the first version of the Education Act, was in court in Rochdale. (34) Some six months earlier a York Citizen's League was brought into existence, its organisers saying they intended to emulate objectors in Leeds and withhold 'that part of the education rate applied to the maintenance of denominationally managed schools.' The Rev Hind, a Primitive Methodist, was elected President; J.M. Gardener (Wesleyan) was made Treasurer; and the Rev A.T. Reissman (from Lendal Congregational Church) was made Secretary. (35)

The City Council awaited the outcome of the formation of the Citizen's League (and put the rates up a little), but by the time the League got to court York had a new Lord Mayor - and a very aggressive, opinionated and unpleasant Lord Mayor he was. He was Vernon Wragge, and his elevation was important to the likes of Reissman because in those days the Lord Mayor became the leading justice during his term of office, and Wragge was to adjudicate on both the passive resisters' cases and some important licensing matters during his year of office. Rarely was he to show that dignified aloofness which is the historic hall mark of the magistracy in this country.

Wragge, who had been a York JP since December 1900, twice fought at Rotherham in the Tory interest, and still had political ambitions, and during his term of office as Lord Mayor it was announced that he might stand a third time as a candidate for Buckrose. (36) Since the time he was last mentioned in these pages he had carried on a busy practice as a barrister and had been a highly controversial chairman of the York Board of Guardians. A detailed study of that body is long overdue, and that study would undoubtedly reveal some splendid shindigs involving Wragge and the likes of Thomas Anderson, representing labour. Wragge could not have felt very flattered by the fact that the Corporation did not initially want him as Lord Mayor (the most senior Alderman 'who had not passed the chair') and had asked the sitting incumbent to stay on. Gray would certainly have presided over the following year with more discretion and decorum than did Vernon.

J.G. Butcher, shortly after the creation of a National Passive Resistance Committee, had warned the citizens of York that, in his opinion, the non payment of rates was 'perilously near a breach of the law, and if it was not a breach of the law it ought to be', but there were York men who were spoiling for a fight. Many of them appeared before Lord Mayor Wragge in December. They clearly relished the experience. (37)

There were 18 defendants taken to court in December for refusing to pay (part of) their rates, and they included Reissman, the Rev William Wheeler, a Primitive Methodist, and Arthur Dearlove of Vyner Street. Wragge, in his inimitable best bullying fashion took a strictly legalistic view of how the court should be run, as of course he was perfectly entitled to do. He asked the objectors if they objected to the legality of the proceedings - which of course none could - and adamantly refused to allow them to give their reasons for refusal. Thomas Parker tried to draw comparisons between himself and his co-accused and the conscientious objectors to vaccination, only to be told, quite rightly, that while the Vaccination Act had made provision for conscientious objectors the Education Act had not. (38) Wheeler, it was revealed, had withheld 1s. 7d, and Charles William Clack 1s. 2d. Clack just 'managed to get in a phrase about objecting to the teaching of Popish doctrine before the guilotine [sic] fell' and Wragge shut him up, while Richard Westrope said he *had* got a legal objection to the rate. The Rev E.C. Penny of the Methodist New Connexion turned his back on the bench, looked at the crowd in court and to them 'expressed his objection to the religious test.' Wragge said to Penny 'would you mind addressing me instead of the congregation' whereupon the defendant replied, 'My Lord, I am so used to addressing congregations.'

Denied a forum in court, the objectors held a public meeting in Lendal Congregational Church. It began with a reading from the fifth chapter of the Acts of the Apostles ('we ought to obey God rather than men') then went on to hear a most extraordinary harangue from Westrope. He demanded that the Lord Mayor should resign from the council and fight him (Westrope) at the next elections. 'The Lord Mayor would not hear him that morning,' Westrope said, 'but he would have to before long. He contended the management representation of the York non-provided schools was a fraud, a snare, and a sham. If Mr Parker ... went to prison, he would not go alone. They would carry their cause to victory or die in the attempt.' (39) This was fiery stuff, but it was not the last time Westrope was to utter such words. '... they were living in a time of revolution', he told a public meeting seven months later, a revolution 'that had been begun by the Government ... that was arousing a spirit in men that in the 17th century met revolution with revolution. The people of England in a few years would be thankful to passive resisters. The old Puritan spirit had been aroused in England, and it would lead on its followers to full and complete victory.' (40)

This kind of language was idiotic, but of course it reflects a genuine, if rather ridiculous, fear about what was going to happen on the part of people like Reissman and Westrope. In the latter's case it almost certainly represented, too, the sheer delight of people like himself at the fact that politically, at last, the government had given them a popular cause with which to attack it. At the time of the Khaki election, when people who thought like Westrope on reform issues were bitterly divided over the war, and when jingo attitudes made sure they would not get a hearing anyway, their prospects looked (were) nil. Now the war had ended and the Education Act had led to something like unity among the opposition, by elections had gone their way, and a successful future seemed to lay ahead. There was no way in which people like Westrope would allow the passive resistance movement to die down if they could help it. It was generally reckoned that a general election was about to be held when he first appeared in court and that a by election might be called in York even before then. It was commonly believed that Butcher would be made a judge and that his seat would be up for grabs.

Many (but by no means all) of the passive resisters were involved in other radical movements as might be expected. Arthur Dearlove, for example, was an active socialist and J.G. Heys was a Primitive Methodist Liberal councillor and member of the York School Board. Westrope, however, epitomised the active enthusiastic radical better than any. He was a socialist supporter of the York Womens Suffrage Society, for example, and on the committee of the York Citizen's Association for Dealing with the Unemployed (of which more later). Westrope was also active in the city's adult schools and a few years later took part in an experiment in adult education when he and Wilfred Crosland became warden and subwarden, respectively, of what became the York Educational Settlement.

The adult schools in York and elsewhere had had something of a renaissance in the early years of the 20th century and then began to change with their social role, providing games facilities and so on, outweighing their educational function. In 1909 Arnold Rowntree decided to set up a centre where future adult school tutors could be trained and the movement therefore revitalised. This was the Educational Settlement, housed in its early days in St Mary's. Rowntree's aims were unfulfilled, but the Settlement rapidly became what it liked to call a 'working man's University', and by the time of the First World War it had an honoured place in the city. It was always popularly associated with the left (except in left wing circles) and during the war engaged in activities which would have done nothing to dispel this impression.

The St Mary's Educational Settlement survived the war and in the 1930s moved to larger premises in Holgate Road bought for it by the Rowntrees. (41) By this time it had forged links with local universities, the Workers' Educational Association and the local Technical College, with which it ran a large languages programme. It continued in existence until 1987, when its grant was finally cut off by North Yorkshire County Council in a stupid cost cutting exercise which ignored the benefits the centre was bestowing on the city with a logic that equalled that of the passive resisters of 1903. (42) A vitrolic hassle accompanied the closure of the Settlement which was let down appallingly by many who could have helped it. (43)

Westrope, Reissman, Arthur Dearlove and the rest of the passive resisters persisted in their campaign against the educational rate (Balfour called theirs the '"cheap illegality" movement') and in March 1904 there was a sale of property seized to cover the unpaid rates. This was in the police yard and J. Crockatt, dyer, of Coney Street was 'the hero of the occasion'. He had owed 3s.11d. but costs had increased that to £1.7s.5d. and curtains had been taken from him. These were 'bought in' by Reissman. (44) Later, in July, Robert Newbald Kay, a well-known York solicitor, was summoned at the East Ainsty Sessions by James Hardacre, an overseer, for not paying a demand of 17s.4d. 'He objected to pay rates for schools where sectarian tests are applied', Kay said, and had a distress warrant issued against him. (45) Less than a week later Kay was in the York court being put down by Wragge while trying to represent that same John Crockatt who had had his curtains seized and bought in in March. (46) It was after this experience that Westrope made his 'fight on to complete victory' speech.

Wragge, who was the most partisan Lord Mayor York had had since George Hudson, went around making snide speeches in which he mocked the absurdity (or what he saw as the absurdity) of people like Reissman protesting, having their goods seized, then having them bought back for them by sympathisers. Had he been a more accomplished politician he would have realised, that, even if he was right, the likes of Westrope and his colleagues were keeping up a constant barrage of criticism of the government which boded ill for the party which had achieved such a remarkable success at the Khaki election and of which Wragge was such an enthusiastic supporter. The Education Act (and other things) was to be a big enough burden for Balfour to carry without having people like Wragge making things worse at a local level. The Liberals must have been as pleased with him as Mrs Thatcher, many years later, must have been pleased with some of the members of her opposition. But it was Wragge's way to shout his mouth off. He could not have been in the position of Chief Magistrate at a worse time for his party. In April he was severely criticised by the *Sheffield Independent* for a speech he made about the objectors of Penistone. (47)

Wragge's indiscretions (if that is what they were) did not only occur when he was sitting in judication on passive resisters. He seemed to find changing horses and sitting in judgement for a year in the court in which he was a frequent pleader a heady draught, and engaged in some mighty indiscretions, (and many unbelievably laboured jokes). He was not an attractive personality, as an unfortunate lady from North Street called Mrs Headley might have agreed. Mrs Headley appeared in the York magistrate's court before a bench chaired by Wragge. She was there simply as a witness against her husband George, a groom who was being prosecuted by the NSPCC for neglecting his four children less than 14. Headley had not worked for four and a half years and his wife described the family income. She earned, she said, between 10s. and 12s.6d. a week and her 14 year old daughter Grace got six shillings for working in a laundry. In the words of the *Evening Press* she got the following rebuke from the Chief Magistrate who ignored the fact that Mrs Headley was only a witness (and he gave the old man six months). 'The Lord Mayor : Are you aware that some families have not more than 17s. a week, and they have a respectable appearance'. (48) What Wragge meant by that is not absolutely clear, but that it was injudicious, offensive and unkind is obvious. The

Lord Mayor had been going the rounds boasting of how he had dealt with the education rate resisters. Now he seemed to be suggesting that 17s. a week was enough to keep a family of six not only well fed but 'respectable'. Tell the citizens of York how this could be done a correspondent to the newspapers demanded of Wragge. Give us a list of how the money could be spent to achieve that desirable result. Doubtless, he went on, it will make 'interesting reading to many struggling families in our midst'. (49) It would have indeed.

Wragge's offensive remarks could not have come at a more opportune time for those who wanted evidence that those who controlled the country's large towns and cities were out of touch, uncaring, ostrich-like bigots. Britain's industry was stagnating, its proportion of world trade in manufactured goods 'fell from 22.8 per cent in the early 1880s to 10.2 per cent in the early 1890s', the value of imports rose, and the figures for unemployment went up to an average of six per cent for the decade 1901-10. (50) Unemployment rose in York too, and there is scattered evidence from the years of Wragge's predominance to flesh out the figures Rowntree had given the nation a couple of years earlier. It will be remembered that then it had been shown that 27.84 per cent of York's total *population was living in poverty*, and that even the (relatively) well paid could fall into dire straits if sickness, under employment or unemployment overwhelmed them.

There seems to have been some sense that, when the war ended there would inevitably be a rise in unemployment, and the opening of the York Soup Kitchen early in the New Year in 1904 was said to be 'in consequence of the great sickness [that prevailed] in the city, and the number of people out of employment'. (51) Within a few days that charity was distributing 1,800 quarts of soup (at 1d. a quart) daily. (52) In February it was recorded that men of the ASRS had had their wages increased from 18s. to 22s. a week, and W. Reynolds a speaker at a meeting where that fact was revealed reminded his listeners of Seebohm Rowntree's findings - that £1 a week 'only meant existence'. (53) The fact that some worked for that existence wage was revealed by the 18 month old York City Hairdressers' Association in March. It announced then that it was going to act as a trade union and appealed to York trade unionists to patronise its members. They were against Sunday trading they announced, and wanted a half day holiday each week. They worked 12 to 14 hours a day, 'and much longer on Saturdays' when they remained open until eleven o'clock at night - and their wages varied from 18s. to £1. (54) It was reported at around the same time that the building trade was 'slack', despite the figures that had been put before the courts for new buildings going up when the brewers wanted new licences, and a well written article on the city's cabbies revealed that they also fell below the standards set for healthy living by Seebohm Rowntree. On 19 March 1904 the *Evening Press* published an account of the *'YORK CABBY, His Work, His Hours, His Wages'*, which showed that there were 200 such people (170 regular) in the city. Their wages were 18s a week. 'Most of the men are married', the report said, 'and the fact that they only earn about two-thirds [sic] of what is now admitted on the authority of Messrs. Booth and Rowntree to be a living wage shows that they must often have a very hard struggle to keep the wolf from the door ... and ... the cab trade is very bad in York now.' A letter published in February 1904 revealed that at the end of December 1903 6.7 of all trades unionists in York were unemployed, compared with 5.5 for the year before and a ten year average of 4.8. (55) These figures would have meant severe hardship for those involved and accompanying these would have been hundreds of the unskilled who were not in unions.

The figures quoted above were publicised by B.S. Rowntree and T.A. Twyman who indicated that much of the unemployment was of a seasonal nature, and, it might be inferred, was among building trade workers. They appealed to the citizens of York to have work like interior painting and household repairs done earlier than usual. Somewhat later they took steps to do something to alleviate the plight of the unemployed.

It is a revealing fact that in the scores of political speeches given in York by Liberal and Tory politicians in the early years of the 20th century there never seem to be any references to unemployment. Old age pensions were being spoken of, but unemployment was not mentioned. It seems to have been accepted as a regrettable continuing fact of life and concern for the unemployed was considered the task of private individuals and charities. All that was to change in the years to come, and labour exchanges were to become a way of tackling the problem. One was set up in York, through private enterprise in 1904.

Percy Alden had visited York and inspired a number of people to try to do something to alleviate distress in the city. A public meeting was called to consider forming a 'Citizens Association' which was presided over by that Rev F.A. Russell of the passive resisters movement. Arnold Rowntree drew attention to the fact that there was now 50 per cent more unemployment in the city than there had been two years earlier, and said that what was needed was a public works programme. However the Council would not provide this (the rates were too high already). So, private individuals would have to do what they could. A committee was set up to create a labour bureau (exchange) and on it, once more, were many of those activists who have already been mentioned as members of the reform group: Richard Westrope was one; J.M. Hogge, then of Sycamore Terrace, became the secretary; Fred Morley of the ILP was a member; as were Seebohm and Arnold Rowntree. Miss May Kendall and a Mrs Bagenall were also members. (56)

In August 1904 Mrs Bagenall read a paper on the experiences in places like Manchester, Leeds and Ipswich and the decision was made to create a labour bureau run by what became the York Citizen's Association for Dealing with the Unemployed. (57) It opened for business on 3 October with premises at 16 Castlegate. On that day crowds turned up, and the papers gave prominence to the first applicant, who was

Walter Anderson of 38, Bright Street, a man 60 years of age. With him was a retired ex-soldier of 66, now out of work and trying to exist on a pension of 1s. a day. (58) To qualify for registration a person had to have been resident in York for six months, and by 12 October the Association had 352 persons on the register (334 men 18 women). Of these half were said to be labourers, with the rest belonging to '63 more or less skilled trades.' (59) At that stage regular work had been found for only four people, and casual work for five. A month later the registered numbers were 789 males and 40 females, and a week later the total was 945. (60) On 19 December it was recorded that Arnold Rowntree had told a conference held at the Homestead (the home of B.S. Rowntree) that 1,258 were registered. (61)

It is quite clear that the figures registered with the York Committee for Dealing with the Unemployed represented nowhere near the whole of the out of work in York. Many trades unionists did not register it was stated, and in fact there were criticisms of it from unionists and labour supporters. A writer who claimed to be a member of the ILP voiced their fears when he wrote to the press to say that the bureau had found work for only a few people who were prepared to labour for less that the prevailing rate. (62)

What practical measures did the York Council for Dealing with the Unemployed take to alleviate distress in the city ? It formally did what B.S. Rowntree and T.A. Twyman had suggested and appealed to firms and individuals to bring forward work which they might have intended for the spring or summer, and it achieved some considerable (if limited) success. Rowntree and Company announced in October that they would only recruit through the bureau and that they had brought painting and other work forward. (63) Later the same firm decided to lay a cricket pitch costing some £600 on a site of some six to eight acres, and give work to 35 men for a period of 20 weeks. (64) Work on the Minster was also brought forward, but all this made little impression on the miserable scenes in York (made worse by the closing down of the York Engineering Company, Leeman Road). In November the Council for the Unemployed recommended all single unemployed men to seek work on the land and hire themselves out for a year at the Martinmas hirings. At these, it was eventually reported, horsemen were hired for £20 to £30; plough lads for £12 to £16; and wagoners for from £18 to £20. (65)

At the November municipal elections of of 1904 Fred Morley stood successfully as a labour candidate in Castlegate and it looked for a while as if he and the other socialists (Councillor Moody, and J.M. Fisher, an insurance worker who stood in Walmgate) might make unemployment an issue. The Independent candidate for Monk (H. Hargrave, a plasterer) wanted rate reductions, and correspondence started in the press when 'OUT OF WORK' wrote to say that this would mean more unemployment through reduced Corporation work, but no great stir was made and despite the fact that the Tory government was under massive attack, the Conservatives were solidly in power, still, when the elections were over. Only rarely did the press give political analyses of the composition of the York Corporation, but it did so in November 1904. There were then, the *Evening Press* reported: eight Conservative aldermen: four Liberal aldermen; 27 conservative councillors; seven Liberal councillors; five labour and one Independent councillor; or a total of 31 Tories; 11 Liberals; five socialists; and one Independent. (66)

Perhaps the York Unemployed Council did its most valuable work by simply drawing attention to the plight of the unemployed, though that surely should have been apparent to anyone walking the streets of the city. In October Richard Hawkin, a Council supporter and a socialist, was given space in the local press to give labour's views on how to solve the problem, and he recommended and urged that the corporation adopt Part III of the Housing Act and build council houses - a move which, he said, would both create employment and have the effect of lowering rents throughout the city. (67) Just after the municipal elections were held the Tories re-selected Wragge for a second term as Lord Mayor and even he had to pay attention to the problem of distress in his speech of acceptance. (68) Shortly after that, and largely as a result of pressure by the labour councillors, the Corporation considered a public works programme for the unemployed. In early November the City Surveyor (A. Greer) drew up a comprehensive list of work which could be done and, in an impressively short space of time, the council did decide to accept most, if not all, his recommendations. (69) In December work had begun (notably on improving Terry Avenue) at just about the time a special meeting was called at the instigation of Fred Morley and his colleagues. There were then 1,195 registered at the bureau, Morley said, a figure which with dependents represented 3,088 persons, and four per cent of the population of York. He dropped a dark hint, and was severel ticked off by Wragge for doing so. 'Up to the present', Morley said, 'the unemployed had been guilty of no disturbance, but there was a limit to their patience. (70)

Christmas 1904 must have been a dismal time for many families in York, a fact which, obvious as it is, can be shown in many ways. The Aged and Poor People's Christmas Dinner Fund was a charitable enterprise, and it reported that demand for tickets was 'abnormal' and that 'in consequence of the unemployed, over 1,200 invitations' were sent out. (71) In January an organisation was set up to provide free meals for school children on a couple of days a week. These were to consist of soup and bread provided at a cost of 1d., but the charity attracted little support. (72) Late in January men at the carriage works of the North Eastern Railway in Holgate Road had to go on short time - starting at 8.30 instead of 6 o'clock in the morning, and many losing Saturday working. (73) Reports of the activities and meetings of many of the city's charities (for example the York Benevolent Society) underline what a dreadful place the city was for many at that festive season. (74)

The work of the York Unemployed Council continued into the new year, and at the end of January it had 1,522 on its register, the bulk of whom were in the age brackets

16 to 20 (196), 21-25 (287), 26 to 30 (247), 31 to 35 (145) and 36 to 40 (137). (75) Heavy snow had fallen in the city during the month and many of the out of work had been set to work clearing the streets and the NER had brought work forward to help the situation - for which it was pubicly thanked by the plasterers' union. (76) In January the Friends' Social Services Committee convened a conference presided over by B.S. Rowntree on unemployment, at which Rider Haggard was the main speaker. His remedy for the evil of unemployment was summed up in one of the *Herald's* headlines - 'SMALL HOLDINGS THE CURE FOR POVERTY' and the meeting passed resolutions demanding that county councils should provide small holdings for the poor. (77) A general election was confidently reckoned to be imminent, and the fact is that one was not all that far away. Land for the poor, and land values taxation were to be important demands at it.

What were the causes of the distress of the post war years ? J.G. Butcher, who now admitted that unemployment caused him 'no little anxiety', thought foreign tariffs were a major cause, and much more was to be heard of this. But allied to unemployment in the eyes of many was (still) the problem of drink. Arnold Rowntree, the president of the Adult School Union, said this when presiding over the laying of a foundation stone of a Wesleyan Club in Melbourne Terrace, (78) and so did a Mr T.T. Whittaker. He had been present at a meeting of a York Medical Society which had heard a paper by a Dr Newsholme of Brighton. He had harked on a familiar theme when speaking on public health. 'At the present time', Newsholme said, 'one of the most serious drawbacks to public health was the fact that a fraction of the community habitually had not enough to eat, and a still more numerous class lived habitually near that "poverty line" and' after even 'a slight accident fell below it.' Whittaker weighed in with an observation straight out of a temperance tract, saying that the average working man's family 'spent 6s.11d. a week on drink, or almost 25 per cent of its income.' (79) He, and people like him just then, were extremely angry about some recent legislation which had had its origins with one of the city's MPs. It had brought down the wrath of temperance reformers on the head of the Prime Minister. The Rev R. Hind of York was - well rather put out by it all, and he told the National Primitive Methodist Conference so. The *Press* reported the speech of Hind, the chairman of Castlegate Ward Liberal Association, as follows (80)

> never before had the mammon fiend fastened its cold steely fingers on the hearts of men in this country with so firm a grip as to-day. Not only was drunkeness more rampant, but it looked as though the brewers and publicans were destined to be masters of England, as they were already one of the great political parties in the country. ... When he saw the conscienceless cynic, A.J. Balfour, sitting in the seat of Mr. Gladstone, he thought it was time they talked rather less of the lapsed masses and rather more of the lapsed classes.

What had the government done that aroused such comments ? Once more it had introduced what seems to be a reasonable bill (which became law), and once more got crucified for doing so. Balfour is generally reckoned to have been an indolent politician, and so he may have been for most of his career. But during the period of the Education Act and licensing reform he was anything but that, and he and his government were taken apart because of the reform projects they then put forward. What had angered the Rev Hind was a measure compensating breweries for lost licences. J.G. Butcher had been in the front line with comprehensive proposals about how it could be done.

It will be remembered that the Tory government in 1901 had introduced (and passed) the Child Messenger Act (the 'Anti-Sipping Act') and that the temperance organisations had recognised then that times were not propitious for root and branch reform and had (temporarily) scaled down their demands. They welcomed the Child Messenger Act and throughout the country had set about trying to persuade magistrates to cut down the number of pubs and other outlets for strong drink in their area. They had had some moderate successes in York when the bench had refused applications for new pubs in the Bishopthorpe Road area - despite pleas (and threats) from R.H. Vernon Wragge (before he was made Lord Mayor). Arnold Rowntree, mixing up his genuine concerns about the problems of bad housing, poverty and booze perhaps, startled an audience when he told them that (this was in January 1905) he regarded pubs as a 'social necessity,' but went on to urge the creation of 'dry' ones like the Cocoa Tree in Walmgate, and the Church Club on the Marygate estate. (81)

Rowntree and his temperance colleagues, with their new attitudes of *realpolitik*, would have welcomed the passing of the Licencing Act of 1902. (82) This changed the date of the Brewster Sessions to 'within the first fourteen days of the month of February', but also enabled the authorities to arrest and prosecute any person 'drunk in any highway or other public place, whether a building or not, or any licenced premises,' and anyone who appeared to be 'incapable of taking care of himself', and impose a fine of £2 or a month inside for being drunk in charge of a child. The Act also provided for a person found drunk and deemed to be a habitual drunkard to be entered on a register (as Screampoke certainly would have been) and thereafter if he or she attempted to buy drink on licenced premises or in clubs within three years, he or she committed an offence, and a licence holder who knowingly sold to such as Screampoke would be 'liable on summary conviction, for the first offence, to a fine not exceeding ten pounds, and for any subsequent offence in respect of the same person, to a fine not exceeding twenty pounds.'

It is perhaps not true to say that the whole of York waited anxiously for the first persons to be prosecuted under the new act, which became operative on 1 January, but had they done so, they would not have had to wait very long. On 2 January a gentleman appeared before the court under the new law and he deserves to be rescued from

S. W. M. Meyer

oblivion, if only for his eloquence. John Foster, 73 years of age, was let out of the York workhouse, managed to get himself smashed, was arrested, and during the hearing of his case kept muttering the immortal words 'Never no more, never no more.' On 'that understanding', the *Press* reported, John 'was dismissed' but he was not a man of his word and 'this morning', the same paper said on 3 January, 'his name again appeared on the charge sheet, as having been drunk ... in the York Union Workhouse.' This time John got 21 days with hard labour at Wakefield. Also in court at the same time, and also charged under the same regulations was 28 years old Mary Emma Temple. Mary had managed to get drunk on two glasses of port (she said) and she also promised never to drink again. She was bound over. (83) Faber, the MP, reckoned the new legislation was good, though when he told a Tory dinner this he was greeted with cries of 'No', (84) and Vernon Wragge thought so too. Addressing the York court on the new act Vernon said that in Cumberland (for example) the drunk was regarded as a harmless and inoffensive person and 'crime was not laid at his door.' Was that fair ? Ninety per cent of workhouses inmates were there because of drink, he went on, and York and the West Riding County Council were about to spend a quarter of a million pounds on building an inebriates' home. So, no messing. The York bench would henceforth fine drunks more than the 2s.6d. and costs which had until then been the going rate. (85)

The first licencee to be charged with selling to a drunk seems to have been Harry Hayes, an ex York City footballer. Harry was the landlord of the Blue Bell, Fossgate, and his prosecution was reported in the *Press* of 5 January. Harry got off on that occasion, but he was going through a bad patch and his activities would have done the temperance cause no end of good. Just a day after it reported his appearance in court for selling to a drunk the *Press* recorded that Harry had appeared in the County Court for kicking over some cooked mussels which Timothy Cattle had been trying to sell to customers of the Blue Bell. Mussels are very tender things which will not bear a lot of knocking about the court was told, and Harry was fined 10s. and costs. (86) He was in a spot of trouble again in February (87) and just before this he had been done for being drunk in his own pub and for not paying his rates. (88) It ought to be pointed out that Harry was not a passive resister, but someone who had simply overlooked his obligations on this occasion. Charles Hudson, of the White Horse, was also fined early in January for serving someone who was drunk. (89) This was the well-known Harry McGinty, who would certainly have got himself on the Chief Constable's hit list sooner or later. Harry made it sooner, rather than later.

The first York Brewster Sessions under the new scheme of things were held just after Harry Hayes' last spot of bother in the courts, and they turned out to be as exciting as those a year earlier. The Chief Constable's report recorded that, as was required by Part III of the 1902 Act, the clubs of York had registered, and that there were 25 of them. The Lord Mayor (90) then welcomed the new act and reminded the court that the licencing bench had ordered a city wide inspection of pubs and off licences and that the police report had been received in March 1902. Two months later, he went on, the bench had definitely decided to reduce the number of York pubs and they had held two meetings with the licencees hoping to get the latter to cooperate with them. Not surprisingly the likes of Harry Hayes and Charlie Hudson had decided not to commit commercial suicide, so Wragge announced that the magistrates would make a start on ridding the Hungate and Walmgate areas of unwanted (as he saw it) drink outlets. There, Wragge said, there were 51 licenced premises for a population of 5,500 - or one to every 107 of the whole population, or one to every 30.5 males over the age of 17. (91)

The Brewster Sessions of 1903 were to be an exciting and prolonged affair. Meetings like that at Southlands Wesleyan Chapel had been held at which the temperance supporters had announced that they were determined to keep the Bishopthorpe Road area free from temptation, (92) and, not only that, there were many others waiting to nudge the bench along their declared policy route and rid the city of at least some drinking establishments. No less than 64 objections were announced at the beginning of the sessions - six to places in Walmgate and Hungate. '... we are rather throng with the licensing gentlemen' the Lord Mayor said as he surveyed the court. Harry Hayes would not have been pleased (or surprised) to note that the Blue Bell, Fossgate was on the hit list.

The objectors to the renewal of licences were the usual temperance supporters and their objections, as always, gave some interesting sidelights on the trade, which would resurface in tracts and arguments in the future. Roland George Hey objected to the John Bull, a pub which came back from the dead in the 1970s. It was owned by a Mr W. Nicholson of Acomb, had been licensed for 70 years with never a conviction recorded against it or its landlord. It was a free house which brewed its own beer (36 gallons a time) three times a week and the tenant then was the splendidly named Harry Robert Trod. Beer then was 1d. a pint it was revealed and the Trinity House Hotel, Trinity Lane, another place objected to, sold between £7 and £8 worth of two splendid beers each week. Frank John Thomas, who a few years later would would have been grateful to his parents for giving him the first of his christian names, objected to the Trafalgar Bay, Nunnery Lane. This was a J.J. Hunt's 'house' for which they charged £32 a year rent and paid £60 a year for the lease. Hunts had just expanded when they took over the firm of Robert Brogden, Sons and Company, of Tockwith (93) and the Crown and Cushion, North Street, was another of their pubs objected to in 1903. J.J. Hunt had bought the Crown for £1,650 four years earlier and charged an annual rent of £22 for it. The place sold 144 gallons a week and W.B. Scannon, the objector, suggested that it was a lively spot. It used to be 'crowded by a roystering crew,' he said, 'shouting and singing and making the place hideous, but it had not been so crowded lately.' This led to the following comments

> The Lord Mayor: The more respectable the place is the less people go
> to it. - Witness: I believe that is so in this case.
> The Lord Mayor: I have heard that theory before.

With the completion of the hearing against the Crown and Cushion, the York bench was only half way through its marathon session. There was still Harry Hayes' pub to consider - and many more.

The Blue Bell was owned by the Tadcaster Tower Brewery Company and it was objected to by J.M. Turner and the ubiquitous Robert Kay of the Wesleyan Men's Class. Their grounds for objection were that the Blue Bell was not 'suitable' or 'necessary' and Robert said that between Pavement and Walmgate Bar there were no less than 34 licensed premises - 'The number of licences in Walmgate was cruel - cruel to the inhabitants', he said, sentiments with which, it seems reasonable to infer, Harry McGinty would not have agreed. Kay also opposed the renewal of the licence of the Red Lion, Walmgate, sandwiched between two other pubs and immediately opposite another. This was a house owned by John Smith Ltd and a Mr Acland, appearing for debenture holders in the company, raised the question of compensation for licences not renewed. This was to become a major political issue. '... the Bench were well aware of the change that had so speedily come over the situation since they first instituted the inquiries that had led to these proceedings', Acland said. He was referring to what was known as the Farnham judgement. After the discussion on the Red Lion Kay objected to the renewal of the Bricklayer's Arms' licence, while the Square and Compass, which belonged to the Tadcaster Tower Company, The Queen's Head, Fossgate, which sold a vast number of glasses of beer a week and belonged to the Albion Brewery, Leeds, the Spread Eagle, and the Bay Horse, Walmgate were also opposed. Police Sergeant Williams said that one of the reasons for objecting to the Bay Horse was that 'the urinal was exposed'. Later the City Arms, Walmgate, was also opposed, as was the Albert Inn in the same area. The Chief Constable rounded off a memorable session by objecting to no less than 20 more licences in the Walmgate/Hungate area, and in doing so trotted out the inevitable statistics and gave voice to a tag about the dangers of the area which was supposed to remain applicable for at least another 30 or 40 years. Walmgate/Hungate was the poorest part of York, the Chief said, and from it came 41 per cent of the convictions for drunkeness. It was so bad that 'The police at night went on duty in couples. Assaults on the police were frequent.' (94)

The proceedings described above related to areas where pubs already existed. In 1903, for the third time, J.J. Hunt and Company applied for four outlets (two pubs, two off licences) on the Bishopthorpe Road estate. An objector was John Richard Swales, who, in a remark that aroused no comment in those more innocent days, said 'he took a great interest in the young men of the district' and thought a pub in an area was 'the first step to slumdom.' The tetchy Vernon Wragge represented the applicants and he uttered what was later represented as a threat. The word had got round, Wragge said, that if J.J. Hunt was refused permission to build pubs again, they would get round the law and build a club.

There was a nasty dispute between Wragge and Alderman Edwin Gray, the Lord

Mayor who was presiding at the Brewster Sessions. In an attempt to stymie the Hunt application one was also made - to build a 'dry' pub - by the York District and East Riding Public House Trust. It had originally intended to make a similar application for the Haxby Road area, and was a company of which the Lord Mayor was a trustee, and the Lady Mayoress a shareholder. The solicitors appearing for the applicants quite rightly asked Gray to stand down, but he refused to do so. Others connected with the Trust were Mr and Mrs Seebohm Rowntree, Sidney Leetham, Lord Wenlock, the Archbishop of York, J. Bowes Morrell and the Bishop of Ripon. It had a capital of £30,000 and its chairman was that Canon Argles who had appeared in the courts as a temperance advocate before. During the Trust's application it was revealed that 235 out of the 265 licensed houses in York were 'tied'.

At the end of the 1903 Sessions the temperance reformers would have considered that they had achieved a considerable victory. The bench turned down both the 'wet and the dry' applications for the Bishopthorpe Road area, so condemning the inhabitants there to a walk of half a mile or so to get a pint (or two). They also turned down the application of George Whiting, grocer, of Leeman Road for an off licence at the junction of Albany Street and Hanover Street; this was his ninth application. The bench also decided to make a start on ridding the city of unwanted boozers and decided not to renew the licences of the Square and Compass; the Black Horse, Walmgate; the Albert Inn, (Baines Brewery); the Hand and Heart (Tadcaster); the Neptune, in the Shambles (Tadcaster); the Duke's Head (Tadcaster); Jacob's Well, Trinity Lane (P.A. Wright); the Crown and Cushion; the Malt Shovel; and the Leeds Arms.

It was inevitable that there would be appeals from the York decisions and at the West Riding Quarter Sessions of April 1903 they were heard. Some licences were renewed (95) and later it was revealed that the appeals had cost the city of York over £242. (96) At about the same time, incidentally, Norman Crombie, the York solicitor, made an appeal to the West Riding Licensing Committee asking that Acomb, which was outside the city's boundaries until just before the Second World War, be declared a 'populous place' under Section 32 of the Licensing Act of 1872. (97) This would have enabled the pubs there to remain open until eleven o'clock and so compete with the clubs which the licensees were always saying had an unfair commercial advantage over them. Harry McGinty and his like would have approved of Crombie's move.

The movement to lower the number of pubs was not confined to York, and looked like going on despite the successful appeals. Mr H.H. Riley-Smith told the Yorkshire Brewers' Association that there were 'No signs' that demands for a decrease would diminish. (98) Manchester had refused a total of 39 and there had been a total of refusals in the counties of 255, and 354 in the boroughs. Of these 331 were appealing and this total of refusals in one year was more than those for the three years 1897-1900 (577 with 66 successful appeals). (99)

The actions of the licensing benches in York and elsewhere alarmed 'the trade', and moves were started to ensure that when licences were not renewed, the late holders were compensated. J.G. Butcher produced a 'Licensing Law Compensation for Non-renewal Bill.' It pleased the trade (naturally). Butcher's bill to compensate licence holders where they had lost their livelihood through no fault of their own was down for the second reading on 24 April. The York and District Off Licence Protection Association supported it, (100) and in April Butcher described its contents to the Primrose League (Edith Milner's branch). There would be fewer pubs, Butcher agreed, but where licences were lost the holders should be given the full value of them from a compensation fund created either by a levy on the trade or by the proceeds of taxation. (101) In the Commons Butcher's bill was opposed by T.P. Whittaker, son of Thomas Whittaker, the 'G.O.M. of the temperance movement' who was once whipped and hanged in effigy at Scarborough. (102)

Butcher's bill aroused the wrath of the York temperance organisations. It formally recognised licenses as a vested interest, they maintained. (103) The Wesleyans publicly condemned it, (104) as did members of the York Temperance Society who supported a resolution to that affect proposed by that Mr Nutbrown who frequently gave them those 'connective readings' (on this occasion they had seen the lantern story 'Come Home Mother'). (105)

Butcher's bill did not become law, but it paved the way for legislation in the following session, and the temperance organisations realised that a government measure was almost a certainty in 1904. At a meeting of the York District Citizen's League which was organising opposition to what they knew would be renewed applications for pubs in the Bishopthorpe Road area, Councillor Sebastian Meyer said it looked as if licences would be converted into absolute property. He was right.

The crackdown on York's drinking establishments did not stop with the actions of the licensing bench. '... there was a great epidemic of licensing reform', Norman Crombie said. This was at the special sessions which were called for renewing and granting music and dancing licenses under the York Extension and Improvement Act of 1884. At those sessions all music and dancing permits for unlicensed houses were renewed, but the pub licenses were only renewed on conditions that no holder of 'any license under the Licensing Acts shall permit any female to be employed or take part in any musical or other entertainment thereby authorised.' (106) Why was this ? The Lord Mayor, supporter of worthy causes that he was, said the bench thought it was not desirable to have entertainment in pubs - 'nothing was more objectionable', he said, 'than dancing in a small room'. There is no record of what Mrs Gray, a supporter of the women's movement and an avid member of the National Union of Women Workers (which held its annual conference in York) thought of her husband's action, and there is no record, either, of what Harry McGinty thought about it. The Rev J.J. Davies, however, might have approved. Just before the lady pianists and singers got the chop he told a meeting that 'The York magistrates deserved their best thanks, for not only had they reduced several licenses, but they also did splendid work in the Bishopthorpe district when they refused the very strong applications made to them to grant a new license (107) on that estate'. (108)

Edwin Gray's act in banning lady performers from York pubs did not go unchallenged by those who would have maintained that pub performances were preferable to Miss Knocker's Saturday pops. In March 1904 the secretary of the Music Hall Artistes Association, a Mr Fearnley, asked that the previous year's decision be rescinded - without any success. (109) A year later the hard working Norman Crombie tried to get the magistrates to change their minds at least as far as four pubs specially constructed for concert purposes were concerned (the Black Bull; the Lamb Hotel, Tanner Row; the Alexandra Concert Rooms, Market Street; and the Wellington Inn, Goodramgate). He revealed that a man and his wife performing there received £3 a week, and that 2d. a glass was put on drinks in the concert rooms. He gave all the assurances about public order and propriety that he could, and got nowhere.

Licensing reform, as Crombie had said, was becoming an 'epidemic' and this may have led to an attempt to get Gray to continue as Lord Mayor for a second term. Certainly he was asked, and certainly he refused, but whether he would have been acceptable to the ruling Tories is another matter. Waiting in the wings to become Lord Mayor was Alderman R.H. Vernon Wragge, the most senior alderman who had not 'passed the chair'. Wragge must have seemed to be just the man to put a halt to excesses that Gray seemed to have started - and, as has been said before, just the man to deal with the passive resisters, who were still causing trouble (even though their leader, the Rev Reissman, had left the city). Those who thought like that were right. Wragge was a barrister, a York Justice of the Peace, and a Tory with political ambitions who would support the party line, and control members of the bench who, seemingly, leaned a little too obviously towards temperance reform. His first term of office was full of incident. He behaved initially rather like a Lord Mayor from an earlier era. Some examples of this have already been given.

Wragge frequently appeared in the York police courts representing brewing and drink trade interests - and it was he, it will be remembered, who said J.J. Hunt would create a club (or clubs) in the Bishopthorpe Road area if the bench did not allow them to build pubs and off licenses there. Wragge set about reassuring the trade and was very indiscreet in that he did it publicly, causing the Rev F. Hughes to tell an audience that 'He would not say a word against the high moral character of Alderman Wragge, but he had no confidence in his judicial capacity', (110) and prompting Alfred Harrison to write to the papers. (111) 'What [a] display of discretion - not to mention impartiality - is there exhibited in the action of a magistrate - and a chief magistrate - who,' Harrison wrote, 'but a fortnight previous to his having to sit in judgement upon the actions of the members of a certain trade, deliberately attends a banquet to the trade, and in a speech says "they have been persecuted in days gone by," but "nothing would be done at the coming Brewster Sessions in the city that would hamper them in carrying on their business."' Harrison's comments were as nothing to the redoubtable Vernon it would seem. A couple of weeks later he criticised the bench at the 59th annual dinner of the York LVA, and he did so in harsh terms. '... it was absolute folly to do anything like the Licensing Bench did at York last year', Wragge said, 'he should hold himself free to act on the Bench as he pleased ... He was not going to be the mouthpiece of opinions he differed from, no matter how large might be the majority against him. (112) Extraordinary.

Wragge found himself to be not quite as dominant as he had thought he was. At the Brewster Sessions an application for a new outlet in Haxby Road was refused and so were the renewed applications for the Bishopthorpe Road sites. When they came up there was a nice little scene which was slighty reminiscent of that in 1903. Then Gray had been asked to stand down because he had close interests in a temperance organisation and he refused. In 1904 demands were made that Wragge should not sit on the Bishopthorpe Road cases on the grounds that he had earlier pleaded for them in the same court and had made speeches in the city saying that they should be given. He refused to give way but said he would take no part in the discussions, unless he had to give a casting vote. (113) (That is not the situation now. The Licensing chairman does not have a casting vote.) He did not say which way this would be given. Well he did not have to, as he had told the city at large already.

Shortly after Wragge had presided over his first Brewster Sessions the government's Licensing Bill, which replaced Butcher's measure, was produced. The bill was intended to reduce the number of licensed premises 'to more suitable proportions.' This was to be achieved in two stages. 'Firstly, all existing licenses were classified as "old on-licenses" for the purpose of extending to them protection against refusal to renew similar to that already enjoyed by the ante-1869 beerhouses, modified by including in the grounds for refusal structural deficiency or structural unsuitability.' Also, and this is what was presaged by Butcher, 'a scheme was introduced to enable unwanted licenses the renewal of which could not be refused on any of the specified grounds to be extinguished on payment of compensation. The compensation was to be raised by "the trade" by a levy on all old on-licenses in each area.' (114)

There had been earlier attempts to create a system of compensation for redundant drink licenses going back to a declaration of Mr Gladstone in 1880 - a declaration which was often, later, quoted against him when his ideas changed. However in 1891 the decision by the House of Lords in 'Sharp v Wakefield' decided that all liquor licenses were held by the year only, and could be refused at the end of the year without any compensation. This seemed manifestly unjust and many benches felt it unfair to proceed without compensation, then, in 1902, problems occurred in Farnham. (115) That place was grossly overprovided with pubs and six renewals were refused, a decision which was upheld on appeal. It was the Farnham judgement which concentrated minds, led LVAs and off license holders' organisations throughout the country to take alarm and first Butcher, then the government, to introduce reform measures. The national LVA lobbied ministers demanding such a measure as Butcher had produced, directing their attention mainly at the Prime Minister and Grant Lawson. (116) Nothing would be produced until after Easter, they were told.

In April 1904 a speech by J.G. Butcher in York was reported in the same issue of the *Press* which recorded the results of a large number of licensing appeals held at Northallerton. (117) A bill would be introduced, Butcher said, which would not suit the extremists on either side of the argument. He was right. Two weeks later, when it had appeared, Councillor Boddy, the York LVA secretary, discussed it at length. It provided that, in places like York, the whole of the bench of magistrates presided over by the Recorder would become the licensing authority. This did not seem to worry Boddy, but he was very concerned that nothing was to be done about what the trade thought was that unfair competition from clubs. One, in York, he said, had a turnover of £2,700 a year yet it, and the others like it, did: not have to pay a license fee; was free from police supervision; could open when it liked; and could close when it liked. (118)

The temperance advocates and the Liberal party were wholeheartedly against Balfour's bill. It was fairly obvious what would be in it, but before it was actually published the York Liberals had, they said, 1,000 canvassers out in the streets to fight it. Nathan Bellerby, the party's secretary, said that 'The latest retrograde measure submitted to the country is a Licensing Bill which proceeds to recognise for the first time a vested interest in licenses, robs the local magistracy, except in county boroughs, of powers which they have enjoyed for centuries, and subordinates the welfare of the country to the interests of the brewers.' (119)

Most of the city's prominent Liberals were also members of temperance organisations, like Henry Tennant, a director of the North Eastern Railway. Tennant told the annual meeting of the North Eastern Railway Temperance Union held at the Railway Institute that he thought the bill's 'main object appeared to be to endow and establish more firmly traps and pitfalls and temptations to excessive drinking.' He said that in matters of licensing the magistrate had been practically deposed and had a conspiracy theory. The bill, Tennant said, was an ingenious contrivance to prevent a substantial reduction in the number of licenses. This was foolish, but statements like these were frequently uttered.

Shortly after Tennant made his speech at the Railway Institute (which was reported in the *Press* of 9 May) a York Temperance Electoral Campaign Committee came into existence. It produced a pamphlet titled *The Drunkeness of York and J.G. Butcher, Esq., K.C., M.P.* which caused a great furore, and Canon Argles was connected with it. (120) Argles' own organisation - the St. Clements Temperance Society - held a meeting on the bill addressed by a J.J. Hatch of Hull. He made much of what he said were to be the diminished powers of the JPs, and the Canon tried to get the meeting to demand that the bill be amended. They would have none of that, however, and resolved that 'this meeting condemns the Licensing Bill, believing it to be detrimental to the best interests of the nation.' (121) The Rev F.A. Russell presided over another protest meeting at the Centenary Chapel at which Joseph Rowntree was the main speaker. He condemned the bill on the same grounds as had Tennant - that it interfered with the traditional powers of the magistrates, that it created a vested interest in licenses, that it made a real, meaningful reduction in the number of licenses impossible, and that it prevented real public 'control over the liquor traffic.' (122) The Rev Hind, a York Primitive Methodist, said Balfour 'had sold himself body and soul to the drink' trade. Lloyd George went even further, describing the Licensing Act as 'a party bribe for gross corruption - an act which Tammany Hall could not exceed'. That was a bit much.

Labour, by this stage in York's history, had a parliamentary candidate of its own, and he was as critical of the Licensing Bill as were the Liberals. The government, G.H. Stuart told a public meeting, 'had gone from bad to worse ... They had given a great deal away to the parsons [over education], as they always did when the parsons press them; they had given something to the African millionaires, and now they were giving something to the brewers.' (123) Many of the city's socialists (this has been mentioned before) were also temperance advocates (and often passive resisters) and this was demonstrated at a conference held in York when the Licensing Bill was going through. Trades unions, and the ILP sent representatives there and among them were almost all the labour leaders in the city: Councillor T. Anderson, who was shortly to become a relieving officer and be lost to the movement; Councillor Fred Morley; and Councillor Andrew Moody. There with them were George Gibbs and Henry Tennant, a manager and director of the NER, the latter a very prominent Liberal. Several of the labour representatives were railway workmen, and it is a fact that labour relations on the NER were then going through a bad patch. The labour delegates at that meeting were there to cooperate with their bosses over temperance, while being at loggerheads over industrial relations, and perhaps in agreement over education. Shortly they were to be asked to cooperate at a general election, while at a Stuart meeting a speaker was saying things like 'the Labour party' had entirely lost faith in the orthodox political parties in 'regard to their intentions to the working classes.' The possibilities of a united anti-Tory front whenever the election came were in reality non-existent.

The Licensing Bill of 1904 became law and the York LVA was delighted, and in July Faber announced that he would not stand for York at the general election which could not be all that far away. (124) Perhaps he thought (almost certainly he thought) that the controversies over education and licensing had roused so much opposition that his return would be in doubt. The LVAs, however, nationally, thanked the government for what it had done, and the drink trade went solidly behind the Tory party. H.H. Riley-Smith, a member of it, was one of those suggested to replace Faber. (125)

The Licensing Bill became law before the end of Lord Mayor Vernon Wragge's term of office. He was then elected for a second term, and it is difficult to avoid the conclusion that he was chosen again because of his willingness to be a partisan chief magistrate, and maybe because his party wanted him there during the general election. When the Brewster Sessions of 1905 was held he received a petition asking again for a reduction in the number of pubs signed by people like Westrope. However Wragge announced that all existing licenses would be renewed, but said the magistrates would look yet again at the situation. He proved the point about him being a biased first magistrate, perhaps, when he said that clubs should be more strictly controlled, and then announced that the York bench had decided that they would impose the maximum scale of contributions to the compensation fund. (126) He then pointed out something that will look surprising to people who recall the English pub prior to the 1970s. Pubs, Wragge said, should sell 'all other kinds of refreshments. A person entering a public-house had a perfect right to ask for tea, coffee, or any other reasonable kind of refreshment, either to eat or drink, and he wished to emphasise the fact that the Act stated that any person systematically refusing to provide such refreshment would render his house to be considered an ill-conditioned house, and the licence could be taken away. Therefore license-holders must be prepared to provide reasonable refreshments of a non-alcoholic character.' (127)

At those same sessions of 1905 Wragge also received a petition from the York LVA. It had to do with what was known as 'the long pull', something that must have been strongly approved of by Harry McGinty and others, but which was certainly illegal. (128) The LVA's petition said that if a person asked for - and paid for - a pint he or she should get a pint, not a pint and three quarters!! Strange as it may seem publicans were frequently 'guilty' of giving the customer more than he or she asked for. There was a great deal that was bad in York society in 1905, but there were isolated areas in which things were good. Harry McGinty would have considered that this was one of them.

The Licensing Act of 1872 enacted that all intoxicating liquor of a half pint or over sold not in a cask or bottle should be sold in measures marked according to imperial standards. Quite frequently licensees were prosecuted for not using stamped glasses, but the 'long pull' must mainly have been used in 'off sales', whether from off licenses or pubs. The York LVA, having drawn his attention to the fact that some people were getting more than they had paid for, met to discuss the Lord Mayor's wishes 'with regard to what is known as the "long pull"' and in April the Association and the York Off License Holders Protection Association declared they were against it, and that after 29 April they would no longer defend any members who were done for this dreadful offence. (129) William Shaw, if he had been a LVA member would have suffered in this respect. William, of St Ann Street, was visited by a weights and measures inspector who ordered a pint and got a pint and a half, and Bill was prosecuted for unlawfully selling ' "... certain intoxicating liquor, to wit a pint of beer ... not in [a] cask or bottle, and ... not ... in a quantity less than half-a-pint, in a certain measure not marked according to the imperial standard ...," or in other words for using the "long pull.'" (130) The chairman told the generous landlord that he was liable to three months imprisonment (but fined him 2s.6d. with costs).

By the time William Shaw was prosecuted the long pull had become a national issue and the National Federation of License Holders meeting at Sheffield urged its members to give up the practice which, it said, 'was detrimental to the well being of society, and contrary to the principles of commercial morality.' (131) At the end of the year, at the York LVA's annual dinner, Boddy reviewed what the Association had done, and said the trade had to get things right before the next Brewster Sessions, which 'will decide the fate of this system of unfair trading.' (132)

1. *Press 24 September* 1900
2. C. Barnett, *Britain and Her Army 1509-1970* (1970) pp 348-49
3. *Press* 1 July 1901
4. *Ibid* 4 July 1901 On Emily Hobhouse see eg J. Fisher, *That Miss Hobhouse* (1971)
5. *Press* 1 July 1901
6. *Ibid* 24 July 1901
7. *Press* 1 November 1901
8. E. Halevy, *History of the English People. (Epilogue: 1895-1905*, Book 2) (Pelican edition 1936) p 115
9. Ensor, *op cit* p 356
10. *Ibid* On the 1902 education controversy see also S. Koss, *Nonconformity in Modern Britist Politics* (1975)
11. *Press* 12 April 1902
12. *Ibid* 5 April 1902
13. *Ibid* 3 April 1902
14. *Ibid* 18 April 1902
15. *Ibid* 8 October 1902
16. *Ibid* 17 October 1902
17. *Ibid* 15 October 1902
18. *Ibid* 23 April 1902
19. *Ibid* 30 April 1902
20. He said this to a meeting of the York Primrose League (Milner Habitation),Edith presiding. *Ibid* 4 March 1902
21. In the St. James's Hall speech *Ibid* 15 October 1902
22. *Ibid* 1 August 1902. In November Herbert Samuel won a Cleveland seat after fighting on the issue of education.
23. Taken from E. Benson, 'A History of Education in York, 1780-1902', Unpublished London Ph. D. thesis.
24. *Press* 28 May 1902
25. *Ibid* 30 May 1902
26. *Ibid* 20 September 1902
27. *Ibid* 14 August 1902
28. *Ibid* 25 October 1902. The Deputy Lord Mayor quashed the objection on the grounds that he had no jurisdiction. He did this at the Guildhall where he was present to hear objections or receive withdrawals in connection with the York municipal elections.
29. On Mawson's meetings, see, eg. *Ibid* 6, 8, 20, 21, 25 October 1902
30. *Ibid* 27 October 1902. He said the Board erected schools costing £14 per head while the voluntary organisations did so for only £4 a head! Scott eventually became chairman of the York Education Committee
31. It finally passed all its parliamentary stages on 18 December

32. *Press* 20 January 1903
33. *Ibid* 7 February 1903. See also issue of 21 March 1903
34. *Ibid* 1 July and 24 December 1903
35. *Ibid* 13 June 1903
36. *Ibid* 3 January 1904. Wragge, as has been said, was already a JP and so already a member of the York bench. So were other Lord Mayors of the period, but Lord Mayors who were not, still became holders of that position of authority. The Act regulating this - making 'every chairman of a district or county council or ... mayor of a borough council ... a JP' for his term of office - was the Local Government Act of 1894. It excluded women, however. See eg B. Broadbent, 'A History of Women on the Bench', *The Magistrate* Vol 46, No 7, 1990. Also P. Hollis, *Ladies Elect: Women in English Local Government 1865-1914* (Oxford 1987)
37. *Press* 16 September 1903 for a letter from Balfour on the resisters
38. *Ibid* 17 December 1903. Wragge also pointed out - a nice debating point - that what Reissman and the others were objecting to was the *School Board rate*. There would be no rate levied under the 1902 act until the following April
39. *Ibid* 18 December 1903
40. *Ibid* 8 July 1904
41. On the history of the York Educational Settlement see A.J. Peacock, 'Adult Education in York, 1800 - 1947' *op.cit*. The site it eventually occupied in Holgate Road was the house once occupied by Henry Tennant
42. It was frequently pointed out that the Settlement was providing educational facilities of a high standard at an incredibly cheap price and that, as a shining example of Thatcherite virtues, it should continue to be modestly supported by North Yorkshire County Council as it had in the past. Logical arguments of this kind got nowhere; a NYCC councillor rose to great heights of eloquence when he told the press that his refusal to support the centre was given in an 'emotional meeting'; and the centre was closed to save £8,000 a year. He eventually lost his seat.
43. There is a MS account of the events leading up to the closure of the Settlement, with details of the appalling lack of support given it in its hour of need, filed with the centre's records in the York City archives.
44. *Press* 28 March 1904
45. *Ibid* 2 July 1904
46. *Ibid* 7 July 1904
47. Quoted *Ibid* 21 and 22 July 1904
48. *Ibid* 28 September 1904
49. *Ibid* 30 September 1904
50. R. Rhodes James, *The British Revolution* (1976) Vol. 1 p 222
51. *Press* 24 December 1903
52. *Ibid* 9 January 1904
53. *Ibid* 8 February 1904. This was at a Labour meeting held in York
54. *Ibid* 1 March 1904
55. *Ibid* 11 February 1904
56. *Ibid* 12 and 28 July 1904
57. *Ibid* 28 July, 15 August 1904
58. *Ibid* 28 September, 3 October 1904
59. *Ibid* 15 October 1904
60. *Ibid* 12 and 19 November 1904
61. *Ibid* 19 December 1904
62. *Ibid* 17 October 1904
63. *Ibid* 22 October 1904
64. *Ibid* 19 December 1904
65. *Ibid* 26 November 1904
66. On the elections, the results and the composition of the council see *Ibid* 31 October, 1 and 2 November 1904
67. *Ibid* 15 October 1904
68. *Ibid* 9 November 1904. Though he made some pretty offensive remarks along the lines of 'the poor are born to labour' lines.
69. *Ibid* 11 and 15 November 1904
70. *Ibid* 13 December 1904

71. *Herald* 4 and 5 January 1905
72. *Ibid* 16 and 18 January 1905
73. *Ibid* 26 January 1905
74. The York Benevolent Society was started in 1792 and in 1904 distributed 4,000 bread and coal tickets to the poor and needy.
75. *The Herald* 21 January 1905 contains a long report on the bureau's unemployed.
76. *Ibid* 7 January 1905
77. *Ibid* 11 January 1905
78. *Ibid* 2 January 1905
79. *Press* 21 October 1904
80. *Ibid* 17 June 1904
81. *Herald* 2 January 1905
82. 2 Edward 7, chap 28
83. *Press* 3 January 1903
84. *Ibid* 9 January 1903
85. *Ibid* 12 January 1903
86. *Ibid* 6 January 1903
87. *Ibid* 2 February 1903
88. *Ibid* 19 January 1903
89. *Ibid* 15 January 1903
90. Still Edwin Gray
91. The proceedings at the York Brewster Sessions can be followed in *Press* 6,7,10,12,13 and 17 January, 2 and 3 March 1903
92. *Ibid* 29 January 1903
93. *Ibid* 30 June 1904
94. In addition to all the foregoing William Matterson, a painter and decorator, opposed the renewal of licences to six pubs.
95. *Press* 8 April 1903
96. *Ibid* 3 July 1903
97. An area of over 1,000 population could be so designated
98. *Press* 25 February 1903
99. *Ibid* 16 May 1903
100. *Ibid* 14 March 1903
101. *Ibid* 17 April, 1903. It is not being suggested that Butcher originated the idea of adequate compensation, of course. That had been around for some time. See eg N. Longmate, *T he Water Drinkers* (1968) chap 22 *passim*
102. *Press* 27 April 1903
103. *Ibid* 3 April 1903
104. *Ibid* 20 April 1903
105. *Ibid* 4 May 1903
106. *Ibid* 9 March 1903
107. They had refused four it will be recalled
108. *Press* 7 March 1903
109. *Ibid* 10 March 1904
110. *Ibid* 30 January 1904. Wragge was made a JP for York, along with six others, in December 1900. See *eg Gazette* 8 December 1900. All seven were local politicians: three had been Lord Mayor; three sheriff. Of the seven, five were Tories, the remaining two were Liberals.
111. *Press* 3 February 1904
112. *Ibid* 16 February 1904. He said this just after the Brewster Sessions, perhaps piqued by not getting his own way
113. *Ibid* 2 February 1904
114. *Patersons op cit* p 9
115. *Longmate op cit* pp 245-46
116 *Press* 16 March 1904
117. *Ibid* 8 April 1904
118. *Ibid* 22 April 1904
119. *Ibid*
120. *Ibid* 19 May, 11 June 1904

121. *Ibid* 31 May 1904
122. *Ibid* 20 June 1904. Hind's remarks following from Ibid 8 July 1904
123. *bid* 4 July 1904. The York labour movement lost another leader when W.H. Shaw, also a railway worker, was made station master at Kildale
124. *bid* 27 and 29 July 1904
125. *bid*. The others were Viscount Helmsley and F.S. Jackson of York
126. Off licenses were not included in the compensation arrangements
127. *Herald* 15 February 1905
128. 'Licensing Acts - *"The Long Pull" - Whether an offence against Act.' Justice of the Peace* 30 July 1904
129. *Press* 21 March, 14 April 1905
130. *Ibid* 4 May 1905
131. *Ibid* 23 March 1905
132. *Ibid* 19 December 1905

CHAPTER 3

THE LAST TORY YEARS

The government's education and licensing reforms had brought it terrible problems and great unpopularity in the two or three years after the Khaki election. By elections began to go against it and, with the war ended, the Liberals began to show something of a united front against it. Unemployment made matters worse, but there was another factor - it was 'Chinese labour', and it was to bedevil the government for the rest of its life.

The Transvaal had been annexed and in December 1903 its Legislative Council decided to import indentured labour to work the Rand mines, overturning a decision of a year earlier when massed protests had been held 'against the Chinaman.' The arguments for allowing the Chinese in were economic - the mine machinery had been renewed and there was 'a shortage of Kaffir labour' - but 'for racial reasons [they] could not be imported as free men; they must be not only indentured, so as to insure that they worked long enough to cover the costs of recruitment and transport, but confined by themselves in compounds and debarred even in non-working hours from the ordinary liberties of life.' (1) The mine owners originally wanted 100,000 'coolies' but eventually 50,000 were taken in for three years. 'The conditions under which [they] lived and worked were unspeakable, and the Government's lack of interest in the subject appalled middle class philanthropists and trade unionists alike. The attitude regarding human labour as a commodity seemed to expose a particularly odious aspect of the Tory mentality, and "Chinese slavery"' was a subject which added to the hatred many already felt for the administration. (2) The Chinese labour scheme was, the Liberal parliamentary candidate said in a speech reported in the *Evening Press* on 28 April 1904,

> an attempt on the part of Conservative employers to get labour in the cheapest possible market [and] work it under the hardest possible conditions in the interests entirely and absolutely of those who had capital invested in the mines. There was no shortage of black labour.

Richard Westrope, that supporter of labour, women's rights, and passive resister extraordinary, someone never at a loss for a rousing word or two, was reported by the *Evening Press* of 7 February 1904, as saying that the government would be known in history as the government of the 'great betrayals ... because all the principles they had valued so highly, and thought they had securely won had during the last few years been practically thrown aside, and bartered for gold, and this last betrayal was the worst of all. It was the betrayal of Judas, for it was the selling of the nation, its honour and its integrity ... the Archbishop of Canterbury [had] called [Chinese labour] ... "a regrettable necessity." ... This was the sentiment not of Christ but of Caiaphas ... The

Archbishop of Canterbury wanted to brutally imprison the Chinese and then Christianise them in their imprisonment. ("Shame.")'

Westrope made his remarks at a Labour party meeting (the headline referring to it in the press read 'Yellow Labour') and the resolutions approved of there said that the Chinese labour scheme was odious, because: it caused incalculable injury to the Chinese themselves; was 'A foul stain upon the fair name of Great Britain as a Christian nation'; was an insult to British labour; and was an outrage on the South African people 'whose wishes are being overridden in the interests of a few mine owners.' The York Central Branch of the Amalgamated Society of Railway Servants attacked it, (3) and so did the city branch of the ASLEF which 'condemn[ed] the action of the City members' in supporting it as 'the conditions suggested are those of slavery.' (4) Just after this members of the South Bank Adult School resolved that we ... as men, call upon the city members to vote against the Government, ... instituting - in land purchased by Englishmen's blood - slavery.' (5) Francis L.P. Sturge sent a copy of several resolutions passed by the Society of Friends to Lord Wenlock. They said - among other things - that the conditions under which the Chinese were to be confined were like prison and 'profoundly demoralising' and alleged that the Rand mine owners had reduced Kaffir wages. (6) Wenlock challenged the Quaker contentions (there was no lack of 'evidence' that conditions in the Chinese compounds - like those seen by Emily Hobhouse - were idyllic) and he did seem to have an answer to the latter charge. The Liberals brought Thomas Shaw to York to address a meeting specifically on the current South African issues, and his appearance was interesting in that it showed how flimsy the united anti-Tory front might be (and how favourable that might be to the Tories) when F.D. Wood wrote to the papers, on behalf of the ILP, complaining about that eminent lawyer politician. Thomas Shaw, Wood pointed out, had been intimately involved in the year long labour dispute at Ballachulish quarry during which it was demonstrated that the operating company had flagrantly violated the Truck Acts, by making deductions from wages for goods supplied, and charging 50 per cent over the market price. (7)

Butcher, like Lord Wenlock, replied to his critics by ignoring the principles involved in the hiring of Chinese labour, disputing facts and using descriptions of his opponents which no longer carried quite the weight they had a few short years ago. Shaw was called, predictably, a pro-Boer and was taken to task, perhaps reasonably, for having said that Chinese labour was introduced to antagonise white labour. It was also pointed out that a deputation to Lord Milner, the governor of the Transvaal and the Orange Free Colony, (8) had said that there would be a grave financial crisis if the solution that was adopted to get the mines working was not used. Faber, at that same meeting, took a rather different line, saying that Chinese labour 'was an evil, but a necessary evil,' a remark that could have raised all kinds of questions about political expediency and political morality. (9) It was not long after this that Faber said he had had enough of being York's representative.

Rhodes Brown

It was inevitable that Labour would be among the harshest critics of the government over the use of Chinese indentured labour, and one of the most unyielding critics of Butcher and Faber over this issue was G.D. Stuart the Labour party candidate. Who was he ? When had the Labour party come into existence in York ?

It will be recalled that in 1902 a United Labour Committee came into existence, and that running a Labour candidate for York was then spoken of. This was when workers were bitterly concerned about what they considered were deliberately hostile attacks on the legal status of trade unions, and when the Education Bill was agitating the nation. Philip Snowden, a famous Labour politician, addressed meetings in the city which were reported in the *Press* under the heading 'LABOUR CANDIDATE FOR YORK. A SUGGESTION', (10) and a couple of months later the United Committee was in existence and its secretary (Albert Lamb) was announcing that A.P. Mawson would be standing for the Council at the November municipal elections. (11) By the end of January a monumental step forward had been taken. A definite decision had been taken to select a parliamentary candidate and the earliest announcements revealed that there were four men up for consideration: a Mr Mitchell of Glasgow; James Connelly, a journalist, also from Glasgow; F. Richards, the district secretary of the Boot Operatives Society; and a representative from the postal workers. (12) This last person turned out to be George Harold Stuart, a 32 year old ex postman who hailed originally from Oldham, and who, from June, was the parliamentary secretary to the Postmen's Federation. (13) At the selection conference held in the Kendrick Rooms, Spen Lane, under the chairmanship of J.C. Robinson, the president of the Trades Council, the choice narrowed down to one between Stuart and Connelly. (14)

Stuart was selected as York's first parliamentary Labour candidate and Keir Hardie was present at his adoption meeting. (15) What of the next election Hardie asked ? They would consider an arrangement in York whereby one Liberal and one Labour candidate stood - 'but there could be no compromise and no working agreement.' From this point onwards Stuart began nursing his constituency, regularly speaking at open air meetings and frequently supported by famous visiting politicians like Fred Cook, the MP for Woolwich. Stuart cleverly mixed up national and local issues in his speeches: denouncing the legal attacks on unions; savaging Joseph Chamberlain's fiscal proposals while declaring himself a free trader; demanding old age pensions; urging better safety measures for railway workers; criticising the Workmen's Compensation Act for not being more comprehensive; demanding better housing; and telling York voters to plump for him and not split - despite what Keir Hardie had said - with the Liberals. (16) Fred Morley uttered similar statements, contending that as Stuart was first in the field he should be first choice of those voting against the Tories. (17) (The Liberals had not yet chosen a candidate or candidates.)

In July 1903 the York United Labour Committee was wound up 'to give place to the new Labour Representation Committee' - the forerunner of the Labour party. (18)

Marris was the LRC secretary (19) and in November 1903 J. Ramsay MacDonald visited the city to speak at a meeting at which the party registered its disapproval of politics as they were by declaring itself against protection, but stating that free trade on its own had failed - 'as is evidenced by the fact that twelve millions ... are on the verge of starvation.' (20) What did they want ? Free trade and wholesale nationalisation was the answer. And why had Chamberlain just started his campaign for tariff reform ? '... to blind the electors to the damaging report of the War Commission' MacDonald said. Chamberlain, of course, had been Colonial Secretary during the Boer War.

From its formation the LRC carried out a continuous campaign in York in what (for it) were favourable conditions. Unemployment continued to cause great and obvious distress and Stuart and his colleagues used its existence - as had MacDonald - to great effect (and quoting extensively, always, from *Poverty*, the author of which was an avid free trader). By February 1904 the first of the ward associations (Micklegate) was set up with Moody prominent as an official and J.R. Hartley president. (21) In March the LRC began issuing copies of a paper called *Labour News* (22) and at the end of the year the local press gave the new organisation the opportunity of stating its views at length when Richard Hawkin contributed a very well written article to it. (23)

The greatest problem confronting society, Hawkin wrote, was unemployment. 'During these last few years of National Prosperity', he went on, 'we have lost sight of this most important problem'. The York Labour Bureau, he claimed, rightly, showed up only a part of the problem in its area, but what was needed ? Relief work? No, Hawkin replied, a wage of 2s. 6d. a day for breaking stones or clearing snow (or something) was not enough. The Corporation should adopt Part 3 of the Housing Act and build council houses and so clear the city's slums, lower rents and create work. Hawkin ended by taking a massive swipe at the jerry builders, who, he said, had built the 'kennels' on the Leeman Road estate.

The York LRC was active at the municipal elections of November 1904, after which they had five councillors, and they began to take a very active part in the piece meal attempts that body made to improve the plight of the unemployed. In February 1905 Keir Hardie was back in the city supporting Stuart and demanding the appointment of a Minister of Labour responsible for finding and starting public work. (24) Stuart agreed saying 'The time had gone by ... when private charity could deal with the question [of unemployment] ... and it was time for the State to step in and do its duty to the people who supported it.' Surely he was right. In June Labour brought more famous politicians to York (Mrs Bruce Glasier, Pete Curran, Philip Snowden and Hardie) who dealt with the same problems, (25) and in July a mass open air demonstration on the unemployment question was held. At that A.P. Mawson demanded some amendments to the Unemployed Bill which the government had produced, (26) wanting a public works programme and quoting J.S. Mill as saying that labour saving machinery had been introduced to the detriment of the workers. (He probably had the case of the NER workers in his mind.) As 1905 went on Labour seemed to be building up a fine head of steam for the general election which everyone had been expecting for well over a year.

The United Labour Committee and the LRC were the products of the combined efforts of the Trades Council and various unions in the city, actively supported by the York Independent Labour Party. The ILP had been formed in Bradford, in 1893, and a branch of it had been formed in York just a year later. The York papers devoted little attention to the ILP, but on one occasion one dropped a memorable clanger when it reported that the party's national convention was being held in Leicester and (this was during the war) that one of the leaders, J. Bruce Glasier, condemned the government's policy in South Africa and said that the war had brought that most hateful of Prussian things - conscription - near. 'Conscription was an abominable expedient ...' he said, being referred to by the *Press* as 'Mr J. Bruce, glazier.' (27)

The York ILP, never a large organisation, worked alongside the other labour organisations and acted as a kind of think tank for the movement, and many of the city's leading socialists were members of it - some being in the LRC as well. Fred Morley was its secretary and Richard Hawkin was a member. These two were splendid publicists and organisers, and they brought people like Snowden to the city, to give a boost to the labour organisations which have been mentioned. The ILP took an active part in the struggle for better conditions for the unemployed, criticising the Labour Bureau and demanding that the Board of Guardians take action on their behalf under the Relief (School and Children) Order, 1905. (28) It always stood for a purer form of socialism than did the LRC and it had an influence far greater than its numbers might suggest. It was to be a thorn in the authorities sides when the Great War came along.

It was inevitable that something like the LRC would come into existence in York in the first years of the 20th century, but the actual decision to choose a candidate and set up a more formal organisation to support one was undoubtedly prompted by the fact that the Liberals were about to choose a candidate of their own. Without doubt the socialists wanted to be first in the field, knowing that if they waited the Liberals might well choose two candidates and that if they did Labour would have to answer charges of vote splitting. It seems almost certain that by moving fast the socialists did stop a second Liberal appearing. Although there seems to be no concrete evidence to support this belief, it does seem certain that, with the government having handed them the issues of tariff reform, education, Chinese labour and licensing, the Liberals must have been contemplating getting both seats.

The same papers that reported that Stuart and Connelly were going before a Labour selection conference, recorded that the Liberals were also about to hold one, and two persons were scheduled to appear before it. The first was Sir Henry J.S. Cotton, and the second was Hamar Greenwood. Cotton gave a spirited address in which he declaimed against the Education Act (while admitting that the government had an undoubted mandate), criticised Chamberlain's proposals for Imperial preference (saying it would lead to increased taxation), and inveighed against what he regarded as wasteful expenditure on the ostentatious Delhi Durbar. (29)

It really is difficult to avoid the conclusion that the Liberals had intended to run both Cotton and Greenwood, but had to rethink their situation when they were gazzumped by Labour. In the event Greenwood was selected, (30) publicly supported by Henry Tennant and Arnold Rowntree. Greenwood, a 30 year old Canadian, and a political science graduate of the University of Toronto, was a member of the Eighty Club and was always spoken of in York as a Rowntree nominee. There seems to be little doubt that Arnold Rowntree was largely responsible for inviting Greenwood to York, but it seems rather unfair to label that young men as a Rowntree lackey. Arnold Rowntree was, after all, secretary of what was known as the Liberal 400, and it would seem to be the most natural thing in the world for a secretary to be given the job of looking for suitable candidates.

Back in the 19th century Joseph Chamberlain had led a revolt in the Liberal party against Home Rule for Ireland and brought into being the Liberal Unionists. There was a Liberal Unionist organisation in York, but it was not particularly active and loyally supported the Tory governments of the time. When, in December 1905, it became necessary to formally adopt candidates for the impending election the York Liberal Unionist Association was represented by James Melrose and W.W. Hargrove at the Tory selection conference. These two voted for the candidates recommended by the executive committee of the Conservative party. (31)

Joseph Chamberlain had the unique distinction of splitting the two great parties of Great Britain. He broke with Gladstone over Home Rule in the 1880s, and in the early years of the 20th century he 'broke' with Balfour over free trade. It was the final gift (if not in point of time) to the opposition, which had been bitterly divided over the war. Lloyd George, the most famous 'pro-Boer', turned out to be Chamberlain's greatest opponent. In the 1880s Chamberlain had followed Lord Randolph Churchill around the country extolling the virtue of free trade when Lord Randolph was temporarily 'toying with Fair Trade'. Nearly 30 years later he was to receive the same treatment from Lloyd George.

Since the days when Chamberlain had pursued and tormented Lord Randolph British exports to the Empire had declined and the value of goods imported into Britain had risen dramatically, while foreign imports into the Empire countries rose. And there was that appalling unemployment at home. Chamberlain had been moving towards some kind of 'Imperial Zollverein' since at least the time of the conference of Colonial Prime Ministers during the Jubilee celebrations, and in 1902 at another such conference held at the coronation of Edward VII. At this 'the Prime Ministers did agree to accepting the principle of Imperial Preference in general terms.' This move forward was to have a 'decisive importance on Chamberlain's outlook.' (32)

Chamberlain, in 1902, was looking for a new national issue, and in that year a registration duty on corn, flour and meal was imposed in the budget, with the Chancellor emphasising that it was to be regarded as a protectionist measure. Chamberlain then proceeded to attempt to persuade the cabinet to respond favourably to a request from Canada for preference, and in November the matter was discussed by it. Chamberlain concluded that the new taxes would be maintained, and that 'preferential remission for the countries of the Empire would be increased', but this was not the interpretation of C.T. Ritchie, the new Chancellor. He repealed the taxes in 1903.

Ritchie took 4d. off the income tax and argued that dropping the corn duty 'was an indispensable equivalent for the indirect tax-payer'. The budget was introduced on 23 April, and, after several weeks of hesitation, Chamberlain delivered what has been described as 'one of the most sensational speeches in modern British politics.' (33) Politics leaped into 'intense life'. Balfour, replying to critics, said that protection would never be introduced silently, without a vote from the country. Chamberlain made certain of that.

Chamberlain's Birmingham speech proclaimed his belief in imperial preference and his 'secession from free trade'. It was dynamite. There were free traders (like Ritchie) in the cabinet and many of these resigned. Chamberlain himself left and Balfour tried a balancing act with a pamphlet of his own, (34) but it was greeted with derision. There had been an attack on free trade - the gospel of half a century of British politics - and the arguments against what Chamberlain meant, what he would do if he got power, and what the results of his new policies would be, took on the form of a crusade in which generalisations and catch phrases meant more than close arguments. ' ... it very quickly [became] apparent', wrote an extremely good popular historian, 'that the unifying influence of an educational question upon the Liberal party was nothing to the unifying influence of a call to the defence of Free Trade.' (35) He was right. Faber and Butcher would have agreed.

The York Liberal Unionist Association (W.F.H. Thomson presiding) rapidly met to consider Chamberlain's proposals, (36) and in August Faber and Butcher appeared in the city to explain them and their attitudes to them - with Faber saying that 'Cobdenism was a splendid thing in its day', but that it was time to look again at traditional policies. (37) The two MPs must have softened the impact of their apparent apostasy just a little when they persistently blamed the current dreadful levels of unemployment on free trade, and they continued to do this in the year and a half that remained before the general election.

Free trade was defended as strongly in York as it was anywhere. In February 1904 Rowntree and Company publicly declared that they were in favour of retaining the old system, (38) and Labour was adamant about the necessity of keeping it (though at the same time wanting a programme of nationalisation). The York Women's Liberal Federation sprung to the defence of free trade, and Greenwood cleverly contended that the reforms suggested by Chamberlain would affect the railways, lead to even more unemployment 'and a diminishing prosperity of York and similar centres. He therefore claimed that he was opposing the iniquities of the policy propounded by Mr. Chamberlain on patriotic grounds.' (39) Chamberlain (and therefore Butcher and Faber) was not only an apostate, but unpatriotic to boot. In vain did York's senior Member try to answer Greenwood by saying that Britain could tax foreign toys, foreign luxuries and foreign motor cars.

Another political party appeared in York as a result of the free trade controversy. Towards the end of 1901 Lord Rosebery, Prime Minister of the last Liberal administration, made a bid for the leadership of the party again, and he made a speech putting forward his current ideas that was almost as famous in its time as was Chamberlain's at Birmingham. This was known as the 'Chesterfield speech' and at the end of the year York Liberals met and welcomed Rosebery's return. (40) They pointed out that war time was a bad time for reform, but recorded their opinion that the areas where reform was most necessary were education (they got the Balfour Act eventually), temperance and housing. A few months later, however, Rosebery announced his 'definite seperation' from Sir Henry Campbell-Bannerman, the Liberal leader, and set up within the Liberal party an imperialistic organisation. This was the Liberal League, which rapidly became known as 'the Liberal Imps.' It gained the adherence of very prominent politicians like R.B. Haldane, and Sir Edward Grey and in April 1903 a branch of the League appeared in York. (41) Prominent among its supporters were the Rev F.A. Russell, Sidney and Henry Ernest Leetham, the well-known local millers, (42) John Bellerby and Henry W. Empson. (43) The Imp's manifesto urged that all sections of the Liberal party should unite as Rosebery had suggested at Chesterfield, and said they had been heartened by recent by election results at Rye, Leeds and Newmarket. They declared themselves imperialists, agreed with the need for educational, housing and temperance reform, and demanded army reform and more support for the navy.

The Liberal League does not seem to have been particularly active in York, though nationally Rosebery caused some considerable embarrassment to Campbell-Bannerman. Rosebery attacked the Anglo-French entente of 1904 (the only leading British politician to do so), and in November 1905 demanded that Sir Henry abandon Home Rule, then publicly denounced him for not doing so. This was on 25 November and it might just have had something to do with Balfour's resignation. The dispute between Rosebery and Sir Henry can hardly be said to have spoiled the Liberals' chances, however, as will be seen.

What were conditions like in York in the last year and a half of Balfour's government, when the attack on free trade had unified the opposition even more, and when an organised labour movement had been added to the political scene ? Had employment improved ? Had anything more been done for the workers ?

Unemployment had remained high and was well to the fore in the speeches of all politicians - with the Tories saying it was the result of foreign competition. In 1905 the government had to be seen to be doing something about it and in that year introduced and passed an Unemployed Workmen Act. (44) During 1904 Walter Lord, then president of the Local Government Board, got on foot in London a scheme of voluntary local unemployment committees linking up borough councils and boards of guardians and in the following year his successor (45) produced the Act to extend and regularise these arrangements. The Local Government Board was given power to establish a 'Distress Committee' in any locality whether or not it received an application to do so. The committee would have to keep a register of unemployed in its area, and it could, out of the rates, establish a labour exchange, collect information, assist emigration or removal, and even acquire land for farm colonies. The committee could not, however, spend money on wages or maintainance unless that money came from private donations. (In York a Lord Mayor's fund for this purpose was rapidly set up.)

It will be recalled that York had a Labour Bureau which had been set up largely through the generosity of the city's Quakers and its work up to the beginning of 1905 has been described. Conditions remained bad even into the summer, and in April the York LRC issued a manifesto which said that prevailing conditions were 'an eloquent tribute to the failure' of 'the efforts of philanthropists' to solve it. (46) The author of the manifesto was Richard Hawkin of the ILP and he gave as the reasons for unemployment not free trade, but the appropriation of wealth by 'the idle class', labour saving machinery, girl and boy labour, under consumption (itself the result in part of unemployment), and the length of the working day. His remedies ? Shorter working days and the implementation of the socialist programme. In July there was that mass demonstration of the unemployed which has been mentioned, then, as the year drew to an end, things got worse again. Late in September (on the 26th) the *Evening Press* carried a news item headed 'Hard Times in York' which made the point. Recently, the *Press* reported, no less than 123 summonses for non payment of rates had been issued in York, and many could not pay simply because they were out of work. 'A defendant from the Leeman-road district said that in such times as had been experienced by workmen lately the summonses drove men to desperation', it was recorded, 'He had not had any work since a year last June, and had not done a week's regular work for five years.' (47) In November the same paper recorded that 'In all parts of the city there are numbers of men out of work with no prospect of obtaining any, and should severe weather set in the pinch of poverty which is already all too keen will be disastrously felt.' (48) Forty men, it seemed, had been discharged from working on the building of the Asylum at Naburn, some of whom had walked to Huddersfield to try to get work

- without success. The day after the story appeared the Board of Guardians reported that unemployment was putting a strain on their resources, with out relief for the year ending 29 September amounting to £7,091, compared with £6,594 the previous year. (49) 'Able-bodied men, in almost wearisome succession, relate the same pathetic story', the guardians said, 'they have enquired daily for work, "at the railway works, at Leetham's, at Rowntree's, at Terry's, at the Corporation depot," and almost always with the same fruitless result'. While 'sentiment plays no part in the granting of a weekly pittance from the poor rates' the guardians went on, in a document which is eloquent of the concern they felt for their customers, 'it is, to say the least of it, pathetic to find a growing body of citizens reduced to impoverishment because they can find no market for their labour.'

The York guardians were, when they issued their report for 1905, deeply affected by a case which had been brought before them, and it illustrates as well as anything the precarious plight of the working class, the truth of Seebohm Rowntree's observations about the rapidity with which disaster could overtake families, and the prevailing attitudes of (most) employers. The closure of the York Engineering Works at Leeman road and its affect on employment has already been mentioned. In October 1905 a winding up meeting of the firm was held. (50)

The York Engineering Company had been very much the result of the business acumen and ability to survive of John Close, one of George Hudson's lackeys. (51) Close had been intimately involved with Hudson throughout that scoundrel's career and was implicated in many of his deals. He stayed in York, however, and such was his ability to survive (or such was the willingness of others to forget) that he became Lord Mayor of the city no less than three times. It is interesting to note that his obituaries make no mention whatever of the foregoing (52) but in the years following his disgrace Close bought the Phoenix works in Fishergate and was later joined by two partners called Ayre and Nicholson. They launched out into the making of railway wagons, a line of business also followed by the firm of Knapton and Company in Aldwark. This firm was eventually bought by Alfred and Joseph Walker who transferred their works to the site in Leeman Road. They sold half that site to Close and Ayre in 1880 who eventually took them over to create the York Engineering Company.

The York Engineering Company prospered, and when John Close died his son, Major Close, took over as managing director. In the two years before its close, however, the company lost trade due to the fact that the railways set up their own carriage works (like that in Holgate Road, York) and it was decided to close down. *Finis* was written to the story of the York Engineering company with an unbelievable payment of 261 per cent to shareholders!!

The YEC's workers had had no pension scheme and redundancy payments were not then even clouds on the horizon, and they entered a labour market which to call depressed would be a monumental understatement. One of them had worked for Close for 35 years and he had been paid off in August. By November that poor man's savings had gone, his furniture had been sold, and he had to apply to the guardians for assistance. (53) His case was reported to a meeting of the board as a whole and Alderman Charles C. Walker, a Liberal, proposed that the guardians send a deputation to Major Close 'to point out the many deserving cases of men who had served him for the best part of their life and were now in need of relief. It was not as though the men had been worthless', Walker went on, 'on the other hand they had been hard working, good servants.' The deputation went to Close and they got nowhere, and the good Major justified refusing to help them in a long letter to the press. (54) The Engineering Company when it was working, Close said, had built workmen's cottages and paid good piecework wages, and,furthermore, had worked at a loss before shutting down. He had no obligation to pay the men anything, he went on, and in a legal sense he was absolutely right. But, Close continued, it would have been useless doing so anyway. When the men were at work few saved - few could have saved it seems - and 'the rest were content to spend their surplus in drink and betting'. During race times the works had had to close down because of the men's addiction to the turf, and the YEC had paid large amounts in rates over the years. Let the guardians support the unemployed, then, out of the rates, Close concluded. There can have been few harsher letters written about his ex workmen by an employer in York. Little wonder that some were saying they had lost faith in things as they were.

The guardians, when they heard about the plight of Close's ex employees, also received that report that men were being turned away from the railway. Little wonder. The work force there had been on short time for many months and what had once looked like a good deal that had been worked out for them had turned sour in practice, and men were frequently taking home far less than what Rowntree said they needed to subsist on.

Workers at the NER had obtained a pension scheme, then in the summer of 1905 it was reported that they had had wage increases. Foremen, it was reported, then earning 3s.9d. a day, were to get 4s. then 4s.3d. a day and drivers' and firemen's bonuses for working on east coast trains were to go up from 8d. to 1s.; and from 6d. to 10d. But this was not all it appeared to be, as a Mr F. Southgate, a trades unionist, rapidly pointed out. (55) Under the new system of working that had recently been started, Southgate said, the men only worked three or four days a week and the bonuses only applied to certain types of engines. Men working the older stock would be doing 50 per cent more work for nothing! '... the men consider the new scale very unsatisfactory, and little better than playing with the subject', Southgate concluded. A month later his contentions were padded out at a meeting called by the ASRS to discuss the union's dealings with Sir George Gibb. On the larger engines conditions were like slavery, the men were told, and some drivers were getting '£1 a week, and [some] firemen 13s., with a wife and family to keep.' The company had 'Americanised' their work practices, and this meant that a fireman had to move three instead of two tons of coal per shift, 'and they had really more work and less wages as more wagons were taken at once, and therefore the firemen were not wanted so many times.' Longer trains had increased the responsibilities of signalmen, but Gibb would not discuss their plight or the pension fund with which the men were dissatisfied. (56) He did tell them that there would be staff reductions, however, and sure enough, a week later it was reported that short time had started, and that many NER men had been moved from York to Darlington and Shildon. (57) A letter published in the *Press* on 12 December said that workers on the NER's private way department had been on short time since August; that they had been laid off at Whitsuntide and during the August races; that they were to be laid off for nine days at Christmas; and that there were railwaymen 'who do not average 16s. per week.' (The General Railway Workers held their national conference in York in 1905, incidentally, and at that conference it was revealed that at Rowntrees, where an eight hour day was in force, 'no married labourer was paid less than 26s. per week.') (58)

So those in work were frequently receiving low wages, and those out of work were forced, more and more, to go to the guardians. The York Labour Bureau had a hopeless task, but then it was taken over when the Corporation decided to set up a Distress Committee under the new Unemployed Workmen's Act. (59)

The Corporation received a report on the provisions of the Unemployed Workmen's Act in September 1905 and decided to set up a Distress Committee. It was agreed that the voluntary body should stay in business until they took it over, and this was done just over a week after the November municipal elections. (60) Money available to it (the product of a halfpenny rate) was to be about £800, and Joseph Fels, a famous millionaire soap manufacturer and follower of Henry George, offered to buy land for the unemployed to work. (61) In December it was announced that the Distress Committee had been offered a farm at a rental of £1 an acre, but it was not taken up initially. (62) Settling people on the land was becoming more and more an integral part of Liberal thinking at that time, and it was to grow in the years that remained before the outbreak of the Great War. J.M. Hogge, who was becoming very important in Liberal circles in York, was fairly typical of the kind of politician who was looking favourably at the ideas of people like Fels, Henry George and Alfred Russell Wallace and listening to the arguments of the English Land Restoration League and the Land Nationalisation Society. At the annual general meeting of the York Citizen's Association Hogge told members of the experiments that the guardians of Poplar, with the assistance of Joseph Fels, and with George Lansbury acting as Fels' 'almoner', had conducted in settling the out of work on land in Essex. Reformers in those days watched the developments at Hollesley Bay with great interest. (Hollesley Bay eventually became a Borstal and is often remembered for being the 'bleeding 'oliday camp' to which Brendan Behan was sent for trying to blow up Cammell Laird's shipyard.) (63)

Between 14 November and 11 December 1905 500 persons registered as unemployed with the York Distress Committee, a figure which had gone up to 736 by the end of the year. (64) Once again Rowntrees and the Corporation brought work forward to help matters and men were taken on at the Naburn Asylum then being built. In January the Committee (of which Edith Milner was a member) discussed the question of emigration as a means of dealing with unemployment and heard a report saying that they now had 831 registered, of whom 493 had wives and on whom 1,061 children were dependent. (65) It was repeatedly said, of course, that these figures did not represent all the unemployed in York and they are certainly not an indication of the amount of distress that prevailed. (By the following March the official figure was 1,152.) (66)

In the winter of 1905-6 people like Richard Hawkin began to organise private relief for the out of work. A York Right to Work Committee was formed and that depressing feature of British history, the unemployed procession, made its appearance. The Martinmas Fair in November was extended to help raise funds, and in one week Hawkin reported that they had been able to relieve 89 persons at a cost of £10.0.6d. (67) The Lord Mayor raised an Unemployed Workmen's Fund and eventually proceeds from this were handed over, supplemented by grants from a similar appeal launched by the Queen, to the Distress Committee. In addition there were many worthy charitable efforts which must have done immense good, and whose activities are an eloquent indicator of the level of distress. The Soup Kitchen opened again, (68) and the York City Mission began to give Sunday breakfasts to the children of the poor. (69) The York Emergency Kitchen for the aid of the sick poor, which had received funds from a charity ball, provided help for the needy, (70) and somewhat earlier a Poor Children's Free Dinner Fund had been started in the city. (71) The old tag about there being 'poverty amidst plenty' would have been apparent as a truism in York around Christmas 1905, despite the efforts of people like the Rev Joshua Mason, who wrote a moving letter to the press saying something had to be done to ease the plight of the out of work and the short of work. (72)

Just before the Rev Mason's passionate letter appeared in the papers Vernon Wragge had been chosen to serve as Lord Mayor for a third successive term, and had then proceeded to take part in as silly a dispute as perhaps any Lord Mayor of York has ever had. It was a gift to the cartoonists, who had hitherto used their talents mainly to mock J.M. Hogge (predictably - very predictably). (73) But Wragge was the darling of the *Yorkshire Herald* and the *Evening Press* - and at one time was spoken of as a possible Tory candidate for the Barkston Ash by election. (74) Nevertheless he was rather reluctantly mocked by his own side - and he deserved to be.

Wragge was spoken of as Lord Mayor for 1905-6 as early as May, (75) and he was duly chosen towards the end of the municipal year. His Sheriff in the past two terms had been Alderman William Bentley, but it seems that Vernon had originally wanted F.A. Camidge; and in October a council sub committee had recommended that man for the next year. A lot of discussion then ensued about whether or not the Lord Mayor should have been asked who he wanted, but, amid some very angry scenes, the Corporation chose Bentley again. Why Bentley should have wanted to serve in the face of Wragge's reluctance to have him perhaps says a lot about the undignified scramble for municipal honours that some people engaged in then and some people engage in now, but he clearly did want to serve and he accepted the office. Then Wragge, the lawyer, wrote some unbelievably childish letters telling Bentley - more or less - to keep in the background at municipal functions at the Mansion House, that he (Vernon) would be responsible for invitations there, and to make sure that Wragge was well away from him in civic processions. When 'walking in procession', wrote the pompous Lord Mayor to Bentley , 'I like to have the opportunity of walking well behind the sword, and shall feel obliged if you will allow me plenty of room to enable me to do this.' These childish effusions from Wragge were sent to the press by the Sheriff and the letter columns were filled with comment for a time. (76) This all took place just a few days before Robert Horton Vernon Wragge was sworn in as Recorder of Pontefract. (77) It was all unbelievably pathetic. But it went on - and on, and on.

York's Military Sunday (it was originally held on Saturday) was held in May and the Lord Mayor and the Sheriff managed to enliven that of 1906. There was a most undignified scene in the civic procession during which the Sheriff showed that he could be every bit as petty and silly as Wragge. The Lord Mayor had invited the Lord Mayor of Sheffield as his most important guest and said that that dignitary 'should have the position of honour behind the civic mace, with the Sheriff and the senior Aldermen and Deputy Lord Mayor, Sir Joseph Sykes Rymer, following.' (78) The Sheriff would have none of this, and 'would not waive his claim to walk beside the Lord Mayor of the City, with the result that the three gentlemen walked abreast, the two Lord Mayors and the Sheriff.'

The undignified behaviour in the Military Sunday civic procession was debated behind closed doors by the City Council, but Wragge would not let matters drop. He consulted Sir Alfred S. Scott-Galter, Garter King of Arms, no less, who said he was right. Your 'Sheriff has no right to walk alongside of you' Sir Alfred told Wragge, (79) as if it mattered. The Sheriff did not agree with that eminent authority however, contending that custom allowed him and the Lord Mayor to walk side by side on such occasions. (80)

Why did the Tories select such a tetchy, opinionated and arrogant a person as Wragge as Lord Mayor for three terms ? It seems that they might have chosen him for the simple reason that as Lord Mayor he automatically became the chief magistrate, and that while occupying that position he might act as a check on the likes of Edwin Gray, his predecessor, who seemed to be dead set on taking on the drink interests, running down the number of pubs in the city and upsetting a trade which was solidly behind Wragge's party. This has been said before. Is it completely fanciful ? Was the York

Licensing bench regularly composed of temperance advocates? Wragge, no less, said it was. He spent a great deal of time assuring the trade that he was sympathetic to it and at the Brewster Sessions of 1906 he actually announced that 'The Licensing Committee was formed very largely of gentlemen who held strong temperance views.' (81)

Wragge's speech at the 1906 Sessions could be used to support a contention that he was less than a totally unbiased first magistrate. He gave vent then to one of the standard binds being made by LVAs and brewing interests in general (one that has certainly been mentioned before). Working Men's clubs (and clubs in general) were not all to the liking of publicans, brewers and people like Vernon, who nevertheless occasionally accepted work from them. The pubs, he said, were still subjected to unfair competition from the clubs, some of which functioned as off licenses and many of which, he contended, rather rashly, were 'drinking and gambling dens.' In some York establishments, he went on, 'there was too much to drink, there was gambling and betting, and there ought to be police supervision.' Norman Crombie agreed, reminding the bench that the clubs had 'better' Sunday opening laws than the pubs. Crombie also reminded Wragge and his colleagues that the LVAs had wanted clubs to be forced to contribute to the compensation fund and had promoted a bill to effect this which had been held over when a general election was announced.

Wragge was even more explicit about his attitude to clubs when he spoke to the 61st annual dinner of the York Licensed Victuallers Association. He was reported in the *Press* of 22 March 1906 as follows under the heading 'York a Sober City'.

> A good deal of comment had been made from time to time with regard to clubs. "I sympathise with you from the bottom of my heart," said Alderman Wragge, amid applause. "There is undoubtedly an injustice done to your trade by pseudo-clubs - places that have no right to be called clubs, that have no right to supply intoxicating drinks and make large profits without any corresponding interest in the revenue of the country, places that are almost unrestricted as to the periods when they should be open, and that altogether abrogate the original intention of clubs by supplying not only members, but also those off the premises.

If the contention that the Tories chose Wragge as Lord Mayor to keep the temperance advocates in check is correct, then he once more found that he was not quite such a powerful man as he may have thought he was. The Sessions of 1906 began with the presentation to the bench of a memorial from numerous York clergymen who declared they were against an increase in the number of licenses in the city and said they wanted a decrease if possible - something they eventually got. Among the memorialists were Westrope, Argles, John Henry Hirst, and that Joshua Mason who had pleaded so eloquently for help for the unemployed. They were led by Arthur P. Purey-Cust who wanted to address the court. He got the same treatment from Wragge as had the passive resisters, and was told to wrap up.

What was to be the bench's policy regarding licenses ? They would make a reduction this year, Wragge said, 'as an indication of the policy which they intended to carry out.' Whether there would have been more had Vernon not been Lord Mayor is unknown, perhaps there would, but anyway the Chief Constable (J. Burrow) objected to the renewal of six licenses. This meant, of course, that the magistrates themselves were objecting, and once more evidence of the number of pubs in York and the magnitude of what people like the Rowntrees saw as one of the city's greatest problems was trotted out. (82) The Three Cups on Foss Bridge was objected to. It belonged to the Tadcaster Tower Company and had another six pubs within 100 yards of it. The Brewers Arms, Walmgate, had exactly the same statistics trotted out on its behalf (or against it). There the tenant made 35s. a week profit, he said, in a good week, and paid £3 to the compensation fund. The Brewers was objected to as were the Black Bull, Walmgate and the Square and Compass, just off Walmgate. The latter's trade was small, not like the Leopard in Coney Street. This was a soldier's pub which took over £603 in a year (paying out almost £344 to the brewery) and contributed £10 per annum to the compensation fund. It was likely that it would be making a claim on that fund because it was opposed, as was the Grapes Beer House, King's Square, owned by Joshua Tetley. This was a pre-1869 beer house which was wholly protected and could only be objected to on the grounds of necessity. The Chief Constable claimed it was unnecessary, and later it was revealed that these six hostelries were regarded as the worst in York. Five of their licenses were not renewed. In May 1906 at the first meeting of the Compensation Committee the question of paying off the tenants and owners was considered. (83) (At the time of the Brewster Sessions of 1906 the fund amounted to £2,386.)

Wragge was intended to be a check on the Liberal temperance reformers - but his supporters may have thought and hoped (correctly) that he would also be a match for the passive resisters against the education rate who were keeping the 'unjust' details of Balfour's Act before the public and getting useful support for the question. They carried on their campaign, even after their leading light, Reissman, left the city for better things. (84)

Reissman had led the rate resisters in 1904, and they kept up their 'fight' in the next two years - with the same old faces involved, receiving the same old fines after making the same old pleas, and being slapped down by Wragge in the same old way. Arthur Dearlove, who seems to have been the only conscientious objector who was not religious had his goods seized in March 1905, along with Westrope and others. (85) A few days later Robert Newbald Kay, himself a resister it will be recalled, appeared in a local court on behalf of James M. Gardiner, alleging that the authorities had seized more than they should have, and threatening to take the case to a higher court. (86) On 16 March it was reported that an attempt to execute a distress warrant against Thomas Parker, a chemist of Micklegate had failed because somehow or other he had no goods to seize. The authorities, ever resourceful, seized Tom instead and he was sent down for 14 days. (87) In August Newbald Kay was in court for not paying 12s.5d. of his rate demand, (88) and in September Arthur Dearlove, Richard Westrope, the Rev R. Morison-Cumming and others were before Wragge once more. (89) Newbald Kay was done again (at the East Ainsty Petty Sessions) in February 1906 (for 14s.5d.) (90) as were Westrope, Dearlove, the Rev Hind (the president of the York Passive Resister's League) and 12 others at York. (91) By this time, however, the government had changed, and Balfour's successor was promising a comprehensive Education Act which might just satisfy the demands of the Dearloves and the Westropes. Certainly that new government would have been much more to their liking.

It is tempting to suggest that Vernon Wragge and some of his supporters may have used a little ploy to defeat the propaganda that the passive resisters hoped to get annually. All of them went along to court, tried to get an opportunity to state their views, were refused it by Wragge, then went out to address meetings about their treatment. This they did, but the impact of what they had to say was somewhat lessened by the fact that usually their fines were paid. The *Press* of 7 January 1905 reported that Reissman's silver had been seized, but that someone had then paid his fine. He was reported to be furious, particularly as the word was put around by the Tories that he had paid it himself! One wonders whether, maybe, those who thought like Wragge had not paid it themselves. It would have been worth doing so. Certainly, after their stuff had been seized, some like the Rev Hind did buy it back at sales in the police yard. But some were made of sterner stuff. Tom Parker was one; Charles William Clack of Scarcroft was another. He got himself sent to gaol at Wakefield classed as a debtor and when he came out there was a meeting at Victoria Bar Chapel to celebrate his and Parker's martyrdom. What a meeting that must have been. 'His Majesty had a very powerful navy', Thomas told those assembled, 'and a very great number of soldiers, but he did not get a penny out of Brother Clack ...'. He said nothing but the truth. (The contention that their opponents might have been paying the resister's small fines does not seem too preposterous, perhaps, when it is born in mind that in Bradford a Passive Resister's Anti-Martyrdom League was set up to do exactly that.)

With the tide of public opinion running heavily against the Tories, November 1905 would have looked like an opportune time to try to dent that Tory monopoly of power in York. The reluctance of the Corporation to adopt council housing schemes to help the health of the city and create work might have led to some optimistic thoughts on the part of the Liberals. Anyway they fielded some exceptionally strong candidates, the first of whom was John Bowes Morrell. (92)

J.B. Morrell was 32 years of age in 1905, and since 1897 had been a director of Rowntree and Company. He stood in Micklegate, for one of the two seats up for grabs. The second and third of the candidates there - it is noticeable that the Liberals did not try to get both seats - were Mawson and W.H.R. Hopkins, who called himself an Independent. Morrell fought his election on the issue of education, health and 'municipalisation.' 'Councils', Morrell said,'should raise money by municipalisation as well as create work.'

The Liberals realised that Micklegate was fast becoming a 'labour' ward and wisely decided not to antagonise the likes of Mawson there. In Castlegate they went all out to get both seats, however, and one of their candidates was Oscar F. Rowntree, son of Joseph Rowntree, the chairman of the cocoa works. He was a graduate of the University of London and also on the board of Rowntree and Company. He was secretary and treasurer of the Bootham Ward Liberal Association and Club and active in the Health and Housing Association. He was also one of the trustees of the Village Trust which was developing the garden suburb of Earswick. Also standing in Castlegate was Councillor W. Boddy, an auctioneer, and the secretary of the York LVA, and J.M. Hogge, the second Liberal.

Hogge had become an important Liberal spokesman in York. He was a graduate of Edinburgh University and a minister of the United Free Church of Scotland who appeared to be unemployed (or of independent means) according to an issue of the *Press* which carried biographical details and line drawings of the municipal candidates of 1905. (93) He was generally spoken of as a 'Rowntree man' and was said to have been private secretary to Seebohm Rowntree. He was an active member of the York Council for the Unemployed, a campaigner against gambling, and an ardent supporter of municipalisation. His employer's book, *Poverty*, he said at one of his meetings, was a challenge 'to the people of York to put their municipality into a better condition.' Take over the gas and water supply industries he urged, and electrify the tram system. (94) Oscar Rowntree agreed with him, but it was Hogge's views on gambling which were his undoing.

Hogge was active as organising secretary of the National Anti-Gambling League, and he had written on the question of gambling. (95) He never missed an opportunity to expound on the subject and in September 1905, for instance, he was doing so to the Bradford and Halifax Primitive Methodists. (96) Shortly afterwards rumours started going round that he would 'do away' with the York races, rumours which he strenuously denied, but which could have done his election prospects no good whatever. Nevertheless Hogge, as well as being a gift to cartoonists, enlivened the election proceedings as a report of the day before polling showed. Arnold Rowntree had presided over an open air meeting at which Oscar Rowntree and Morrell spoke first (97)

> Mr J.M. HOGGE, who was the last speaker, also desired to take the opportunity of denying the statement that part of the Progressive municipal policy was to sweep away York races. It was another of the foolish falsehoods that the "Herald" and the "Press" had attempted to circulate against the Progressive candidates. In the columns of the "Herald" was also published a letter saying that there were too many

J. B. Inglis.

Quakers standing for the City Council, (98) and naming Messrs Rowntree, Morrell, Baker and himself as Quakers. That was not true. Mr Morrell was a Wesleyan and he was a Scotch Presbyterian. The only excess of Quakers there would be on election day [sic], when the Tory party would quake when they saw the result of the poll. "Don't you make any mistake," he went on, "we have in the City Council far too many old men, who have been [there] far too long, and what you want is to infuse a lot of fresh blood. It is the young men who are standing throughout the city - Mr. Rowntree and myself and Mr. Morrell - who, if you return us will do our best to put some Progressive spirit into the dry bones at present in the Council chamber.

Hogge mentioned a Mr Baker. He was George Baker a candidate in a by election in Castlegate which happened to be taking place at the same time. Baker was a Quaker whose father had had an 'extensive' drapers business in Pavement. He was an accountant and a director of Brown Brothers and Taylor, 'the York furnishing firm', and had been educated at Bootham and Ackworth. He was a vice president of the York Temperance Society.

Another of the Liberal (Progressive) candidates in 1905 was R.G. Heys. He has been mentioned in these pages before as a member of the York School Board. He had been educated at Elmfield College, York, and the University of Leeds, and after graduating had had a number of teaching posts in various places. In January 1892 he returned to York to become headmaster of his old school, and was elected a city councillor in 1902. R.G. Heys was president of the York and District Band of Hope Union and treasurer of the York Free Church Council. He stood for re-election in his old ward of Monk.

Sebastian William Meyer was a sitting Liberal councillor who was returned unopposed in 1905 for Bootham, and the last of the party's new candidates was K.E.T. Wilkinson who was seeking election in Walmgate along with the retiring Liberal councillor W.H. Birch, the youngest member of the council.

Wilkinson was the son of the late E.T. Wilkinson, once the Official Receiver in Bankcruptcy and for many years a councillor for Micklegate. K.E.T. was born in 1871 and was educated at St Peters School, York, and Gonville and Caius College, Cambridge 'where he took honours in the classical law tripos.' He had been extremely active in the York Liberal party for over a decade, and in 1900 had been the Master of Elibank's election agent. At the time of the 1905 municipal elections Wilkinson was working as a solicitor in partnership with his uncle William Wilkinson. In the 1920s he became (after having been thrown off the Council) a very active member of that York Educational Settlement which was closed in the 1980s. (99)

This strong Liberal contingent fought when things were going very well for the opposition, and they avoided a clash with Labour. The campaign managed to get itself centred around Hogge and his alleged threat to the races, however. Perhaps this was partly his own fault. 'Hogge,' the *Press* said, 'around whom the election fight mainly rages, is a Scotchman of very extreme views, and with a very ready tongue which he uses with greater vigour than discretion.' Whether that was fair or not Hogge lost, coming second to Oscar Rowntree and Boddy in Walmgate. Heys came second to a Tory in Monk and got in - with W.M. Marriss (Labour) coming last. Morrell and Mawson got in for Micklegate; while Birch came second to a Tory (R. Richardson) in Walmgate, with K.E.T. Wilkinson at the bottom of the poll and unelected. The result of the election was two gains for the Liberals - but the council remained overwhelmingly Conservative. (100) (29 Tories; 13 Liberals; five Labour; one Independent.)

What were the issues that concerned the Corporation at this time ? Unemployment has been mentioned, as has the Council's unwillingness to embark on a council house building programme. What else was there ? One issue, on which the Tories, Liberals and Labour agreed, was the electrification and municipalisation of the city's trams. Moves to effect this had started.

York had a tram service which was horsedrawn and something of a joke. The city had rejected proposals to buy the system in the early years of the century, (101) but the issue had not gone away. The York Tramway Company bought new cars in the summer of 1905 but 'Smarter cattle would be a decided improvement', commented one of the local papers, 'York is a great horse centre, and the capital of the great horse breeding county, and a better type of horses would look well in front of the new cars.' (102)

The York Tramways Company's horses were a scrawny lot, and they were mocked in a celebrated series of postcards which aroused some hostility when they first appeared - a punning York reporter saying that they 'delittled' the city. (103) Their owner had come into existence in 1879 (to become the City of York Tramways Company in 1886) and had as its major shareholder Major Close, the son of George Hudson's sidekick, and the man who had refused help to the workmen who had lost their jobs with the York Engineering Company. At the company's half yearly meeting of 1906 the chairman told shareholders that the firm was relaying rails but that prospects were not rosy. The York Corporation seemed determined to take them over, he said, 'The receipts had been very low ... He understood that the trade of York was not improving ... He had nothing encouraging to say.' (104) Six months later he revealed that negotiations were still going on with the Corporation, but that the latter had definitely decided on a takeover using the Tramways Act of 1870, (105) 'which gave every local authority power to purchase the line 21 years after it had been authorised, and at the end of every seven years after the 21 years.' (106) This meant that purchase could take place at stated intervals as the York line had been authorised in 1879 (from Fulford to Castle Mills Bridge) and 1881 (for the Mount to Castle Mills Bridge). However, the chairman concluded, he hoped the purchase could be made by agreement. (107)

It seems strange to read descriptions of the deliberations regarding the York tram system and to see beside them news items that featured acccounts that showed where the real way forward was. The appearance of the motor car in York has been mentioned and the prosecutions for speeding went on unabated in the first years of the century. Pressure groups demanded a raising of speed limits and the registration of cars, and Balfour's government duly brought in such things, making the streets perhaps just that little more dangerous for the likes of Harry McGinty (or perhaps Harry made things more hazardous for the drivers). In May 1903 there was a blitz in York on drivers exceeding 12 miles an hour, (108) but the number of vehicles increased, as did complaints about them. But if private vehicles were now practical and (relatively) reliable, why not supplement the tramway system with motor omnibuses ? Were there such things ? Of course there were and in May 1905 vehicles built by the Wolseley Tool and Motor Car Company were displayed in York, and Sheriff Bentley said he was sure they would replace the horse drawn trams someday. (109) Very shortly afterwards such ideas were discussed in council, with members debating whether they should have motor buses or electric trams. Sebastian Meyer, surprisingly for someone connected with transport in a professional capacity, disagreed with Bentley and so did the Lord Mayor. (110) (This may have been an additional factor causing friction between Vernon and his Sheriff.)

Very shortly after the Council's debate mentioned above, a definite announcement appeared that motor buses were to start running in York. These were to be operated by Messrs Vincent Brothers of Tudhoe, Spennymore; were to carry 30 persons; were to be of nine horse power; and were to ply for trade from Haxby Road to the railway station. (111) In July 1906 steam auto cars began a service from York into the countryside with one going from York to Ulleskelf and back each day and another going to Strensall and back, each carrying 60 passengers in a carriage towed behind the vehicle. (112) In July 1907 a motor bus service between York and London started. This was operated by Messrs Teste and Lassen of Regent Street and vehicles left Regent Street at 9.30 a.m. and arrived in York at 6.30 p.m. A stop was made for lunch at Grantham and another for tea at Barmby Moor. The return fare was four guineas (there were no singles).

These were clearly not the only buses running in York at that time. There were others doing 'pirate' work, as is shown in the court case in which James Emerson was prosecuted as an unlicensed bus driver. Emerson had on board some football players who he was taking to a match and he gave in to temptation. In Coppergate he picked up people who paid to go to Leeman Road, for which he was fined half a crown. (113)

In none of the meetings of the Tramway Company that were reported in the press is there an indication that shareholders or management recognised that the real threat to them was to come from road vehicles. People like Meyer thought the threat was non existent and people like J.H. Hartley simply demanded electrification and that labour be represented in the take over negotiations with the tram company. This was in his election speeches of 1906.

Hartley also demanded better pay for Corporation workmen, a demand which was not welcomed enthusiastically by his fellow councillors. Just before he was up for re-election Hartley became the spokesman of the clay carters working for the Council who sent in a memorandum (prompted by the ILP it was said) asking for an increase. This was put before the Streets and Buildings Committee and eventually debated by the full council. Streets and Buildings had not gone along with Hartley's demands but recommended that when vacancies occurred among the night scavengers the day porters could apply for them and so get a penny an hour more (6d instead of 5d). Hartley wanted 6d an hour for day men. He 'was convinced', he said, 'having tried it, that men were unable to run a home on less than that.' Councillor Pearson agreed. He knew, Pearson said, 'that it was impossible for a family man to live decently on less than 6d an hour.' (114) The Council deferred the matter, with Vernon Wragge saying it had been introduced deliberately to influence the November council elections.

Wragge and Hartley had taken part in a rather unpleasant episode in March 1906 that did nothing to endear the Labour member to the likes of Vernon. It was decided to make J.G. Butcher an honorary freeman of the city, a decision with which few could cavil, but, at a time when the unemployed thronged the city's streets, the Council decided that Butcher's parchment should be given to him in a silver casket. It was a heartless thing to do and Hartley was furious, and said so at the confirment ceremony. He was, Hartley said, a temperance man, but Butcher, 'in the House of Commons, had ... pulled in the other direction.' That was perfectly true, but Hartley also complained of the underhand way he said it had been decided to give Butcher his present. It had cost between £40 and £50 and had, through the rates, been subscribed to by hundreds of men who were 'unable to provide the necessities of life for their families.' Hartley asked Butcher to refuse the casket amidst tremendous uproar. (He asked unsuccessfully.) (115) A little later Hartley got into another row when he protested against schools drilling on Empire Day with dummy rifles. '"I am going," he said amid protests [in the Council chamber], "to be a passive resister, and to refuse to allow my children to attend any school in this city in which dummy rifles and Union Jacks are used."' (116) All good stuff, but Hartley seems to have got his facts (about the rifles) wrong on this occasion. (117) The Tories were to get their own back on him. But that was many years ahead.

Butcher had been honoured by the Tory Corporation of York because of what had happened at a recent general election. The freedom ceremony not only reflected the insensitivity of that body; it reflected, also, the acute sense of embarrassment and anger the majority of councillors felt at what had happened then. Butcher had been chucked out.

1. Ensor *op.cit.* p 376
2. Rhodes James *op.cit.* p 210
3. *Press* 3 March 1904
4. *Ibid* 21 March 1904

5.   *Ibid* 22 March 1904
6.   *Ibid* 24 March 1904
7.   *Ibid* 17 March 1904
8.   The Orange Free State
9.   *Press* 28 March 1904
10. *Ibid* 15 August 1902
11. *Ibid* 6 October 1902
12. *Ibid* 16 January 1903
13. *Ibid* 19 January 1903
14. *Ibid* 17 January 1903. Both Mitchell and Richards found other constituencies.
15. *Press* 27 February 1903
16. Eg *Ibid* 29 June, 1 and 3 July 1903
17. *Herald* 29 May 1903
18. The *VCH op.cit.* p 301 deals only briefly with Labour politics, but is rather misleading, saying, eg, that 'the Labour Party' emerged 'into York politics during the 1890's'.
19. On Marriss see earlier
20. *Press* 28 November 1903
21. *Ibid* 9 February 1904
22. *Ibid* 18 March 1904
23. I*bid* 15 October 1904. Hawkin is sometimes described as Richard Hawking, frequently as Hawkins. See eg *Ibid* 24 January 1906 (letters column).
24. *Herald* 1 February 1905
25. *Press* 26 June 1905
26. See later. In March 1903 the ILP's national conference was held in York.
27. *Press* 8 April 1901
28. *Ibid* 16 November 1905. The guardians did not do what the ILP wanted.
29. *Ibid* 15, 16 and 17 January 1903
30. *Ibid* 6 March 1903
31. *Ibid* 29 December 1905
32. Rhodes James *op.cit.* p 208
33. *Ibid*
34. *Economic Notes on Insular Free Trade*
35. R.H. Gretton, *A Modern History of the English People 1880-1922* (1930) pp 627-28
36. *Press* 17 July 1903
37. *Ibid* 17 August 1903
38. Public announcement by Seebohn Rowntree. *Ibid* 27 February 1904. The York Women's Liberal Federation meeting on free trade, mentioned later is reported in *Ibid* 23 September 1903
39. *Ibid* 11 October 1904
40. *Ibid* 20 December 1901
41. *Ibid* 22 April 1903
42. On the firm see eg the report of its annual general meeting in *Ibid* 18 March 1905. The year reported on then had been one of 'great prosperity and progress' it was said, with the firm showing a profit of £81,000, putting £20,000 into reserve, and paying $7^1/2$ per cent on ordinary stock and 5 on the guaranteed shares.
43. *Ibid* 22 April 1903
44. 5 Edward 7, chap 18
45. Gerald Balfour
46. *Press* 7 April 1905
47. *Ibid* 26 September 1905
48. *Ibid* 7 November 1905
49. *Ibid* 8 November 1905
50. *Ibid* 5 October 1905
51. On Close see A.J. Peacock. *George Hudson. The Railway King* (York 1989)passim. The Major Close referred to in the text had originally lived in a house on the site of the Royal Station Hotel, and the NER built a new one for him called 'The Hollies' on Tadcaster Road. It became the Chase Hotel. M.H. Pocock, *They Lived in Dringhouses* (York nd) p 25.
52. Eg *Press* 16 September 1896, where it simply says Close had been connected with the York and North Midland Railway.

53. *Ibid* 9 November 1905
54. *Ibid* 21 November 1905
55. *Ibid* 16, 19 and 23 August 1905
56. *Ibid* 18 September 1905
57. *Ibid* 27 September 1905
58. *Ibid* 19 and 20 June 1905. Marriss was the York representative at the GWR conference and he made some very lukewarm remarks about the situation at Rowntrees.
59. *Ibid* 21 and 29 September, 17 October 1905
60. *Ibid* 9 November 1905
61. On Joseph Fels see eg M. Fels, *Joseph Fels, His Life Work* (1920)
62. *Press* 15 December 1905
63. B. Behan, *Borstal Boy* (1958)
64. *Press* 11 and 30 December 1905
65. *Ibid* 11 January 1906
66. *Ibid* 22 March 1906. In October Arnold Rowntree had said there were 2,000 out of work in York. *Ibid* 30 October 1905
67. *Ibid* 27 November 1905
68. The work of this organisation would be a splendid subject for a dissertation
69. *Press* 13 November 1905. On an annual meeting of the Mission with a description of its normal work see eg *Ibid* 25 March 1905
70. *Ibid* 22 March 1906
71. *Herald* 1 and 22 February 1905
72. *Press* 8 November 1905
73. See eg *Ibid* 2 November 1905
74. He did not stand.
75. Press 3 May 1905
76. Eg *Ibid* 31 October, 9 and 13 November 1905
77. *Ibid* 17 November 1905
78. *Ibid* 28 and 29 May 1906
79. *Ibid* 12 June 1906
80. *Ibid* 13 June 1906, letter from W.A. Pearson, the under-Sheriff.
81. *Ibid* 12 February 1906. The Licensing Committee in 1906 consisted of the following persons - the first two of whom certainly were very active temperance reformers: J.S.Rowntree, Henry Tennant; J.R. Hill; Alderman Agar; Alderman McKay; Alderman Sykes Rymer; Alderman Foster and J.W. Proctor.
82. *Ibid* 7 March 1906. Report of adjourned sessions.
83. *Ibid* 29 May 1906
84. He resigned from Lendal Congregational Church in April 1905
85. *Press* 6 March 1905
86. *Ibid* 9 March 1905
87. *Ibid* 16 March 1905
88. *Ibid* 12 August 1905
89. *Ibid* 28 September 1905
90. *Ibid* 10 February 1906
91. *Ibid* 22 February 1906. The details of Brother Clack's incaceration and Thomas Parker's speech in *Herald* 14, 18 and 24 January 1905
92. On Morrell see eg A. Vernon, *Three Generations* (1971). This is a very slight piece of work, as is the same author's biography of Arnold Rowntree. Both are full of the most appalling trivia.
93. *Press* 27 October 1905
94. *Ibid* 27 September 1905
95. There was a York branch of the League, naturally, of which B.S. Rowntree was treasurer and in which Hogge was active. See *Herald* 19 January 1905 for a report of its annual general meeting.
96. *Press* 29 September 1905
97. *Ibid* 30 October 1905
98. See also *Press* letter signed "HARD KNOTT" 28 October 1905 wherein it was said that Morrell, Hogge, Rowntree and Baker were 'strong anti-gambling fanatic[s]' who would 'drive the "races out of the town" ... '.

99.   *Press* 4 March 1954, 5 December 1955. Wilkinson was extremely active as a lecturer at the York Settlement as well as being the chairman. He wrote a guide to the Education Act of 1918.
100. *Ibid* 2 and 4 November 1905
101. See chapter 1
102. *Press* 6 July 1905
103. A pun on the name of DeLittle, the firm which published the cards *Ibid* 13 November 1905. On the cards see J. Dickinson, *York on Old Postcards* (Ruddington 1989)
104. *Ibid* 14 February 1906
105. 33 and 34 Victoria, 1870 sec 43
106. *Press* 5 September 1906
107. *Ibid*
108. See eg *Ibid* 9 May 1903
109. *Ibid* 23 May 1905. These early buses are not mentioned in K.A. Jenkinson, *The York City Buses* (1984)
110. *Press* 6 June 1905
111. *Ibid* 4 July 1905
112. *Ibid* 2 July 1906. The *VCH op.cit.* p 478 said the 'trams were not challenged by buses until 1914'. The announcement of the starting of the London to York service appeared in *Press* 9 July 1907
113. *Ibid* 8 March 1906
114. *Ibid* 2 October 1906. W.A. Pearson was an interesting person who had been absent from the council after he volunteered to go to the front during the Boer War.
115. *Ibid* 10 March 1905
116. *Ibid* 29 May 1906
117. See the replies to him from the schoolmasters involved. *Ibid* 9 June 1906

CHAPTER 4

THE LIBERAL REVIVAL

A.J. Balfour resigned on 4 December 1905. The Tory government which had been returned so sensationally at the election in 1900 (brought on in part, it has been suggested, by events in York) had had a terrible time since the end of the Boer War. It had introduced much needed reforms, and all of them had brought it unpopularity, it seemed. Not only that, but they had united the Liberals. Attacks on the unions had prompted the Labour movement to organise a national party, as had the dreadful levels of unemployment which had followed the end of the war. For a brief period in 1905 - when Campbell-Bannerman enunciated a 'step by step' policy towards Home Rule for Ireland - it looked as if the Liberals might split again over that issue (Rosebery had disagreed with and attacked the Campbell-Bannerman policy). But there was no split and Balfour's party had to fight something like a united opposition, and it did so with disastrous results. Balfour himself was rejected. So was York's senior MP.

Campbell-Bannerman accepted office, formed a government, then dissolved Parliament. The general election was held on various dates in January.

The York Tories ran the two sitting members, J.G. Butcher and G.D. Faber. The latter had announced in the summer of 1904 that he would not stand for York again, and H.H. Riley-Smith of Tadcaster (and others) had been mentioned as a replacement for him. Faber had stayed, however, and had been as active in the constituency as Butcher. Hamar Greenwood remained the Liberal candidate; G.H. Stuart was to represent the Labour Representation Committee.

The Liberals were not - even in 1906 - out to get both York's seats. Their fortunes were in the ascendant, and had been for nearly four years, but there was a threat to them on the horizon that was somewhat larger than a man's hand. Those years which saw the decline of the Tories' fortunes had also contained attacks on the Labour movement which had led to the formation of what came to be the Labour party, and it was from here that ultimately the threat to the Liberals was to come. People in York realised that was the case. Joseph Rowntree, for example.

Perhaps it was inevitable that labour would eventually form its own political party - the Liberals in disarray would have seemed to have had little prospects of power in the early years of the century, and anyway were the party of free trade and the manufacturers. But the York Liberals left it late in the day before they made an attempt to make any kind of an electoral alliance - very late indeed. Maybe they thought the threat from Labour would go away, and that the working class would support them 'when the time came'. Perhaps the majority thought like that - or did not bother to think at all, but some realised the true facts of political life. One of the Quakers, for example, and some of the professional workers. Joseph Rowntree spoke to members of the Yorkshire district of the Society of Certified and Associated Liberal Agents and 'urged that some effective union should take place between the Liberal and the Labour Party' - but this was a week after it had been announced that a selection conference was to be held to select a Labour candidate for York. (1) Speeches at the meeting of the Liberal agents make it quite clear that those present realised what a threat was presented to them, but things had gone too far. When Rowntree spoke much attention was being given to a long drawn out and bitter strike at Denaby Main and events there had prompted Ben Tillett - a famous Labour leader - to say that 'it was time for labour to take off the gloves' and go it alone. (2) At the meeting of the Liberal 400 in February 1903 K.E.T. Wilkinson took up Rowntree's theme and urged on the likes of Sebastian Meyer, J.B. Morrell and Arnold Rowntree the need for the Liberals and the socialists to unite. (3)

The York Labour Representation Committee refused any alliance with the Liberals, and at a meeting in York at which the famous Will Crooks spoke (making an old age pension his major demand) Stuart emphasised that he was standing alone, and resolutely refused to ask voters to split between him and Greenwood. (4) Wilkinson again demanded an electoral pact (5) but to no avail. This was in the summer of 1903 and thereafter nothing more was heard publicly of such a pact. Certainly there was never any question of the Liberals (or the socialists for that matter) running two candidates, but it might have been to Stuart's benefit had there been something of a rather more formal nature.

What was Stuart's campaign like ? What issues did he choose to highlight ? Education, though still of great importance to some people, did not seem to concern Stuart all that much, but he declared himself unequivocally a Home Ruler and against conscription. (6) Helped by national figures like Pete Curran, Stuart also demanded the full socialist programme of nationalisation, and maintained that the (impressive) Tory reforms they had seen in the past few years had been forced from them. Unemployment rightly figured largely in Stuart's speeches, so did the attacks on the trade unions and the question of tactical voting. What should York electors do with their second vote ? Stuart, with all the understandable enthusiasm of a pioneer, had high hopes of topping the poll and had taken a 'devil take the hindmost' attitude, maintaining that the Liberals were no better than the Tories. He reiterated his statements of as long ago as 1903 and said 'no deal' with the Liberals. Were there none among his supporters suggesting otherwise ? There were, and one of them got heavily clobbered for doing so.

There can have been few more genuine radicals in York in the first decade of the 20th century than Richard Westrope - a passive resister and a tireless worker for housing reform, temperance, women's suffrage, and the Labour movement. Westrope appeared regularly on Stuart's platform, and it seems that he urged Labour supporters to split between Stuart and Greenwood. Why not ? But Brother Richard as he came to be known (7) was criticised. Someone from the ILP called George Brown (the LRC said he did not exist) wrote to the *Press* saying that Westrope was a mole. He was 'controlled by Mr. Rowntree, the most influential member of the Liberal Association.' We 'and our candidate have been sold', he went on, 'sold to the Rowntree party - the capitalists, and I want to know who is to blame ?' (8) If Westrope was urging his Labour colleagues to split with Greenwood - and it does not seem an unreasonable thing for him to have done - then he was only doing what his alleged masters were urging publicly anyway. 'I and all my family are going to vote for Mr. Stuart' Arnold Rowntree declared. (9)

What of Greenwood's campaign ? He dealt largely with what he saw as the attack on free trade, and what he saw as an inevitable rise in food prices if a system of protection was introduced. 'Vote for Greenwood and the big loaf' was one of the prominent slogans used by the Liberals. Every 'vote given to the Conservatives was a vote for the Protectionist party because the Conservative party was pledged to protection', he said. Greenwood ignored the fact that there were Tory free traders and some who were opposed to taxing food. Butcher and Faber for example. They both proved that they had declared against food taxes, and K.E.T. Wilkinson had to apologise to them pubicly. Greenwood also spent a lot of time talking about Chinese slavery, and got rather a drubbing in the process.

Greenwood took part in a well-publicised argument with D.L. Pressly, the editor of the *Herald*, who certainly did seem to score heavily against the Liberal by shifting the discussion away from matters of principle to matters of detail, and rattling him in the process. The compound system had gone on for 30 years at Kimberley, Pressly contended; it was not an invention sanctioned for the first time by the Balfour government. And should the Chinese stay there, having gone there voluntarily ? That should be for the people of the Transvaal to decide, Greenwood said. It was an unimpressive performance by Greenwood, who was further embarrassed, as were Liberals everywhere, by the persistence with which the Tories pointed out that systems of slavery similar to that in South Africa went on in other parts of the Empire, and that the Liberals had never criticised them. Lord Helmsley, speaking on behalf of Butcher and Faber, delighted a York audience when he told them how Griffith Boscawen had read out clauses from an official document about the importation into South Africa of foreign labourers, pausing after each quotation and asking 'Is that slavery ?' To that question he always got a positive reply, then revealed that in fact he was reading pieces from the British Guiana ordinance which had been passed by a Liberal government! (The *Press* published articles during the election 'proving' that the Chinese in South Africa were happy, contented, were dressing 'IN THE HEIGHT OF FASHION' and were 'SURROUNDED BY LUXURY'.) Chinese slavery was an emotional subject which, however much people like Boscawen pointed out Liberal inconsistencies, did immense harm to the Tories. Richard Westrope could usually be relied upon to turn in an emotional speech when called upon, and he gave one on Chinese slavery. It was probably typical of hundreds that were made throughout the country. He inveighed against the introduction of it as an incalculable injury to the Chinese, a foul stain upon the fair name of Great Britain as a Christian nation, an insult to British labour and an outrage on the people of South Africa, whose wishes are being overridden in the interests of a few mine-owners. Mr Westrope said the Government would be known in history as the Government of the great betrayals - (applause) - because all the principles they had valued highly, and thought they had securely won had ... been practically thrown aside, and bartered for gold, and this last betrayal was the worst of all. It was the betrayal of Judas, for it was the selling of the nation, its honour and its integrity'.

Greenwood and Stuart were the attackers in 1906. How did the Tories deal with great issues of the day ? How did they deal with Chinese slavery, for example ? Faber rubbed home the point made by Lord Helmsley rather effectively. Greenwood had been driven from his earlier position on Chinese slavery after his mauling by Helmsley and Pressly, Faber said, for if it was slavery in South Africa it must logically be slavery in the West Indies where it was employed or used by the very people who had brought him to York - the Rowntrees. Butcher dealt with the issue by contending, also, that it had had beneficial results. Chinese labour in South Africa, Butcher said, had led to an increase of between 5,000 and 6,000 jobs for white men. Not only that but it was necessary, because white men would not work down the mines. Here things got very nasty, with the two Tories using very unpleasant expressions. Butcher told an audience that white men had 'refused to do nigger's work', but Faber said some had tried then stopped, saying 'they were not niggers and would not do the work.' Faber, in a reply to a questioner, said 'You know quite well that in South Africa no white man can work alongside a black-skin or a yellow-skin. You wouldn't.' Butcher also contended that the Chinese had to be used because native labour would not go down the mines. '... the Chinese were doing only the unskilled labour which the Kaffirs had done before the war, but which they were too well off to do now, and which whites could not and would not do.'

Butcher, one of the prime instigators of the compensation system for defunct drink licenses, was disliked by temperance advocates like Councillor Hartley, and he had to spend some time dealing with the 'evils' of drink. 'Intemperance' he said, 'was one of the most disgusting of vices, but if a man wanted to drink a glass of beer in all moderation, he should not be prevented because his fellowman was not thirsty.' That seems very reasonable, and the licensed victuallers thought so too. Early in January George Woolford, president of the York LVA, and licensee of the Clarence Hotel, Davygate, declared that the Association recommended support for the Tories. On almost the same day the city's Roman Catholics (who approved of the Balfour Education Act) also urged support for Butcher and Faber.

106

Faber and Butcher both emphasised that they were against food taxes, and Faber declared he had first been returned to the Commons as an imperialist and that he was still an imperialist - 'and a big loafer too.' Both Tories were against Home Rule for Ireland, and Butcher linked the question of unemployment with the need for imperial preference. The one was caused by the lack of the other. What they 'were suffering from in York and other parts of the country was want of employment,' Butcher said, 'owing to the unfair treatment of foreign nations who would not let our manufactured goods ... go into their markets. The Radical policy from beginning to end was destructive. They were going to leave this question of unemployment untouched and they were going to destroy the Voluntary schools, and ... the union between Great Britain and Ireland.'

If Butcher's diagnosis of the causes of unemployment was correct then he was right to say that the Liberals were not proposing measures to create jobs, for there was no way in which they could alter the free trade system. The populace chose to believe that any interference with that time honoured system would lead to increased food prices, and that was the main issue at the general election. What happened? One of the greatest landslide election victories in British history took place. The Liberals won no less than 377 seats - a majority of 84 over all the other parties combined. What happened in York?

On the night of 14 January a crowd of 10,000 gathered outside the De Grey Rooms to await the results of the poll. (Already many of them had the news of the defeat of A.J. Balfour, the ex-Premier.) During the day 12,906 out of the 13,890 on the electoral register voted, and when the declaration was made at around midnight the city's senior Tory was out. Greenwood came top of the poll followed by Faber, the man who had declared he would not stand, some 3,000 votes behind. Butcher was third just 14 votes behind his colleague and Stuart was last. 'Butcher out, and by fourteen votes! How loyally the unionists have polled' bleated the *Press*. Later that night the inquests began with Councillor Boddy, of the LVA, being particularly uptight about Butcher's defeat. Labour spokesmen said they would never trust the Liberals again. What did they mean by that? They had not been loath to say that they regarded the Liberals as in some ways no better than the Tories, and certainly people like Arnold Rowntree had not let them down. He had voted for Stuart. He publicly said he would. But then he should have, because he was in on an important secret.

The poll showed that Stuart had received 421 plumpers, but that Greenwood had received well over 2,000. What did this mean? Stuart had a conspiracy theory which he revealed in *The Postman's Gazette* in February. (10) He had started off by refusing to advise people how to vote (beyond giving him one that is). Then the Liberals had begun to persuade 'our people' to split with Greenwood, doing this both within the Labour organisation (through Westrope for example) and from the ranks of the Liberals. Stuart had to some extent been won over, then the Liberals used a letter from

Will Crooks allegedly written to Greenwood but really written to Arnold Rowntree. (Rowntree eventually apologised.) It was placarded around York and persuaded many Labour voters to give their second vote to Greenwood - but Greenwood's supporters did not reciprocate. '... having induced our folks to vote for their man,' Stuart wrote, 'they didn't vote for me. That's all. To the number of 2,082 they plumped for Greenwood, and he was returned at the head of the poll.' But the Liberals could not force people to split in his favour, and it has been shown that some urged folk to do so. The plumpers for Greenwood may have been Liberals who bore a resentment against Labour dating back a long way Stuart suggested. Many harboured a resentment dating back to 1892 when Keir Hardie 'went dead against Sir Kit [Furness]' at a York election which he lost by only 11 votes.

Perhaps this resentment goes a long way to explaining the voting patterns of 1906. Many Liberal sympathisers resentful over licensing, Chinese labour or education maybe could not face the prospect of voting Tory, but were afraid of Labour with its large scale plans for nationalisation. Whether in 1906 they still harboured resentment for what Hardie did in 1892 seems doubtful, but remembering it might have reinforced their fears of the likes of Stuart.

It seems, really, that the Liberals did not engage in the scheming Stuart suggested, but there were also some splits between the Tories and Greenwood. Richard Hawkin said that Greenwood's split votes got him elected. But why on earth should an elector cast one of his votes for Butcher or Faber - protectionists and food taxers (11) - and the other for the free trader Greenwood ? It is difficult to comprehend. Could they have thought that Butcher was unelectable, because he had been in office longest and took most of the Liberal flak, and that Greenwood and Faber was better than Greenwood and Stuart? Perhaps. Butcher had alienated the temperance advocates while Faber, sensibly, hedged his bets on that one.

But given the way the Balfour government had been shooting itself in the foot, and given what happened elsewhere, it must be conceded that the Tories did remarkably well in 1906 - Stuart, himself, said so. He wrote of 'the wonderful efficiency of the Conservative machinery in York. To poll as they did, in the face of the wave which [was] going over the country, was wonderful' he recorded. (12) In the aftermath of the election Labour took a look at its opponents and reorganised itself. Ward organisations had been created in the city before the election, but just a few weeks after it the City of York Labour Association was brought into being. W.M. Marriss was its secretary and it already had a paid organiser in the energetic E.B. Rose, an ex Liberal agent, who turned out to be a most effective propagandist. The Association was said to be like the old LRC but 'perhaps a little more serious', and was to have paying individual members, and affiliated organisations, with delegates from those. Rose announced that he hoped for 1,000 paying members within six months and revealed that they hoped they could build or buy a Trades Hall at a cost of some £10,000. (13)

The analysis of the 1906 poll, over which the arguments about interpretation were to range, is as follows. (There were eleven spoilt papers.)

	Butcher	Faber	Greenwood	Stuart
Plumpers	62	37	2,082	421
Butcher and Faber	5,852	5,852		
Butcher and Greenwood	122		122	
Butcher and Stuar	58			58
Faber and Greenwood		167	167	
Faber and Stuart		52	52	
Greenwood and Stuart			4,042	4,042
TOTALS	6,094	6,108	6,413	4,573

Labour, as has been said, felt bitterly let down by the Liberals, and their protests were loud and long. He thought there would be another election before very long, E.B. Rose said, though how he could think this is difficult to see, and when it came they would 'act a little less like bally fools than we have done.' 'We've been sold, betrayed' asserted a Stuart supporter just after the declaration, 'We'll never trust the Liberals again said another' and others said that in future 'there was to be "no more chocolate, or cocoa-nabs."' But is this totally fair ? Surely not. Rose (for example) to begin with ignored the fact that there were many kinds of Liberals - some of whom he could surely not have expected to vote for Stuart - and to have assumed that the majority of splits between Stuart and Greenwood were Labour supporters who, in a one member constituency would have simply voted Labour was not logical. They, or the majority of them might have been Liberals first, who obeyed the requests of Arnold Rowntree, Westrope and others. Two thirds of those who voted for Greenwood also voted for Stuart, and that seems an impressive enough figure to excuse the Liberals of bad faith - and if there really was a conspiracy it would have taken a great deal of organising, even with the adult school movement having been whipped in to help as Stuart said. The splits between Butcher and Stuart and Faber and Stuart shown in the poll analysis look extremely bizarre.

The bitterness of many Labour supporters, however, must seem just a little more understandable when it is born in mind that York in 1906 was in fact a part of an 'arrangement' which had been reached at the very highest levels between the Liberal party and Ramsay MacDonald. (14) The latter and Herbert Gladstone (with the approval of Campbell-Bannerman) drew up a list of constituencies in which Labour would be given 'a free hand' or in which (two Member constituencies) representation would be shared. York was one of the latter and, of course, the deal was honoured. Not only that, but people like Arnold Rowntree did their level best to persuade Liberals to go the next logical step and split between the two parties. They did all they could to make the arrangement work beyond the original deal not to oppose each other, but could not force their followers to vote as they wished.

The election over, Greenwood's parliamentary career got off to a very promising start. In March it was announced that he had been appointed parliamentary private secretary to Winston Churchill. It was not long, however, before he displayed that rashness with matters of detail which he showed during the election over Chinese labour - and he got severely handled for doing so. Everyone waited for the first Liberal budget to be introduced by H.H. Asquith and later Greenwood commented on it, saying that the tax on sugar had been reduced. This was not so and a tetchy correspondent to the *Evening Press* - Charles A. Thompson of St Paul's Square - pointed out that whereas the tax on tea had been reduced and that on coal abolished, 'not one farthing has been taken off sugar since its impost in 1901.' (15)

Reducing taxes was essential for the new government, and it had other debts to pay. Important politicians like Lloyd George, now president of the Board of Trade, had inveighed against the Education Act and had done much that led to the movements of passive resistance throughout the country. It was essential that nonconformist grievances should be removed, and Augustine Birell duly produced a bill to do so. Its introduction started one of the most shameful episodes in British political history. Balfour - now back in parliament after his initial rejection and leading a party which in the Commons had only 157 members - deliberately set about emasculating the Liberal government by making the House of Lords, wherein there was a huge Tory majority, throw out legislation sent up to it. Very sensibly the Lords, 'Thinking of little but party tactics' and recoiling 'from increasing the hostility of organised labour towards them', let the Trades Disputes Bill of 1906 through unscathed. (16) This reversed the Taff Vale judgement which had been so important in leading to an organised Labour party and exempted trades unions from all actions for tort. The Education Bill, however, and the government had 'an unusually clear mandate' to amend the Act of 1902, (17) was killed stone dead by their Lordships. (They also killed off a Plural Voting Bill intended to stop the owners of several properties voting more than once.)

Birell's Education Bill was intended to remove the grievances of people like Newbald Kay, Reissman and Arthur Dearlove. It was a complicated measure, (18) and it met with great hostility from English churchmen. The Lords drastically amended practically every clause; the Commons rejected the amendments; and the Lords then

J. M. Hogge.

insisted upon them; whereupon the government announced on 20 December, that it would proceed no further with the Bill. Thus started a fundamental political contest, with the Lords doing Balfour's bidding, and negating legislation passed by a government that had been returned with an unbelievable majority. The contest went on for years.

Campbell-Bannerman wanted to dissolve parliament after the rejection of the Education Bill and fight a new election on the issue of 'the Lords versus the people', but he was overruled. E.B. Rose had said he expected another general election quickly, but he could have hardly anticipated one as early as this. It must surely be a fact that the Liberals missed a great opportunity in 1907. Their Education Bill was truly a shambles, but the appalling behaviour of the Tories would have obscured that in a general election fought over the behaviour of the Lords, and in that election it would have been interesting to see what Labour did in York. Stuart, or whoever stood, would not have made the mistakes he did earlier.

The Church of England in York mustered its forces against the Education Bill. At one protest meeting in the Bedern School Canon Watson called it monstrously unjust and elsewhere in the city, on the same night, the Rev E.E. Nottingham, of the Diocesan Training College, the Rev E.C. Owen, the headmaster of St Peter's School, and Alderman H.V. Scott, chairman of the York Education Committee vied with each other to do the same. (19) A little later Canon Argles - he of the temperance movement - presided over a meeting at which W.F.H. Thompson, the Liberal Unionist, told his hearers that 'of all the Bills that were ever before the country ... this is the most astonishing, [the] most impudent, and [the] most impossible.' (20) These were but a few of the protests held in York. What was the attitude expressed towards the Lords when they began their programme of wrecking legislation sent up to them ? Towards the end of the year the Ripon Diocesan conference was held at which those assembled thanked 'the Archbishops and Bishops for their action in the House of Lords in defence of the principles of justice and religion.' (21) How those eminent clerics could have contended that the Lords were defending principles of justice in rejecting the Education Bill (22) defies logic, but J.G. Butcher, a trained lawyer, went even further. Balfour had set the Lords to work as wreckers, but not in Butcher's book. He blamed everything on the Liberals. '... the Radicals were engaged at their old and congenial occupation of manufacturing a constitutional crisis', he said. 'He had no doubt that sooner or later they would be faced with the grave constitutional question of what was really the function of the House of Lords in the English Constitution', he went on, 'No doubt the agitation against the House of Lords would go on, but it would not succeed.' (23) This was an extraordinary speech, and it was as wrong as it was silly. Butcher's conspiracy theory was miles wide of the mark and, although the struggle with the Lords did go on, it certainly did succeed.

Augustine Birell became Irish Secretary early in 1907, and was replaced at the Board of Education by Reginald McKenna. He introduced 'A feeble ... Bill' which 'was cursed by both sides, and was ignominiously withdrawn.' (24) It gets rarely a mention in the political histories and biographies, (25) but its abandonment meant things were just as they were before the general election. The passive resisters must have thought badly of the House of Lords. (Arthur Dearlove would have abolished it.) They carried on their protests as they did in Balfour's time.

In September 1906 Dearlove, Heys, Hirst, Aldridge and others appeared in court again, only to have their cases adjourned for six months - until an appeal decision had been handed down by the Lords. (26) This involved the West Riding County Council, and the point at issue was 'whether ... the respondents were entitled to refuse the payment of such part of the salaries of teachers as represented the time devoted to the imparting of religious education.' (27) This was decided in December 1906, and Arthur and the others were back in court in March - with Arthur owing 4s.4d. this time. (28) Once more they appeared before Wragge who reminded them that the Lords had in fact decided against them. The Lords had decided, Wragge said, that 'it was illegal for educational authorities to withhold any part of a teacher's salary because he gave religious education in the school.' Orders were then made to confiscate goods, but two of the York protesters had arranged things so that they had nothing to seize, and commitment orders were issued against them. The Rev Hirst had decided that the fight should go on when the Lords destroyed the Education Bill. He owed 15s.8d. and he was arrested as he was in the act of performing a marriage ceremony for a member of the York constabulary. Inspector Williams was off to arrest Aldridge who owed 10s.4d. when he saw him on his bike and nicked him. (29) The two were put on the 12.12 for Wakefield where they did their bird. On his release Hirst told a meeting at the Victoria Bar Primitive Methodist Chapel of his experiences inside. He rather resented being dealt with by a bench that included an ex-Methodist (Vernon Wragge) and two magistrates connected with the drink trade, he said. (30) One of these was J.J. Hunt.

The likes of Aldridge expected much from the Liberals in the way of education reform (and would have got it had it not been for the Lords). They were also 'into' temperance, and expected Campbell-Bannerman to deliver in this respect also. In 1907 the government announced a Licensing Bill, 'but Ministers became increasingly appprehensive' about fighting the Lords on temperance reform and they contented themselves with passing a resolution that in the case of conflict between the two houses the will of the people - the will of the Commons - must prevail, with the Prime Minister producing what R.C.K. Ensor called a 'typically English' method of solving any disputes. (31)

So in 1906 and '7 the long awaited drink reform, so desired by people like Argles and the Rowntrees, had not appeared, and, as with the education struggle, men had to fight on a local level as before. The logic behind the temperance justification for their attempts to reduce the number of pubs is hard to find, high levels of drunkeness did not seem to have any obvious connection with the number of outlets, but the annual demonstrations in courts kept the issue alive and were useful from that point of view. They continued in York.

Vernon Wragge had presided over the Brewster Sessions of 1906; his much insulted Sheriff should have presided over those of 1907. To their everlasting credit the York Tories had chosen Bentley to succeed Wragge as Lord Mayor - though not straight away. Alderman A. Jones, the senior member of the bench was about to leave York and Alderman C.C. Walter was unwell, so Bentley was selected. (32) Bentley was a temperance man who had never been reluctant to speak his mind in public, and his elevation to chief magistrate was viewed with considerable alarm in the trade. This was demonstrated at the fourth annual dinner of the York Licence Holder's Protection Association when J. Broxup attacked the new incumbent '"... we do not seem to have found in him a friend,' Broxup said, 'He taunts the trade and everything connected with it at every turn, and he never ceases to speak ill of it. I do not think it is well for the chief magistrate, as chief magistrate of all classes, to keep one section of the community under his foot, and let all the others alone.'" Bentley was not a free agent, as Broxup should have realised, and in those days it was necessary for local politicians to take a stand for or against drink, but he may have thought that with a new Liberal government in power with an avowed aim of producing licensing legislation, the going could get rough for him and his colleagues in the future, particularly with a temperance Lord Mayor. Well the House of Lords helped Broxup and his fellows as will be seen, and poor Bentley, who looked like being an extremely good Lord Mayor (Broxup notwithstanding) was not to serve out his term of office. He died late in January 1907,(33) to be succeeded, eventually, by Alderman Border. Alderman Agar presided at the Brewster Sessions, held at a time when the temperance movement had expanded its aims just a little to demand the 'Sunday Closing of Public Houses.' (34)

In the short time that he held office as Lord Mayor Bentley had an undignified, stand-up, public row with Wragge - the first of many one would have thought had his term of office run its allotted length. It had to do with licensing and the press reports of one of them was headed 'A POLICE COURT INCIDENT.' It was unpleasant, said much about Wragge, now sitting as just a member of the bench and not chairman, and a lot about the passions that temperance issues gave rise to. In itself it was about very little, but Wragge saw fit to criticise his colleagues from the bench! A Mr Stott of the Old George Hotel, Fossgate, applied for an occasional licence to run a bar at the Albany Hall, Goodramgate, where the Agricola Lodge of Freemasons were to hold their annual ball. Stott wanted to go on supplying liquor until 3 a.m. but Bentley announced that he would have to close an hour earlier. The magistrates agreed to this by a majority of five to two, and Vernon was clearly in the minority. For someone who had been a justice since 1900, was a Recorder, had been three times Lord Mayor and for many years a practising barrister, he then engaged in an unseemingly outburst (and got away with it).

Alderman Wragge said he thought the time had arrived when a firm stand should be taken in this matter. He did not think that the social life of York should be interfered with in this way. It was absurd that at a function of this kind the people attending it should be unable to get refreshments during the last hour before going home. He wished it to be known that he dissented from the decision of the Bench.

The Lord Mayor said he thought it was a piece of impertinence on Mr. Wragge's part to interfere with the opinion of the majority of the magistrates present.

The Chief Constable's report to the Brewster Sessions of 1907 mentioned the campaign against the 'long pull' which had been referred to by Wragge a year earlier. (35) Two licensees had been reported for giving their customers good measures, the officer reported, 'It is a practice which does not tend to sobriety, besides placing those licensed persons who are undesirous of introducing the system, at a disadvantage.' Councillor Boddy appeared in court on behalf of LVA members and he made a request which drew attention to an aspect of policing the city which is not without interest. If a person like Harry McGinty was guilty of refusing to quit licensed premises, Boddy said, it was expected that they should be prosecuted - and they were. But it was the licensees who had to bring the prosecutions, and this was proving expensive. He wanted the police to prosecute but was told by Agar and the clerk of the court that this was a matter for the Watch Committee. Canon Argles - fresh from helping to defeat the Education Bill - was also present in court and so was the ubiquitous Westrope. They wanted no new licenses and still more reductions in the number of pubs in York,he said, and sounded very modern when he said he wanted these to be 'especially' among 'those whose structural deficiencies made effective supervision difficult.' Objected to were the Anchor Inn, the Staiths, (Bentley); the British Tar, North Street, (Tadcaster Tower Company); the Newcastle Inn, North Street, (J.J. Hunt); the Turk's Head, King's Square, (Tadcaster Tower); and the Garden Gate, Hungate, (Johnson and Bainbridge, York).

At the adjourned sessions in March the bad news was given that all but one pub had stopped long pulling - but that splendid place was unfortunately not named (though no doubt Harry McGinty would have known it). Once again some nice pieces of information about the minutia of York's history were given to the court. William Martin of the Newcastle, for example, said he was a muffinman as well as a licensee and that he sold tea, coffee and cocoa as well as booze. The sand barge men used his pub, he said, and had their dinners cooked for them on the premises, as people had done at bakehouses in North Street in the 19th century. (36) Martin's trade amounted to £12 a week - small stuff when compared with the Garden Gate where it was 'voluminous.' Norman Crombie said the Gate had sold an average of 539^{1}/$_{2}$ barrels a year over the last six years; £45.14s.2d. worth of bottled beer and stout; and minerals and cigars worth

£25 per annum. The bench renewed the Garden Gate's license, but refused to do so for the other places objected to. H.F. Anderson applied on behalf of J.J. Hunt for the licenses for the South Bank area which Wragge had once submitted. These were successfully opposed by Newbald Kay acting on behalf of the South Bank District Citizen's Association.

The bench announced in 1907 that, as before, it would levy the maximum amount it could for the compensation fund, and it might be of some interest to record what early awards that body made. The people representing the Leopard Inn had claimed £1,345.5s. - 'The rent paid by the tenant was estimated at 18 years purchase, trade profits at 10 years purchase, and the estimated rental value of the building without a license at 14 years' purchase.' (37) Eventually the Commissioners of Inland Revenue 'determined ... the sum of £960 [as] the amount which should be paid as compensation ...' Of this £200 was for the tenant; the balance for the lessees. The Three Cups was assessed at £100 for the licencee and £310 to the lessees. The British Tar, the Turk's Head, the Anchor and the Newcastle had not submitted claims when the committee met in June but in July they were awarded £220, £800, £425, and £1,100. Martin got only £100 of the latter sum which does not seem much (but then he still had his muffin trade).

These awards were made well into the life of the first year of local government after the fall of Balfour. The York Tories had too large a majority for them to be turned out of office, but what had happened in November ? Had York gone anti Tory as the country had in January, or had a year of Campbell-Bannerman's administration lessened enthusiasm for change ?

In 1905 the Liberals had fielded some strong candidates in the local elections, and Hartley had enlivened proceedings. In May the rates were reduced by 4d., something the Council was able to do now that the initial heavy expenditure following the Balfour Education Act had been made. (38) This would have helped the Tories, and they would have been elated when the annoying J.M. Hogge lost his qualification at the York Revision Court in the late summer. (39) He would almost certainly have stood if qualified, but for Castlegate the Liberals in 1906 selected Harry Miles of Hazell and Miles, Coney Street, and Samuel Henry Davies, of White Cross Lodge. These two were chosen to replace a Councillor who did not want to stand again and Councillor Blakey who, like Hogge, had lost his qualification. (40) Miles told his selection meeting that he was mainly interested in housing reform and Davies, who was employed by Rowntree and Company as a chemist, demanded better housing, allotments and the electrification of the tramways. Nearer the election Miles was to say that the York City Council was 'as antique as the tram cars which ran through the streets', (41) which was not quite fair as it was the horses and not the cars which were antique. (42) This prompted a letter in the *Press* which reminded readers that Harry had made some very outspoken remarks during the Boer War (to the effect that everyone who fought the Boers ought to be shot). (43) It could not have helped his campaign.

K.E.T. Wilkinson stood again and John Henry Hartley, the railway shunter, was up for re-election. His championing of the Council carters and his demands for a wage increase for them - an election gimmick the Tories said it was - has already been referred to. He was in the field as early as September (the carters question blew up a month later) and he put a comprehensive programme forward. Hartley, as well as increased wages for Council workmen, demanded: a municipal cemetery; better street lighting in areas where 'the "box hat people"' did not live; pavements in South Bank; the widest possible interpretation in York of the Unemployment Act; and Labour representatives in the take-over of the tramways negotiations. Hartley during his campaign of 1906 maintained publicly that both the Tories and Liberals were working to 'crush him out of the Council Chamber', and he and Rose bravely tackled the problem of telling electors that a municipal programme of the kind they wanted would necessitate higher rates. What did this matter, Rose asked in a speech which was headlined 'The Bogey of High Rates' in the *Press* of 8 October. What was needed was more money spent where it was needed. There should be no waste or ostentatious banqueting while the streets were full of the unemployed. Rose was surely right and he had in mind that gift to Butcher of a while back. 'Money raised by the rates', he said, should not be spent on such things, but 'should be properly expended. Balls, banquets, caskets, kegs of whisky, "and pineapples at 15s. a time," should' become things of the past. He had in mind, he said, a recent 'historic Ouse survey jaunt.' Later Rose was to say that he had been misreported and that he had said 'pegs' and not 'kegs' of whisky, and his attack lost just a little of its sting when someone pointed out that Labour members had been on the 'historic Ouse survey jaunt.'

Hartley was the most prominent of the Labour candidates of 1906. In addition to him there were Fred Winspear, a railway signalman and John Glasby Parker, another signalman, who stood in Walmgate, and John William Sharp, a railway guard, who stood in Micklegate. The Liberals also selected a railway candidate. He was Benjamin Stoker Wales, a carriage builder, who was nominated for Bootham, by, among others, Joseph Rowntree, J.B. Morrell and O.F. Rowntree.

Hogge, although he could not stand, took a prominent part in the elections of 1906 and got a great deal of press coverage through pointing out - reasonably it seems - that whereas the Corporation could raise £3,000 to help host the annual meeting in York of the British Association, (44) it could not raise anywhere near that to help the unemployed.

The candidacy of Wilkinson is of a special interest because he was attempting to get the seat which had once been that of Thomas Anderson. Anderson was one of the group of extremely capable Labour supporters who had stood for office in the early years of the century and taken part in the activities of the Trades Council, the School Board, the guardians and the creation of the Labour Representation Committee. But Anderson's abilities and contacts made him aware of other work and capable of doing something better paid, and, it will be recalled, he became an employee of the guardians and was lost to his movement. This happened frequently, and there is no doubt that Labour frequently suffered from the simple fact that the abilities of their leaders opened up opportunities for them which, in the conditions of the first decade of the 20th century they could not refuse. Anderson left the movement in York and the movement was weakened by his going. There were others. Andrew Moody for example. He has been frequently mentioned in these pages as an active railway trades unionist and a councillor. In the early months of 1906 Moody left York after being made stationmaster at Pilmoor. (45) The same thing was to happen to Hartley. But that was several years ahead.

There were 8,245 voters on the municipal register in 1906, and of them 6,175 - 75 per cent - voted. Wilkinson was returned second in the poll for Walmgate, behind John Atherly, the landlord of the Phoenix Inn, a Tory. Fred Winspear and Parker were well behind. (Atherley 1,094; Wilkinson 1,010; Parker 331; Winspear 271). J.W. Sharp was bottom of the poll in Micklegate. (James Birch, plumber, Conservative 1,233; Hartley 901; John Thomas Clarke, commercial traveller, Liberal 807; Sharp 764.) In Castlegate another member of the Birch family, Frederick William, also a plumber and a Tory, beat S.H. Davies into second place. Harry Miles was bottom. In the three remaining wards there were no contests.

The Liberals had made one significant gain in 1906 (Davies for Anderson) but they still had a long way to go to get control of York. The situation in November was that the Tories had a majority of 14 over the combined opposition (31 Conservatives; 13 Liberals; four Labour). It is interesting to note that one of the first tasks of the 'new' council was to do something dear to the 'Progressives'' hearts - municipalise the city's tramways.

Negotiations and discussions about municipalising the York tramway system had gone on for many years - and some of them have been described. They went on to a successful conclusion (that is if using or adapting an already outmoded system rather than going for buses as Bentley wanted is successful) with Alderman Wragge, no less, taking a prominent part in the negotiations. He was chairman of the council committee dealing with the tramway question, and it seems strange to see that hard-line Tory acting on this occasion as an enthusiastic 'municipaliser'. Whatever differences they may have had with Wragge, and there must have been dozens, the Rowntrees, the Wilkinsons and the Grays could not have faulted him over 'trams'.

Hugh Murray in his monograph on York's Horse Tramways (which would have been improved beyond measure by the use of footnotes) (46) has dealt with the last years of the Tramways Company. Perhaps he should have stressed that the *Yorkshire Gazette's* articles 'Towards a Municipal Policy' which were published as a booklet in October 1905 were written by opposition Liberal politicians (like Sebastian Meyer) and that the trams had become even more of a joke than they had been before. Harry Miles' statement that the Corporation was as 'antique as the tram cars which ran through the streets' has been quoted (and challenged) and in January 1907 the Market Committee of the Corporation heard an alarming report that all the tram horses (stabled next to those of the 11th Hussars) had got the mange and would have to go to the knacker's yard, and in the same month Frederick Young, the tram company manager, was prosecuted by the RSPCA for cruelly treating one of them a month or so earlier. Arnold Rowntree got severely ticked off for joking about the tram company's mangy nags, (47) and in March 1907 great hilarity was caused when Tramcar No 8 broke down in Bridge Street and three of the company's horses were unable to remove it for repairs. (48) In December the company was prosecuted for using a horse when it was lame. (49) All this probably made the proposals to take the tram company into public ownership a little easier to sell. There were some minor snags, however, which from the vantage point of the 1990s, make the take-over look a little odd. There was a last minute attempt to get the tramways taken over by a private company - an attempt which was resisted by Wragge and others.

In June 1906 the York Council set up a special Tramways Committee which had Wragge as its chairman. Its task was to expedite negotiations, but then a private organisation appeared on the scene. In August a London firm of solicitors asked if they could meet Wragge's committee to explain a client's intended application to Parliament for permission to build and work a tramway system in York. Wragge angrily dismissed the Western Counties Electric Railways and Tramways Company as 'interlopers', 'pirates' and 'intruders'. (50) The Tramways Committee refused to meet the Western's solicitors, but the company decided to carry on nevertheless. Huge front page advertisements were taken in the local papers urging the city to say 'No' to municipal trams and saying that privatisation would mean electric trams in York by Christmas 1907. (51) Details of their bill was made public, and the names of the proprietors revealed. These included Henry Leetham, the miller, and the man who had put up the money for the Liberal Club in Clifford Street; John E. Oldfield, a well-known York wine merchant; James Backhouse, the Quaker nurseryman of Acomb; and W.F. Thompson, that ardent campaigner against the most recent Education Bill, who was the eldest son of Archbishop Thompson. At the half yearly meeting of the York Tramways Company held not long after the Western Company appeared on the York scene Joseph Kincaid said that he and his fellow directors knew nothing of its proposals. When it was revealed that a new company was 'coming to make application ... for power to construct new tramways and take, compulsorily or by agreement the existing tramways', the 'present company', he said, 'were entirely taken by surprise, and knew nothing about that application.' (52) This seems extraordinary. Kincaid also told shareholders that things were very bad. It was 'an exceedingly bad time for business', he went on, 'The [York] Engineering Company's works had closed, and the works of the railway company had decreased, and such things as these reacted very much upon the prosperity of the company.'

The Western Company's intervention concentrated minds wonderfully, and the tramways issue was debated in depth. A by election was held in Bootham caused by the elevation of Captain Pearson to the Aldermanic bench and two candidates there dealt at length with the tram question. John Fenwick, a printer, the Liberal, was in favour of municipalisation, contending that the system could be run at a profit. His opponent, Arthur Brown, a house furnisher, seemed to favour privatisation, and a supporter (Councillor Lambert) was not so sure about Fenwick's point about profitability - look at what was happening with the electricity supply, he said. (53) Letters and articles appeared in the press saying what had happened elsewhere. One, headed 'Object lesson for York', drew attention to the losses being made in Halifax. (54)

Mr Murray has made the point that the Western Company's scheme had 'considerable advantages' for the city of York, but the city of York, Tory dominated though it was, ignored it. The terms (55) for a municipal take-over were made public in December 1906, (56) and the agreement embodying it was carried overwhelmingly in the Council on 7 January with only seven dissenting votes. (57) The purchase price was to be £11,000 to be paid on 13 July 1909 'or within three calendar months after the Corporation shall have obtained power to work the tramways, or to reconstruct and work the same as a light railway, as the case may be, whichever shall first happen.'(58)

The Western Company made some last ditch efforts to attain its objectives, but in February the Council finally approved the purchase of the tram system. (59) A year went by, then in February 1908 the Council's application for an order 'to "make, maintain, work and use light railways" within the city and also in the parish of Fulford' was heard by the Light Railway Commissioners meeting in the Guildhall. (60) The application was granted, Board of Trade approval was given in October, and the way was clear for electrification to begin. Well almost; there were still details like whether the work should be done by direct labour or contract to be decided. There was also the necessity for a poll of ratepayers. That was held in the spring of 1909.

No doubt there were many in York who hoped that when the tramways were electrified it would mean an increase in work in the city, for it is a fact that the dreadful problems of unemployment and under employment still persisted. When he became Lord Mayor Bentley spoke of the evil (61), and appealed for funds for the 'Muncaster House scheme.' (62) Unemployment, Bentley said, was 'being felt very keenly in the City.'

The Muncaster House Scheme was one being considered by the York Distress Committee. The Muncaster House estate had been bought by the Council for £1,800 and in February 1906 the Distress Committee began to look at the possibility of using it as small holdings on which to employ some of those registered with it. (63) (At this time the committee had 1,152 on its books, of whom 609 were married with 1,445 children.) (64) By August 1906 details of the scheme the Distress Committee had in mind were public knowledge. After the land had been broken up it was anticipated that 75 men could be given permanent work - three per acre. A Mr Rushworth reckoned they could make an annual profit of £30 per acre after the first year. There had been 140 applications for the post of gardener, it was reported. He was to be paid 28s. a week with a house and rates plus a bonus of four per cent on all produce sold. (65)

People like J.H. Hartley regularly demanded the widest possible use of the Umemployment Act, but the York Distress Committee had two major problems. The first was that funds raised from the rates could not be spent on schemes like the Muncaster one, and the second was Robert Horton Vernon Wragge. The scheme had to be started - if it was to be started at all - with private donations, and Wragge opposed it anyway. J.W. Hogge, a great advocate of such schemes (and annoyed no doubt that he had just lost his qualification to become a councillor) fulminated in public about the unwillingness of the Corporation to help the unemployed. Wragge, he said, had 'damned' the Distress Committee's plans. (66)

To add to the public's unwillingness to subscribe to it and the opposition of Wragge, there was a third problem for the Distress Committee - Edith Milner. Now that the Liberals were in power at Westminster, Edith was even more politically active than before and well into the career of regular letter writer to the press which reached a hysterical crescendo in the 1914 war. (Her letter of congratulation on the *Press* achieving its 25th anniversary is totally political - and at one, in fact, with the opinions of the *Press* itself.) (67) Edith had been against the Muncaster scheme and she angrily resigned from the Distress Committee (presumably because of it) in October 1906. (68) Anyway by February 1907 the Muncaster scheme was dead, a fact which led to an angry letter in the press from J.M. Hogge in which he said that 'It may interest those [who] killed the Muncaster House scheme for dealing with the unemployed to know that Peterborough cleared a profit of £1,000 last year from the growth and production of celery.' This profit 'was made from 23 acres, in spite of the fact that prices all round were low and supplies excessive.' Hogge's claims did not go unchallenged, however. (69)

Hogge, along with people like Meyer and Mawson, had supported the Muncaster scheme and opposed the use of money for emigration for the unemployed, (70) and he eventually attacked the whole concept of 'charity' and the kind of work the energetic Edith Milner was doing. She was involved in all kinds of good causes - for which she deserves credit - and some of her activities have been mentioned. At about this time she was engaged in running a thrift club, as well as being involved in the activities of the Hungate Mission, (71) the York Emergency Kitchen for the Sick Poor, (72) arranging holidays for deprived town children, and much more. This was all worthwhile; but to Hogge it seemed all wrong. The sick and the poor should be looked after by the state he thought. Charity was demeaning, patronising, out of date, and certainly undemocratic. Edith replied to him in a letter published in the papers in February 1907.

(73) In it she outlined her beliefs - hardened no doubt by having had to live for 12 months under a reforming Liberal government. They were almost identical to those of Charles Loch and the leaders of the Charity Organisation Society, which is not surprising as Edith was an active worker for the COS in York. (74) They, and she, believed that only the 'undeserving' should be helped by the state and that the 'deserving poor should be helped individually, voluntarily, temporarily and constructively.' 'Self-dependence' was an expression frequently used by the COS spokesmen and underlying their beliefs was an assumption that self-dependence was possible for (nearly) all men. If they failed to achieve it, the fault lay with them. 'The possibility that the fault could lie, wholly or in part, in the economic set-up of society did not enter the collective mind of the C.O.S.' (75) Things like old age pensions were an anathema to the likes of Charles Loch and they adopted a 'the poor will always be with us' attitude - based on an assumption that all was well with the economic and social arrangements of society. Surely there were times and situations when 'social conditions' would not allow men to meet their responsibilities Helen Bosanquet asked rhetorically in a book published in 1903 ? (76) Not so, she said. Social conditions *would* permit them to do so. Their efforts to help themselves would be enough to solve their problems. This was simply dotty and a walk round York in 1905, '6, or '7 would have shown hundreds of men who were incapable of helping themselves in the way the admirable Bosanquet said they could. They were unemployed because the engineering works had closed, because the NER had shut down part of its operations, and because there was a slump, maybe caused by free trade if Edith's political associates were to be believed. Her letter, which could have come straight from the highest eschelons of the COS is as follows. It was headed 'The Greatest of These is Charity.' 'When the distress committees protest against charity and fail to get State grants', Edith wrote,

> they promptly appeal for "voluntary contributions" to start schemes for making work for the unemployed. In other words creating a want, but at the same time, whatever they call it, they are asking for "charity." I think the State-aid scheme is already carried too far. I think the English working man was in a much finer position when he helped at least to pay for his own children's schooling. I am sure it will be a further downward step if he accepts free meals for his children from the State. I draw a very sharp line between the "unemployed" who parade the streets, and in many cases would refuse work if they could get it, though they accept "charity," and the brave artizans out of work, hiding their trouble and bearing it bravely. I know many such whom it is a privilege to help, and who do not scorn the "charity" that prompts it. I am prepared, and others are prepared, to meet this present cry of the children, but we should like to do it thoroughly and with properly organised help.

The likes of J.M. Hogge would have said that adequate help for the needy could *only* be 'thoroughly' and 'properly organised' by the state and, of course, Edith did not address herself to the obvious fact that what she and others were doing and had done was simply, obviously, not enough. She applauded 'Mrs Edwin Gray's scheme for providing milk for breakfastless children in the schools', thanked the organisers of the 'Charity Ball, promoted last night' and the workers at the Emergency Kitchen for the sick poor. I know what good this work has done, she concluded. All that was needed was more of the same thing.

Following the defeat of the Muncaster House scheme for the unemployed the Distress Committee considered another scheme put forward by a Liberal lady who could not have been a bigger contrast to Edith Milner. This was Almyra Gray (Mrs Edwin Gray) the supporter of women's suffrage, the ex Lady Mayoress, and the most prominent person in the York Health and Housing Reform Association. (77) Mrs Gray wanted the unemployed to be put to work building a recreation ground 'on the side of the Foss, near Hungate', at a cost (according to the deputy city surveyor's estimate) of £2,468. There were funds available (presumably from the Lord Mayor's appeal for the Muncaster scheme) and Councillor J.B. Inglis, a Tory for Guildhall, wanted to use it. But any initiatives of this kind would be met with opposition, he said, in a moving speech. 'It was painful', he said (78)

> to think that they had all this money lying idle whilst people were walking the streets unable to get anything to do. Probably the site would be more adapted for buildings than for a recreation ground. [But] If the Distress Committee were composed of angels, with the angel Gabriel as chairman, the proposals they brought before the Council would meet with opposition.

They seemed to have made up their minds, Inglis went on, that the Distress Committee was incompetent, 'and were determined to oppose them, whatever line they adopted.'

In March the Hungate scheme was abandoned like the Muncaster one before it. (79) (The Distress Committee would not have been made more acceptable to the Tories by the fact that for some time Councillor Fred Morley of the ILP was its chairman.)

There were no schemes for tackling unemployment on a national level, and those devised locally in York were killed off by the likes of Edith Milner and Vernon Wragge. So what relief there was for the distressed was of the same voluntary kind as before. How people could have reckoned that private munificence was adequate is mind blowing given the overwhelming evidence of suffering in York. In February 1907 rate arrears in the city were well over £2,000, (80) and in that winter, once more, workers at the Hope Street Adult School provided free breakfasts for the unemployed. (81) Edith Milner's favourite newspaper the *Yorkshire Herald* ran long articles on the state of the children in some areas of the city. Things were still bad in the summer of 1907, as a letter from Arthur Brown showed, (82) and, as always, got worse in the winter.

Hamar Greenwood was challenged about the prevalence of unemployment when he spoke to railwaymen in January, (83) and in the following month the Trades Council urged the Corporation to adopt clause three of the Provision of School Meals Act and spend the product of a halfpenny rate on feeding needy children. It drew attention to the 'serious prevalence of unemployment in this city', and the *Herald* asked for subscriptions to enable the voluntary provision of school meals, using the system established a few years before. (84) (In the April before the Trades Council made its demand the City Council had actually reduced the rates by 5d. to a level of 7s.5d.) (85)

Writers frequently comment about the coexistence in Victorian and Edwardian society of poverty and affluence, and those contrasts were as great in York as anywhere. Every now and then things happened which seemed to highlight first the plight of the underprivileged, then the seeming callousness of (most of) those in authority. The Ouse Navigation junketing while men were out of work in their hundreds was an incident like that, as was the gift of that silver casket to J.G. Butcher. These incidents surely demonstrate bad planning by those in power as well as much else. So too did an incident which took place just as Hartley was pushing the case of corporation workmen again early in 1907. The very meeting of the Council which had to discuss the carters' salaries also had to deliberate on a wage rise recommended for the staff of the public library. The appropriate committee had decided to ask for salary increases for the chief librarian (then receiving £4.4s.7s. a week), the chief assistant (getting £2.2s.3d.) and an assistant (earning 35s.) when it was quite certain there would be rows about a modest amount for the council workmen. Regardless of the fact that only a few people were maybe involved here, and regardless of the fact that in global terms the council's budget would not be affected all that much, bringing the librarians' increases forward did seem heartless - and at least one citizen said so publicly. 'I protest,' wrote W. Shilleto, 'These very men who are going to ask for this increase, voted against giving Corporation Carters an increase of 1d. per hour. ... It would be far better for the Council to grant this £50 increase asked for, to relieve some of the distress in the city.' (86) Surely he was right, and given such demonstrations it seems surprising that there was not a tremendous swing against the local leaders. But there was not.

The library salaries question was debated for two hours in the council early in March. (87) Clearly some members agreed with Shilleto, and some of them said they would filibuster and speak 'against time all night.' Several others protested against those 'farcical proceedings', and ultimately the librarian got an increase of £20 instead of the £30 suggested. Hartley (it seems fair to give him the credit) got the corporation carters a modest increase also.

When Hartley had taken the carters' issue before the council in October 1906, just before the local elections, he had found an ally in Capt Pearson, and the matter was shelved temporarily, though not before the full council had voted for a wage rate of 6d. an hour. The Streets and Buildings Committee had then decided that the carters' wages were satisfactory! No-one questioned the propriety of this, it seems, and maybe it was perfectly proper, but they reported that while they paid their men 5d. an hour for a week of 53 hours, the average elsewhere in the city for similar work was 5.07d. per hour. However, they went on, making some perfectly reasonable points, the council workmen did have some advantages not enjoyed by those they were being compared with. To begin with their employment was regular, and this must be reckoned as of great consequence. Men at the NER, for example, were frequently put on short time, and private carters also had to 'supper up' each night which the corporation workers did not. Sunday duty was a regular feature for those in private employment, while for the corporation men (who got time and a quarter for overtime) this cropped up only once in eleven weeks. (88)

The Streets and Buildings Committee sent the question of the carters' wages to the Council's Depot and Provender sub-committee where time was taken up comparing the wages the men got with what was paid by the local Cooperative Society. Back at the Buildings Committee Hartley said that - despite what the Council had decided - he was getting nowhere, and opted out of further discussions. But in the full Council meeting the men were not without friends, and Councillors Mansfield and Birch proposed that they be paid 6d. an hour. This was defeated but a recommendation for 5d. an hour proposed by W.H. Birch and seconded by Sebastian Meyer was carried by a substantial majority. (89) This would give the men just over 24s. a week.

Just before the Council debated the question of the carters'wages the York Trades Council, clearly in an attempt to influence the discussions, passed a resolution heartily endorsing Hartley's recent campaign. Chairman on that occasion was one Will Dobbie, someone destined to be of great importance in York's history in the future. (90)

Both Hartley and Dobbie were railwaymen and it looked very much as if they would be involved in a major strike at around Christmas 1907. The dispute had to do with wages, of course, and much to do with union recognition. There had been negotiations in 1905, it will be recalled, (91) which ended with some wage increases, but left the work force extremely dissatisfied. From then onwards there had been simmering discontent, made worse, in York, by short time working in the winter months of 1905 and continuing low wages for the less skilled workers. In February of the following year a correspondent to the *Press* revealed something about what short time working meant. The men had to be at their work place even when officially laid off. The working week at the NER was then 53 hours, and men were duly spending 53 hours there because of the aforementioned rule - but getting nowhere near a full week's pay. 'I am sure it would better for us to work four days a week and get four day's pay', the writer said, quite reasonably it seems, 'Hoping that this will meet the eye of some higher official ...' (92)

In February 1906, not long after the general election, a meeting of NER men was held in York at which yet again evidence was given of increased work loads, long hours, (93), staff reductions and low wages well below Rowntree's subsistence figure. Many, according to W. Reynolds, were getting from 16s. to 18s. a week. (94) A month later a deputation met the NER directors and demanded, among other things: time and a quarter pay for night duty; a 2s. a week advance for lower paid workers; the abolition of what were called 'twelve hours signal boxes'; and the dropping of a pay 'system' which, it was contended, meant a reduction in pay of 3s. for passenger guards. (95) The deputation got nowhere and the NER management took up what the *Press* called 'A THREATENING ATTITUDE', (96) which led to speculation about a possible strike involving 20,000 workmen. (97) 'The agitation for a reconsideration of what have been described as irksome and irritating working conditions, amounting in many cases, it is alleged, to unfairness and injustice, has been growing for some time', said an account of the report-back meeting to York men from the deputation to management. (98) The directors had refused to discuss these grievances and men were dissatisfied from the Humber to the Tweed. It added, ominously, that the directors had said that the NER had 15 per cent more men than they needed. (99)

The NER had a new general manager in 1906 - Alexander Kaye Butterworth. Shortly after he took up his post, changes were made in the company whereby the permanent way and locomotive departments were reorganised, with the transfer of men to Hull and Darlington, and a consequent severe loss to York of spending power and rate income. (100) The men's demands were enshrined in what came to be known as 'The Darlington Programme', and the NER did eventually make some concessions or offers to some parts of the work force. Passenger guards' hours of working, for example, were reduced by an hour a day; shunting firemen got a modest wage rise; Sunday allowances for signalmen in busy boxes were increased; platform porters' wages went up modestly; and more time was allowed for putting engines away. (101) These were put before the men, many of whom were still angry over the 'American' methods which had been introduced, and some of whom spotted in them something similar to what had happened with the York carters. While men were getting nothing but refusals or niggardly offers, a Mr Sykes of Leeds said, the 'increase of officials' salaries went up from £43,000 to £63,000, with no corresponding increase to workers.' It was a good point to make, but not one to calm things down.

The concessions mentioned above (which were to cause great trouble eventually) were referred back to union members with Richard Bell, the ASRS secretary recommending acceptance, saying they were the maximum that could be got at that time. (102) He was condemned by one of the York branches, (103) and in November three of the city's Labour activists (J.M. Nutbrown, Hartley and J.W. Sharp) attended an ASRS conference about the awards in Birmingham. (104) For many years the railwaymen's campaign had been known as the 'All Grades Movement' and in December Sharp gave some figures of union membership to a meeting in York at which their basic aims were said to be 24s. for lower paid workers and a ten hour day. There were in the industry, Sharp said, 7,219 drivers in the union out of a total of 20,965. The corresponding figure for platelayers were 4,941 and 50,919. (105)

Throughout 1907 the railway crisis simmered, and in October Hamar Greenwood attacked the directors of the NER for their intransigence and for refusing to recognise the unions. Also in October the York branches of the ASRS held a mass meeting in the Victoria Hall presided over by William Hallaways. There J.W. Sharp launched a bitter attack on Richard Bell only to be ticked off by someone who was to become very famous in British history. J.H. Thomas said 'Never was any man more unworthy than Mr. Sharp has proved himself this evening.' (106)

It looked as if there would be a rail strike over Christmas 1907, then help came from a person Edith Milner would certainly not have approved of. It was the President of the Board of Trade, David Lloyd George.

Richard Bell gave a detailed account of what he said was the most momentous year in his union's history in its annual report published in April 1908. (107) The intransigence of the railway companies (not just the NER) was criticised in the Commons, huge public meetings were held in May, membership began to increase, then in the autumn a third appeal for union recognition was refused. Faced with this, the national executive of the ASRS decided to ballot members about strike action. The results were unambiguous: some 98,000 voting papers had been issued; 88,134 unspoiled ones were returned; with 76,925 men voting in favour of handing in their notices. A national strike looked a certainty, but by the time Bell made the ballot results known the government had stepped in. (The smaller General Railway Workers' Union also balloted its members.)

Lloyd George began negotiations with both sides in the railway dispute in October, determined, if necessary, 'to introduce a measure making Arbitration in railway disputes compulsory' if 'the Directors refuse conciliation'. (108) When the meetings began, one fine book on union history said, quoting the findings of a Royal Commission, 'it quickly emerged that the crucial issue was the demand for [union] recognition, and this was the only topic discussed,' but this is not the way Richard Bell saw it only a short time after the event. Bell gave Lloyd George credit for bringing about a peaceful solution to the dispute of 1907, (109) but also said, correctly surely, that the president had diverted the All Grades Movement away from the national programme of better wages and conditions to one about conciliation and arbitration. (110) Elsewhere, however, it has been said that Bell, an MP, had said that he would not press for union recognition if he got 'a satisfactory method of dealing with grievances.' (111)

Lloyd George had a formula for ending the railway dispute even before Bell gave his revelations of the results of the strike ballot at the Albert Hall, and on 6 November he put it before the railway chairmen. They accepted it and so did the unions, and Bell

William
Bentley.

has been praised for having the wisdom to postpone demands for union recognition. (112) For years the NER, for example, had been able to delay claims, and the new scheme improved that. Or did it ? The new scheme was complex and in fact necessitated using the old traditional methods of petition and deputation before grievances could go before a 'sectional board' on which workers, elected under Board of Trade supervision, sat. Any dispute (about wages and hours only) which could not be settled there, went to a central board and if agreement could not be reached there, 'or if either the directors or the men refused to accept the board's settlement, the matter could be referred to an independent arbitrator.' (113)

Eleven of the major railway companies signed up with Lloyd George's scheme on 6 November 1907, and 35 others signed later. The North Eastern Railway Company, however, decided to go it alone and set up a scheme of its own. There was to be trouble over that in 1908.

During the developing railway crisis most of the publicity in York centred on the ASRS, which certainly had the most prominent labour figures among its members, but there was also a York branch of the General Railways Workers' Union, and the two unions adopted identical attitudes. At one of the GRWU's meetings a Rev P.H. Greaves presided and he launched a tremendous attack on the NER, justified, if the example of management practice he gave is true. A Mr Cotsworth, a clerk in the statistics department of the company, had formed a branch of the Railway Clerks' Association, Greaves said, and a week later the president and secretary resigned. Cotsworth, the vice president, did not, and a week later he was sacked! At that same meeting the results of the York ASRS strike ballot were given, showing that 3,025 men were for industrial action and only 84 against, and Hartley engaged in some straight talking which was very widely noticed. He had been told, Hartley said, that their demands, if met, would cost the railway companies seven and a half million pounds. So what ? '... when he came to study the matter', Hartley said, 'he felt ashamed at the smallness of this amount, because it was ridiculous to ask for so small a sum when the railways paid their shareholders last year over forty millions.' What Edith Milner thought is not on record, but it is not beyond the powers of imagination.

The militancy shown by the ASRS following the general election of 1906, of course, had more than a little to do with the passing of the Trades Disputes Act of 1906 - the one the Lords had sensibly let go through unmolested. The Taff Vale judgement resulted from incidents during a strike on the Taff Vale railway, when Richard Bell had organised picketing to prevent the employers from importing blackleg labour which it had arranged to get through the National Free Labour Association. The union had been sued and eventually it was decided that the funds of a union were liable for damages inflicted by its officials. This had a devastating effect on the unions and their chances of successful strike action in the future. It was of paramount importance in turning the unions towards the infant Labour Representation Committee. The Liberal Act of

1906 restored the legal immunity of trade unions and ushered in a period of industrial militancy, but in 1907 the spectre of the Free Labour Association still hung around. At the meeting at which he said their claims were not enough Hartley attacked the FLA as did a Mr J. Kelly. He spoke of the Association 'as being financed by "blood suckers" and "crime originators".'

During the rail dispute a great deal of evidence about current York wage rates was given out, and once more it was conclusively shown that many workers were well below the Rowntree levels of subsistence. According to the ASRS (114) the average wage of engine cleaners was 14s.8d., of ticket collectors 21s.6d., goods porters 19s.8d. and carriage cleaners 18s.6d. Just before Lloyd George intervened to end the dispute a controversy arose over hours for women workers at the factory of York's best and biggest employer. A letter appeared in the press saying that girls at Rowntrees had been ordered to work until 8pm on Tuesdays, Wednesdays and Thursdays. This was not to the liking of the writer, but why did she or they not complain at work ? Because things were not as liberal there as was sometimes thought, she said. '... some people wonder why we do not protest at work instead of through the paper', she wrote, 'and in reply I would say that if any girl dared to protest she would be told to clear off.' But what about wages ? Were they not good at Rowntrees ? Piece work prevailed there, the writer said, and if 'we want any wage we have not to waste our time, but have to work twice as hard as the proverbial nigger.' (115)

A reply appeared to the above giving the hours the girls had to work at Rowntrees-7.30am-6.00pm on Mondays; 7.30am-5.00pm on the remaining days; except Saturdays 7.30-12.00. Only two rooms had been ordered to work until eight o'clock it was revealed, and this was only for five weeks at the most. Another writer objected to claims that Rowntree girls simply walked the streets until ten o'clock at night, after leaving work, and said that overtime working should be voluntary. She also made the reasonable claim that they should be paid more during overtime periods because they were then tired and incapable of working as hard as earlier.

With labour issues to the fore the Labour party tried to seize seats at the November municipal elections, running no less than three prominent railway trades unionists - W. Dobbie, J.W. Sharp and that J.W. Hallaways who had presided over the mass meeting at the Victoria Hall when Sharp had got slapped down by Jimmy Thomas. They all did very badly. Fred Morley did not stand in 1907 and Hallaways was put in to replace him in Castlegate. There were 2,258 voters in that ward and Hallaways polled only 390 - well over 400 behind the second successful candidate. (116) Dobbie and Sharp were well behind a Tory and a Liberal in Micklegate, the one area where Labour had a good ward organisation.

Labour had clearly run out of steam somewhat since the general election. It was rumoured that there had been some internal troubles in the party, but that the disputes over the strays (117) had brought some renewed support, but if it did this did not manifest itself at the municipal elections of 1907. Perhaps the electorate saw that Labour's municipal programme was hardly different from that of the Liberals and went for the stronger party. Perhaps Dobbie and the others suffered from the stance they were taking in their industrial dispute. Perhaps the Liberals benefited from the stand they were taking on the Council and the Distress Committee on behalf of the unemployed. Certainly the most outspoken of those on the Distress Committee was returned in 1907, taking Fred Morley's place on the Council. (118) He was J.M. Hogge, the darling of York cartoonists.

Hogge topped the poll in Castlegate, much to Edith Milner's alarm, it is certain. (Hogge 852; R.A. Knight, Tory, 823; Hallaways 390). He was not long before he made his mark in the Council Chamber as will be seen. He joined Hartley as an *enfant terrible* of York politics.

Just before the elections of November 1907 a special council meeting had had to consider filling six Aldermanic seats, their occupants' terms of office having been completed. Five of the sitting tenants were re-elected immediately, a proceeding which angered Hartley who wanted to wait until the new council met (perhaps expecting Labour gains) and demanded a Labour alderman anyway. A great deal was talked about the time honoured process whereby each alderman became Lord Mayor, it being contended that this prospect stopped some members joining the bench, and it was agreed that some attempts would be made to alter the existing 'system'. Sebastian Meyer and Councillor G. Mansfield were both spoken of as possible Liberal aldermen to fill the remaining vacancy. Meyer was eventually chosen

Meyer's elevation, and that of Norman Green, another Liberal, meant two by elections - in Bootham and Guildhall. In the former Labour ran John Fisher, who made impassioned demands for municipalising the trams (the draft order for the scheme was published in December), (119) and the Liberals put up W.H. Sessions. Fisher did no canvassing, had no transport and fared as badly as had Dobbie and the others, coming in over 700 votes behind Sessions. (Sessions 1,043; H.Hopkins, Tory, 953; Fisher 303.) In Guildhall, for some extraordinary reason, the Liberals did not put up a candidate, and Arthur Richmond Fox, a genuine independent, non-politiclal candidate beat the Tory Edward Allen (460:437). (120)

A little while before the by elections a Mr Hodgson had written a letter to the press showing that the gap between the parties on the city council was closing and complaining that the representation on the various committees did not truly reflect the state of the parties. There were then, Hodgson said, 20 elected Tory councillors and 16 opposition members. (121) Despite this, representation on the Finance Committee was 11 to four in the Tories' favour, on Streets and Buildings the Tories had a 12 to five majority, and on the Watch Committee the situation was eleven to five.

The Liberals and the Labour party at this stage in York history stood for 'municipal socialism', the details of which have been frequently mentioned. Both Mr Murray (who gives the ILP far too much credit for planting the idea of municipalisation as far as the tramways are concerned) and Mr Hills infer that the Liberals were in fact stealing Labour's policies, but this is surely not the case. Demands for municipal control by the Liberals pre-date the appearance of Labour, though of course individuals like Thomas Anderson were putting them forward at the turn of the century. Conditions in the cities were deplorable and municipal socialism was an obvious way of improving them - no one group can claim sole credit for coming to that conclusion. Of course the Liberals' current ideas were in conflict with their traditional thinking about government and free enterprise and they would have made excuses for deviating from their traditional beliefs on the grounds of necessity, or by declaring that the issues they had to deal with were special. They had done the same thing earlier in the case of railways, and before that over the corn laws.

What the Liberals wanted in and for York is clear. What was the attitude of the party in office ? What attitudes dominated the York Tories who had been in power for so long? K.E.T. Wilkinson, admittedly not an unbiased observer, said that for only a slightly earlier period the 'Tory Party was committed ... to a policy of doing as little as possible and keeping down the rates', (122) and that would seem to be a fair judgement. In fairness it ought to be remembered that they *were* the party of free enterprise and that they *had* been regularly returned to power and so were justified in assuming that a *laisser faire* attitude to government was in accordance with the electorate's wishes. They certainly did keep the rates down, but the city's problems multiplied. There were terrible slums, but the council resolutely refused to use the Housing Act. There was great suffering amongst the unemployed but, if one of their own members is to be believed, the Tories actually hindered the work of the Distress Committee. Surely these were special cases where the Council might have - should have - deviated from their dogmatic beliefs ? Maybe, but they did not, except in the case of the tramways. Perhaps one reason was simply that had they done so they might have been seen to be adopting the opposition's policies - so they hardened their attitudes. The debates on the taking over of the trams show some of the ruling party being quite explicit about being seen to be implementing the ideas of others. Councillor Lambert objected to taking over the city's transport because of the risk of burdening the city with debt, and because the likes of Hartley were advocating doing so. 'If anything had convinced him that the Corporation should not acquire the tramways', Lambert said, 'it was the manifesto of the Labour party. ... The municipal debt had already reached the enormous sum of three-quarters of a million, and everybody in the city was quite of the opinion that they should not enter upon another speculative enterprise.' (123) It seems only right to point out that people like Meyer were saying that the trams could be run at a profit and that the profit could be used for the city, but others took the opportunity of joining Lambert and saying one thing was enough. The *Press* recorded that 'Councillor PINDER, Councillor RICHARDSON, Councillor HIBBETT and Sir JOSEPH SYKES

RYMER protested against any attempt at introducing the thin end of the wedge of municipalisation.' They got an early opportunity of registering that enough was enough when S.H. Davies and Oscar Rowntree proposed setting up a committee to get a municipal cemetery in April 1908. This had long been a 'Progressive' demand, but the councillors would have none of it and Rowntree's and Davies' demands were unceremoniously kicked into touch.

Not only had the Liberals been slowly eating into the Tory majority on the Council, but many of their gains had been made by younger men (like Morrell, Wilkinson and Oscar Rowntree) of considerable ability, and to them was now added J.M. Hogge. He heightened political tensions in April, lining up with Hartley over the question of salary increases for corporation officials (again).

Late in March it was announced that there would be no rate increases, and that there were recommended salary rises being presented to the full council for such people as the Town Clerk, the Treasurer and others. (124) Perhaps it was thought that presenting the two together would help matters, but the day before the Council meeting a letter appeared in the press objecting to what was being proposed. (125) At the Council meeting Hogge wanted the whole question of salaries put before a committee, demanded properly recognised scales, and also 'pleaded for the workmen, who had', he said, 'received scurvy treatment from the Corporation.' This caused an uproar and Hogge was supported only by Mawson and Hartley. The latter then took up the question of workmen's salaries again and demanded to know why a petition from them sent by one of their union leaders had not been considered. He was bitterly attacked by Wragge and then a vote on the petition was taken with the Lord Mayor (now Sykes Rymer) announcing there had been a majority in favour of ignoring it. Hogge wanted to know what the voting figures were and who had voted against, and this was refused. Those names would have been very useful in the future and, not getting them, Hogge launched what Councillor Mansfield said was the worst attack on a Lord Mayor for 24 years. Hogge stuck to his guns and complained bitterly that members were putting forward 'every obstacle' they could to prevent a discussion of wages. He was right. A little later Hartley asked for a return of corporation workmen's wages. This was also refused.

Twice the York Corporation had allowed substantial wage demands for higher officials to go to the full council while their own men were in dispute. It looked bad; it was bad; and it says little for the tact of the Tory party organisers. On this occasion the result was (almost) the same as before, and a couple of days after the Hogge/Hartley demonstration it was announced that the Town Clerk was to get one increment instead of three; the Treasurer was to get nothing; and the other recommendations for the lower grades were knocked down. (126) A great deal is heard in the 1990s about local councils being 'caring authorities.' It was felt in many circles that the York authority of 1908 was also a caring authority, but that it restricted its caring to its 'own kind.'

Whatever it felt about municipal initiatives the York Corporation had to take one that came to fruition early in 1908. One of the statutes the Liberals got through in 1906 was the Education (Provision of Meals) Act. The York Trades Council urged the local Council to adopt the Act and, to its everlasting credit, it did. In February 1908 the Education Committee began providing 'MEALS FOR NECESSITOUS CHILDREN' consisting of soup and bread, and worth 1¹/₂d. In one week, the *Press* reported, 2,912 meals were given to 753 children. (127) The funding was found from - or was the equivalent of - a half penny rate, and Edith Milner, it will be recalled, regarded the acceptance of free school meals as 'a downward step', but from the figures given above and from the comment that follows it will be seen that voluntary workers and voluntary schemes were providing but a quarter of what was clearly necessary. Sykes Rymer, Hibbett and others might well have thought of this also as 'the thin end of the wedge of municipalisation', but it was necessary and it was good. 'Nearly one thousand children are being fed every week-day in York by these school committees and voluntary helpers', that *Press* report said, 'It is a staggering total, for behind those figures lies concealed a vast amount of poverty and misery.'

The Tories did little to try to attract new industry to York to help relieve the depressed state of the city, but there were some initiatives taken. They, it must be admitted, achieved little, but one perhaps deserves to be mentioned, if only because it could be said to have been as farsighted as any, given what has happened to the city in the second half of the 20th century. In March 1907 J.B. Morrell and J.T. Clarke, one of the councillors for Micklegate, told the annual meeting of the ward's Liberal organisation of the work of the Committee for Promoting the Commercial and Industrial Development of York. They had hopes for an iron works in the city, they said, but were also discussing advertising York as a tourist resort. It was not then on the railway register for week-end tickets, while Malton was! York as a tourist centre? Clearly that was an idea to pursue. (If this has echoes of the 1970s and '80s in it, so does the archaeologists' protest against the damage that might be done in the work to be undertaken laying the new tram lines.)

It seems paradoxical that while the Liberals were slowly gaining ground in York local politics the Liberal government was losing popularity. That got worse as the Lords continued their course of wrecking the legislation sent up to them, but just when things were looking rosier for his party and its prospects for the next general election good, York's Tory MP announced that he would not stand again. Faber, who was a moderate, popular figure in York, and one who certainly did not blindly follow the party line as Butcher did, clearly did not like being a Member for Old Ebor. It will be recalled that he announced he would not be standing in 1906, but changed his mind and was preferred by the electorate to Butcher. In November 1907 he announced in a letter to Charles E. Elmhirst, the Conservative party chairman, that he would not stand for York again, and that he would try to obtain a seat in the south. (128) This must have been a blow to the party, and it organised a 'mass' lobby of Tory working men to try to get Faber to change his mind. He refused, giving various reasons for wanting to move. He did not tell them he was already well into negotiations with the local party at Clapham - and just two weeks after he wrote his letter to Elmhirst he was adopted at that place. (129) He was replaced fairly rapidly by one of the people spoken of as a replacement for him before - H.H. Riley-Smith of Tadcaster. He must have looked a splendid choice at that time because the Liberal government was about to launch yet another 'attack' on 'the trade'.

Henry Herbert Riley-Smith was the eldest son of Henry Wilkinson Riley Smith of Harrogate 'whom he succeeded in the management of the famous brewery enterprise at Tadcaster known by the name of John Smith's Tadcaster brewery'. He was a barrister, a Justice of the Peace for the West Riding of Yorkshire and, at the time of his adoption, chairman of the board of directors of John Smith's. Riley-Smith was said to have made his first appearance in York as a public speaker at an LVA dinner some 20 years before his adoption, and he had taken a prominent part in the various campaigns launched by the trade, whether to support or reject proposed legislation. He had also been a member of a Royal Commission on Licensing and was said to have been much in demand as a speaker and a candidate.

Riley-Smith was adopted at a joint meeting of the York Conservative Association and the York Liberal Unionist Association - the two were politically indistinguishable now, but the presence of W.W. Hargrove representing the Unionists is a reminder of the days before Home Rule split the Liberals. Elmhirst, now a major figure in York politics, presided at the selection proceedings with Councillor G. Fowler Jones and Lord Deramore prominent. The parties, naturally, decided to run two candidates whenever an election was called and J.G. Butcher was to be Riley-Smith's running mate.

The main domestic themes of British politics in the years 1900 to 1908, the period covered in this study so far, were the decline of the Tory party (nationally), the re-emergence of the Liberals after the Boer War, the attacks on Labour (Taff Vale in particular), the emergence of the Labour party, temperance, education and unemployment. The prevalence of unemployment, the unwillingness, seemingly, to do anything about it and the consequent suffering have been highlighted in these pages. But there were sections of the working class which, when in work, were able to indulge themselves occasionally. What was there that they - and those better off than themselves - could find to do in the way of entertainment ?

The front pages of the York newspapers in 1908, where the entertainment industry advertised its wares, look sparse by the standards of a few years later. The Theatre Royal and the Empire were the only two permanent venues appearing in the entertainment columns of the *Evening Press* of 1 January 1908, for example, and popular prices for the latter were given as 3d., 6d., 1s., and 1s.6d. Since its opening a few years earlier the Empire had developed into a splendid music hall and it, and the Theatre Royal, had brought many of the most famous names of the day to York. The Theatre Royal provided fairly standard fare, with performances of Ibsen, Shakespeare, and Gilbert and Sullivan and shows like 'Floradora', and 'Sapho' and over the years performers like Sarah Bernhardt, Mrs Patrick Campbell, Vesta Tilley, Fred Karno and Marie Lloyd appeared either there, at the Empire, the Exhibition Hall, the Victoria Hall or the Festival Concert Rooms, all of which staged professional shows or performances on an irregular basis. Sousa's Band played in the city, as did Bessies O'the Barn, the most famous brass band in the world. Sousa's Band performed pieces which were to become jazz classics and recorded such glorious tunes as Kerry Mills 'At a Georgia Camp Meeting', Neil Moret's 'Hiawatha' and 'Creole Belles'. (130) He undoubtedly included such numbers in his York concerts and it must have been a marvellous experience for those fortunate enough to have been there. But the city had had at least one opportunity to hear such music before. 'Georgia Camp Meeting' and 'Creole Belles' are cakewalks, and the most famous exponents of the cakewalk had appeared at the Theatre Royal in 1904. (131) In August 1904 'In Dahomey' featuring Dan Avery and Charles Hart was played at the Theatre Royal, with Will Marion Cook as the musical director. Cook was a serious black musician who worked hard to erase the current condescending image of the black performer but who 'economic and social pressures forced ... to work' as a commercial tune smith or jobbing musician. (132) He eventually teamed up with Joe Jordan, a famous ragtime pianist and composer, and recorded with Ethel Waters, but in 1904 he was touring Europe with the all black show 'In Dahomey'. 'The cake walk (the real thing) is a feature of the play', an enthusiastic *Press* told its readers, 'and is alone worth seeing.' (133) It must have been. (Many years later the York Educational Settlement reintroduced live ragtime music to York.) (134)

A great feature of the Theatre Royal's season in the 1990s is an annual production by local amateurs of a musical or light opera, and it was so in the years before the Great War. In 1908 the production was the musical comedy 'San Toy' (someone always seemed to be performing 'San Toy') which gained rave reviews. Proceeds went to charity and Edith Milner would have felt very much at home on the last night, when W.A. Forster Todd, the director, accepted the plaudits of the crowd and R.B. Lambert, that Tory opponent of municipalising the trams, and Riley-Smith, all made speeches. On that last night Clifford Segler, the star of the show, 'added a couple of verses to his "pidgin" English song.' They were about Winston Churchill. The government had been reconstructed after Sir Henry Campbell-Bannerman was replaced as Prime Minister by H.H. Asquith and, as was the custom in those days, Churchill had to resign and seek re-election after his appointment as President of the Board of Trade, Lloyd George's old post. Churchill was rejected at Manchester, a fact Segler dwelled on in his 'capital topical verse.' (It was over Chinese labour, which Segler referred to, that Churchill made his famous remark that 'To call it slavery is "a terminological inexactitude".') Churchill rapidly found himself a seat for Dundee, however, and Segler's masterpiece went as follows. (Joynson-Hicks was the successful candidate at the Manchester election.)

Winston Churchill, little sweet,
Dapper coat and dapper feet.
                    Ah!
Plenty fibber, champion kidder -
Teller crams to keep his seat.
                    Ah!
Chinese slavery was his cry
Now we know it was a lie.
                    Oh!
Manchester is now awake,
Winston can his hookee take.
                    Oh!
Oh, Winnie Churchill swell,
Him ringee great big bell,
The colonies and workingmen him sell;
And now he's lost his seat,
For Joynson-Hicks him beat,
And Winston Churchill now can go to Dundee.

It was not to be many years before every home had to have a gramophone - and when the war came and the economy picked up nearly every home (and nearly every trench) got one (it seems). The first issue of the *Press* of 1908, from which theatre prices have been quoted, carried advertisements for gramophones - with Pathephone offering one with an unwearable sapphire needle at 45s. In July of the previous year a free gramophone concert at the Exhibition Buildings was arranged as part of a sales campaign by Messrs J. Gray and Sons of Coney Street and it is of some interest not only because of the performers and performances chosen, but also because one of them was by a York dignitary. (135) Records of Eli Hudson, a famous piccolo player, who was no relation whatsoever to George Hudson (as far as one can tell) were played, as were others by Dame Nellie Melba, Caruso, Adelina Patti, Clark's London Concert Band and Olly Oakley. The latter (whose real name was James Sharpe) was a magnificent banjoist who began recording in 1903, performing many ragtime compositions, (136) but perhaps Canon Fleming's rendition of Edgar Allan Poe's 'The Bells' was more to the liking of that York audience than Olly Oakley's marvellous rendition of 'Creole Belles'. Fleming was the precentor of York Minster and when the Queen (an ardent 'gramophonist') heard that he had recorded Poe's work she rushed out and bought a copy (the *Press* said). Others surely followed.

The great popular form of entertainment for half a century or more, however, was to be the cinema, and the first showing of films in York (featuring the fire brigade and the trams) have been mentioned. What was the state of that art in 1908 ? In January 1903 it has been recorded that animated pictures were part of the show when Carl Systo, the Handcuff King, topped the bill at the Festival Concert Rooms. In December 1905 the New Century Animated Picture Show was put on at the Festival Rooms, this time without the added attraction of the likes of Mysto. But why book Mysto when 'Rescued by Rover', which had only been generally released in July, was available ? (137) That film, beloved by film historians, documentary makers and film society secretaries in the 1940s and '50s, played to crowded houses and was supported by one of the visit by the Prince and Princess of Wales to India and another showing a fight between a mongoose and a cobra. (138) Good Christmas fare. In March 1906 C.E. Elmhirst presided at a showing of a rather more instructional kind when 'living' pictures of India were shown at the Exhibition Buildings (cost of admission 6d.). (139) In January of the following year Parlato's Sacred animated pictures were screened at the Victoria Hall, (140) but the fare offered to York's citizens was usually pure entertainment. In June 1907 the Alliance Bioscope Combine directed by C. Egerton Burnett and Harry Tindell - one of the largest cinematograph concerns - booked the Theatre Royal for a series of twice nightly shows. They would be good, the *Press* assured its readers, and would include films of the Niagara Falls and the Derby. You could get in for as little as 3d. (or as much as 1s.6d.). (141)   At Christmas 1907 Sidney Prince's 'Prince Edward' animated pictures were showing at the Victoria Hall with at least three 'pantomime' films for children. In addition to the Forty Thieves, Aladdin and Cinderella, pictures of the Olympia Horse Show and motor racing in France were put on. Over 40 miles of film were used by the operators, and there was an additional attraction. 'By a clever arrangement the characters on the screen were made to "talk"', said the *Press* , 'thus adding to the enjoyment of the audience.' (142) All these shows, however, were by travelling companies and nothing in the nature of a cinema had appeared in York yet - or had it ? If the definition of a cinema is a place where films are regularly - not exclusively - shown it could be said that York had had one since 1905.

From August 1905, at least, the Empire had been showing films on the 'Empire bioscope' as a regular feature of its weekly programmes. 'The bioscope operator winds out humour by the yard' a reviewer of the week's show in May 1907 said, (143) and a little earlier readers of the local papers had been told that '"Playing Truant" is a very laughable film showing on the Empire Bioscope.' (144)

There were occasionally films shown in York, however, that were not quite of the same kind as 'Rescued by Rover' and featured tangles of a rather different kind than mongoose versus cobra. At the York Martinmas fair of 1907 there were no less than three tent shows advertising films on the Thaw case, an American murder, reports of which had filled columns of newsprint for weeks on end. Harry Thaw had been tried for murdering one Stanford White on the roof garden at Madison Square during a performance of the light opera 'Mam'zelle Champagne.' Thaw's wife had told him of the treatment White, a famous architect, had subjected her to in Paris (where else) and Harry had done White in during a night at the opera. Involved in the case, which went on from 2 February to 12 April 1907, was the notorious lawyer Abe Hummel, who got a year inside for 'subordination of perjury.' The trial was said to have cost £70,000 and the jury could not agree. The case was heard again in 1908 when Thaw was acquitted but declared insane and committed to an asylum. (145) A John Gulland wrote to the papers and protested at the representation of the case shown in the York Market Place. (146)

Gulland's letter was answered by the proprietor of one of the tent shows. This was Councillor G. Tuby of Doncaster, 'one of the best known and respected men in ... show business in the north.' Gulland had been to the wrong show, Tuby said. (147) There were two film versions of the Thaw case; the one which his organisation was showing was perfectly alright, but the other left a lot to be desired it seems. What effect did Gulland's letter have ? The inevitable. People rushed to see what it was all about and trade boomed, yet there were enticing things (to judge by the titles) that should or might have got them there even if Gulland had not played Mrs Grundy. 'Gentleman in a lady's Bedroom' was showing in one of the tents and looks interesting, as does another which was playing called 'Lady's troubles with a rat in bed.' Neither of these appear in *The British Film Catalogue*, and surprisingly Edith Milner did not write to the papers about these apparent masterpieces.

For most ordinary people, for most of the time, their entertainment was of a more homespun, do it yourself kind. The adult schools, to the chagrin of their benefactors, were places of recreation rather than learning. The YMCA was active in the city and the Working Men's Clubs - soon to be attacked again by the government and the likes of Vernon Wragge - were more and more into providing entertainment. Some pubs did so also, but without lady performers it will be recalled. For many, however, their social life was based on their chapel or their favourite organisation. The various temperance movements would have provided an almost continual round of social evenings, and for those of a serious turn of mind there were, in addition to the night schools provided by the local authority, educational courses of an impressive kind. The Railway Institute was particularly active in this respect providing lectures on such topics as Robert Burns, chemistry, the optics of photography and glass making. (148) In June 1907 Albert Mansbridge visited the city and a York branch of the Workers' Educational Association was set up. (149) There was already in existence a York University Extension Society.

The bicycle had made its appearance in York during the 19th century, and it was not long before competitions were organised and cycling clubs founded. They proliferated in the first decade of the 20th century and were an amazing liberating influence for the working class. Prior to the appearance of the bike a person was restricted in the few hours left over after work to his own locality. With a bike he could go miles, and he did. Edith Milner's branch of the Primrose League had a cycling 'corps' and Rowntrees had a club. Also in existence were, among others, the York Harriers, Clifton and Guildhall organisations, the Holgate and District Club and a Layerthorpe and District Club. Each year all the cycling organisations in the city held a parade in aid of the Hospital Fund, and cycling competitions became popular spectator sports. The York City and Suburban Bicycle Club, for example, organised the Garrowby Hill Climb, which, in 1908, it was considering putting on on a Saturday to cater for the crowds, and in the same year the York Harriers held their fifth annual gymkhana. Just a few days after that a five mile handicap road race was held which was won in an actual time of 14 minutes 27 seconds, and in August York riders took part in the 24 hour Northern Roads unpaced cycle race in which serious attempts were made on the record of 327 miles. The race started at Wellington Hill, Leeds, and was of particular interest because a Miss Green was a participant, and one of the prospective record breakers.

The roads the Harriers and the others rode over still left much to be desired and were criticised almost as frequently as the York pavements were and are. Sebastian Meyer demanded that they should all be macadamized, and he may not have been concerned only about getting an easier ride for the Harriers. Frequently in the first decade of the century worries were expressed about the bad effects of the clouds of dust thrown up by traffic (the number of prosecutions of motorists for speeding did not go down, even although the speed limit had gone up). In 1906 Dr E.M. Smith, the Medical Officer for Health in York, said in his annual report that the death rate in the city in 1905 was the lowest on record, (150) but that the incidence of diptheria had increased - the result of polluted air and soil he thought. Is it the result of the dust 'so copiously, unnecessarily, and almost incessantly raised by motor car traffic on our numerous macadamised streets and roads in dry weather', Smith asked ? 'I think it not improbable', he concluded. (151) There were also frequent complaints in these years of the chaos and damage caused by another form of mechanical transport. In May 1907 an irate citizen wrote to the press complaining of 'ponderous traction engines laden to their full carrying capacity travelling through our narrow thoroughfares.' (152) Others did so too.

Cycling was clearly popular in York and was a healthy alternative for some to the club or the pub (or the temperance meeting), but the fact remained that the pubs were important centres where people could get entertained as well as get drunk. Then, as now, they were centres of competitive activities, and perhaps the name of Jonathan Temple should be added to the list of York achievers. He was a 65 year old shoemaker who for 20 years had been the English champion at brasses who in 1908 played for the Alexandra Hotel Club. (153) Temple's career was outlined in an *Evening Press* article on brasses, and a little earlier it had carried an equally long feature on another unbelievably popular activity which has now, thankfully, disappeared. (154) Hardly a week went by during the 'season' when the press did not carry reports of linnet singing competitions and the aforementioned *Press* feature explained the elaborate staging and marking of these contests. Their popularity might perhaps be gauged by the fact that in June 1908 the Bricklayers Arms in the salubrious area of Hungate held its 31st annual Whitsuntide competition. (155) The papers spoke of the number of birds 'hung up' when they reported the competitions, as they always did, and it is nice to be able to record that a Mrs Peckett did her bit for the women's movement in 1902 when she won the 29th annual competition at the Lord Nelson. (156) There was an active RSPCA branch in York and several natural history organisations but none of them seem to have protested at this activity. It was still as popular as ever during the Great War.

In 1908 at least two new organisations came into being in York which must have added to the recreational outlets for young men, but which have a little more significance than might appear at first sight. In March the North Eastern Railway League of Riflemen held its first meeting. This was a rifle club which would enter local competitions, but it was that and a little more. Lord Wenlock was present at that first meeting and he made it quite clear that he had some kind of military purpose for it in mind, and the chairman was also quite explicit on the matter. (157) He hoped, he said, that the men would devote some portion of their leisure time to the drill which ought to some extent to accompany the training in shooting, and thus make the men 'more useful to their country.' Just a few days later Riley-Smith opened the York Minature Rifle Club. It had a range in the Bedern, in the Yeomanry Headquarters, and was equipped with Bisley and running man targets. (158)

As Lord Wenlock's remarks show rifle clubs were beloved by the advocates of people like himself who were concerned about the state of the British army - people who were, in fact, ardent workers for conscription, or, as they always called it, national service. The experience of the Boer War, and the revelations that came out of investigations into it, had led Balfour's government to make some attempts at reform. First William St John Broderick, the Secretary for War, then his successor, H.O. Arnold-Foster, introduced schemes of reform, but their work floundered, (159) and the Liberals took office. In the years that they held office L.S. Amery, who claimed a great deal for himelf and his influence as a writer on army reform in the *Times*, went to 'a meeting at Apsley House, under the Duke of Wellington's chairmanship' where they 'definitely started' the National Service League as an 'effective organisation.' (160) They persuaded Lord Roberts, 'Old Bobs', Britain's favourite soldier, to become its president.

The National Service League had been formed in 1902, and it owed a great deal to the publication of George Shee's book *The Briton's First Duty*. It spent a great deal of time stressing Britain's 'vulnerability', contending that the navy could not prevent an invasion, and calling for universal military training for all young men between 18 and 23. (161) Roberts' appointment breathed extra life into the movement, and one of his first speeches advocated the formation of rifle clubs on a national scale. In March 1908 it was announced that the first steps were being taken to form a branch of the League in York. It was dominated, nationally, by Conversatives and it seemed that it would be in York. C.A. Thompson, that man who tripped Greenwood up over sugar duties, was prominent at the inaugural meeting, as was C.E. Elmhirst. Lord Wenlock would become president it was announced. (162)

Arising out of the same feelings of dissatisfaction with the British state of preparedness for war came another organisation which also took root in York. This was the Legion of Frontiersmen, formed in 1904 'to keep tabs on veterans of the Boer War so that they would be available for service in any emergency.' (163) It was started by Roger Pocock, who wrote a weird book on its history which must rate as one of the greatest oddities of Edwardian literature. (164) Anyway the idea caught on, and in August C.T. Cutcliffe-Hyne, a well-known author of the day, appeared in York to see about forming a 'command' of the Legion there. (165) The Legion had been officially recognised by the Secretary of State for War in March, and just over a week after Cutcliffe-Hyne first appeared in York an inaugural meeting was held at the De Grey Rooms. (166) Present there was the 'organising officer' Captain Lionel Palmer, son of Sir Charles Palmer, head of the Tyneside Shipbuilding Company. Palmer had served with the West Yorkshire Regiment and had once been heavyweight boxing champion of the Royal Canadian Mounted Police. He was a colourful character but paled into insignificance by comparison with another present, the commandant of the London command. This was Colonel Manoel Herrera de Hora who was supposed to have stolen a battleship (the *Huascar* ?) when he was 23 which was then sunk by *HMS Shah* after it had fired the first three torpedos 'ever fired in naval warfare.' (167) He was also supposed to have raised a force of 600 and commanded it in Johannesburg until handing it over to Lord Roberts, and found the Maghellan treasure!

The Legion of Frontiersmen in York had the active support of F.J. Munby who was its treasurer. Munby was clerk to the York magistrates and later, at one of its meetings, the Legion had the support of the Lord Mayor, Colonel R. Bewicke-Copley of Northern Command, and Lord Deramore, who gave a speech advocating conscription. (168)

What were the aims of the Legion ? It claimed that it was not out to interfere with enlistment in the regular forces or (when they appeared) the Territorials, and it restricted its membership to those with previous military training who 'were unable or ineligible to serve elsewhere.' The Frontiersmen were out to 'indoctrinate the nation with the need for loyalty and military preparedness' and they set up three classes of membership - 'those pledged to take up active service anywhere; those pledged to take up home defense if called upon; and those merely sympathetic to the aims of the Legion. Providing', in fact, 'a pool of experienced men prepared to augment His Majesty's forces in time of war.' (169)

The Legion of Frontiersmen became a feature of York's life for many years. It is unlikely that the ILP approved of it, and it is certain that the Quaker element among the Liberals did not. Edith Milner would have. The League took part in a military tournament in Cambridge in September, where Trooper Jackson, a giant of six feet three inches, excelled himself at tent pegging and other competitions.

The appearance of the Legion of Frontiersmen in York meant that the issue of national service would be kept before the public, but what of that other great 'movement' of these years - that for women's rights ? What had happened to the organisation that Almyra Gray had been connected with ? Was it still in existence ? It was, and it followed the same tactics as ever. Mrs Gray and her colleagues were moderates and they undoubtedly expected much from the Liberals - many of whom, Lloyd George for example, were 'male suffragists.' The year 1907 was said by one of the historians of the suffrage movement to have been a year of 'delusion', (170) yet women did, in that year, get the right to sit on town and county councils. (The Act giving them this privilege must be one of the shortest ever passed.) (171) Did Mrs Gray's ladies thereafter put up members to contest York seats at the November elections ? They did not, and why will remain a mystery. Surely this would have been a golden opportunity for them ? If it was, they did not take it. It seems strange.

The York Women's Suffrage Society was in existence by 1901 and taking part in activities outside York by 1903. (172) The members continued in their constitutional, self effacing way in the years that followed, loyally supported, particularly, by Richard Westrope. (173) No doubt speakers like Mrs Bruce Glasier, who regularly visited York to take part in ILP meetings mentioned votes for women in her speeches, (174) but the Suffrage Society did nothing, as far as one can see, at the general election of 1906, and Hamar Greenwood does not seems to have been asked to commit himself as many Liberal candidates were. (And no-one in York did what Miss Alwyn Bussey did at Little Titchfield in the Marylebone constituency - but then they could not have. Miss Bussey had found herself on the voters list with vote number 6,036 and she simply went along and used it.) (175)

Most ladies who supported the York Suffrage Society were Liberals, like Mrs Gray, and in the year that they obtained the right to sit on borough and county councils, the Yorkshire Council of Women's Liberal Associations met in York, and the ladies gathered there noted that something new had crept into the women's movement. They were all, no doubt, expecting Campbell-Bannerman to do something about women's suffrage (something more than giving them the municipal vote that is) and they condemned the more militant campaigners who had appeared on the scene, saying that they were 'impairing the fundamental English ideas as to the manner in which social changes should be brought about. They believed', they said, 'in using their sober second thought ... and in persuading the men that women were capable of giving intelligent votes.' (176) This was the attitude of Mrs Gray and her colleagues, but happenings elsewhere spurred them into activity, and in April 1907 the York Women's Suffrage Society issued *An Appeal to Reason*. In this they recognised that much of the new militancy was being resorted to simply because, after winning the arguments about the vote for decades, many of the ladies had run out of patience. Their 'constitutional' methods seemed to have got them nowhere (much) and they had adopted new tactics 'in pursuance of reasonable convictions and a settled purpose for which they know not how else to gain, from the mass of men, so much as a fair hearing'. (177) Shortly after the appearance of the *Appeal* Mrs Gray told a public meeting - at which Mrs Philip Snowden also appeared - that she admired members of the 'new wave', even if she was not willing to adopt their methods herself. Another of her colleagues on the platform that day was Mrs G.H. Wilson of Halifax who, as a result of her activities, had been imprisoned both in Armley and Holloway. (178)

The York Women's Suffrage Society (whose secretary in 1908 was Miss Mary Cudworth) was a part of the National Union of Women's Suffrage Societies and in June 1908 - by which time it must have been clear to everyone that pressure needed to be put on the Liberals if they were to fulfill their destiny and emancipate the women - it sent delegates to a mass meeting at the Albert Hall. Before they went they displayed their banner in York, (179) and also, just before they went, a meeting was held in the city to form a branch of the National Women's Social and Political Union (the NWSPU). (180)

The NWSPU was founded in Manchester in 1903 by Mrs Emmeline Pankhurst and run dictatorially by her and her daughter Christabel. They had moved the centre of their activity to London and it was they who had begun to interrupt proceedings in parliament and, at the general election, harass such prominent politicians as Winston Churchill. The Union was the 'physical force' arm of the Suffragette movement and gained a great deal of publicity from incidents like assaulting a policeman guarding the house of H.H. Asquith (and the subsequent court appearances). The campaign of the NWSPU was to become more militant in the years ahead, but their methods and how they would develop must have been obvious when they first appeared in York. Then they heard a speech from a Mrs Martel from Australia and got words of encouragement from Richard Westrope - who clearly preferred the Pankhurst to the Gray methods of conducting an agitation. The attendance at that meeting was kept low by the 6d. entrance fee it was thought, but those who attended heard words from Una Dugdale that were remarkably like those of Mrs Gray's *Appeal*, but with this difference. Una, and those like her, were going to pursue the new methods, and why not ? Their militant action during the last two years had done more than 50 years of 'quiet and dignified persuasion' Una said, 'This was to be their supreme effort, it was [to be] a fight to the finish, and she did not think it would be long before women obtained the vote.' It depends on what Una meant by 'long', but in fact it was to be over a decade before the first legislative steps were made towards her objective. On 10 June the *Evening Press* compared the NUWSS and the WSPU for its readers. Both, it said, 'have the same object in view, but their methods are entirely different. The National Union of Women's Suffrage Societies, although no less keen for female suffrage, works with quieter methods, and hopes to "arrive just as early" to use an Americanism.'

When the WSPU branch was formed in York it was, in fact, the third suffragette organisation in the city. Two days before Westrope and Dugdale held their meeting

Fred Morley.

at the De Grey Rooms another was held at the ILP rooms, St Sampson's Square, to form a branch of the Women's Freedom League. The celebrity present there was Mrs Edith How Martyn, the first lady to go to prison for suffragette activities, and little was said about the organisation except that it had nothing whatsoever to do with the Pankhursts and that it demanded the vote on the same terms as men. (181) That raises an interesting point. It has been raised before.

Why the suffragettes did not seize their opportunity (in York) to run for municipal seats at the very first opportunity (given that most of them were ardent Liberals) is puzzling. (Perhaps they did not want to spoil their party's gradual march to power.) Why the Women's Freedom League should be satisfied with equality with men - if by that they meant by getting the franchise as it stood at that point in time - is equally puzzling, because only 58 per cent of adult males then had the vote! (182) This is a fact that is not stressed nearly enough by historians writing about Edwardian Britain. Voting in York (at parliamentary elections) was dictated (as it was in boroughs everywhere) by the Representation of the People Act of 1867, and paragraph three of that Act said that 'Every man shall' thereafter 'be entitled to be registered as a Voter, and ... vote for a Member or Members to serve in Parliament, who ... qualified' in a number of ways. (183) These were: that he had to be of full age; and on the last day in July and for 12 months had been 'an Inhabitant Occupier, as Owner or Tenant' of a house in the borough; and who had been rated to all Rates (if any) made for the Relief of the Poor in respect of such Premises; who had, furthermore, paid his rates. Paragraph four of the 1867 Act dealt with lodgers who qualified if they resided 12 months in a property of £10 and upwards if let furnished. This excluded many, giving, as has been said, a vote to only 58 per cent of the male population. What did this mean in York ? It is difficult to be precise but the voters register for the York constituency in 1901 contained 13,045 names, while the census for the same year showed there were 20,789 residents over the age of 21 residing in the city and borough. The parliamentary and municipal boundaries were not exactly the same it is realised, and the latter included figures for parts of York which were actually in the county, while the former included people who had qualified elsewhere. Nevertheless they are a rough guide showing, as John Grigg has said, that the electorate was still predominantly middle-class.

It seems reasonable to assume that the 42 per cent of adult males without a vote, from the poorer sections of the community, would have contained a large majority of potential labour supporters. Why then did not the labour candidates continually agitate for the old Chartist demand of universal male suffrage ? It seems strange, but they did not - or at least they were not reported as doing so. Given the foregoing, and the smallness and composition of the electorate, Stuart's performance in 1906 looks most impressive.

The suffragettes, however, were simply interested in 'the vote', but there those of the fairer sex who did not want to be emancipated. Edith Milner, of course, was one.

In June 1908 the Milner Habitation of the Primrose League went on a river trip on 'The River King', a pleasure boat, to Beningbrough Hall. It was on the same day as the Women's Freedom League was formed and Edith gave a speech of thanks to Lord and Lady Dawnay. She spoke about votes for women. '... members of the Primrose League,' she said, 'were opposed to votes for women. A short time ago she received a cheque for £15.15s. from a gentleman who said he was sending the money on instructions from his wife. In acknowledging the donation,' Edith went on, 'she wrote him that there was no necessity for women's suffrage when men were so obedient to their betters.' (184) Edith was anti- suffrage, anti-school dinners, anti-state aid for the unemployed, and anti much else. In the troubled years ahead it was a dead certainty that she would be anti Lloyd George and pro the House of Lords, and she certainly would not have approved of the Women's Freedom League, even although it was not connected with the Pankhursts (though it was militant).

The Women's Freedom League represented in fact a breakwaway from the NWSPU. Mrs Pankhurst, with all the assurance of a despot, had demanded absolute power in the Union, and this had caused a split led by Mrs Charlotte Despard, Mrs Theresa Billington-Greig, and Mrs How Martyn. They formed the WFL, taking with them 'about a fifth' of the WSPU membership. (185) The League, it was said, developed some original ideas, and it was three members of it who chained themselves to the grille of the Ladies' Gallery of the House of Commons. The League also invented some other 'original schemes' a history of the women's movement contended. 'One of them was refusal of house-owners to pay taxes, and Charlotte Despard's admirers grew quite used to haunting the auction rooms to buy back her furniture which had been sequestered for non payment of tax.' (186) Arthur Dearlove, Richard Westrope, Reissman and Brother Clack had been passive resisting like that in York for years.

1. *Press* 22 and 23 January 1903
2. *Ibid* 2 February 1903
3. *Ibid* 19 February 1903
4. *Ibid* 1 July 1903
5. *Ibid* 30 July 1903
6. The details of the election campaign can be followed in the local press from December until polling day. Most of the quotations used in the following description are from *Ibid*
7. He produced a number of digests of the classics under this name
8. *Press* 4 January 1906
9. *Ibid* 17 January 1906, letters column
10. Quoted *Ibid* 5 February 1906
11. Despite their protests people regarded them as food taxers
12. *Postman's Gazette* quoted *Press* 5 February 1906
13. *Ibid* 7 February 1906
14. See eg, H. Pelling, *Labour and Politics 1900-1906* 1958 and F. Bealey, 'Negotiations between the Liberal Party and the Labour Representation Committee before the General Election of 1906', *Bulletin of the Institute of Historical Research*, XXIX, 1956
15. *Ibid* 26 February 1907
16. Ensor *op.cit.* p 392
17. C. Cross, *The Liberals in Power, 1905-14* (1963) p 41
18. There is a good summary of its provisions in Gretton *op.cit.* pp 700-1
19. *Press* 16 May 1906

20. *Ibid* 19 May 1906
21. *Ibid* 21 November 1906
22. They did not actually reject it; it was abandoned as has been said earlier. Effectively their actions had this effect however.
23. *Press* 10 December 1906
24. Rhodes James *op.cit.* p 233
25. Eg S. McKenna, *Reginald McKenna 1863-1943* (1943). Details can be found in the *Annual Register 1907*
26. *Press* 6 September 1906
27. *Ibid* 14 December 1906. The point involved only voluntary schools - Church of England and Catholic mainly. The Council was responsible for teacher's salaries but questioned whether it should pay for time taken in denominational religious teaching.
28. *Ibid* 7 March 1907
29. *Ibid* 3 April 1907
30. *Ibid* 2 May 1907
31. Ensor *op.cit* p 394
32. *Press* 12 October 1906
33. *Ibid* 31 January and the following issues for biographies of and tributes to Bentley. The details of the row with Wragge in eg *Ibid* 7 January 1907
34. *Ibid* 13 February 1907 Meeting of the York Temperance Society. The 'Police Court Incident' which follows reported in *Ibid* 7 January 1907
35. *Ibid* 12 February 1907. Wragge lived on until 1933, and served another term as Lord Mayor. He began life, like George Hudson, as a draper's assistant and was in business in York before taking up the law. There are articles on him and an obituary in *Gazette* 3, 10 and 29, 1933. See also C.A. Manning, *Yorkshire Leaders: Social and Political* (1908), *Yorkshire Who's Who* (1912) and W.H. Scott, *The North and East Ridings of Yorkshire At the Opening of the Twentieth Century* (Brighton 1903)
36. *Press* 6 March 1907. The notice for the Brewster sessions gave Martin's name as Tom
37. *Compensation Authority. Minute Book* (At present in the possession of the author)
38. *Press* 8 May 1906
39. *Ibid* 8 and 11 September 1906. *Herald* 25 October 1906
40. *Press* 19 September 1906
41. *Ibid* 24 October 1906
42. See earlier
43. *Press* 25 October 1906
44. *Ibid* 24 October 1906
45. *Ibid* 3 March 1906. The men mentioned in the text are presumably those Mr R. Hills had in mind in his essay, 'The City Council and Electoral Politics 1901-1971' in Feinstein *op.cit.* p 262
46. Mr Murray gives Vernon a hyphenated name (Vernon-Wragge) which is not correct (at this time anyway)
47. *Press* 14 and 23 January 1907. The letter in which Arnold Rowntree was taken to task is in *Ibid* 25 January 1907. In the same paper is a letter applauding Rowntree and Company for the way they looked after their animals
48. *Ibid* 24 April 1907
49. *Ibid* 19 December 1907. It is only fair to record that the case was dismissed
50. Quoted Murray *op.cit.* p 95
51. See eg *Press 21* January 1907
52. *Ibid* 13 February 1907
53. Wragge, who was returning officer, made a very outspoken speech about what was going on at the declaration in Bootham. Councillor Lambert's remarks about electricity were: 'They had municipalised the electric light undertaking, and the result was that besides the loan debt being increased by £122,000, there was a deficit balance of £6,000, although £920 had already been paid out of the rates in relief.'
54. *Press* 15 February 1907
55. *Ibid* 21 December 1906
56. Mr Murray says that negotiations were 'delayed by the municipal elections and the consequent reconstitution of the council and the Committees', but this seems hardly likely. Murray *op.cit.* p 96

57.   *Ibid* pp 96-97. One of the four dissentients was Councillor Lambert who had opposed the takeover publicly at the recent by election. He thought £11,000 too high a price. Mr Murray is wrong in saying there were only four dissentients - there were seven as stated in the text. 'The report was ultimately adopted by 33 votes to 3, four being neutral.' *Press* 8 January 1907

58.   *Press* 30 January 1907. The date given in the text is different from that given by Mr Murray. Murray *op.cit.* p 97

59.   *Press* 13 and 19 February 1907

60.   *Ibid* 25 February 1908

61.   *Ibid* 9 November 1906

62.   *Ibid* 14 December 1906

63.   *Ibid* 19 February 1906

64.   *Ibid* 22 March 1906

65.   *Ibid* 30 August 1906

66.   *Ibid* 24 October 1906

67.   *Ibid* 2 October 1907

68.   *Ibid* 25 October 1906

69.   See the letters saying he had got his calculations and facts wrong in *Ibid* 11 February 1907. His original letter appeared on 8 February

70.   *Ibid* 11 January, 8 and 9 February 1906

71.   See eg *Ibid* 28 March 1906. On the thrift club see eg *Ibid* 15 October 1906

72.   Eg *Ibid* 22 March 1906

73.   *Herald* 13 February 1907. *Press* 13 February 1907

74.   On these see eg K. Woodruffe, *From Charity to Social Work in England and the United States* (1962) Chap 2 *passim*

75.   *Ibid* p 34

76.   H. Bosanquet, *The Strength of the People. A Study in Social Economics* (1903)

77.   See eg *Press* 6 February 1908 for a report of its seventh annual general meeting

78.   *Ibid* 21 February 1907

79.   *Ibid* 12 March 1907

80.   *Ibid* 14 February 1907

81.   *Ibid* 24 December 1906

82.   *Ibid* 16 July 1907

83.   *Ibid* 22 January 1908

84.   *Herald* 11 February 1908

85.   *Press* 15 April 1907

86.   *Ibid* 28 February 1907

87.   *Ibid* 5 March 1907. Fifty three hours seems to have been the prevailing length of the working week for many years - that is there had been no reduction for 30 years or more. See *The Story of a Printing House William Sessions Limited* (York 1965) p 16 where wages for 1878 are said to have been 3d. an hour for a 53 hour week

88.   *Ibid* 15 February 1907, interview with Hartley

89.   *Ibid* 5 March 1907

90.   *Ibid* 1 March 1907

91.   See Chap 3

92.   *Press* 9 February 1906. The NER actually recognised the unions. See eg W.W. Tomlinson, *Tomlinson's North Eastern Railway. Its Rise and Development* (Newton Abbot 1907) pp 748-52

93.   50,000 railwaymen worked a 12 hour day, it was said

94.   *Press* 26 February 1906

95.   *Ibid* 21 March 1906

96.   *Ibid* 2 April 1906

97.   *Ibid* 5 April 1906

98.   *Ibid* 23 April 1906

99.   See the table showing the decline in jobs on the NER in R.J. Irving, *The North Eastern Railway Company 1870-1914* (Leicester 1976). The background to the NER's industrial relations can be found in Mr Irving's book and in other histories of the railway unions, eg P.S. Bagwell, *The Railwaymen: A History of the National Union of Railwaymen* (1963). See also G. Alderman, 'The Railway Companies and the Growth of Trade Unionism in the Late Nineteenth and Early Twentieth Centuries,' *Historical Journal* Vol 14, 1971

100. The loss of the railwaymen meant more empty houses in York. In May 1906 here were 796 compared with 564 the year before - these were assessed at £6,200 a year
101. *Press* 14 and 15 May 1906
102. *Ibid* 6 July 1906
103. *Ibid* 4 July 1906
104. *Ibid* 26 November 1906
105. *Ibid* 24 December 1906
106. *Ibid* 14 October 1907. J.H. Thomas became organising secretary of the ASRS in 1906
107. Long extracts from it published in *Ibid* 10 April 1908. Also on the dispute see H.A. Clegg, A. Fox and A.F. Thompson, *A History of British Trade Unions Since 1889*, Vol.1 (1964) pp 423-28
108. Quoted Clegg, Fox and Thompson *op.cit.* p 425. 'Conciliation at first, but, failing that, the steam roller', Lloyd George said to his brother about the way he intended to arbitrate. J. Grigg, *Lloyd George. The People's Champion 1902-1911* (1978) p 113
109. Bell wrote a study of the most famous case his union was involved in - *The Taff Vale Case and the Injunction* (1902). There is a long entry about him in J.M. Bellamy and J. Saville, *Dictionary of Labour Biography* Vol 2 (1974)
110. On the ASRS annual report. See fn 107 *supra*
111. G. Askwith, *Industrial Problems and Disputes* (1920) p 121. Askwith, later Lord Askwith, was the head of the Board of Trade's railway department and claimed to be the go-between.
112. Bagwell *op.cit.* p 277
113. Clegg, Fox and Thompson *op.cit.* p 426. The account of the meeting which follows involving the GRWU from *Press* 4 November 1907
114. *Press* 4 and 5 November 1907
115. *Ibid* 4, 7 and 8 October 1907
116. The rest of the electorate then was: Micklegate 3,217; Monk 2,049; Walmgate 2,869; Bootham 3,278; Guildhall 1,157
117. On the strays, a long running cause of dissension in York, see W.W.M.. Nisbet, *The Strays of York and their Management through the Ages* (York nd)
118. Election results in *Press* 1 November 1907
119. *Ibid* 9 December 1907
120. On the by elections and the results see *Ibid* 15, 20, 28 and 29 November 1907
121. *Ibid* 15 November 1907
122. Quoted R. Hills in Feinstein *op.cit.* p 256
123. *Press* 8 January 1907
124. *Ibid* 2 April 1908
125. *Ibid* 6 April 1908. The council meeting mentioned immediately afterwards reported in *Ibid* 7 April 1908
126. *Ibid* 9 April 1908. The account of the report of the Industrial Development Committee later is from Ibid 21 March 1907. See also Ibid 30 June 1908
127. *Ibid* 17 February 1908
128. *Ibid* 13 November 1907. *Herald* 13 November 1907
129. *Press* 26 November 1907
130. The band recorded 'Georgia Camp Meeting' at least seven times between 1899 and 1908. That marvellous piece is equally well known as the 'Georgia Cake Walk', and for those who like jazz the rendition by Pete Daily is magnificent
131. The cakewalk was not introduced by 'In Dahomey'. There are British recordings of cakewalks from 1898
132. W.J. Shafer and J. Riedel, *The Art of Ragtime* (1977 edition) p 21
133. *Press* 11 and 20 August 1908. Picture of Cook in latter issue. The following comments about 'San Toy' are taken from *Ibid* 21 and 27 April 1908. Will Marion Cook has another claim to great fame as far as English jazz is concerned. After the war he brought over to England a huge ensemble called The Southern Syncopated Orchestra. It was not a jazz or even a dance band but among its members was Sidney Bechet, a jazz giant. Bechet's genius while playing with Cook's orchestra was recognised by Ernest Ansermet, the conductor of the Suisse-Romande orchestra, who wrote a famous article about him. See eg B. Rust, *The Dance Bands* (1972) pp 14-15
134. With a series of concerts by the famous jazz pianist Neville Dickie. This led (a note for future historians) to a sadly short-lived (though not too short-lived) appearance of ragtime performances in some of the better pubs of York. The recreator then of the beautiful music of Scott Joplin, James

Scott and others was the late Brian Sourbut, a lecturer at St John's College and the York Educational Settlement. Ragtime absorbed the cakewalks, to become the next major musical style in American art. Jazz followed

135. *Press* 11 April 1907
136. See eg E.S. and S. Walker, *English Ragtime. A Discography* (1971)
137. D. Gifford, *The British Film Catalogue*: 1895-1970 (Newton Abbot 1973). The film is categorised and described as 'ANIMAL Dog trails gipsy who stole baby and returns home to fetch father.' Rover was played by 'Blair'
138. *Press* 23 and 27 December 1905. In 1905, and this shows how popular the film show was becoming. Two travelling companies put on shows in York at the Christmas season. The New Century Company is mentioned in the text. At the same time the Royal Canadian Animated Picture Company was putting on performances at the Exhibition Buildings and did good trade over a three week period. Highlights of their show were 'Life in a Coal Mine', and 'An Elopement by Strategy'. *Ibid* 19 December 1905
139. *Ibid* 20 March 1906
140. *Ibid* 21 January 1907
141. *Ibid* 29 June 1907
142. *Ibid* 10 December 1907. The films being shown here might have been Chronophone Films or Cinemataphone Singing Pictures. Quite a number of these were issued in 1907, described as 'MUSICAL Synchronised to gramophone records.' Vesta Tilley, Peter Dawson and Gus Elen all appeared in them. Details in Gifford *op.cit.*
143. *Press* 21 May 1907
144. *Ibid* 9 April 1907. One travelling show at least combined live entertainment with films. This was Sidney Carter's New Century Pictures which were shown at the Festival Rooms. Top of the bill then were 'Dumb Sagacity' a film in the 'Rescued by Rover' mould ('Pet dog fetches horse to save girl cut off by the tide.') and 'The Adventuress, or the Female Spy.' These were supported by a series on the life of the trout (!) and the Zambesi and some music hall acts. *Ibid* 26 November 1907
145. The trial was fully reported at great length in the York papers. See eg *Ibid* 3 February 1908 for the verdict. The Thaw case is regularly rediscovered by journalists. See eg 'The Fatal Triangle, Harry Thaw', *Murder Casebook* Issue No 44
146. *Press* 26 November 1907
147. *Ibid* 27 November 1907
148. *Ibid* 8 January 1908
149. *Ibid* 27 June 1907
150. 14.2 per 1,000. Infant mortality was 130 per 1,000
151. *Press* 10 July 1906
152. *Ibid* 20 May 1907
153. *Ibid* 10 June 1908
154. *Ibid* 21 April 1908
155. *Ibid* 9 June 1908
156. *Ibid* 31 March 1902
157. *Ibid* 27 March 1908
158. *Ibid* 31 March 1908
159. Barnett *op.cit.* pp 353-59
160. L.S. Amery, *My Political Life* Vol 1 (1953) p 214
161. On the League see the excellent account in R.M. Rosenthal, *The Character Factory* (1968) Chap 7. J.E.B. *Seely, Adventure* (1930) p 92
162. *Press* 28 March 1908
163. Rosenthal *op.cit.* p 257
164. R. Pocock, *Chorus to Adventurers* (1931)
165. *Press* 14 August 1906
166. *Ibid* 22 August 1906. For a short account of the *Shah/Huascar* incident see eg E.H.H. Archibald, *The Fighting Ships in the Royal Navy* (1987) pp 86-87. There the *Huascar* is described as a Peruvian armoured turret ship! It will be seen from this account that the *Shah* did not fire torpedoes and the Huascar was not sunk!
167. Pocock *op.cit.* p 26
168. *Press* 3 December 1906
169. Rosenthal *op.cit.* pp 207-8

170. Fulford *op.cit.* p 136
171. Gretton *op.cit.* p 720. The Act giving women the right to sit on borough and county councils is the Qualification of Women (County and Borough Councils) Act 1907. (7 Edward 7 cap 33.) It consists of two clauses only - the second of which simply gives the name by which it was to be known
172. See earlier
173. Eg *Press* 6 October, 7 December 1905
174. For some of Mrs Glasier's meetings see *Ibid* 11 November 1905 and 12 May 1906
175. *Ibid* 17 January 1906
176. *Ibid* 14 March 1907. See also the 'funny' letter about suffragettes in the issue of the following day
177. *Ibid* 3 April 1907
178. *Ibid* 5 April 1907
179. *Ibid* 1 and 10 June 1908
180. *Ibid* 6 June 1908
181. *Ibid* 4 June 1908
182. Actually Mrs Martyn said they wanted the vote on the same terms as the men as it was or as it might be. It is not suggested that the women's movement and the Labour movement did not, sometimes, demand 'adult suffrage', they did, but not effectively, and they did not press it in York. In the early days of the suffrage movement in the 20th century the NWSPU and the ILP were very close, and the latter continually demanded adult suffrage, while the women anted support for female advancement in any form. See eg J. Liddington and J. Norris, *One Hand Behind Us. The Rise of Women's Suffrage Movement* (1978) chap 10 *passim* on the demands for adult suffrage and the disputes it led to. There was also in existence an Adult Suffrage Society, with which was connected Margaret Bondfield, then a shop assistant's union organiser.
183. 30 and 31 Victoria, 1867, cap 102
184. *Press* 4 June 1908
185. Liddington and Norris *op.cit.* p 209
186. J. Kamm, *Rapiers and Battleaxes* (1966) p 159

CHAPTER 5

OLD AGE PENSIONS, UNEMPLOYMENT, AND A RATIONAL DIET

1908 began with a sensational court case in York. The press, as it showed with the Harry Thaw case, was not averse to a good crime, and in 1908 it got a home-made one which it made the most of! It broke about three days after Thaw's second trial started, it involved a prominent York figure, and it nearly caused rioting in the streets and a nearby village.

Charles George Golden Rushworth was a solicitor who, in 1908, was secretary to the York Education Committee. He and his wife, Sarah Catherine, lived at Poppleton. She was a daughter of the Rev Jackson, who for 40 years was the vicar of Filey, and she had once been married to a Captain Scott. He died, she married Rushworth, and they went to live at Nether Poppleton, some 25 years before they were charged. The two of them were tried at the Eastern Ainsty Petty Sessions in January on charges that they did jointly wilfully illtreat and neglect Olive Mabel May and Dora Cress. A third charge was brought against Mrs Rushworth alone, alleging that she caused Olive to be ill treated and neglected in a manner likely to cause unnecessary suffering and injury to her health. The proceedings against the Rushworths were brought by the NSPCC under a Prevention of Cruelty to Children Act. (1)

The Rushworth case (in which Vernon Wragge appeared as one of the lawyers for the defence) revealed some interesting facts about Edwardian Britain and how vulnerable some small children then were. It also revealed a dreadful story of hypocrisy by a major York public servant and showed that the Edwardian crowd had not lost all resemblance to that of a century or so before. (2)

The Rushworths decided to be tried summarily (by magistrates rather than by a jury) and it was immediately revealed that so much interest had been shown in them, and so much hostility expressed towards them, that the charges had been investigated in London and that 'outside' counsel had been moved in to prosecute them. The case against them was shocking. What had happened ?

The Rushworths had a large house in Nether Poppleton and a son (aged 22 at the time of their trial). They had several servants at one stage, but these either left or were sacked and eventually replaced by Dora and Olive Mabel. How were these children found and engaged ? In 1903 or thereabouts Mrs Rushworth put an advertisement in a newspaper asking for a child for her to adopt. A Mrs Wilson replied. She had Olive to dispose of, who she had obtained through answering a similar advertisement to that of Mrs

Rushworth. She had answered that first letter, Mrs Wilson said, and met a man and a woman at York railway station. She had taken Olive, who seemed then to be about five years of age, and had paid £10 for her. The little girl was with her for three years.

Mrs Wilson met Mr Rushworth who said 'he was looking out for a nice-looking child whom he would treat as his own daughter, and bring up at his house, as he had no daughter of his own.' Mrs Wilson then met Rushworth's wife and Olive went to stay for a few days at Poppleton. About six months later the little girl went to live there. Five years went by and, according to the prosecution, Olive went out of the house on only one occasion in the whole of that time.

On 6 July 1905 the Rushworths received Dora Cress, who they had seen at Hull. She, too, was handed over to their care on York railway station.

The villagers of Poppleton engaged in gossip about what might be going on in the Rushworth's house, but with the exception of one neighbour none of them (or none of them willing to do anything) saw the two little girls. The postman said they were scared and always frightened of him, but he too did nothing . Then in November 1907, one of the little girls was seen scrubbing the front door step dressed in filthy clothes and wearing odd shoes. Mrs Rushworth was seen to hit her. What happened then is not completely clear, but someone, at last, it may have been John Leaf, who was also employed by the Rushworths, called in the authorities. Leaf let Inspector Campbell of the NSPCC into the house on 28 November - when Mrs Rushworth was away in Scarborough - and Olive and Dora were taken to the York Rescue Home. Miss Bennington of that establishment gave evidence of their condition, as did a doctor called in by the NSPCC. Olive, they said, was dirty, undersized, badly clothed, anaemic and enuric. Moreover she was badly scarred. One of her scars, counsel said, was seven inches by five and a quarter inches in extent and was caused by being burnt with a flat iron; others were caused by what the children said was 'a French dog whip.' Olive's enurism had ceased when she was taken away. She then weighed five stone one and a half pounds, she could not read and was 'wholly illiterate in every way.' In his opening statement the chief prosecutor said that Olive had suffered 'excessively, continuously and for a long time.' Dora, to begin with, had been treated better (and encouraged to beat Olive by Mrs Rushworth), but eventually she began to be treated badly. Mrs Rushworth had made her write home saying she was happy at Poppleton but when her mistress went to Scarborough she wrote to her mother and told the truth. This was another possible way in which the case was brought to light.

Counsel told the bench that Olive had been forced to sleep on the stone floor in the kitchen and John Leaf confirmed that the poor child slept in filthy conditions - on 'Half a bag with a little straw'. Leaf, who became something of a local hero, and who worked for the Rushworths from March to December 1907, said he had told Mr Rushworth (who he drove to work in York each day) about the state of the children and their treatment, but he did nothing. Leaf said he had seen Olive fishing food out of a pig tub on 'Many occasions' and that the girls were always half starved. The food he was given was frequently inedible. Why had he done nothing he was asked by the defending lawyers (the Rushworths pleaded not guilty) ? He had done all he could he said, and, as has been said, he may have called in outside help eventually. He was severely reprimanded for letting Inspector Campbell into the house, and Mr Rushworth, Leaf said, told him 'he would give me £10 if I could stop this.' This seems to have been an attempt to get Leaf to give evidence for the defence (and Mrs Rushworth and her son made similar attempts) but Leaf refused, and he was sacked some two or three weeks later. (The well-known Dr W.A. Evelyn wrote to the *Herald* on 14 January applauding Leaf's action in rescuing Dora and her friend from 'white slavery'.)

During the prosecution case evidence was given of neglect and cruelty towards the girls of 'the very grossest kind' by Mrs Rushworth. There were stories of dowsing them with water, thrashing them with that 'French dog whip' and burning them with a flat iron and a red hot poker. Under examination, when she gave evidence for herself, Mrs Rushworth maintained she was being framed. Who by ? Leaf and the NSPCC were her major suspects.

Mr Rushworth was never accused of cruelty towards the children of the gross kind his wife was. But how was it possible for him to live in the same house as they did and not see that Dora and Olive were filthy and had been beaten ? Rushworth simply denied that they were filthy and suggested that the burns resulted from the children having accidents. Why did he take no notice of Leaf's protests ? Rushworth resorted to that well-known ploy of blackening your accuser's character. Leaf, he said, boozed (as he did) and was unreliable. But there was another thing. Rushworth, as secretary to the York Education Committee, was responsible, as Alderman Pearson eventually said at a meeting of the committee, for dealing 'with York citizens for failing to send children to school, while he himself had children of school age at his home as household drudges without providing education for them.' (3) How could this have happened he was asked in court ? There was no way that he, a solicitor, could be ignorant of the law. Rushworth lamely said that he thought Olive was so backward (no wonder) that she could not have been 'accommodated' anywhere. What about Dora ? Rushworth had no explanation.

The dreadful revelations about what happened to the little girls went on for several days, then findings of guilt were brought in on all the charges. The husband was fined £50; Mrs Rushworth was sentenced to nine months imprisonment in the second division. Eventually some extraordinary stories about Mrs Rushworth were published - one alleging that she had been arrested in Paris as a spy and thrown out of France. The stories suggested that all was not well with her sanity, and during her trial it had been contended that she had an insane desire to inflict cruelty on others.

During the trial of the Rushworths crowds had assembled outside the courts, putting the participants in fear, and at night the house in Poppleton had been besieged by crowds shouting insults and 'tin canning' its occupants. Rough music was a traditional way of the crowd registering its disapproval of persons - particularly in villages - who had transgressed in some way (or were thought to have done so). British history is full of such incidents, (4) and it is interesting to see it persisting in (or near) York so late. After Mrs Rushworth was sentenced she was waited for by a huge crowd, but the police smuggled her away. A special edition of the *Evening Press* had been rushed out giving the verdict on the Rushworths and there were further crowds at York railway station where Mrs Rushworth was put on a train. Vernon Wragge travelled with her, and there was another demonstration at Leeds where a crowd of women tried to get at the guilty party. She was successfully got into a cab which took her to Armley gaol.

York had not been the centre of so much national attention since the time of the by election which did so much to precipitate the Khaki Election. Just how great interest was in the Rushworth case can be gleaned from the following press report. (5)

> One effect of the trial ... was to cause an extreme pressure of work upon the telegraph officials at York Post Office. Reports of the case were telegraphed to all the principal daily newspapers in the United Kingdom, Not only was it reported in the English newspapers, but many in Scotland and Ireland published long accounts of the proceedings.

> An unusually large number of Press messages were despatched from the Post Office. The total number of words wired during the three days [the trial took] was over 80,000. The heaviest day was Friday when about 38,000 words were telegraphed. This, we believe, constitutes a record for the York Post Office, that figure not having been approached on any one previous day, not even during the visit of the British Association to York.

With Mrs Rushworth gaoled, decisions had to be made about her husband, the man who had prosecuted people for not sending their children to school while keeping Dora and Olive away. He had earlier been clerk to the School Board and when that went out of existence he had been granted a pension of £120 a year, which was suspended while he worked for the new education committee. (6) Could he be sacked? The *Press* wondered if he could - pointing out that, unlike his wife, he had only been found guilty of a misdemeanour, an offence created 'within the past few years by Act of Parliament, viz., an act of omission in not taking measures to stop an evil.' (7) The Education Committee, at which Pearson made his speech about Rushworth's hypocrisy, nevertheless decided he could be. (8) Quite clearly - they said so - many would have liked to have stopped his pension also.

Rushworth was deeply involved in education, of course, and the educational resisters continued their protests into 1908 - maybe giving a lead to the followers of Mrs Despard and Mrs How Martyn. In late February orders for non payment of (what they said) was an education rate were made against Hind, Arthur Dearlove (of course) and Brother Samuel Clack (of course), (9) but the drink question, not education, was to be predominant that year. The very papers that reported Brother Clack's and Arthur Dearlove's latest court appearances revealed the contents of the government's new licensing bill. Just before that, however, a court case in the city revealed a little more about the complex system of licensing in Edwardian Britain. It involved Norman T. Crombie, that solicitor who was then specialising in matters relating to the trade. He had been present at the Tory selection conference which chose Riley-Smith and Butcher as York's next Tory hopefuls.

Allen Davis, of The Old Number Five, Bridge Street, was prosecuted, and his premises held a six day license. Through section 49 of the Licensing Act of 1872 this meant that he paid less taxes, but had to keep closed on Sundays. Section three of a subsequent act defined Christmas Day as a Sunday, but Davis - and nearly all the other six day premises as well - had opened on Christmas Day, which in 1907 fell on a Wednesday. Crombie, acting on Davis's behalf, pointed out that his client was not charged under the provisions that defined Christmas Day as a Sunday, and contended that section 49 was not appropriate. The case could have been arguable, Crombie said, if the summons had alleged that Davis kept open in prohibited hours, but it did not, it said he had been unlawfully selling drink without a licence. ' ... how could Wednesday be regarded as a Sunday?' Crombie demanded rhetorically and went on to say that the law was an old one (it was not that old) and that 'no one [else had] had the temerity to bring a case like the Chief Constable had done.' The case would be a test case, Crombie concluded, and it was dismissed.

Who decided to prosecute Davis? The York licensing bench was predominantly of a temperance disposition, and perhaps the Chief Constable acted on their advice or demands. The Watch Committee was overwhelmingly Tory, so it seems unlikely that the initiative started there. Perhaps, then, the Chief Constable simply acted on his own initiative; or maybe he had been pressurised by the temperance organisations and the upholders of that dreadful bequest to the 20th century the Victorian Sunday. They would certainly have contended that Wednesday equalled Sunday (in 1907).

The 1908 Brewster Sessions had a familiar air about them. The Rev James Brightling of the York Evangelical Free Church Council (and an active supporter of the York Anti Vivisection Society), (10) Argles and the LVA submitted petitions and Newbald Kay represented the South Bank Citizens Association in (successfully) opposing a new off license in Queen Victoria Street. (11) Objections were also made to the renewal of the licences of: The Beehive, Peter Lane; The Engine Driver's Rest, Mount Ephraim, Holgate Road; and The Trumpet Inn, the Groves. At an adjourned meeting the bench heard details of these three places, some of which are eloquent of the economic state of parts of York, others of which illuminate aspects of the law and, in one case, demonstrate how the courts were now concerned (since 1902) with the structure and character of a property. The Engine Drivers, the Chief Constable said, had been visited no less than 17 times when no one was to be found using the place. Why ? Charles Green, the landlord, explained that since the NER had 'removed so many men from York there had been no chance of making a success of the house.' The Trumpet, the court heard, had only one room - and it should have had two - while The Beehive, a beerhouse, could only be objected to, because of its status under the Beerhouse Act of 1869, on the grounds that the buildings were unsuitable. Limericks were very much in the news at that time, (12) and Crombie quoted an old one about the Beehive (a John Smith's pub) 'which showed', he said, 'there were limericks' in the 1860s - after saying that it, too, had fallen on hard times 'in consequence of trade depression and the removal of railway men from York.' Crombie made no claims about the quality of his verse, which is just as well, and it does not appear in the marvellous anthologies of this art form compiled by G. Legman, which is not surprising (and if it had it would not have been quoted). Anyway, Crombie dared to read to the court lines which declared

> In this house we all live;
> Good liquor makes us funny;
> If you are dry,
> Step in and try,
> The flavour of our honey.

It is not known whether Crombie's versifying influenced the bench, but the Beehive, the Engine Drivers, and the Trumpet got the chop, and the Compensation Committee considered their value in June. (13) Crombie at that time, was lending his considerable talents as a public speaker to the campaign against the Licensing Bill. If the 'Goverment did not bury the Licensing Bill,' he said from one platform, 'it would bury them. They came in', he said, in a nice phrase, 'as free fooders; they were now freebooters, and he hoped the people would give them the boot freely.' Councillor Boddy, on that occasion, gave some indication of the pitch which this particular controversy had reached already (in March) when he cryptically said the bill embodied 'Hypocrisy, robbery and hatred'. (14)

Boddy's remarks about the Licensing Bill being 'robbery' were made in March 1908, after its contents were known, but that was well into the agitation against it. That had begun, in fact, before its details were known - though everyone certainly had a good idea of what they might be. (15) It has been suggested that Riley-Smith was regarded as a particularly good choice for York at that time, as he represented brewing interests, and he was campaigning against interfering with the trade (again) early in the year. In January he was the principal guest at a meeting of the Leeds LVA, and he told a sympathetic audience that the next parliamentary session would be 'memorable. They were met with a gigantic wave of Socialist-revolutionary interest', he said, graphically, 'which threatened the foundations of all property alike.' (16) The Bill did not do that, as was shown when it appeared in February, but Riley-Smith roundly condemned it out of hand as 'downright robbery'. Not only that, the Bill had also been introduced, Riley-Smith said, as a part of the government's war against the House of Lords. The peers had continued to wreck Liberal legislation sent up to them, and it was frequently said that at this point of time measures were being sent for them to reject. All to discredit the Upper House and to pave the way for a drastic reform to either abolish it or severely reduce its powers. The Licensing Bill, Riley-Smith said, was 'another item in "the filling up the cup" of the House of Lords'. (17) It might have been, but it was much more as well. The Liberals had great obligations to those in the temperance camp.

What was proposed in the Licensing Bill of 1908 ? H.H. Asquith, who was to become Prime Minister six weeks later, introduced it in what is always described as a triumphal speech on 27 February. It 'struck at the root of legislation passed by Balfour's Government', one of his biographers said, referring to the Act of 1904, 'which had for one main object the raising of the status of the Licensee. Balfour was furious about it.' (18) Balfour had set up the system of compensating licensees who had lost their houses, and four years later Asquith set about altering it. Balfour's Act, intended partly to suppress 'unnecessary' licenses, was reckoned to be proceeding too slowly, and Asquith therefore proposed to get rid of more than a third of the pubs and beer houses of England and Wales by imposing a sliding scale which would allow one licence to every 400 persons where the population averaged two to the acre, one to every 500 persons where the population was from two to 25 an acre, up to one per 1,000 in crowded cities where the population averaged over 200 to the acre. All excess licenses would be suppressed over a period of 14 years, with compensation to be shared out by a central commission. The local licensing benches would decide which places to close and, after the 14 years had elapsed, all licenses would be regarded as new and could be refused renewal without compensation. Local option, a word popularised by the Rowntrees, would come into force immediately for the issue of new licenses, should there be such things, and any area could vote itself 'dry'. Asquith also proposed some minor changes 'including stricter control of clubs', something the York LVA had been demanding for several years, 'shorter Sunday opening hours and a great increase in the power of justices, who could shut down additional public houses by negotiation, and make stringent conditions before granting any license. These might include total Sunday closing, a ban on sales to children or on the employment of women, and - a vital provision - refusal of a license to a 'tied house.' (19) All this was proposed in that long, impressive speech on 27 February, and the story of Asquith being asked for his notes for it by an admirer who wanted them as a souvenir is often told. Asquith simply handed over a scrap of paper on which was written the three words 'Too many pubs'.

Balfour accused the government of building 'upon a foundation of injustice', and

Riley-Smith's early comments on the Licensing Bill have been noted. In March a sensational by election was held at Peckham in which a Liberal majority of 2,300 was turned into a Conservative one of approximately the same size, and in York the arguments over the merits (or otherwise) of the Bill were as bitter as they were anywhere. Riley-Smith spoke at that meeting where Crombie and Boddy made their remarks. 'Mr Asquith's Bill, he said (20)

> was absurd and foolish. ... The framers of [it] had fallen into the same error as Sir William Harcourt did over the Local Veto Bill; (21) they had mistaken the temper and the character of the British people. ... If the door of his accustomed public-house was banged in his face, the Englishman would find other means of gratifying the requirements of his appetite, and he would take care to remove himself to a place that was out of the reach of the arm of the law. ... If ... the Bill was passed, 30,000 licensed victuallers, their wives, and those dependant upon them, would be suddenly cast into a state of poverty.

What Riley-Smith meant by the Englishman finding other means of gratifying his thirst was revealed in a lecture on the history of licensing which he gave to the York branch of the Junior Imperial and Constitutional League reported in the *Herald* on 28 November. The Bill, if passed, he said, would transfer drinking 'from the licensed and controlled public-house to the unlicensed and uncontrolled club, [and] retard rather than ... hasten the progress the country is ... making in the direction of increased sobriety'. This may or not have been true, but it was all good knockabout stuff, and he went on the stump. He was in demand as a speaker at places like Middlesborough and Darlington, and in September was chairman of platform No 12 (sharing it with Will Dyson of *The People*) at the huge Hyde Park rally called by opponents of the Bill. (22) (Other speakers from York were George Woolford and Councillor R.B. Lambert.)

The Tories waged a huge campaign against Asquith's Bill, seemingly unaware of the damages that rejection might have for them. They were jubilant at the results of the Peckham by election where a Unionist recaptured a seat lost in 1906, and Wragge and Boddy headed a huge crowd assembled at the York Conservative Club to await that result. (23) But in York, as might be expected, there was tremendous support for Asquith. In March, for example, the York Free Church Council publicly declared its support for a measure which, it said, would restore the freedom of action 'of the Licensing Justices so ruthlessly destroyed by the Bill of 1904.' (24) A few days earlier the York Wesleyans had declared their support, as had the workers connected with the Central Mission, Peaseholm Green. (25) The Society of Friends acted similarly, supporting resolutions proposed by Theodore H. Rowntree, (26) and the 25th annual meeting of the Liberal party declared that 'The Licensing Bill is a bold and statesmanlike endeavour to cope with a gigantic evil, which, whatever be the fate of it, does honour to the Government that introduced it.' (27) Their MP agreed. After saying that

Balfour's Bill had been 'a bargain ... between the plutocrats of the liquor trade and the Tory party' Greenwood declared that 'The [Licensing] Bill, once it got on to the Statute book - as it would do - would never be taken off again, for progressive measures were never replaced.' Greenwood's optimism was ill-founded.

In April the supporters of the Licensing Bill, with Newbald Kay, the passive resister, particularly prominent among them, decided to coordinate their activities. A York Citizen's Council was formed, and the Archbishop (who refused) was asked to become a vice president.(28) Kay, K.E.T. Wilkinson, Councillor R. Petty and S.H. Davies addressed meetings with the latter saying the bill was 'a real temperance measure' which enabled magistrates to close pubs at election times, though it was weak on clubs. T. Storey at one of the Council's gatherings said that feelings about the Bill had got to a pitch where the Tadcaster Tower Company demanded to know whether their suppliers were for or against Asquith. (29) Later in the summer the Council conducted a village campaign, during which A.P. Mawson and Harry Miles were prominent. (30)

What happened to Asquith's Licensing Bill of 1908 ? It provoked immense opposition, as has been shown, and it undoubtedly heightened political feeling and set the scene for dramatic events that were to come. Or perhaps it would be more correct to say its rejection did, because the Lords - despite the fact that it could have been said to have had features about it that were of a financial nature - rejected it. The third reading in the Commons, had been completed on 20 November and the Bill then became the responsibility, in effect, of Lord Lansdowne, the Tory leader in the Lords. He was urged by King Edward ('the very antithesis of a teetotaller') to amend the Bill rather than reject it, but the Tory peers would have none of that, and at a meeting in the ballroom of Lansdowne House they overwhelmingly decided on rejection. After three days of debate, during which some unbelievably silly remarks were made, the Lords divided 'and at 7.20 p.m. on Friday, 27th November ... the Bill that was to crown eighty years of effort by the temperance movement was thrown out by 272 votes to 96. It was the House of Lord's last great triumph.' (31) It was a decision as stupid as some of their Lordships' remarks. Lucy Masterman recorded how one famous government politician viewed it; it meant that now the government would have to attack the Lords head on. Lucy was dining at the House of Commons and found herself sitting next to Winston Churchill. '"He was perfectly furious at the rejection of the Licensing Bill by the Lords, stabbed at his bread, would hardly speak"', she recorded in her diary. '"We shall send them up such a Budget in June as shall terrify them", he thundered; "they have started the class war, they had better be careful."' (32) In York the announcement of the Lords' act was splendidly stage managed. Riley-Smith was giving his lecture on the history of the licensing laws to the Junior Imperial and Constitutional League when he broke off, having just been given the news. ' ... the end had come', he said, and 'no one was better satisfied than he was.'

The Lords had rejected other Liberal measures, but they had had the good sense to leave 'labour' legislation alone and they also desisted from interfering with the Old Age Pensions Bill. This was separate from the Finance Bill, and was Asquith's responsibility.

Asquith had been Chancellor of the Exchequer in the Campbell-Bannerman government and he introduced the budget in 1908, even although Lloyd George now held that office. In 1907 Asquith had differentiated between earned and unearned income, and, thanks largely to the efforts of R.B. Haldane at the War Office, had a surplus of over £5 million. Asquith decided to demonstrate that the Liberal policy of 'retrenchment' was not being pursued solely for its own sake, but also as 'the concomitant of Reform' and he decided to set aside some of the surplus for non contributory old-age pensions to be introduced the following year. (33) Pensions had been spoken of for many years, but the scheme of 1908 (the pensions were to be paid from 1 January 1909) was modest by any standards. The *Evening Press* explained the sliding scale of relief to its readers, and the rules and regulations that entitled a person to a payment. (34) The pensioner had to be over 70, and must have been a British subject for at least 20 years. He was disqualified if he (or she) was in receipt of poor relief; had habitually failed to work; was a lunatic; or was convicted of a criminal offence. Payment would not be paid to a person in receipt of an annual income of over £31.10.0 and the largest sum that could be received was 5s. The scale declared that where the pensioner did not receive £21 he would get 5s. Receiving from £21 to £23.12s.6d. he would receive 4s. Getting from £23.12s.6d. to £26.5s.0d. entitled him to 3s. Receiving an income between £26.5s.0d. and £28.17s.6d. would give him 2s. An income from £28.17s.6d. to the maximum entitled him to 1s.

This meant that, in weekly terms,

> An income of 8s.1d. gave a full entitlement.
> An income of 9s.1d. produced a pension of .... 4s.
> A weekly income of 10s.1d. produced a pension of .... 3s.
> 11s.1d. entitled a claimant to .... 2s.
> With an income of 12s.1d. a person could get .... 1s.

It will not escape the notice of anyone that a person on full entitlement could receive no more than 13s.1d. a week - and what could this buy was highlighted in York in 1905, and of that more later. Did a couple living together both become entitled to a full pension ? They did not. 'In imitation of the income tax's penalties on marriage, the pension for two old married people living together was thriftily cut down to 7s.6d.' (35)

How many people in York would be over 70 when the pensions became payable, and how many would qualify for aid ? The question fascinated the press, and in September Thomas Anderson went to an obvious source for an answer. At the time of the last census, he said, there were 2,016 persons over the age of 70. Deduct those who would be ineligible for having received poor relief (and Anderson was a poor law official) and this would bring the figure down to 1,664. What of those in possession 'of an income in excess of the maximum' allowed? This was difficult to estimate, Anderson said, and guessed they might be a third of the total, though some said a half would not apply. (36) In early September the city corporation discussed the implications of the new Act. Three local pensions sub committees were appointed, and in December it was stated that there would be 500 pensioners in York. (37) When the final adjudications had been made, and on the day that the pensions were first paid out, it was revealed that 827 claims had been successfully made in the city. (38) The *Press* told its readers what this momentous innovation meant (nationally) in sheer weight of coin.

Claims admitted	528,000
To be paid today [1 January] (say)	500,000
Average pension	4s
Amount required	£100,000
Approximate weight (in silver coin)	13 tons

How had the York politicians received the Old Age Pensions Bill ? The Liberals, of course, welcomed it, coupling it with the Licensing and Small Holdings Bills of 1908 as being among the major legislative innovations of the government so far. Faber, however, had opposed state pensions long before Asquith's positive proposals of 1907 and '8. In March 1906 he had attacked what he said were the government's intentions and drawn attention to what he thought was the dilemma of its adherence to concepts of both retrenchment and reform. (39) Payment for Members was not started for another five years, but Faber clearly thought it was imminent. (40) ' ... the first movement in the direction of retrenchment', he said oddly was the payment of Members. It means, he went on

£200,000 a year, but what is that for the party of retrenchment ?" ... Then there is the franking of letters and "free breakfasts for school children." Old-age pensions amounting to twenty-six millions a year at 5s. a week for two millions [sic] people was another item of retrenchment. "I say", asserted Mr Faber, "as a man of business and finance, that this nation cannot find the money ... "'

When the Old Age Pensions Bill was before parliament Faber had practically abandoned York and was concentrating on his new constituency of Clapham, (41) but Butcher had been reselected to stand in his old constituency. He had opposed old age pensions when Joseph Chamberlain spoke of them earlier in the century, and in 1907 and '8 he was busy defending the House of Lords' policy of wrecking the government's proposals. He left most of the speaking on the Licensing Bill to Riley-Smith and devoted much time to the problem of unemployment - contending that fiscal reform was the only remedy for that evil. What did he think of Asquith's plans for (really rather niggardly) state pensions ? He had modified his views a little, he said, but he did not like what was being proposed in 1908. Nobody would object to a scheme which did not 'impose a crushing burden of taxation upon the people', he said, while leaving few in doubt that he thought this one would. He went on to say that he thought it wrong that the thrifty and the unthrifty should be treated alike, then made a criticism with which few today would disagree (surely). 'It was very hard,' Butcher said, 'that the sick pay or superannuation which a man got from his friendly society should be reckoned against him when he came to ask for his old age pension'. (42) Edith Milner, no doubt, would have, like Faber, lumped old age pensions with free school meals for the needy as evidence of the decline of a once great nation. (43)

Just after the details of the level of old age pensions and how to apply for them were made known to York's elderly, the plight of the city's unemployed and underemployed was highlighted yet again. Winter was approaching, and elsewhere there had been serious incidents arising from demonstrations by those out of work and those sympathising with them. Nothing like that had happened in York, but things were no better there than they had been in the years since the ending of the war, and the Distress Committee over which J.M. Hogge presided reported early in October that the expected 'stress of unemployment' had 'already set in.' (44) There was now a branch of the National Right to Work Council in York, (45) but what modest relief measures there were in the city were as before. The Distress Committee detailed them early in the New Year, just as appeals for funds for the soup kitchen went out. (46) Men had been found work road sweeping; some had been found part-time work at the Post Office; and Rowntrees had employed 22 men making a playground in Palmer Lane, Hungate. (47) In addition to this men had been employed dumping refuse from the municipal destructor on the site of the Municipal School for Girls (Queen Anne's) then being built at Sycamore Terrace. This had been taken there by barge and some 2,079 tons had been delivered and dumped in the three months before the Distress Committee issued its annual report. 1,170 dinner tickets had also been distributed. A summary of the Committee's report spoke of the city in 1908.

> The following general observations were made regarding York. The conditions of industry were bad, and there was little employment for men of the unskilled and casual labour class. There are no factories in the district, and building works were restricted. Work was provided by the Council in digging and levelling land, and laying out a bowling green, with an average period of three days to three weeks work per man at 5d. per hour. The quality of the work was very inferior, notwithstanding extra supervision, this was largely due to the physical incapacity of the men.

The problems of distress and lack of employment were highlighted in ways other than through the official reports from Hogge and his colleagues. The soup kitchen, as has been said, was at work again, free breakfasts (as well as school meals) were being provided, and in February the *Press* carried an editorial in which it revealed that the plight of the unemployed had led to some suicides in the city. (48) PC Clarkson, in a case at the York magistrates court involving Thomas Cunningham, an eleven year old who was prosecuted for begging, revealed that many youngsters like Tom loitered about 'near Terry's [restaurant], some in their bare feet.' (Young Cunningham was threatened with the birch for his behaviour.) (49) Another case involving Arthur and Lily Chapman, who lived in Bootham Row, revealed a tragic state of affairs. They were prosecuted for neglecting their child and during the hearing it was revealed that the husband had a wage of 18s. 3d. a week - but had been on short time! In February and March there was a severe bout of bad weather which peaked when nearly six inches of snow fell in less than 24 hours, causing chaos. It was the most severe storm York had seen since 1879, but it was welcomed by the unemployed and those temporarily laid off. Thousands [sic] 'clamoured for work at the Foss Islands depot' it was reported, and over 500 were engaged (making a total work force of nearly 900 working on clearing the streets). So desperate were the men for work that it looked as if trouble might ensue. A report said that

> The scene at Foss Islands ... was one of great animation. Thousands of unemployed men were crowded at the gates of the cleansing department, and when the gates were opened there was an ugly rush, which might have proved serious. So anxious were the men to secure employment, and thinking that the first few might only be favoured, each strove to get in front of his neighbour.

Incidents on the North Eastern Railway also, at this time, showed how desperate men could become (at least according to a critic) and how they were, still, at the mercy of their employers. During 1908 the NER's conciliation scheme was a constant source of discussion and negotiation, while many employed at the carriage works in York were on short time (and having to go into work when they were not paid it will be recalled). Towards the end of the year a dispute broke out among the waggon builders at New Shildon over the price the men were to get for a new order of some 400 vehicles, and the management dug in its heels and moved the work to York, where men were desperate. What was the result ? The waggons in December were being built at York at '24s. - or 2s.6d. below a living wage' according to someone who should have known. (50) This was J. Bermingham, the organising secretary of the General Railway Workers' Union, who made some brave and impassioned appeals to railwaymen at lunch time, factory gate meetings. It seems that men had drifted out of the union. Out of 100 waggon builders at York there were now only five in 'the Society' Bermingham said. 'York had ceased to be democratic', he went on, 'the autocrat had got hold of York and was squeezing the life out of its [sic] dupes.' He had been told, Bermingham said, 'that the York men could hardly make their salt upon this transaction ... They deserved the condemnation of the whole of the railway workers throughout the country. ... The management were trying ... to defeat the men ... .' For 'ten or eleven weeks', Bermingham said the York men had been knocking about the shops on "short time," waiting for something to turn up which would enhance their wage-earning capacity ... The company had kept them in the gas oven for a long time, and had squeezed all the substance out of them before they were asked to take on the present job. He cried shame upon them ... York [was a] ... black spot ... He hoped the men at York would ere long be sitting in sackcloth and ashes repenting of what they had done ...

Bermingham may have been right about management tactics, and he was undoubtedly right about the York men accepting work from Shildon. But it was near Christmas, they were on short time and there were no other jobs in York. It must have appeared to many of them that maybe they were 'defeated', in spite of all the talk about conciliation boards and better labour relations on the railways. The Lord Mayor recognised the hopeless plight of many of his fellow citizens and pledged himself to do what he could during his term of office to help them.

James Birch, a councillor, one of three with the same surname, was chosen as Lord Mayor in 1908-9. (51) He was a plumber, a Liberal, who had last fought an election in 1910, when he was returned for Micklegate along with J.H. Hartley. Birch was an extremely attractive personality and early in his mayoralty he announced that he would not hold an official inaugural banquet as was the tradition, but that he would give the money that would have been spent on it to a fund set up to relieve the poor. (52) As a means of swelling the coffers of that fund a mammoth whist drive involving hundreds of people was held in the De Grey Rooms (53) over several days in January. On one evening alone 1,056 players took part, (54) but the event was not without its critics and a nice little row about it developed involving J.M. Hogge, who the *Herald* called the 'bletherer in chief' of the York Corporation.

A similar fund raising event to the York Civic Whist Drive for the Unemployed was to be held in the north east and it was discussed in the Newcastle Presbytery. Some of the clerics assembled there were hostile to it, and a Rev J.B. Cantley spoke disparagingly of the York event as 'a huge public gamble' which should be condemned. (55) Hogge attacked Cantley in his usual blunt way, then the roof fell in on him, with critics having a field day at his expense and pointing to his rather ambiguous attitudes to such things as betting. Hogge welcomed the whist drive because it would produce money for the Distress Committee, of which he was chairman, but he was also a very active dignitary in the Anti Gambling League. That spoil-sport organisation, Hogge's opponents rapidly pointed out, had blown hot and cold in condemning the current craze for the limerick competitions which some papers were running. These required some skill (perhaps greater than the composer of the one Norman Crombie quoted to the licensing bench) newspaper correspondents pointed out. How could Hogge condemn them, yet support the De Grey Rooms event ? He had angrily demanded a little earlier that the Corporation should stop advertising in the *Herald* on the grounds that it was prejudiced, and its editor must have welcomed such an early attempt to get his own back on the man who C.A. Thompson called the 'well-informed world-wonder from Castlegate'. (56) He took it and did indeed expose Hogge's inconsistencies. (Another great concern of the anti-gambling lobby in these years were the 'football coupons' which had just made their appearance.) (57)

When Birch told the Corporation of his decision to make helping the poor a feature of his mayoralty he was speaking to the Council newly elected in November 1908. What had happened then? Had the reforms of that year brought support to the Liberals? Did they edge a little nearer to getting control of the city? They did not. The Tories in fact made a gain of one, though losing one councillor to an independent, (58) and Labour lost one of its two remaining seats on the Council.

In Bootham W.H. Sessions (Liberal), who had been returned only a short time before at a by election, was returned without a contest along with the Tory Henry Hopkins. In Monk two Liberals were allowed a walkover, and in Walmgate W.H. Birch (Liberal) and Frank Rickaby (a genuine Independent) beat Councillor R. Richardson, but in the so called Liberal stronghold of Micklegate, the largest ward, with an electorate of 3,305, the Tories made a remarkable gain. (59) There Dr Sanderson Long (1,305 votes) beat J.B. Morrell (1,021 votes) into second place, ignominiously ousting A.P. Mawson (844 votes). With his defeat only J.R. Hartley (Hogge's Sancho Panza the *Herald* called him) represented Labour on the Council.

The most active of the Tory candidates in 1908 was that R.B. Lambert who had taken such a prominent part in the struggle against the Licensing Bill. He had been returned at the top of the poll in Guildhall. His Tory running mate then, who came third, was a man who was to make a great impact on York politics in the years to come. This was his first appearance as a politician. He was Henry Rhodes Brown, who, in the Great War, became the scourge of the local conscientious objectors.

With the Licensing and Old Age Pension bills as a backcloth, what did Lambert (and Sanderson Long) concentrate on during their municipal campaigns? A great deal of argument was then going on about the projected removal of St Margaret's archway from Exhibition Square, but Lambert spent most of his time in defying his party's line and continuing his objection to the Corporation taking over the tramways. Despite the results of the poll of 1902 he pointed out, quite reasonably, the Corporation had decided to take them over. Lambert wanted another poll before this was done. (60) Vernon Wragge, the chairman of the Council committee dealing with the tramways, came under criticism at about this time when a Mr Arthur Humphreys wrote to the press saying that an 'Electro-bus' company had made an offer to run vehicles in York which had not been considered. Wragge denied that this was so, but a colleague, Alderman Norman Green, said it was. The truth seems to have been that an offer was made to Vernon Wragge which was not passed on to the committee. (61) Rhodes Brown agreed with Lambert about the trams, saying they should be run by a private company contracted to buy its electricity from the York generator. ' ... he thought municipalisation of every kind was a plank of Socialism', Rhodes Brown said, 'and he was emphatically against it.'

Lambert and Rhodes Brown also made the standard demands for economy and low rates during their campaign of 1908. His 'chief aim', the latter said, 'his only pledge, would be economy.' Lambert said York needed new industries, and the only way to get them he contended, was by lowering the rates. An interesting experiment in creating a new enterprise was in fact taking place when he made his remarks.

There was still a modest amount of river traffic in 1908, but in the autumn it was announced that the London and York Steamship Company would inaugurate a direct sea service between Old Ebor and the capital. Hitherto, the initial announcement said, goods had to be transhipped at either Goole or Hull and thereafter brought up on barges to York, with a consequent rise in transportation costs. Now a regular service would start from London to York on Fridays or Saturdays. (62) In December the company's new steamer *The Repetor* arrived at the King's Staith, the largest vessel ever to have appeared in the city at that time. She was a schooner rigged steamer of 250 tons burthen, with a crew of seven. She had been built by Messrs John Crow Ltd of Sunderland, was driven 'by compound engines of the latest type, and steam[ed] at $9\frac{1}{2}$ knots per hour. She [was] built with ballast tanks, and [was] 109 feet long by 22 feet beam.' (63) The company announced that it hoped to have a second steamer by the early days of 1909.

Almost as soon as the London and York company announced its regular services, a competitor appeared. This was the City of York Steamship Company which announced a service using the *S.S. Glenco* from Butler's Wharf, Southwark each Wednesday and from the King's Staith each Saturday. The company had offices at 1a Low Ousegate. The *Glenco* arrived in York for the first time on 24 November.

An acrimonious press correspondence broke out between supporters of the two companies, with some allegations of sharp practice levelled at one of them. (64) During that correspondence it was revealed that there was great dissatifaction (real or imagined) with the rates for carriers being charged by the NER, and that the steamers were hoped to effect reductions all round. However it was generally felt that unloading facilities were inadequate and great demands were made for shedding to be built on the King's Staith. The Council was criticised for not acting quickly, but this seems a little unfair as a shed being constructed out of corrugated and galvanised iron was nearly complete at the end of the first week of March. The contractors were A.J. Main and Company of the Clydesdale Ironworks; the building was 35 feet by 20 feet; and the cost of it was £108.

Another form of transport concerned the citizens of York, and in October 1908 the splendidly named Ponsonby Moore Crossthwaite presided over an enquiry about it. Traction engines working in and to and from the city were a cause of great complaint, and some of those complaints have already been mentioned. Some streets had been prohibited to these vehicles under the Locomotive Act of 1898 and some had been restricted between the hours of 9am and 5pm. Complaints about the nuisance and the damage done by the engines were the subject of memorials presented to the Council in 1906, and two years later the authority had decided to seek a change in the by-laws to regulate their use further. J.R. MacDonald of the National Traction Owners and Users' Association gave evidence to the enquiry and much was said about whether York's bridges could carry these vehicles and the extra cost incurred by businessmen in having to use devious routes because of the restrictions already imposed. R.B. Lambert, who lived in High Ousegate, had his house lit by electricity, and he told the enquiry that each time an engine went by it broke the filaments of his light bulbs, and many others described, in what turned out to be a very jolly enquiry, how they were shaken in their beds in the early morning by the comings and goings of the 'leviathans'. George Sharp, president of the York Master Builders' Association, however, told the enquiry how efficient they were compared with horses and carts. They cut the cost of haulage, Sharp said, by no less than a half. (65)

George Sharp was a partner in the building firm of Parker and Sharp, and they had carried out prestigious work in the city including the new law courts in Clifford Street, the filters and reservoirs for the York Water Works Company and the Castle Mills lock. Sharp had political ambitions and in early 1909 he got an opportunity to stand for the Council. A vacancy on the Aldermanic bench was caused by the retirement of W.A. Pearson and it was decided that James Birch, the Lord Mayor, should fill the vacancy. Sharp and Charles E. Tee, a baker, and a Liberal, who had come fourth in the election for Guildhall in November, contested the vacancy in Micklegate. Dr Sanderson Long had captured a Labour seat there in November and Sharp beat Tee there in January (1,221 votes to 979). (66) He accused Tee of being a 'nominee of a large firm who [sic] sought to be monopolists in the city of York' and declared 'He was not a keen partisan himself', but then went on to show he was, making much use of a little local difficulty one of the MPs was experiencing at the time. Hamar Greenwood, Sharp claimed would be sent packing as soon as a general election was held. Although he was 'not a keen partisan', he went on, 'he was a strong Churchman, and when Mr Greenwood went out of his way to insult the Church people of York and utter blasphemies against the leaders of the Church he made one of the greatest mistakes any man could make.' What had Greenwood done? In a comprehensive speech to the Liberal party during the Licensing Bill campaign Greenwood had poked fun at what he said was the undignified scramble among prelates of the established church to become Archbishop, and said it was strange that H.H. Asquith the Prime Minister should be involved, as he was a Congregationalist. (67) His remarks brought forth many angry letters of complaint including one from A.P. Purey Cust and another from Edith Milner. (68) (What had prompted Greenwood's remarks, was the fact that the Archbishopric of York had become vacant.) (69)

Greenwood had come under fire for mocking the higher dignitaries of the Church of England and Hogge, who was never far away from controversy anyway, had angered the likes of C.A. Thompson for attacking the Rev Cantley. Another Liberal was also at the centre of controversy in 1908 - unfairly as it turned out. This was Seebohm Rowntree, and the controversy had to do with some recommendations from the York Health and Housing Reform Association that were certainly well meant.

The York Health and Housing Reform Association produced a chart for use by the poorer sections of the community which an ILP member dubbed the 'minimum scientific starvation diet' sheet. It was thought that it was produced by Seebohm Rowntree, but it was actually the work of S.H. Davies, and it claimed to show that 'a working man' could 'supply all bodily needs' for himself, his wife and three children for 12s. 9d. a week! *The Daily News* thought that what was suggested was an 'ample diet' and Edwin Gray said 'The dietary ... will supply just sufficient nourishment to keep a family of 5 (three children, ages 11, 8, and 5) in full health.' The costs in the diet sheet, Gray said, were estimated at the prices prevailing in the autumn of 1907, and he realised they had since gone up - and that many families had to live on £1 a week or less. F.A. Brain, the ILP member mentioned above (70) analysed what was in the diet: skim milk at 1¹/₂d. a quart; scrap beef at 4¹/₂d. a pound; dripping bones; six ounces of 4d. jam (for a family of five); ¹/₂ pound of 3d. figs; tea at 1s.3d.; and mutton at 4¹/₂d. a pound. Why 'should the wealth producers of this country be trained to stint and starve' Brain asked , adding that he had experienced poverty amid plenty personally. W.A. Fowler of Heworth also attacked the chart and a B. Lasker said that it demonstrated - as it certainly did - 'that for the lowest classes of unskilled labour the wages actually paid in York at the present time are entirely insufficient to maintain a family (71) in physical efficiency and reasonable comfort.' (72)

One reader wrote to the press saying that he had adopted the Housing Association's diet sheet. 'I am working for only small wages', he said, 'but since my wife adopted the diet table we have been able to go to Scarborough on Whit-Monday and had a few shillings at the weekend.' If he or they really did so with a family of five, then they were remarkable administrators, particularly when what another perceptive critic pointed out is taken into account. The chart had been worked out wrongly, he said, because the figures were given for standard measures - and working class people did not buy in those quantities. 'A poor man can only afford to buy an ounce of tea at a time', he wrote, 'and pays at least 6d. per pound more for the convenience.' This was a valid point, and one which should be taken into account in any effort to determine working class standards of living. The writer also said that the poor working man bought his coal in stones, so putting the price up from 19s.6d. to £1.8s.0d. a ton.

At the 1909 annual meeting of the Health and Housing Reform Association, reported in the *Evening Press* of 17 March, Seebohm Rowntree spoke of the diet chart and was at pains to correct some misunderstandings about it. He also gave some figures for wages and standards in York which it seems reasonable to assume that careful investigator had produced fairly recently (that is they were not those he had collected for *Poverty* nearly a decade earlier). The Association chart, Rowntree said, did not detail amounts deemed sufficient to feed a family of five properly - it was simply a guide to the best way 12s.9d. could be spent. He knew only too well of the appalling suffering in York. He agreed with Lasker and said that

> As the result of investigations in York he had found that unskilled working class families were actually living on food 25 per cent. below that which was necessary for the maintenance of mere physical efficiency. Trained artisans were receiving just about enough, while families of the middle classes were receiving 15 per cent. more than was necessary for physical efficiency ... the standard of living of the unskilled classes alluded to was *25 per cent. less than that of the paupers in the workhouses, and 29 per cent. less than convicts [got] in our English prisons.* (My italics.)

How families on low incomes or short time managed to exist at all is a constant source of amazement, but from the turn of the century there had been a growth in the number of outlets selling a hot nutritious and (one hopes) relatively cheap food which might have done a little to help the poor. The number of fried fish shops had increased in York from 15 in 1901, to 37 in 1905 (when there was one in the Shambles), to 46 in 1909. (73) Perhaps it might be inferred from the case of Thomas Henry Sanderson that this kind of food was reasonably priced - that is if market forces worked as they should have. Sanderson had a fried fish shop at 12, Lord Mayor's Walk, and in August 1908 he failed, owing, he said, to 'severe competition, price increases, and illness.' (74)

As the examination of Sanderson showed, prices were rising in the early years of the Liberal government and wages may have risen a little, though that seems unlikely. While there are reports of council officials, electricity company officials and a few privileged groups getting rises, there seems to be few of working men getting substantial increases, if indeed they got anything. (75) The railwaymen got some minor awards, but for many of them (certainly if their union leaders are to be believed) they were worse off because of bad piece rates. What was the extent of the price rises in these years which made life even harder for many ? The Cooperative Wholesale Society produced some comparative figures which included tea and sugar, the duties on which had been reduced by the Liberals. (76) Coal prices, the CWS said, had gone up by over 33 per cent since 1908 and cotton manufactured goods had gone up by 25 per cent between 1898 and 1906, then gone down a little since. A table included the following. (77)

	1898 Per lb	1908 Per lb
Bacon and Hams	4.96d	6.15d
Butter	11.35d	13.08d
Tea	16.17d	15.65d
Sugar	1.49d	1.86d
Cheese	5.24d	6.68d
Flour	1.39d	1.29d

In 1908, and again in 1913, government reports were published on the *Cost of Living of the Working Classes* which contained information about York and the rise of prices, wages, rents and so on. (78) The second of them showed that between 1905 and 1912, while rents remained steady, wages rose only a little (skilled builders +1; labourers 0; compositors +3;) and retail prices went up alarmingly (meat + 12; other foods +16; coal +24). An overall prices index of the earlier report, compared York with the capital and other towns and cities.

	Rent	Prices	Rent and Prices Combined
London	100	100	100
York	53	96	87
Wigan	50	88	80

Wage tables using the same comparisons were given

	Building		Engineering		Furnishing	Printing
	Skilled Men	Labourers	Skilled Men	Labourers		
London	100	100	100	100	100	100
York	85	89	83	-	-	79
Wigan	95	93	84	79	-	83

The above table compared wage rates with London. What actual levels prevailed in York when the government investigators gathered their statistics ? The following examples show that when they were in full time work (and the builders lost a great deal of time in these years - and indeed for many years afterwards) they were reasonably well-off and easily able to afford the city's entertainment.

Weekly wages in York

	Occupation	Wages in s.
Building	Bricklayers, Plasterers	39.9
	Masons	37.2
	Carpenters, Joiners	36.5
	Plumbers	30.4
	Painters	30.11
	Labourers	24.9 and 26.6
Engineering	Fitters	33
	Turners	33
	Smiths	33

Information was also gathered and tabulated about working class housing. Twelve per cent of working class housing it was said was 'back to back', but building of that kind had been prohibited by a by-law since 1870. The bulk of these properties were two storey houses, there were few cellars in the city, and no sub letting.

Working class housing in York

Size of Houses	Number	% of working class Houses	% of total Houses
One room	284	2.4	1.8
Two rooms	1,401	12.1	9.2
Three rooms	1,264	10.9	8.3
Four rooms	4,501	33.9	29.5
Five rooms	3,607	31.2	24.3

What of rents ?

Working class rents in York

Size of houses	Rent per week in s.
Two rooms	2.3
Three rooms	3s 6d - 4s
Four rooms (older type)	3s 10d - 5s 3d
Four rooms (newer type)	5s 6d - 6s 3d
Five rooms	6s 3d - 7s 9d

Frequently (particularly from organisations like the Health and Housing Reform Association) figures were given about the number of empty houses in York. The first of the government reports also did so, saying that these amounted to 796 in March 1906, and mentioning that the removal of the NER men to Darlington had had deleterious effects on York's economy.

A great deal has been said about wage rates, prices and rents. The first of the two government reports of the pre-wars years gave a table relating average incomes, size of families and expenditure on food on a national basis. It showed that as incomes rose the percentage spent on food, naturally, went down.

	Under 23s	23s and under 30s
Average weekly income	21s 4^1/2d.	26s 11^1/2d.
Average children at home	3.1	3.3
Total expenditure on food	14s 4^3/4d.	17s 10^1/4d.

1. There were two recent Prevention of Cruelty to Children Acts: 57 and 58 Victoria cap 41; and 4 Edward 7, cap 15, 1904
2. The proceedings in the Rushworth trial are reported in *Herald* 10, 11 and 13 January 1908 and *Press* 9, 10, 11 and 13 January 1908
3. *Herald* 18 January 1908. See also letter to the same effect in the same issue
4. On rough music see eg the interesting account by W.R. Meyer, 'The Huntingdon Charivari' in *Cambridge Local History Council Bulletin* No 34, 1979. The *Press* 5 September 1906 reported

a lovely case involving rough music in Swansea
5. *Herald* 13 January 1908
6. *Press* 16 January 1908
7. *Ibid* 21 January 1908
8. *Herald* 18 January 1908
9. *Press* 27 February 1908
10. For a meeting of the Society at Holgate Hill House, Henry Tennant's residence, see eg *Ibid* 1 April 1908. Arnold Rowntree was a supporter.
11. Brewster Sessions proceedings in 1908 reported eg in *Ibid* 11 February, 11 March 1908.
12. The Anti Gambling League and other organisations were regularly protesting at the 'Limerick Competitions' (for cash prizes) which were being run by some popular magazines and newspapers.
13. *Press* 10 June 1908
14. *Ibid* 27 March 1908. The occasion was the annual dinner of the LVA. *The Licensed Victuallers Official Annual, 1906*, subtitled "The Blue Book of the Trade" describes Boddy as Councillor W. Boddy, Auctioneer, The Estate Sale Rooms, 4, Lendal, and secretary of the York LVA
15. A Licensing Bill had been announced in the King's speech for 1907, but it was postponed.
16. *Press* 24 January 1908. Speech by Riley-Smith
17. *Ibid* 28 February 1908.
18. B.E.C. Dugdale, *Arthur James Balfour* (1936) p 29
19. Longmate *op.cit.* pp 248-49.
20. *Press* 27 March 1908.
21. Sir William Harcourt, the Chancellor of the Exchequer, had introduced a Liquor Traffic (Local Control) Bill in 1873. It never received a second reading.
22. *Press* 23 and 25 September 1908
23. *Ibid* 25 March 1908
24. *Ibid* 28 March 1908.
25. *Ibid* 26 March 1908.
26. *Ibid* 13 March 1908.
27. *Ibid* 27 June 1908. Greenwood's statement which follows from *Herald* 6 November 1908.
28. *Press* 3 April 1908.
29. *Ibid* 13 and 14 May 1908.
30. *Ibid* 12 June 1908.
31. Longmate *op.cit.* p 256. On Landsdowne and the Licensing Bill see Lord Newton, *Lord Landsdowne A Biography* (1929)
32. Quoted S. Ross, *Asquith* (New York 1976) p 109.
33. *Ibid* p 80
34. *Press* 3 and 24 September 1908.
35. Ensor *op.cit.* p 408
36. *Press* 1 September 1908.
37. *Ibid* 3 September and 4 December 1908.
38. *bid* 1 January 1909.
39. *Ibid* 24 March 1906.
40. This is rather strange because payment of Members was really triggered off by the famous 'Osborne Judgement'. The Walthamstow branch of the ASRS sued the union through W.V. Osborne, alleging that the union's levying of compulsory contributions for Labour party purposes (the party paid MPs from them) was illegal. Osborne's contentions were upheld in the Court of Appeal on 28 November 1908, and by the House of Lords on 21 December 1909.
41. See eg *Press* 7 January 1909.
42. *Ibid* 11 June 1908.
43. Edith resigned from her position of ruling councillor of her branch of the Primrose League at about this time. She continued to write reactionary letters to the newspapers, but she was 'into' preparations for the York Historical Pageant which was being prepared for 1909. Perhaps this was a reason for her resignation. See *Ibid* 16 December 1908. There is a photograph of her, from the collection of Hugh Murray, in *Gun Fire* No 10 (no date)
44. *Press* 3 October 1908.
45. *Ibid* 30 October 1908.
46. *Ibid* 27 January 1909.
47. *Ibid* 23 November 1908, 22 January 1909. The Dean of York, A.P. Purey Cust, wrote to the press

at this time saying that because of winter coming, and with growing unemployment, a public works programme should be started. He wanted the walls round the castle demolished (they had been ridiculed from the day they were put up, he said) and a walkway built with the stone going from Lendal to Baile Hill. *Ibid* 29 September 1908. The government issued returns relating to all the Distress Committees in England and Wales in the summer of 1908. For a summary of them see *Ibid* 25 August 1908.

48. *Ibid* 2 February 1909. The case of Joseph Dale, aged 38, was particularly tragic.
49. *Ibid* 2 and 7 September 1908. It was reported that the magistrates had ordered six strokes of the birch, and this prompted a furious and justified letter to the press from J.T. Mahoney, who complained about 'that malady (peculiar to the genus homo only) called flagellomania.' In actual fact Tom had not been birched. He had said he was begging to get enough to go to the Opera House incidentally. (The Chapman case and the incidents at Foss Islands reported in *Ibid* 4 February and 4 March 1909.)
50. *Ibid* 17 and 18 December 1908.
51. The other two were W.H. and F.W.
52. *Press* 9 November 1908.
53. Moved there because the Exhibition Buildings had been declared unsafe.
54. *Press* 13 January 1909.
55. *Ibid*
56. *Ibid* 28 December 1908.
57. For prosecutions involving them at, eg, Hyde and Consett see *Ibid* 5 and 12 January 1909.
58. In Walmgate, see later.
59. Details of the candidates and results can be seen in eg *Press* 26 October and 3 November 1908
60. *Ibid* 13, 20 and 23 October 1908.
61. See *Ibid* 26 and 30 November 1908.
62. Advertisements in eg *Ibid* 6 and 26 November 1908.
63. *Ibid* 22 December 1908.
64. See eg the letter from J.T. Clarke in *Herald* 24 November 1908, also *Press* 22 December 1908, and subsequent issues. The building of the Kings Staith warehouse reported in *Press* 8 March 1909.
65. *Press* 21 October 1908.
66. *Ibid* 21 December 1908, 12 January 1909.
67. *Herald* 6 November 1908.
68. Eg *Ibid* 7 November 1908.
69. It was filled by the election of Cosmo Gordon Lang (1864-1945)
70. He was then acting secretary of the York ILP.
71. Of the size Davies had in mind presumably.
72. *Press* 25 June 1908. See also issues of 18, 19, 22 and 26 June 1908.
73. *Kelly's Directory of the North and East Ridings of Yorkshire.* Editions of 1901, 1905, and 1909.
74. *Press* 4 August 1908.
75. On wages in York see C. Feinstein, 'Population and Economic Development' in Feinstein *op. cit.*, and the sources quoted in fn 78.
76. The sugar duty had been put on in 1901 at 4s.2d. and reduced to 1s.10d. in 1908. Tea duty had been put up to 6d. in 1900 and reduced to 5d. in 1906.
77. *Ibid* 12 February 1909.
78. Cd 3864, *Parliamentary Papers*, 1908, CVII and Cd 6955, *Parliamentary Papers*, 1913, LXVI

CHAPTER 6

THE PEOPLE'S BUDGET, TRAMS, AND J.W. HOGGE

1909 was to be an exciting year in British politics and in York it began with a frenzied bout of activity by the 'Progressives'. It had to do with municipalising the tramway system.

The York Corporation, Tory dominated, was none the less dedicated to the idea of municipalising the tram system - none more so than that diehard Conservative Vernon Wragge - but there were some members of the ruling party who were determined to resist 'creeping socialism'. The leader of these was R.B. Lambert and he, Rhodes Brown and Sanderson Long had used the municipal election campaigns of 1908 to demand a citizen's poll about the future of the trams. In this they were successful, and one was fixed for 30 April. In March the old private company was wound up, (1) still to the accompaniment of complaints about the state of its horses and their use - particularly on Micklegate Hill. (2)

Shortly after the old (horse drawn) tram company was wound up an agitation in the press brought up the question of a system of electric buses for York (instead of trams) again, (3) and in March Arthur Brown, the Tory candidate in a Monk ward by election caused by the death of a sitting Conservative councillor, made clear his opposition to taking over the trams in the way then being proposed. The rates were too high to attract new industry Brown said, and the municipal electricity concern (which just then got permission from the Local Government Board to raise a loan of £27,000) (4) was 'an absolute failure.' Perhaps scared that people like Lambert and Sanderson Long might win over their party, the Liberals took to the streets and J.B. Morrell put a resolution to the Council proposing that it should recommend to the citizens that when the poll was taken they should vote for action under sub section 1(a) of section 85 of the York Corporation Light Railways Order of 1908. This meant that they should recommend what was their avowed policy anyway - that the Corporation should construct and run an electric tramway system.

By the time Morrell's proposals were voted on, the street campaign for municipalising the trams was well under way, but the outcome of the vote was extremely odd. Rowntree, Meyer, Morrell and others made well-argued cases for corporate ownership but they were defeated: 18 for the resolution; 24 against; two neutral. People like Sykes Rymer, who agreed with Morrell and the others about what should be done, found reasons for not recommending it to the voters. (5)

People like Arnold Rowntree, Sessions, S.H. Davies, J.T. Fenwick, Morrell and, of course, Hogge were prominent in the street campaign for municipalising the trams, and

Hartley and the ILP took part also. Hogge put forward closely reasoned contentions for a corporation scheme. What were they ? The system planned for York could be put down for £109,000, he said, and the trams would pay 'if they could carry their population 52 times [a year] at a penny.' If they did this they would earn £18,416 gross, and expenditure, which Hogge said was estimated for these purposes at a ratio of 63 per cent to gross profit, would be £11,648. Depreciation was estimated at a penny a mile or £2,083 and these figures would leave the city with a handsome profit. Was the initial estimate reasonable ? Hogge said some towns carried their populations 88 times a year. How many people had the old horse trams carried ? Hogge said he had been told that 'for the last ten years' they had 'carried no fewer than 850,000 passengers ... on a hen roost system ... extending from Fulford to the Mount.'

Having set up the citizen's poll Lambert and his supporters were seemingly taken aback by the spirited Liberal campaign, but as the poll approached they started to hold meetings of their own and started a press and poster attack. What did they say ? There was no opportunity, this time, to vote against an electric tram system for York - the voting papers did not allow for that - so they urged the populace to poll for a network to be built by a private company and leased to and run by a private company. Why ? To do otherwise was 'pure socialism'. A municipal building and operating programme would be pure speculation according to Councillor J.B. Inglis, and a Mr Hutson drew attention, as always, to losses the electricity company made and the rise in the rates he said a tram system would cause. Another speaker angered the Liberals by calling some working men 'serfs' of Rowntree and Company and meetings held by the opponents of municipalisation were broken up by hostile crowds. Hogge, as always, suffered in a predictable way; so much that he said his opponents appeared to be suffering from 'swine fever'.

What was really behind the opposition of people like Lambert ? Morrell said 'the real' reason was that they were all shareholders in the gas and water companies, and were scared that a successfully run transport system might lead the populace to demand the taking over of their services. He may well have been right, at least in part. At one of his street corner meetings, Hogge had compared the York and Leeds gas undertakings. Both, he said, charged 2s.2d. per thousand feet of gas, but in York private owners pocketed the profit, whereas in Leeds £14,000 went towards reducing the rates.

During the street campaign (6) tenders were received for constructing Yorks new tram system. No decision had been reached about what methods were to be used but the lowest estimate for an overhead power system was £89,233 and the highest £129,726; while a surface contact system attracted estimates that included £129,458 and £115,239. The *Press* told its readers that the tenders included estimates for work including strengthening Lendal bridge, raising an archway in Leeman Road, altering such things as manholes, drains and gas and electricity mains, widening the road, opposite the railway station, supplying cables and 20 cars.

On the eve of the poll the York papers carried huge expensive advertisements urging citizens to resist the Progressives' demands, and vote for what came to be known as 'Option C'. Voting papers enabled voters to vote for: a tram system to be constructed by the Corporation (Option A); a system constructed by the Corporation then leased to an operating company (Option B); or a system to be constructed then (possibly) leased by a private company (Option C). The result was a decisive win for Hogge and his colleagues. (Option A - 6,297 votes; B - 78; C - 3,734.)

Hogge, Hartley, Rowntree and the rest of the Progressives were elated at the result of the 1909 poll. They had not done well in the November election, but now it must have looked as if their fortunes were about to change. The small group of newcomers to the Liberal ranks (including Morrell, Sessions, and Wilkinson) had shown themselves adept at political campaigning and there had been something like a united front forged with the labour movement. The Labour party, at this time, seems to have been a spent force, but the ILP had lent its support to the campaign about the tramways, and the opposition must have looked forward to making inroads into the Tory majority at the next municipal election contests. However, there were to be political sensations galore before then. The very issues of the York papers which contained those huge advertisements urging citizens to vote against 'Option A' carried details of the 'People's Budget'.

The House of Lords had wrecked the Liberal legislation of 1908, their actions had infuriated the government, and there had to be a show down. How long could a non-elected second chamber be allowed to thwart the legitimate intentions of a popularly elected government ? No longer, it was clear. The Liberals had to take on their Lordships in 1909 (they should have done so earlier). Lloyd George's budget was to bring the conflict with them to a head. He had 'a serious revenue problem' when he set about producing it. Most of Asquith's surplus of the previous year had been spent 'not on building up a fund for old age pensions ... but [on] ... reducing the sugar duty - an orthodox Free Trade gesture for which there was no urgent practical need.' (7) So, the Chancellor had to find money for pensions, at a time of recession, and he had to do it 'within the Free Trade system,' while realising that rising unemployment was leading people to look more favourably towards tariff reform. This was a situation vastly at variance with that of five years earlier when Joseph Chamberlain had launched his campaign for tariff reform. Then, as John Grigg said, he had had 'the misfortune to run into a period of prosperity, which seemed to make a mockery of his argument that Free Trade was ruining the country.' Now those palmy days were over, as the gloomy, depressing reports from the York Distress Committee regularly revealed.

Where could the Chancellor get his revenue ? 'I have no nest eggs at all', he said in a famous remark, 'I have got to rob somebody's hen roost ...' Shortly after this the Lords rejected the Licensing Bill, and public alarm at the growth of German naval power made it 'inevitable that the range of taxation in the 1909 Budget should be far wider than Lloyd George initially hoped or desired.' An extra £3 millions had to be found for naval expenditure, meaning that the Chancellor would have to find around £13 millions in new or higher taxation while making up the estimated deficit with £3 millions from the Sinking Fund.

> The new taxes were to include a super-tax of sixpence in the £ on the amount by which incomes of £5,000 or more exceeded £3,000; a 20 per cent tax on the unearned increment of land values, an annual duty of a halfpenny in the £ on the capital value of undeveloped land, and a 10 per cent reversion duty on benefits to lessors at the termination of leases; motor vehicle taxes varying according to horsepower, and a threepence per gallon tax on petrol; and, finally, a general tax on liquor licences amounting to roughly half the annual proceeds from the sale of drink. ... In addition, income tax was to go up from 1s. to 1s.2d. in the £ on unearned incomes, and on earned incomes if over £3,000 a year, while estate and stamp duties were to be increased substantially, as were duties on tobacco and spirits. ... The tax on licenses was to be accompanied by a reform of the licensing system, and the land taxes by a valuation of land ...

How many people would be affected by Lloyd George's major proposals ? Liquor and tobacco taxes would yield a higher percentage of the revenue raised than before, but in 1909 only about one million paid income tax, and among them only a small number would be affected by the proposed tax rises. 'At most 12,000 people would have to pay super-tax, and only about 80,000 were liable to estate duty. Land taxes, stamp duty and the taxes on motorists - then a very small class - had a similarly restricted incidence.'

Budget day 1909 was 29 April, and Lloyd George introduced his proposals in a speech of four and a half hours. 'This is a war Budget', he said, 'it is for raising money to wage implacable warfare against poverty and squalidness.' Four days later Balfour began the Tory onslaught on it, condemning the land taxes and cleverly ridiculing the liquor duties. Throughout the summer the struggle for the budget went on with the increased possibility that the Lords might reject it beginning to be mooted, despite the fact that it was an established constitutional rule that they should not interfere with financial matters. The budget finally passed through its last Commons stage on 4 November (with a majority of 379 to 149) and was sent to the Lords. There it was rejected on the second reading by 350 to 75. 'THE NATION TO BE CONSULTED' the *Evening Press* told its readers, jumping the gun just a little. The day after that headline appeared (2 December) a resolution was carried in the Commons by an enormous majority saying that the Lords' action was 'a usurpation' of the Common's powers. Thereafter a general election was inevitable.

The Tories of York attacked Lloyd George's budget proposals from the moment they appeared, with Riley-Smith first in the field. (8) How did they present it, and what was their attitude towards what the Lords should do (and did) ? Both Butcher and Riley-Smith throughout the long months of the campaign insisted that Lloyd George's proposals would do nothing to deal with unemployment - indeed they said they would increase it. What was their alternative ? Tariff reform. Free trade, Riley-Smith said, was 'an antiquated system', (9) and the nation should follow Balfour's lead. He also persisted in presenting the budget as a socialist measure. The electors' choice was between tariff reform or 'Socialism and destruction, he said on one occasion (10) and on another declared that 'The sole issue before the country at the present time was between Socialism and ruin under a Radical Government or orderly progress and prosperity under a strong and patriotic Unionist party.' (11) On yet another occasion Riley-Smith said that (12)

> the present Budget was not a Budget in the usual meaning of the term; it was a programme, a manifesto, a portmanteau of wild legislative schemes under which taxation was to be heaped upon the country, not to meet the financial requirements and necessities of the year, but to further and facilitate the future intrigues of Mr. Lloyd-George and his newly adopted associates and friends.

So the budget, to Riley-Smith and Butcher, was socialistic and one that would make unemployment worse. Given the nation's well-known fear of socialism these were not bad cards to play, but what about the Lords rejecting proposals that were sent to them with a huge Commons majority, and were of a financial nature anyway ? Their Lordships, Butcher in particular maintained, were actually helping the democratic process! How ? The proposals contained in the budget were of such profound importance, Butcher said, that the electorate should have the right to vote on them. A referendum was not constitutionally possible, so the Lords should reject the Finance Bill and give the nation the right to vote on it. (13) Presumably he would have gone on to say that the Liberals had not got a mandate for this measure. They certainly had for the legislation of 1907 which the Lords had rejected, but maybe Butcher would have argued even then that they were helping democracy (or something).

The rejection of the People's Budget was a short sighted, bigoted and appalling piece of political activity, but people like Butcher had prepared the way for it well, certain that they would win the ensuing election (all the current by election results were extremely favourable for them) and that then all would be well. Organisations like the York LVA stated that 'we earnestly trust that the House of Lords will reject the [Finance] Bill', (14) and when they did the city's Conservative Association welcomed their action. (15)

Throughout the spring, summer and autumn countless 'budget' meetings were held in York, and Butcher and Riley-Smith siezed every opportunity to broach the subject at dinners, prize givings, Primrose League bunfights and straightforward campaign meetings. They both addressed the local ILP, (16) and the Budget Protest League made its appearance in Old Ebor. (17) The Liberal Unionists were at one with them, and they held at least one mass meeting in St Sampson's Square to declare that they viewed Lloyd George with as much alarm as did the Tories. (18)

Hamar Greenwood also took to the street, defending the People's Budget, and attacking the Lords. 'If the Lords now rejected the Budget', he said in October, 'they were bringing about a revolution in the custom and the constitution of the country.' What would happen if they did reject the Finance Bill? Then an election would be held, which the Liberals would win with a mandate to change the whole nature of the Upper House. Greenwood reminded his listeners that their Lordships had not only got their eyes on the budget, but that they had been carving up the Irish Land Bill and the Housing and Town Planning Bill as well, a fact which angered the York Health and Housing Reform Association. (19)

What about the allegations that Lloyd George's proposals were unfair? Greenwood said '"Don't worry about the Dukes"', and people like Harry Miles thought that their silly behaviour in forecasting ruin (for themselves) was actually helping his cause. '... the dukes' Harry said, 'instead of cutting down their subscriptions to charities and dismissing their men (20) should spend less money in wine, in going abroad, and in yachting cruises, and should be willing to reduce their racing studs. He thought that they were doing great service to the cause of the Budget.' (21)

Harry Miles was speaking at an open air meeting and, like the Tories, the Liberals were helped by national organisations set up to fight the cause of the People's Budget. Strafford B. Whitby, of the Free Trade Union, appeared in the city, for example, declaring that the election, when it came, 'would doubtless be the bitterest and the keenest of modern times.' (22) Earlier Sessions and Morrell (who referred to himself 'as an advanced Liberal') and others appeared on platforms speaking for the Budget League. (23)

If the general election was to be as important as everyone predicted (and it had to be) who would be the candidates for York? Riley-Smith and Butcher had been selected long since, and there was no chance this time of a Liberal/Labour deal as there was in 1906. Greenwood, the sitting Liberal, would stand. Who would be his running mate? The *Press* suggested it was likely to be J.M. Hogge. He was deeply into the budget campaign and had had a hectic year. Whether what he had done (which looks completely honourable) and the way he had done it (which was simply disastrous) would have made him a good candidate for York is questionable. (The Tories said his intervention at Malton had lost the Liberals that seat in 1906.) (24)

Why in York politics the governing party frequently allowed opposition councillors to occupy key positions in local government is a constant source of amazement. (George Hudson never did in his time.) In 1909 Sebastian Meyer, a Liberal, was important in this respect, and so was Hogge, who was chairman of the Distress Committee. Maybe the Tories reckoned that it was an unpopular post, that as chairman Hogge would demonstrate his ability in the art of foot in the mouth, and that they would benefit. They were half right if this was the case. Hogge was a splendid champion of the unemployed but he undoubtedly helped the warnings of creeping 'socialism' being regularly put out by the likes of Riley-Smith to gain a little more credence.

Shortly after the taking of the citizens' poll, in which claims of creeping socialism were heard, tenders from Messrs Dick, Kerr and Company were accepted by the tramways committee for 'the construction of track and electrical equipment' for the York tramways, (25) and in June by the Council. (26) Then, at that meeting, an attempt was made to get the tramways constructed 'by their own workmen' - an attempt which was defeated, with Sebastian Meyer pointing out that to do this would necessitate the creation of a council works department. At that same meeting Hartley, Hogge and others caused a rumpus over a proposal to spend £100 on street decorations when Princess Louise and the Duke of Argyll visited the York Pageant in the summer.

The horsedrawn trams of York stopped running early in September. 'No more shall the jingle of the bell and the clatter of equine hoofs resound along the paved thoroughfare between Fulford and the Mount' recorded the *Press*, no more will the 'driver crack his fearsome whip and shake the reins to urge his tired steeds along. The old order has given place, or is going to give place, to the new, and soon the whirr of the electric car, speeding from end to end of the city, will be heard ...' (27) Work soon began on laying the new lines, but within no time at all there was industrial trouble. The Distress Committee reported that the contractors were not paying the agreed rate of 6d. an hour (but 5d.) and that some men the committee had sent along had been sacked when the strikers returned to work. (28) At the City Council Hogge and Hartley alleged that Dick, Kerr had imported 'foreign labour' and J.B. Morrell took up the question of wage rates. Hogge demanded that men should be taken from the Distress Committee's register, and Meyer revealed that in fact 57 per cent were from the city. (29) Hogge attacked the contractors from election platforms, saying they had broken a pledge given to the Council. (30)

Hogge and the Liberals (or most of them) had the laudable aim of wanting to make the York Corporation a 'fair wage' authority, paying their own men fair rates, insisting that their contractors did so, and setting an example for the area. The earlier attempts to do this will be recalled, and Hogge and Hartley continually tried to persuade the Council to their way of thinking. Hogge linked his demands to attempts to get work for the city's unemployed, of whom there were 1,475 registered with 2,704 dependants when the Distress Committee reported in December. 'SAD TOTAL OF 4,179' was a

Press headline. (31) Hartley got himself into a spot of bother for his part in the fair wage agitation.

Hartley was due for re-election in 1909, and in the run up to polling day he dropped some bricks. To begin with he told a public meeting that he had conned the Council into accepting a tender for a contract to widen Holgate and Acomb roads wherein there was a proviso saying that the wages the contractor had to pay would be those agreed by the Federated Builders Labourers' Union (that is 6d. an hour). (32) The accuracy of this claim was questioned in the press, but then Hartley lost his cool and lashed about with all the recklessness of his mate Hogge. He and Will Dobbie attacked Dick, Kerr, and Company, then Hartley laid into some of his fellow politicians. Two aldermen had refused to become Lord Mayor, he said, one of them on the grounds that he had too many children! Arthur Brown, he said, was a reactionary Tory and so was George Mansfield. Moreover, some of the Liberals were no better. Take the case of Councillor Wales. He had tried to get an eight hour day for workers on the tramways, Hartley said, and had proposed one on the tramways sub committee. He did not even get a seconder, and Wales supported a 60 hour week! Not only that but Wales had wanted to employ 12 year olds as conductors at 12s. a week. (33) He had then put the starting age up to 14. Hartley was attacked for leaking information from a sub committee, but he was unrepentant. "'I cannot allow a man like Ben Wales to preach at street corners as a Progressive and then go one point worse than the most reactionary Tory in the whole city when he gets behind the walls of the committee room'" Hartley said. (34) Later he repeated the charges. Wales had relented somewhat, he said, but had still wanted 18 year olds to work 60 hours for 12s. Most would now get £1, but 'work that out per hour,' Hartley said, 'and you will see that it is not very much.' (35)

Whether it was right of Hartley to leak committee secrets or not, it does seem extraordinary that Wales, a member of the same party as Seebohm Rowntree, should have supported such niggardly wage proposals. Hartley was right to be angry, but he should have looked over his shoulder, and was made to pay dearly for his outspokenness. Alderman Green revealed that he was the man with a lot of kids who did not want to become Lord Mayor. But he went on to tell a tale about when he and a party of councillors went to Lancashire to look at tramway equipment. Hartley was a member of the group, but would not travel with the rest. Nothing wrong in that, but Hartley paid 9s. for his ticket with his concession pass. Now 'The railway fare to the town we visited was 28s.6d.', said Green, and 'Mr Councillor Hartley pocketed the difference.' (36) Not only that but Hartley was always anxious to go on visits and moreover received 7d. or 7¹/2d. an hour for the time he spent on Council work. He 'really began to wonder whether Mr Hartley was not looking after his own personal interests', Green concluded.

This was dynamite. Hartley, the man who had objected to drilling in schools on British Empire day, who stood up to Wragge for better working conditions in general, who had opposed the street decorations for a royal visit and who had tried to stop the city giving an expensive present to J.G. Butcher, had seemingly been on the make. The Labour party called a public meeting at which he explained all. (37) That he got 7d. or 7¹/₂d. an hour, he said, was a 'deliberate lie.' All that happened was that the local Labour party reimbursed him for lost earnings. But what about that municipal visit to Lancashire ? He had had to have three days off work, and had lost his wages, Hartley said, and that was why he pocketed the difference between his concession fare and the full fare. This was painful, yet nobody seems to have pointed out that if what Hartley had said earlier was true - that his party made up his wages - he lost nothing!

When Hartley offered his explanation to the city the municipal elections of 1909 were but a few hours away. During his campaign Hartley (along with S.H. Davies) had demanded better conditions for the police force, (38) and had urged the need for a bridge over the Ouse from Water End to the Leeman Road area, work which was not done until well after the conclusion of the Second World War. (In April 1909 the Corporation took steps to bring to an end the expenses fiddles which had clearly got out of hand. Hartley took no part in the debate about the abuses, a debate in which it was revealed that the aldermen were the worst offenders.)

The municipal elections had gone hand in hand with the budget campaign and had been as vitrolic as some of those of George Hudson's day. With their demands for better wages and their exposés of the apparent reluctance of local contractors to pay reasonable amounts Hartley and the Liberals might have expected to make inroads into the Tory majority on the council. But then Hartley's indiscretions and Hogge's ranting may have had a bad effect on their chances, and on the very eve of the poll Hogge engaged in some very dangerous 'joking' which caused a real furore. He had had a dream he told an audience. What was it about ? It fair 'took away the breath of his hearers' according to the *Press*. Hogge was in Walmgate, and he told his listeners he had dreamed he was in hell, and if some of his teetotal mates were to be believed he could actually have said he was in hell. But it was a dream? What was Hades like ? There were a number of rooms there, Hogge said, in which various groups were being tortured and tormented. In one were teetotallers and in another there were 'anti-gamblers.' In another room Hogge saw the editor of the *Herald* 'reading all the articles that he had ever written against me', but in the last place there were York people hanging up on hooks. Who were they ? Why were they hanging up ? They were the people who had voted against clause A in the municipal poll about the tramways, Hogge said. 'They are too green to burn, so they are hanging up to dry' he was told. (39)

Hogge's Dante-esque 'joke' looks pretty tame - and very laboured - today, but it caused a tremendous outcry at the time (and later). A.P. Purey-Cust wrote to the papers protesting against Hogge's 'VULGAR PROFANITIES' and suggesting that if people wanted to read such utterances they should issue special 'Garbage Supplements'. (40) This was over the top stuff and Purey-Cust might just have considered that, however he did it, Hogge was at least drawing attention to the evils of unemployment and the ostentatious plenty amidst poverty that was there for all to see, and about which Purey-Cust's political friends seemed resolutely determined to do nothing. Hartley too was surely right to draw attention to a decision of the council to pay appalling wages well below what Seebohm Rowntree had proved was necessary to sustain life at even a subsistence level.

Hogge at this time was often spoken of as the 'leader' of the Liberals on the Council. What the internal organisation of the party was like is unknown, though the Tory group was only very loosely ordered, it seems. (41) Outside the council chamber Hogge had replaced Richard Westrope as the leading local firebrand. What had happened to him?

Westrope had almost disappeared from view, though he was still active in the York Anti-Vivisection Society. His name no longer appeared among the list of passive resisters who still, each year, held back a part of their rates, nor did he appear at meetings for female suffrage. He had in fact changed direction, and in 1909 he became Warden of the York St Mary's Educational Settlement. Westrope's colleague in this new venture was Wilfred Crosland, a man with as radical a background as 'Brother Richard' himself. (42)

The York Educational Settlement was very much a 'Rowntree' venture, though it had the very active support of the Rev E.C. Owen of St Peter's school, (43) who was also involved in the York Workers' Educational Association. Its objects have been described at some length in a study of adult education in York, (44) and what they were was summed up in the press heading 'EXTENSION OF THE ADULT SCHOOL MOVEMENT.' Westrope told the Settlement's inaugural meeting that he 'hoped to realise the dream of Bishop Westcott in his book on "Social Aspects of Christianity."' (45)

Westrope's (or Westcott's) dream did not get the publicity that that of his friend did. What effects did Hogge's outbursts have on his career as a local politician ? Well it is not possible to say how seriously he was being considered as a York parliamentary candidate (the announcement that he was may even have been a Tory scare tactic), but he was not chosen - and neither did his party do all that well in the municipal elections. There were extraordinarily heavy polls, 81 per cent voting in Micklegate, with but one Liberal gain (46) in what had once been the solidly Labour or Liberal ward of Micklegate. Hartley was beaten into second place by George Sharp, the builder, with a Liberal failing (Sharp, Tory, 1,293 votes; Hartley 1,236; Charles E. Tee, Liberal 966). (47) K.E.T. Wilkinson came first in Walmgate; S.H. Davies second in Castlegate.

The heavy polls of November 1909 reflected the heightened political feeling of the time and are notable for registering the almost complete devastation of the Labour party. Hartley was now the only labour representative on the council. There seemed no possibility whatsoever of a Labour candidate for 1910 - the way was open for two Liberals. Who was selected to run with Greenwood ? The party chose Arnold Rowntree. It was said later that Asquith himself had suggested Arnold as a candidate.

Rowntree, Hogge and an unnamed person from Manchester had been spoken of as Liberal candidates to fight York alongside Greenwood, but Rowntree was adopted early in November at a meeting of the York Liberal Association at which Hogge (the treasurer) was present. (48) Would he be a good candidate ? There were conflicting views in the city about the Rowntree influence, and indeed the motives of people like Arnold helping to create places like the Settlement were questioned. But what of his political views ? The election, whatever Lloyd George may have desired, would be fought partly on the issue of free trade versus tariff reform, and Arnold was a loyal supporter of the free trade party - but, as a businessman, he benefited (at least according to his opponents) from protection! The *Herald* was quick to point this out. Rowntree could not possibly stand as a free trade candidate, it said, because he was a representative of a protected industry. Foreign cocoa had a duty levied on it of £99 a ton, and the state received some £300,000 a year from it. Both Asquith and Churchill had condemned the duty, with the Prime Minister saying that it did indeed smack of protection.

Arnold Rowntree declared that he had entered the contest of 1910 to fight the Lords, doing so, his opponents said, so that he could avoid having to defend free trade. The Lords, Rowntree told his first public meeting as a candidate, were 'contemplating a great Constitutional crime', and Greenwood declared that the Liberals intended to reduce their delaying powers to one year. (49) Nevertheless Rowntree was continually questioned and heckled about the cocoa duties throughout the campaign and went on record as saying that he did not think his firm had benefited from them and declaring that he and Greenwood would vote for their abolition. He went on to the attack on the question of tariffs, demanding to know from Butcher and Riley-Smith exactly what they would tax and to what extent. Butcher replied that only manufactured goods would be taxed, and that raw materials from abroad would be let into the country free. (50) The Liberals persisted in saying that food would be taxed - 'TARIFF REFORM MEANS DEAR BREAD' one of their campaign slogans said. (51) Using figures from *The Birmingham Post* Rowntree told his hearers that the likes of Butcher and Riley-Smith would levy 2s. on foreign corn; five per cent on butter and meat; and five to 15 per cent on manufactured goods. (52) Towards the end of the campaign Rowntree had a heated dispute with Messrs Leetham's, the millers, with whom he did business. It was over whether a tax on corn would be passed onto the customer. The Leethams said no; Rowntree said that France had started with a 2s. tax on corn which had then risen to 12s. (53)

For some time the cocoa manufacturers had been under attack for using the products of slave labour. This too was dragged up by the dirty tricks department of the Tory party. One of their slogans read (54)

COCOA SLAVERY, 1901-7, A Proved Fact!
CHINESE SLAVERY, 1906, A Fiction

Chinese slavery was, of course, an issue at the election of 1906, and since then arguments about it had run on and on. 'Cocoa Slavery' was an even longer running issue as the dates above indicate, and it had ended up with a sensational legal action in the year that Arnold was selected as a parliamentary candidate. For around 20 years the firm of Cadbury Brothers of Birmingham had received cocoa from the Portugese equitorial islands of San Thomé and Principe before it was made aware of serious concern about labour conditions there - which, if true, amounted to slavery. William Cadbury visited Lisbon to discuss the charges with the planters and was assured that the charges were untrue, but that any minor abuses would be eliminated by a Labour Decree of 1903. (55) Cadbury Brothers decided to carry on buying cocoa for a year, during which the decree could take effect, then investigate for themselves. At this stage they involved Messrs Fry of Bristol and Rowntree of York in their campaign, and when the time came they sent Joseph Buritt, a Quaker, to look at conditions in San Thomé and Principe (and other places) for them. Buritt reported in July 1907 and made it quite clear that 'The labourers ... in San Thomé and Principe were in a real, if not a theoretical, state of slavery.' (56) Many were captured in the interior of Angola and sent (often shackled) to the coast, where a farcical signing of contracts was engaged in. Buritt's report concluded by saying (57)

> I am satisfied that under the servical system as it exists at present, thousands of black men and women are, against their will, and often under circumstances of great cruelty, taken away every year from their homes and transported across the sea to work on unhealthy islands from which they never return. If this is not slavery, I know of no word in the English language which characterizes it.

The Foreign Office persuaded the cocoa manufacturers not to make Buritt's report public while they tried to effect reforms on the Portugese islands, but, not knowing this, the Liverpool Chamber of Commerce called on the government to take steps to end slavery and on the cocoa manufacturers to stop taking supplies from the slavers. William Cadbury explained their inaction to the Liverpool merchants, to their entire satisfaction, but the issue was now public, and the cocoa firms began to be bitterly attacked, on the one hand by people at home who thought they should immediately stop buying raw materials from the Portugese, and on the other by the Portugese themselves.

Cadbury and Buritt allowed themselves to be fobbed off with promises of reform again, and in September 1908 it was announced that W.H. Cadbury and Buritt were going to the islands and Angola to see if the promises had been carried out. On their return they announced (on 17 March 1909) that 'no adequate steps' had been taken 'to remedy the evils [already] proved to exist' and that Messrs Cadbury, Fry and Rowntree would cease buying 'cocoa produced in the Islands of San Thomé and Principe.'

During all the years in which conditions in the Portugese islands had been argued about there had been periodic press attacks on 'the Quaker houses' for using slave produced cocoa, but always, when the facts were pointed out to them, retractions and apologies were issued. (58) *The Standard* of 26 September 1908, however, had published a leading article wherein it accused Cadburys of not acting quickly enough over the conditions in San Thomé and Principe and contrasted the solicitude the cocoa firms showed for their workers at home in places like Bournville and New Earswick with their alleged indifference to the sufferings of the native labourers. 'Counsel was consulted and a case for libel entered in the High Court.' (59) The article was a 'fine specimen of satanical invective' in the words of H.W. Nevinson. (60)

The case of Cadbury versus *The Standard* involved some of the most famous names of the day, including Rufus Isaacs, Sir Edward Carson, Sir Edward Grey (a witness) and John Simon. It turned into a question of whether the cocoa firms had been involved in what the judge called 'a dishonest sham ... for the purpose of making profit when they ought not to do it, and it was their duty to stop.' The jury retired, then returned with a verdict for the plaintiffs with damages of one farthing!

The Cadbury case ended in December 1909, in the run-up to the election, and it cannot be supposed that it did Rowntree's cause any good whatsoever.

Riley-Smith and Butcher continued to campaign in the way they had started, contending that the Lloyd George budget would cause unemployment, applauding the Lords for their democratic action in chucking it out, maintaining that only tariff reform would bring down the numbers out of work, and arguing that tariffs would not be passed on to the consumers. 'FREE IMPORTS have made BRITAIN the DUMPING GROUND of all Nations' declared one of their advertisements. (61)

TAXATION GONE MAD. TAX tobacco and beer, TAX tea and sugar, TAX trade and enterprise, and thus TAX work and wages, TAX anyone, TAX anything, BUT *DON'T* touch the Foreigner! The plan of the Radical Means taxation gone mad. DOWN WITH THE BEDLAM BUDGET!

How did the various pressure groups line up in 1910 ? The LVA, naturally, urged support for Butcher and Riley-Smith, (62) and the Labour party, which was not very active at all, supported the Liberals. The ILP did so also, and held meetings attacking the Lords at some of which Mrs Charlotte Despard - the sister of the later Field Marshal Sir John French - was the star attraction. (63) The Roman Catholics were urged to vote Tory, (64) which seems rather odd, as the Liberals were the party of Home Rule, and a large group of the York clergy, including Purey-Cust and C.C. Bell, publicly announced their support for the Tories. Why? They were concerned about the fate of the Established Church in Wales and the future of church schools, they said, and neither Rowntree or Greenwood would give them any pledges on disestablishment or disendowment.

Greenwood and Rowntree (but not Riley-Smith and Butcher) were prepared to give their support to another cause, however. The York Women's Suffrage Society demanded to know of all the candidates whether they would support their cause, and both York Liberals said they would. (65) This may have called off a determined women's campaign in York.

It will be recalled that in the summer two new suffrage societies had been formed in York. Little or nothing was heard of them thereafter, but during the budget campaign the YWSS decided to add to the political fever prevailing in the city by holding meetings and organising a petition. (66) The first signature was that of Almyra Gray, and the meetings were often addressed by a Mr E.P. Holmes, of 55, Wentworth Road, and Mary Fielden, the Yorkshire secretary. (67) The ladies had committee rooms at No 10 Feasegate, where their petition lay for signatures. (68)

The York Suffrage Society was of the non violent variety and the candidates of 1910 would have had little to fear from it. In December, however, Miss Adela Pankhurst, representing the more (much more) militant section of the women's movement turned up at Scarborough declaring that she was going to intervene in the election there. Not only that, but she had York in mind as well. When 'I have concentrated my forces at Scarborough', Miss Pankhurst said, 'if it is at all possible, I shall also lead an attack on Mr. Hamar Greenwood at York, and if we can cause Mr. Rea and Mr. Greenwood to lose their seats at the next election we shall have done good work.' (69) This intention to go for and defeat Liberal politicians was the tactic used by the militant women in 1910 and it looks rather strange, given the attitudes of most Tory politicians and the ILP background of the Pankhursts, but Greenwood was spared the attention of the militant ladies. Perhaps his reply to the approach to him and Rowntree satisfied Miss Pankhurst. Anyway York did not see the exciting scenes that some places did.

The candidates of 1910 were nevertheless frequently questioned about votes for women, and very frequently about old age pensions. The People's Budget had much to do with raising money for pensions, and Rowntree and Greenwood were often asked whether they thought pensions should be paid to people who had been unfortunate enough to have been in receipt of poor relief and who were now denied assistance. (70) Rowntree said that he thought such a reform should be made, and surely he was right. Shortly after the pensions had begun to be paid in York the fact that poor people were frequently put into a Catch 22 situation was highlighted again and again. K.E.T. Wilkinson, speaking as a member of the York Out-Relief Union, had given some instances of this happening as long ago as April. (71) One old lady, Wilkinson said, had been refused a pension because she had received relief in 1908, and when he spoke she was starving and selling off what pieces of furniture she still had. Because she had done something wrong some years earlier, Wilkinson went on, she could not get outdoor relief. Presumably this old lady was desperate to stay out of the workhouse, understandably, and Wilkinson spoke of the case of a family he visited with the father out of work. When he had been in employment he had earned 12s. a week, but the family would not seek relief because of their fear of the workhouse. Wilkinson spoke of another old lady who, like the first one, had been refused an old age pension because she had received relief in 1908. Three or four months before he made her case public the old lady had had to go into the workhouse and when he spoke she had been out for three weeks, and unable to obtain either relief or a pension. (72)

A week after Rowntree promised to do something about the dreadful restrictions on pensions entitlement the candidates for York were officially nominated. The list of 'Assentors' for Rowntree and Greenwood contains no surprises, but that of Riley-Smith and Butcher is interesting. Among the names to be seen there (73) are those of Vernon Wragge, Elmhirst and Purey-Cust, as well as that of George Sharp, the contractor. Sharp was the candidate for municipal office who had so vehemently protested that he was an 'Independent' only a short time earlier. Also 'assenting' to the nomination of the two Tories were a number of working men employed by the railway company. One of these was C.H. Akers, a clerk. Another (also a clerk) was that E.P. Holmes who was active in the suffrage movement in York. His name looks somewhat out of place.

Voting in the general election of 1910, as before, was spread over a long period, and York went to the polls in January. The contest turned out to be a close run thing, necessitating a recount, at which 95 per cent of the electorate polled. When it was over it was seen that the city's senior MP had lost his seat; the 'second' Liberal had topped the poll; and a long-serving Member had made a remarkable come-back. The results were

Rowntree	6,751
Butcher	6,741
Greenwood	6,632
Riley-Smith	6,495

An analysis of the poll revealed the following (the number of plumpers for Butcher was the subject of serious comment later in the year).

Plumpers

Rowntree	31
Butcher	136
Greenwood	12
Riley-Smith	7

Splits

Rowntree and Butcher	130
Butcher and Greenwood	38
Greenwood and Riley-Smith	29
Rowntree and Greenwood	6,564
Butcher and Riley-Smith	6,436

Shortly after the election was over the *Press* reported rumours that Arnold Rowntree (then on holiday in Cannes) might resign. Several government ministers had been defeated, and it was said that Asquith was looking for seats for them. (74) If Rowntree resigned, the *Press* said, there would be a contest, but nothing happened and Arnold was very quickly into the struggle with the Lords, taking a very prominent part.

An interesting if unimportant fact about the general election of 1910, as far as York is concerned, is that it saw a second one, the day after Butcher and Rowntree had been returned. On that day York was a voting centre for the freeholders and out-voters of the Thirsk and Malton constituency. Acomb was then entirely within that rural division; there were some 2,000 voters in the district; and five York polling stations were opened. One voter - and this is reminiscent of the days before the 1832 Reform Act - travelled from Switzerland to record his opinion on the People's Budget, tariff reform and much else.

The election of 1910 was a tremendous defeat for the Liberals. Before the dissolution they still had, despite by election set-backs, an overall majority of 76. When the last results were in, in February, they had only two seats more than the Unionists (275:273) and henceforth would only have a working majority with the support of the Irish and Labour Members. In trying to explain the apparent unpopularity of the People's Budget, the fact that the British electorate was still extremely limited must be born in mind. That still only 58 per cent of adult males had the vote has been mentioned before.

A new feature of the 1910 election was that the candidates found themselves a part of the programme of one of the city's centres of entertainment. Mr Bert Rutter, the energetic manager of the Victoria Hall, used photographs and slogans from the four candidates as a part of one of his film presentations in January. (75) (A little later he organised a special showing and a collection for the city's Crimean veterans.) (76)

The Victoria Hall was showing films regularly, and in the summer of 1909 it had pulled off something of a scoop. In July final dress rehearsals for the York Historic Pageant were being held, and these were filmed. Rutter wanted to show them on a Sunday (maintaining the record amounted to a 'sacred film'); this was refused; but the Victoria Hall put them on to good houses on weekdays. (77) Those fortunate enough to have been there would have certainly seen pictures of the redoubtable Edith Milner in the role of Queen Ethelburga. (Edith, incidentally, lived up to expectations during the general election campaign and roused the ire of J.M. Hogge when she - a governor - allegedly told the kids at a local school that David Lloyd George, he of the People's Budget, was 'a very wicked man'.) (78) Perhaps prompted by the York Pageant, another interesting public entertainment was provided for York citizens at Christmas 1909, when the Rev C.C. Bell, the vicar of St Olaves, revived the ancient York Mystery Plays and had them performed in the St Mary's Hall, Marygate. It is often suggested that they were first revived in the early years following the end of the Second World War.

Competition in the entertainment industry had hotted up somewhat and from 1909 Rutter and the Opera House had another place showing films and competing with them for business. Early in the year the New Street Palace of Varieties opened its doors. Like the Opera House this place included variety 'turns' in its programme, while giving over the main part of its shows to films, mixing 'weepies' with adventure, comedy, and educational and sporting offerings. Nothing quite as sensational as that played a few years earlier at the Martinmas Fair went on at New Street (quite rightly as the place had once been a chapel), and in January typical fare included film of the recent earthquake at Messina and the world heavyweight title fight between Tommy Burns and Jack Johnson. (79) The Victoria Hall was showing the Burns-Johnson brawl in the same week. In April the Palace of Varieties was announced to be under new management, and the place was renamed the New Hippodrome.

Film going had become extremely popular among those who could afford to go, but there was another craze that swept the country. It took some time to get to York, but when it did roller skating became as popular there as it did anywhere.

The first proposals for a roller skating rink in York were for a building to be put on land between 'Walkers training ground' for horses and the North Eastern Railway's hotel entrance in Leeman Road. (80) This fell through when the NER refused a lease, but in May 1909 the York Roller Skating Rink Company announced that it had obtained a permanent site. This was 'on the Sycamore Estate, close to the Scarborough Railway Bridge.' (81) It was built very rapidly, got itself a drinks licence in June, and was opened by none other than Edith Milner in July, (82) to the delight of many and to the considerable annoyance of its neighbours. A military band was hired to accompany the skaters, and races and hockey matches began to be held there. In March 1910 at the York City Music and Dancing Transfer Sessions the licence of the Sycamore rink was objected to. It was renewed, however, but with provisos that the

191

place did not open on Sundays and that it closed at 10.45 pm. (83) (The rink later became known as the Sycamore Skating Rink.)

At the Brewster Sessions of 1910 the Sycamore Terrace Rink was compared (unfavourably) with a competitor. (84) Shortly after the announcement that it was hoped a skating rink would be built next to the Station Hotel, Sidney Bacon of the Victoria Hall venture, Frank C. Bostock and Fred Ginnett announced that one would be laid in a large tent at the back of Fishergate School, and that, eventually, a permanent structure would be built round it. (85) This was to be 180 feet by 90 feet and in May it (the York Roller Skating Pavilion) was opened by Mrs Preston of Middlethorpe Manor. The Lord Mayor was present on that auspicious occasion, saying that 'There was an old saying that York was always the last to start anything new.' (86)

York may have been late in getting itself a skating rink, but when it did move it got two, then a third appeared to replace the Pavilion. This place came under new management in July 1909, (87) but then work was begun on the City Roller Skating Palace situated on land between the glassworks and Blue Bridge Lane. It comprised a skating area of 25,000 square feet and was built to plans drawn up by Messrs Dugdale of Blackpool and constructed by Messrs Parkins and Sons of the same place. Work was almost complete in early October and the opening date was fixed for the middle of the month. Before this happened the prospectus of the City Roller Skating Palace Ltd appeared. Skating, it said, had 'taken a keen and firm hold on the public fancy ... and is a favourite form of recreation with all classes.' Skating, it went on, had become 'delicious ... by reason of the use of ball-bearing skates on maple floors.' A dividend of 80 per cent (!) was confidently predicted and the Palace rink (215 feet by 98 feet) would accommodate 1,000 skaters and 300 spectators. The company had a capital of £7,000 and was formed to get the lease of land with 'a footage in Fishergate' of 106 feet and an area of 22,788 square feet. (88)

Late in the day or not, skating in York became as popular as it did elsewhere. Speed competitions were held, a hockey club was formed, 'historical pageants' were put on, and so 'feverous' did the craze for skating become, according to the *Press* in February 1910, that Miss Edith Rawdon, the daughter of Canon Rawdon of Stockton on Forest, attired her four bridesmaids in 'skating costume'. (89) The *Press* published a line drawing of these ladies and two days later another of a skater doing the cakewalk. Whether this was intentional or not was not revealed.

At just about the time that the first skating rink was being considered for York another movement was started in the city. In February 1909 the first Boy Scouts group was formed, and in June at least two were in existence. (90) In September Baden-Powell took the salute at a rally at which between 300 and 400 scouts put on a marching display 'consisting of "The Spiral March," "The ZiZg [sic] Zag," and "The Windmill."'

The drill movements performed by the York Scouts would have done nothing to dispel the beliefs of those people like J.H. Hartley and Arthur Dearlove (91) who believed that they were militaristic and that the Scouts were a part of the same 'movement' as the gun clubs, the Boys Brigade, the Frontiersmen and the National Defence League. Whatever the rights and wrongs of that argument, however, an outlet for great activity and pleasure had been given to the city. In this study so far several other outlets for pleasurable activity have been mentioned, with perhaps a noticeable exception. What of the oldest activity of all ? This has been studied for an earlier period in some detail. (92) Were there still red lights districts as there once had been ? York was a garrison town. The thirst of the soldiers and citizens was more than adequately catered for. Did York's hospitality stop there ? The answer must be a definite negative, and a trawl through the police court records show that to be so. In May 1909 Mrs Emma Richardson, of Fitzroy Terrace, for example, was charged with keeping a disorderly house and given a month with hard labour. (93) A month later Edwin Severs, of Hungate, the red light area par excellence, was fined £5 and costs (in default a month inside) for permitting his premises to be used as a brothel. (94) There are numerous other examples of the foregoing scattered through the columns of the York press. Strange to report, however, York's streets were free of the ladies of the night soliciting for custom. (That is if letters to the press in January 1911 are to be believed.) Maybe they confined themselves to touting in the pubs. It seems likely that they did, yet this was never put forward as a reason for closing a hostelry.

With the election out of the way York turned its attentions to the tramways again. Work on erecting the overhead cables went on and by November 1909 the tracks had been laid from Fulford to Clifford Street and from Dringhouses to St George's Place. (95) By the end of January four and a half miles out of the planned six miles were opened for business. (96) 'York has now come into line with the more progressive cities in the matter of tramways', the *Press* told its readers, then went on to give them some fascinating technical details. (97) Windby anchor chains had been used to hold the tracks, it said, and the joints had been welded by the Thermite process. The rails used had been No 3 British standard, which weighed 100 pounds per square yard and had been made by Messrs Bolckow, Vaughan and Company of Middlesborough. The points and sharpest curves had been made in manganese steel by Messrs Edgar Allan of Sheffield, and for most of the system the roadway between the rails, and 18 inches on either side of the tracks, had been paved with creosoted wood blocks. The radius of the 'quickest' curve on the York network was 10 feet and the steepest gradient was one in 18 over a length of between 170 and 180 yards on Holgate Hill.

The trams began running, then a row started about them which is reminiscent of an earlier one of 70 years earlier which had had tremendous consequences. Then there was a dispute on the board of the York and North Midland Railway Company about the running of Sunday trains, and in the aftermath of it the Sabbatarians left in a huff - and left the way open for George Hudson to embark on a tremendous career of shady dealing. The dispute over Sunday trams in 1910 was nowhere near as important, but perhaps it was as predictable. The trams began running late in January, and in early February the Methodists objected to them working on the one day when working class people were able to go out and about. In one week the Clifton Methodist Church, the Wesley Mission Men's class and the Groves Wesleyan chapel all registered their objection to Sunday trams. (98) Later sermons were preached against Sunday running, but the bigots did not get it all their own way, and letters saying that York on a Sunday was bad enough already made their appearance. (99) Eventually a debate was held in the Council with Sir Joseph Sykes Rymer and Alderman Agar leading the kill-joys, and they were only beaten by two votes (20 to 18). (100) Shortly afterwards the line to Dringhouses was opened, (101) and Sunday travel proved to be extremely popular. On one Sunday late in March it was reported that eleven cars had run 790.66 miles; and taken £71.2.1d. in fares from 13,230 passengers. (102)

The dreadful Victorian Sunday had been ushered in in York largely during the Mayoralty of a Methodist, and the Methodists were prominent in the 1910 effort to retain that day in all its awfulness. (103) They failed (narrowly) and of course J.M. Hogge was prominent in the debates (voting for the running of Sunday trams it is pleasant to record). He was also to the fore as a critic of the new government very early on in its life. Late in February he went on record as saying that he was furious with the Prime Minister who was seemingly reluctant to deal with the Lords once and for all. If it were possible, Hogge said, he would withdraw the vote he had given for the Liberals. (104) What had been happening ?

It had been assumed by most Liberals that Asquith had obtained 'guarantees' from the King before the dissolution saying that if the Lords attempted further resistance to the budget he would sanction the creation of new peers as in the Reform Bill crisis. On 21 February Asquith revealed that he had not received such a guarantee and that in fact he had not even asked for it. It was this that made James Myers Hogge so angry. He was, Hogge said, 'a Single Chamber man, and would have the House of Lords swept altogether out of the constitution.' (105)

Hogge had every reason to be angry with Asquith. The general election had seemingly been fought mainly over the question of the Lords, and Arnold Rowntree had made that his main issue. Now it seemed that, even with a mandate, their Lordships would not be attacked head on - and in fact the King in December 1909 had said he would not create Peers en masse until after a second general election. Had this been known at the time, it is said, the King's attitude could have had profound political effects.

The budget was disliked by the Irish, and they imposed conditions for their support. First there were to be passed 'a group of resolutions in the Commons to set out the principles of Lord's reform; second a Finance Bill to carry the 1909 budget into law;

third, actual legislation on Lord's reform.' (106) The timetable was implemented. The resolutions were introduced, the budget was passed by the Upper House in a single sitting, and a Parliament Bill based on the resolutions was introduced on 14 April. At this point a 'major distraction occurred' when King Edward died suddenly and unexpectedly. What should be done now ? Was an undertaking given by one King binding on his successor ? George V suggested the parties should call a truce and try to settle their arguments by negotiation and in June the first meeting of a constitutional conference' was held. It held 21 sittings and it eventually broke down in November on one point. The Tories were determined to block Irish Home Rule and they insisted that all 'Constitutional' legislation should be subjected to a referendum. The Liberals were prepared to consent to this for bills affecting, for example, the Protestant succession of the crown, but, now dependent on the Irish vote, they were adamant that Home Rule should not be included. Prior to this 'On almost every other point agreement was reached; the Lords could not reject Money Bills, and if other measures could not gain the support of both Houses two years running the matter would be settled by a Joint Sitting, with the Lord's representation scaled down so that a Liberal Government with a majority of fifty could gets its legislation through - after a time.' (107)

Many Liberals, like Hogge, were furious at the delay in dealing with the Lords, but the constitutional conference in effect imposed a party truce. While it sat, however, Hogge was rarely out of the public eye in York. He took part in a prolonged and acrimonious wrangle about the appointment of a head teacher at the municipal girl's school, (108) and in a long controversy (particularly involving Rhodes Brown) about whether workers were better off in free trade Britain than they were in protectionist Germany. Hogge also carried on his work with the York Distress Committee and the Labour bureau which, sadly, had as much work to do as ever. The problems of under employment and low wages were as acute in York as ever, and in 1910 the Distress Committee had helped with financial grants for people taking work in the Bradford mills. (109)

The Distress Committee and the bureau had done something to alleviate suffering in York and the city had every reason to be thankful to the likes of Hogge and Hartley. However things were to change in the autumn of 1910. Winston Churchill and William Henry Beveridge had determined to set up a national network of labour exchanges under the control of the Board of Trade, legislation enabling them to do so was passed in 1909, and in August 1910 Lt J.B. Adams, a well-known arctic explorer, but then an Inspector for the Board of Trade, addressed a meeting called by the York Trades Council and sought to allay trades unionists' fears about the new bodies - one of which was to be set up in York. Trades unionists, Adams said, were worried about wages and strikes (and Britain was experiencing an epidemic of those at the time). The new exchanges had nothing to do with wages, he pointed out, and explained what should happen if workers were sent to places where a dispute was in existence. (110) J.H.

Hartley was anxious that trades unionists should be appointed to the local advisory committee.

The York Labour Exchange was established in property which had been empty for two and a half years at the corner of Jubbergate and Parliament Street, and when it opened the Labour bureau in Castlegate closed. The new body had no more powers to create work than had the old one, and the only new industry proposed for York at this time was turned away (for very good reasons). In May 1910, after a great deal of discussion over the preceding months, the Council discussed the proposal by Messrs Oppenheimer for a gut-scraping factory on premises belonging to the Yorkshire Bone Products Company, Hull Road. (111) They turned them down.

Just before the Council discussed the proposed gut scraping factory (and the Retreat's objection to it) Councillor George Mansfield died and a by election became necessary for Monk ward. Labour's representation on the Council had dwindled to one and the party determined to try to start a come-back. Almost before poor old Mansfield was in the ground they nominated an excellent candidate - the first Labour candidate in York who was not a member of the working class. This was Dr Peter MacDonald, who held the degrees of MA and MD from the University of Aberdeen. He had first appeared in York some 16 years earlier and had worked as a physician at the Dispensary for some two and a half years. After that MacDonald had gone to Bradford, then returned to the York area and worked as a GP in Acomb. At the time of the 1910 municipal by election he was a consultant and honorary opthalmic and house surgeon to the ear, nose and throat department of the County Hospital. (112)

MacDonald fought an able campaign, with radical demands about fair wages and municipalisation. He applauded the recent Medical Inspection of School Children Act, but regretted that it only provided for inspection and not treatment. The day after MacDonald's nomination the Liberals set up T. Allison Booth and the Tories selected J.W. Dixon, a builder of Hempland, Heworth. (113)

J.W. Hogge criticised Labour for setting up a candidate, seeing, of course, that the opposition would be split and that not for the first or last time the Tory would be let in. Hogge was both right and wrong in 1910. The radical vote was split, but Dixon got more than the other two combined. (Dixon 854; MacDonald 374; Booth 288.) The result was bad for the Liberals and bad for Labour, and it came at a time when Hogge was looking for a larger political stage on which to parade his talents.

The next general election in York would undoubtedly have been a livelier affair than it was had Hogge been able to take part in it - but he was not. In August 1910 James Myers was selected as their Liberal candidate by the Camlachie Liberal Association, and the reports of his adoption meeting make it quite clear that his brand of radicalism went down well in (at least some parts of) Glasgow. Their chosen man was 'in

Parliamentary parlance, "a whole hogger"', the chairman said in a rather predictable phrase. 'There was no dubiety about his politics. He was none of the suppple-backed, weak-in-the-hind legs politicians. ... He was a straightforward Radical.' (114) Very true, and a little later Hogge made it quite clear that he did not deviate one tiny bit from the main belief of Liberal orthodoxy. 'All over the world at this moment', he said, 'there was a widespread revolt against high prices, and high prices were the result of Protection. High prices meant low wages' he went on, 'low wages meant decreased demand, decreased demand meant less work, and consequently more unemployment.' (115)

Hogge's selection meant that there would be excitement in at least one Scottish constituency when the general election came along, but before that he had to seek re-election to the York City Council. He did extraordinarily well. He stood in Castlegate and he and William Page, a coal merchant of Holgate House, easily beat two Conservatives. (Hogge, 1,044; Page, 923; John Strangman Shannon, schoolmaster, 846; Dr Arthur Kemp, 746.)

Hogge fought an uncompromising campaign in November 1910, boasting that the tramways were now paying, (116) and advocating more municipalisation - in particular of the Water Company - (117) and a publicly owned cemetery. (118) Elsewhere in the city, however, the Tories held their own and the balance of power remained more-or-less as it was. That Henry Rhodes Brown with whom Hogge had been arguing topped the poll in Guildhall and in Micklegate two Labour candidates finished bottom, well over 300 votes behind the successful Liberal John Thomas Clarke. The two Labour men were Dr MacDonald and the veteran Andrew Pattison Mawson.

It must have seemed to Labour after November 1910 that it stood little chance of advancement until the electorate was enlarged, particularly as its programme was still almost indistinguishable from that of the Liberals. It remained to be seen what their attitude towards the parliamentary election - which could not be all that far away - would be.

The Labour party was still in existence in 1910, but as inactive as it had been a year earlier. The ILP continued to invite prominent speakers to the city and the Trades Council got an accession of support when a local branch of the Musician's Union was formed in the spring of 1910. (119) But Labour fortunes were bleak. It seems strange that in that year of intense political activity and excitement the party of the future did so little. The year 1910 also saw massive political activity by the suffragettes - but not in York.

Mention has been made of the fact that 1910 saw an enormous amount of labour unrest, with disputes in the ship yards and the cotton industries attracting tremendous attention. There was also great trouble on the railways, and for a short time it looked as if York's railway workers would strike. It would have been a fascinating dispute had they done so, given that there was great unemployment and that the unions were in reality representing only a fraction of the NER's workers. What had happened? It all centred round 'Shunter Goodchild'.

Goodchild worked in the north east; he was ordered to move his place of work; he refused; was suspended; and a strike started which seemed likely to spread. The York newspapers were full of it and great concern was expressed about the possible effect on business in the city. (The effects of the removal of NER men a few years earlier were frequently recalled.) (120) Both the ASLEF and the ASRS in York were in favour of striking and they issued an ultimatum saying that if a settlement had not been reached by 3 pm on 21 July a walk-out would take place. (121) But would it be effective? To be so many who were non-unionists would have to take part, run the risk of being sacked, and being replaced by men who were unemployed. As the crisis time approached, the *Press* said, crowds of men assembled outside the works 'mainly composed' of 'unemployed men obviously waiting to step into the shoes of the goods-yard employees intending to come out.' (122) Fortunately the strike was called off, though the company refused the men's demands for the immediate reinstatement of the erring shunter. (123)

The NER made a great deal of the fact that it had recognised the men's unions and had conciliation procedures, but it was more than capable of acting harshly - and there is plenty of evidence that this is so. Some examples from earlier periods have been given, and in the aftermath of the 1910 dispute there were allegations that it victimised strikers. Mineral guard Levitt of Middlesborough, for example, was suspended for a month and at a public meeting at which his case was discussed there was talk of an 'official tyranny.' Kaye-Butterworth refused to discuss Levitt's case with a deputation of his colleagues. And why had guard Levitt been suspended? Because he had been one of the first out during the recent troubles Levitt maintained. (124) He was probably right.

The rail unions in 1910 were discussing amalgamation and were weak in York anyway, and what conditions on the railway were really like were regularly revealed when James Bermingham visited the city. He, it will be remembered, regarded the York men as something akin to blacklegs, and urged them to unionise. His speeches were always revealing, though they showed little sympathy for the men who would have undoubtedly been worried about the crowds of unemployed at the gates. Bermingham made it clear that most of the men in the waggon works (who seemed now to have been on full time) worked piece work, and in October he said that the company was up to its old tricks. Earlier the York men had taken work from Shildon at a cut rate - now the company were out to perpetrate 'a gigantic crime' and force a reduction of one shilling on a five shillings job - reducing wages from 30s. to 24s. a week. If there was ever straight talking in York at this time it came from Bermingham. 'If you permit them to do it', he told the railwaymen, 'you are unworthy of the name of free citizens of one of the greatest nations in the world, because you are not free. The next thing I recommend the Company to do', he said in a nice phrase that must have touched many a raw nerve, 'is to erect a compound, and when you disobey they could give you the Chinese march.' (125) Not only was it difficult to persuade men to unionise, however, for the very good reason that they were afraid, but when they did, the NER had a nice way of punishing them and cooling their enthusiasm. As soon as there was a tendancy to organise in York, Bermingham said, the company 'removed the leaders from one place to another, and reduced men from piece work to day or ordinary time, thus reducing their wages.' (126) In November Bermingham was back in York claiming that his prophecies of a month earlier had been fulfilled. Piece work rates for painters on the NER, he said, had been lowered with 10d. being knocked off every 5s.10d. job. (127) Bermingham seemed to regard York as a challenge (which it was) and he reappeared to castigate the city's railwaymen in early 1911. (128) He was now able to report that men elsewhere (5,000 since Christmas) were joining unions, but the NER had sacked 200 in January. Why ? The 'reason given them', Bermingham went on, 'was slackness of work. [But] They did not believe that, because the men were re-placed by others from outside contraction, and it was known that the contractors paid those men 2d. per hour more, as well as their railway fares, and in many cases their lodgings.' If what Bermingham was saying was true, and he was never shown up as a liar, he was asking men to risk their jobs or at least their wages, with them helpless in the face of a harsh employer. In the harshest condemnation of his 1911 'season' Bermingham really went for the Yorkies.

"'The railway workers at York," said Mr Berminkham [sic], "are the worst organised body of men, and the most apathetic specimens of humanity I have ever met. They won't even turn out to a meeting that has for its object something for their own good; they won't do anything to assist each other, but they have a tendency, on the other hand, towards backhanded work. Carrying tales to the foreman," proceeded the speaker, "will never get you up; the foreman knows that if you are not a man to your own class you will never be a man to him. ... Anonymous letter writers who disclose what takes place at branch meetings are not appreciated."'

York's railwaymen had been in the forefront of those moves at the beginning of the century to make labour an important force in York politics. With that agreement about the 1906 election it must have looked as if they would make great advances - even with the restricted electorate which surely disqualified many of their potential supporters. Since then, though, things had gone wrong. With policies that were practically indistinguishable from those advocated by people like Hogge; with unemployment (surely) making people scared of adopting attitudes that might result in them being picked off by employers; with people like Hartley giving their opponents opportunities to point the finger at them; with tariff reform now looking like a reasonable weapon with which to tackle unemployment, and given the British working class's well-known distrust of 'socialism', 'labour had gone into the doldrums.' There had been no suggestion of a parliamentary candidate in the general election at the beginning of the year; municipal election results were disastrous; and there was now only one Labour representative on the Council. The party, when it did make a move, was accused (justifiably) of splitting the anti-Tory vote. What would it do if and when another general election was called ?

When the constitutional conference broke down Asquith decided on a dissolution, and this time did get a secret understanding with the King that 'in the event of the Government being returned with a majority at the General Election, I should use my prerogative to make Peers if asked for' to swamp a recalcitrant House of Lords. (129) But were prospects good for the Liberals ? No government since 1832 had ever won three times running, the five-monthly truce during the constitutional conference had seemingly weakened the popular demand for reform, and the death of Edward VII had delayed political events to the detriment of the Liberal cause. What would happen in York ? The answer was not long delayed. The parties simply decided there would be no contest.

The dissolution of Parliament was announced for 28 November and rumours went round York that Arnold Rowntree would stand again with either Hamar Greenwood, who would also be a candidate at Sunderland, or Chiozza Money (130) as a running mate. (131) Three days later a joint meeting of the York Conservative Association, the Liberal Unionist Association and the Junior Imperial League met to choose their candidate or candidates. They received a message from Riley-Smith who urged them to make an arrangement with the Liberals whereby if they agreed to run Rowntree only, the Tories would only put up Butcher. (132) Riley-Smith was ill at the time (he had several serious operations shortly afterwards), but did not mention this as a reason for not wanting to stand himself. In a letter dated 15 November he revealed that he had been bitterly disappointed by the results of the last contest. Then, he noted, 136 Conservatives had plumped for Butcher. Why ? It certainly does look an extraordinary fact. Why did they not split with Riley-Smith ? He said it was because they were Tory temperance supporters. 'My conclusion,' Riley-Smith said, 'is that there are a certain number of Conservatives in the city [who] won't support a brewer on principle.' (133) He may have been right, and that being the case he refused to stand. By not doing so, he said, Butcher would be saved something like £1,000.

The Liberals agreed to do a deal, so for the second time in less than five years, York was the subject of an 'arrangement' between the parties, but this one was conditional. If Labour entered the fray the Tories would regard their candidate as an ally of Rowntree and they would then, they said, run a second man. But Labour did not nominate anyone, and Butcher and Rowntree were returned unopposed. It would be interesting to know whether the Liberals had had talks with the likes of Hartley and Will Dobbie.

The decision to do a deal was not without its critics. Had Hogge been in York he, no doubt, would have opposed it, and some Tories suspected that there would be last minute moves of the kind George Hudson used to engage in. C.H. Akers was one. 'The Radical Party in York on a former occasion "did" the Labour party,' he said, 'and if they got the chance they would "do" us tomorrow.'

The second general election of 1910 hardly altered the balance of the parties at all, and the Liberals continued in power having to rely, still, on the support of the other parties. What happened to York's number one politician, the man the Tories loved to hate ? Hogge found himself fighting a Tory, a socialist (J. O'Connor Kessack), and a candidate supported by the National Union of Women's Suffrage Societies and the Scottish Federation of Suffrage Societies. This was William J. Mirrlees who said he was in 'general agreement' with the Unionist candidate! The contest was exciting (as it had to be with Hogge taking part) and was a close-run thing, with Mackinder, the Tory, the eventual winner. In Sunderland Hamar Greenwood was returned.

Not long after the election was over Riley-Smith appeared as the principal speaker at a York LVA meeting, promising gloom and doom for the drink trade now that the Liberals were back in power. 'It did not require much common sense to realise that if the Veto of the House of Lords was abolished their trade would be largely at the mercy of any transient, eccentric or fanatical majority in the House of Commons,' he said, 'and that their only safeguard against intolerable oppression, if not final extinction, would entirely disappear.' There would be more pub closures Riley-Smith said, but he did not live to see them. He never recovered from his surgery and died in May at the age of 48. (134)

The veto of the House of Lords was not abolished, as Riley-Smith feared it would be. It was, however, modified. In February Asquith introduced a Parliament Bill which completed its passage through the Commons in May. In the Lords it encountered die-hard opposition, and attempts to modify it, which the Commons rejected. Finally it passed by a majority of 131 to 114. By its provisions the Lords' powers, which they had used so recklessly since 1906, were curtailed. The British electorate, seemingly of the belief that the second election of 1909 had settled the matter, showed little interest in the culmination of the fight between the two Houses.

1. *Press* 10 March 1909
2. See the letter from a Dr Shann, *Ibid* 16 March 1909
3. Eg *Ibid* 19 March 1909. Letter from Hogge
4. *Ibid* 30 March 1909
5. *Ibid* 26 March 1907
6. The campaign can be followed in issues of the *Herald*, the *Press* and the *Gazette* from about early April

7. Grigg *op.cit*. Chap 6 *passim*. The following description of the creation of the People's Budget is based on this source
8. See eg *Press* 14 May 1909
9. *Ibid*
10. *Ibid* 27 November 1909
11. *Ibid* 2 December 1909
12. *Ibid* 16 October 1909
13. *Ibid* 1 October 1909
14. *Ibid* 23 November 1909
15. *Ibid* 2 December 1909
16. During the campaign Riley-Smith was asked what wages he paid his workers. His reply was 21s. to 22s. a week
17. *Press* 22 September 1909
18. *Ibid* 9 October 1909
19. *Ibid* 8 October 1909
20. A reference to an oft reported action of one of their Lordships
21. *Press* 30 September 1909
22. *Ibid* 26 November 1909
23. *Ibid* 3 September 1909
24. Letter in *Ibid* 13 November 1909
25. *Ibid* 13 May 1909
26. *Ibid* 8 June 1909
27. *Ibid* 8 September 1909
28. *Ibid* 16 September 1909
29. *Ibid* 5 October 1909
30. *Ibid* 8 October 1909
31. *Ibid* 16 December 1909
32. *Ibid* 15 October 1909
33. *Ibid* 25 October 1909
34. *Ibid* 27 October 1909
35. *Ibid* 28 October 1909
36. *Ibid* 30 October 1909
37. *Herald* 1 November 1909. *Press* 1 November 1909
38. *Press* 30 October 1909. They wanted the officers to have one rest day in seven instead of 14 days.
39. *Ibid* 1 November 1909
40. *Ibid* 2 November 1909
41. This can be inferred from a speech at a meeting at which Councillor E. Walker was readopted as a candidate for Guildhall. 'Ninety-five per cent of the speeches delivered in the Council were more or less of a political nature,' Walker said, but 'when they as Conservatives were adopted as candidates, they had an absolutely independent hand. They could vote on any discussions as they chose, and could exercise an independent opinion and vote according to their conscience. Unfortunately such was not the case with the opposition.' *Ibid* 19 October 1909
42. We strope got this name from some small digests of the classics he produced called 'Brother Richard's Bookshelf.'
43. *Press* 5 October 1909
44. A.J. Peacock, 'Adult Education in York, 1800-1947' *op.cit*.
45. *Press* 4 October 1909
46. In Bootham
47. Sharp, of course, called himself an 'Independent'
48. *Press* 13 November 1909
49. *Ibid* 27 November 1909. 'When requested to stand on previous occasions,' Rowntree said later, 'I have felt clear that my work lay in other fields.' However, he went on, 'the country is [now] faced with a dangerous and unprecedented situation. The House of Lords is challenging the established right of the House of Commons to exercise supreme control in questions of finance. If this claim were established it would reduce the House of Commons to impotence and would deprive every elector of a large part of the value of his vote.'
50. *Ibid* 7 January 1910
51. *Ibid* 5 January 1910

52. *Ibid* 10 January 1910
53. *Ibid* 14 January 1910
54. *Ibid* 8 January 1910
55. I.A. Williams, *The Firm of Cadbury 1831-1931* (1931) p 193. See also A.G. Gardiner, *The Life of George Cadbury* (nd) and G. Wagner, *The Chocolate Conscience* (1987)
56. Williams *op.cit.* p 194
57. *Ibid* p 196
58. See eg *Daily Graphic* 24 October 1907
59. Williams *op.cit.* p 206
60. H.W. Nevinson, *More Changes More Chances* (1925) p 87. Nevinson was a journalist who frequently wrote for the Cadbury newspaper *The Daily News*. His book *A Modern Slavery* was frequently quoted in the trial in which he was to be a witness. He was not called
61. *Press* 5 January 1910
62. *Ibid* 23 November 1909
63. *Ibid* 27 and 30 November 1909
64. *Ibid* 15 January 1910
65. *Ibid* 27 December 1909
66. *Ibid* 2 November 1909
67. *Ibid* 8 December 1909
68. *Ibid* 12 January 1910
69. *Ibid* 6 December 1909
70. *Ibid* 7 January 1910
71. *Ibid* 1 April 1909
72. Wilkinson maintained that if a person had received only *medical* relief they should not be disqualified
73. *Press* 14 January 1910. It seems to be around this date that the newspapers began to spell Riley-Smith's name with a hyphen. The poster for the 1910 election did so. I have used this version of his name throughout this work
74. *Ibid* 28 January 1910
75. *Ibid* 18 January 1910
76. *Ibid* 11 March 1910. *Herald* 14 March 1910
77. *Ibid* 22 and 28 July 1909
78. *Ibid* 19 February 1910. Councillor Petty alleged that remarks of this kind had been made when at an education committee meeting - Hogge then blamed Edith, though there was a Miss Milner on the staff. The Rev Jones sprang to Edith's defence and denied the charges against her. *Ibid* 24 February 1910. The following reference to the York Mystery Plays is from *Ibid* 29 December 1909
79. *Ibid* 19 January 1909
80. *Ibid* 1 April 1909
81. Prospectus in *Herald* 17 May 1909
82. *Press* 24 June, 19 July 1909
83. *Ibid* 21 March 1910
84. The other place, as will be seen, was not in a residential area like Sycamore Terrace
85. *Press* 20 April 1909
86. *Ibid* 17 May 1909
87. *Ibid* 31 July 1909
88. *Ibid* 2 and 7 October 1909
89. *Ibid* 3 February 1910
90. The Fulford and the YMCA groups. There were eight groups by December. See eg *Ibid* 28 June, 25 September and 9 December 1909
91. On the Dearlove/Hartley type of attitude toward the Scouts - perhaps from a more 'respectable' source - see eg the lecture on militarism given to the Wesleyan Brotherhood in *Ibid* 18 July 1910. The Boys Brigade was well established in the city and the 3rd company at this time started a rifle club! On the Brigade see eg *Ibid* 30 September 1910. On the first annual meeting of the York and District Scouts organisations see *Ibid* 21 March 1910. New groups were still being formed. See *Ibid* 12 November 1910 for the formation of the St Paul's troop
92. F. Finnegan, *Poverty and Prostitution in York* (1979)
93. *Press* 20 May 1909
94. *Ibid* 7 June 1909

95. *Ibid* 15 November 1909
96. On the tram routes see Murray, *Tramways op.cit.*
97. *Press* 20 January 1910
98. *Ibid* 15 February 1910
99. *Ibid* 3 March 1910
100. *Ibid* 10 March 1910
101. *Ibid* 17 March 1910
102. *Ibid* 21 March 1910
103. For typical Sabbatarian attitude at this time see the speech by J. Melrose, JP, at a meeting called to raise funds for a Clifton Church Institute in *Ibid* 30 September 1910
104. *Ibid* 23 February 1910
105. *Ibid* 12 November 1910
106. Cross *op.cit.* p 113
107. Rhodes James *op.cit.* p 249
108. This controversy (in which Hogge seems to have been completely in the right - wanting to choose the best qualified candidate) ran and ran in the press. See eg *Press* 19 August 1910
109. *Ibid* 18 November 1910
110. *Ibid* 19 August 1910
111. *Ibid* 24 May 1910
112. *Ibid* 27 and 31 May 1910
113. *Ibid* 28 May 1910
114. *Ibid* 6 August 1910
115. *Ibid* 10 September 1910
116. But a letter writer said he had not included figures for depreciation in his calculations. *Ibid* 31 August 1910. An interesting criticism of the Corporation at this time was that they were buying tram uniforms from Manchester while many York tailors were 'disengaged'. *Ibid* 3 November 1910
117. *Ibid* 12 October 1910. In September the Council had decided they would try and purchase the waterworks. *Ibid* 23 September 1910
118. The establishment of such a place was recommended and agreed by the Council in September then 'referred back' in November *Ibid* 23 September and 15 November 1910
119. *Ibid* 4 April 1910
120. A fruiterer went bankrupt in 1910 and at his hearing blamed his troubles on the removal of the NER men from York
121. *Press* 21 July 1910
122. *Ibid*
123. *Ibid* 22 and 30 July 1910
124. *Ibid* 23 and 27 August 1910
125. *Ibid* 27 October 1910
126. *Ibid* 28 October 1910
127. *Ibid* 22 November 1910
128. *Ibid* 25, 26 and 28 April 1911
129. H. Nicholson, *King George V - His Life and Reign* (1952) p 129
130. Chiozza Money, a famous Liberal politician, author of several influential books
131. *Press* 19 November 1910
132. *Ibid* 25 November 1910
133. *Ibid*
134. *Ibid* 19 May 1911, obituary. He was buried at Newton Kyme. Funeral reported eg in *Ibid* 22 May 1911

CHAPTER 7

'MOB LAW IN YORK'
(AND SUNDAY TRADING)

Riley-Smith had prophesied that there would be attacks on the licensed trade and was concerned by the campaign to reduce the number of pubs. At the Brewster Sessions of 1911 the renewal of the licenses for five houses (1) was opposed, and eventually two of them were closed, one belonging to J.J. Hunt and the others to the Albion Brewery Company. (2) Once more attempts were made to get licensed houses in the Bishopthorpe Road estate, which failed, and once more great criticisms were made of the city's working men's clubs. Those had been steadily increasing in number as a return showed. (3)

Year	Number of Clubs	Members
1903	31	5,380
1904	30	5,244
1905	31	5,380
1906	31	5,243
1907	32	5,379
1908	34	5,458
1909	35	5,661
1910	37	6,346

The 'trade' was worried about the competition of working men's clubs, and their unfair trading position. It was also concerned about that phenomenon of the 'long pull' which still persisted. The Lord Mayor of 1911, Alderman T. Carter, (4) a butcher, said what many must have thought in his comments following the Chief Constable's report. 'If somebody came into my place for one pound of steak', Carter said, not very grammatically, and 'I gave them a pound and a half nobody would interfere ... but it appears that in the case of the long pull there is a penalty of £10.' How much more did you get than you paid for if you were lucky enough to hit on a long pull pub ? There do not seem to be any figures for York, but the *Press* of 10 March 1911 reported that in the Kirkham magistrates' area some publicans 'gave ... almost a gill over measure.' They would undoubtedly have found their way into *The Good Beer Guide* had that valuable publication existed then, and quite rightly so.

The Chief Constable presented his usual statistical report to the justices. There were now 312 licensed premises, (5) he said, one to every 249 persons using the 1901 census figures, one to every 286 on current calculated population statistics. Those figures were to be made precise in 1911 when the decennial census was taken in April. The suffragettes had been told of the WSPU's policy of resisting the census by Adela Pankhurst when she visited York, (6) but nothing was done in York (as it was in places like Cardiff, Bristol and Reading). Preliminary census returns showing a population increase were published as early as May. (7)

Population of York		
1901	1911	Percentage increase
77,916	82,297	5.63

The census of 1911 showed that York still refused to become an industrial city and prospects of that happening were not enhanced when yet another rate increase was decided on in April. (8) The Tories were still in power, of course, and the rate rises were a considerable embarrassment to them - so much so that one of their leading members, Sir Joseph Sykes Rymer, declared that, whereas he had succeeded in knocking a penny off the 1911 increase, this 'is the last time I will move the adoption of a report that means an increase in our present high rates.' (9) How high were they, and what had the recent increase been ? The proposal for 1911 was 8s.2d. - 3d. more than a year earlier, and 6d. more than in 1908. (10) How did York compare with neighbouring places ? The answer is reasonably well. In 1910 Halifax had collected 9s; Bradford 8s.10d.; Huddersfield 8s.4d.; and Leeds 9s.4d.

Why was Sykes Rymer so concerned about the rates (apart from the fact that as a businessman he would have to pay more himself) ? He was worried about the oft repeated fact that it was considered that 'high' rates were keeping industry away from York, but he was also concerned about possible political consequences. The parties were fairly evenly balanced on the Council, but with the Tories safe with a majority of Aldermen. But they could take no chances, and a swing could oust them from power. But where was the swing to go to ? Not the Liberals, surely, as they advocated even more municipal expenditure with a Rowntree (for example) wanting to free Skeldergate bridge of tolls and Davies wanting a municipal cemetery. (11) No, the fear at that time was that some kind of Ratepayers Association might come into existence. There were letters in the press suggesting the formation of one. (12)

Just after the latest rate rise had been announced a municipal by election was held in the Liberal ward of Micklegate. It was to show that the split between Labour and Liberals was now complete, and the splitting of the anti-Tory vote letting in the Tory looked a distinct possibility. Labour decided to run John Francis Glew, a goods checker, of the Amalgamated Society of Railway Servants, and the Liberals put up Arthur Wilkinson, a works manager of East Mount Road. The Tories ran Thomas Powell, a licensed victualler of 55, Blossom Street. Wilkinson made a great deal of the need for trams into the South Bank and Leeman Road areas, (13) and he had the active support of J.M. Hogge.

Defeated at the general election Hogge had returned to enliven and entertain the city of York again, speaking a great deal of commonsense, yet managing to put people's backs up by the way he said it - a not all that rare phenomenon. He had had a cracking row with Charles A. Thompson (who spoke of his 'gyrative megrims' in the Council chamber) over spending on naval armaments, (14) and had been dragged into arguments over the new Holgate railway bridge. Why did not the talkative Mr Hogge object to that monstrosity being put up to carry 'his' tramways people asked ? Did he approve of it ? (15). This was yet another example of people doing nothing when they should have, and complaining when it was too late, but Hogge sided with them, and he was right. The thing which the *Evening Press* called 'a ponderous erection', (16) in a phrase which in later times would certainly have appeared in 'This England' or *Private Eye*, was and is an eyesore. It was opened in August. 'The bridge, which is about 150 feet in length, if not in appearance such as might satisfy all aesthetic tastes, is of itself a veritable triumph of engineering skill', one of the papers said, making as much of a virtue out of necessity as possible and neglecting to say why *it* had not opposed it. The ponderous erection had cost £3,500 and had been built by Handyside of Derby.

Hogge had also been involved in a splendid row about the city's coronation celebrations. He and Councillor Rowntree had objected to money from the rates being spent on decking out the city, (17) and he reverted to this topic in speeches on behalf of Wilkinson in the Micklegate by election. Why not put the money to better purposes - like helping the poor and needy Hogge asked ? And why had only Messrs Rowntrees been approached for gifts of chocolate and cocoa. 'Why didn't they [the Corporation] go to Alderman Sir Joseph Sykes Rymer and ask him to give free coals or Alderman Purnell to give packets of "Woodbines" ?', Hogge asked. (18)

Edith Milner also got herself into a spot of bother over the coronation. Edith who was well into her letter writing to the press penned a strange missive saying that she had solicited small sums for a coronation gift from the Boy Scouts and had got very little. 'It was felt the George effort should be left to the men', she said, 'If the women win the chivalry of England will gladly recognise their superiority, and bow to them in all loyalty.' (19) This strange letter prompted a stinging rebuke from a Scout official, who said she had ticked off his charges for not digging deep into their pockets. (20) His letter seems a little unfair, but it is good to see Edith getting a taste of the treatment she dished out - and continued to dish out (particularly during the war) to others.

Edith Milner would have approved of Powell's candidacy for Micklegate, but that gentleman's chances of election might just have been spoiled a little by what looks like - at this remove of time - charges that the ruling party in the city had been doing its friends a favour. The Council had spent £1,000 on doing up a property which was then let for £110 a year to the Conservative party for a club. The figure that should have been charged was really £140, an irate writer to the press said, before going on to say that one of those involved had wanted to pay tram conductors a paltry 3d. an hour. (21) He also objected to decking out the streets at the ratepayers' expense, saying that Skeldergate bridge should be freed of toll with the coronation money.

What happened in Micklegate ? Surprisingly the Liberals won easily with Wilkinson over 200 votes ahead of Powell, (1,072:819). J.F. Glew was third with 628 votes. He was to have a great deal on his plate in the very near future.

The summer of 1911 was unbelievably hot, with tremendously high temperatures in York, (22) and during those oppressive months an international dispute (23) dragged on, coinciding with the 'final crisis over the passing of the Parliament Act.' Not only that but the country 'witnessed the onset of the gravest strike movement that till then' it had known. (24) York was to be affected, despite its non-industrial character, and the city was to witness some of the most exciting scenes in its modern history.

The judgement in the courts in what came to be known as the 'Osborne case' had swung the working class movement away from parliamentary to trade union action. W.V. Osborne had been the secretary of the Walthamstow branch of the Amalgamated Society of Railway Servants and he had sued the union, holding that it was wrong for a union to provide for parliamentary representation through a compulsory levy. The court agreed and the decision was upheld on appeal (November 1908) and by the House of Lords (December 1909). Labour MPs immediately found their salaries were cut off and industrial trouble ensued on an unprecedented scale. In that 'summer of extreme heat', a historian of the time recorded, 'industrial tempers' went 'from bad to worse. Not only was there, as it seemed, a kind of running fire of strikes ... but every strike was attended by violence.' (25)

James Bermingham and people like him had been haranguing York crowds for years to get them into unions, but without success. Spurred on by price rises, the behaviour of the Lords maybe, the examples elsewhere, and local factors, workers began to move in 1911 as never before, however. Many were non-unionists, others decided to join the unions after they had struck. It all made for a very exciting long hot summer of discontent. When one looks, once more, at what many were earning it is again a cause for amazement that they did not strike or organise earlier. That they did not do so must be explained by fear (of reprisals and the sack), and that great pool of unemployment that already existed in the city.

The incidents to be described mainly involved the unskilled or semi-skilled, and the first strike of 1911 started at the flour mill belonging to Henry Leetham Ltd, and rapidly spread to the Ebor Flour Mills, Skeldergate. Leethams was frequently referred to (by the likes of that great wag J.M. Hogge) as 'Siberia' because the wages had been 'frozen' there for many a year. (26) During the general election the Leethams had had a prolonged dispute with Arnold Rowntree over tariff reform, it will be recalled, and they had also said then that they would donate a huge sum to the County Hospital if it could be shown that they paid less than 25s. a week. Hogge reminded his listeners of this at a meeting in support of the strikers and told the Leethams to get their cheque book out. Now it was seen, Hogge said, that they were paying $3^3/_4$d. an hour for a 59 hour week.

Between 400 and 500 employees at Leetham's struck, including millers, labourers, packers, watchmen, fitters, joiners, and 'the girls in the sack department.' They demanded increases of $^1/_2$d. an hour and, in the words of the *Evening Press*, they were 'not associated with any Trade Union, but it is said that they intend to join one immediately.' (27) To begin with they spoke of joining the Millers' Union, but they then considered forming a branch of the Gasworkers' and General Labourers' Union, which was particularly strong in Leeds. This was eventually formed and Francis Reilly, the secretary of the Disputes Committee which was set up, became secretary.

In addition to Reilly a Mr Wood from the union helped the Leetham workers and J.H. Hartley and Will Dobbie of the Trades Council were active as speakers and organisers. What attitude did the employers adopt ? They pointed out that the men were given an extra hour's payment a day ($12^1/_2$ hours pay for an $11^1/_2$ hour day), but refused to negotiate at all. The firm also pointed out that their men did not lose 'wet time'.

What had triggered off the dispute at Leetham's ? The knowledge that the firm had made a profit of £89,000 during the last trading year was not lost on the men, and when the firm put its prices up (taking advantage of a dispute in Hull) they seem to have regarded this as almost a provocation. There was also some talk about a proposed decrease in wages which, if true, shows the management up in an extremely insensitive, perhaps aggressive, light.

The Leetham's strike became violent. Superintendent Woolnough of the York police was injured in a stone throwing incident in Hungate and a man called Baynton was put in fear of his life. Baynton was an extremely unpopular foreman and crowds waited at the mill gates to get him. Will Dobbie went in with a police escort and got Baynton out and made safe in the police station and similar treatment had to be dished out on behalf of a man called Brown. He was a timekeeper who had fled from the mill and taken refuge in the Liberal Club from whence he was taken under escort. (28)

Leetham's mill was eventually closed down and then the employers had to meet a deputation (consisting of Reilly, Dobbie and Wood) whether they liked it or not, and the men secured most of their demands. The extra hour's pay was to remain, as was the length of the working day, and $1/2$d. increase was given all round. (29) Union recognition was not conceded, it seems, and new wage rates per hour seem to have included: $5^1/4$d. for wagon loaders; $4^1/4$d. for warehousemen; 5d. for head packers and $4^1/4$d. for mill labourers.

The Leetham's strike lasted less than a fortnight, and was remarkable. Several hundred unskilled men, who had resisted the blandishments of trades unionists over the years, had come out on strike, used some force, and gained nearly all their demands. Not only that but a new union had been formed and the strikers had had considerable public sympathy. That was demonstrated when Dobbie eventually published the accounts of the strike committee which showed that a collection of £158 had been made, from which modest strike payments had been made to nearly 500 persons. (30) The mill strike was sure to be copied. It was.

The next group of workers to strike in that hot summer of 1911 were the York sand catchers - the men who dug sand from the river beds and brought it on barges to the city for use in the building trade. Over the August Bank Holiday about 30 men struck for more wages. What were they receiving at the time ? They said they were getting 30s. in the summer and only 10s. in the winter months. (31) The sand catchers were rapidly joined by many of the city's carters, who were said to have been receiving a mere £1 a week (with 6d. an hour overtime), and who demanded 25s. Both groups joined the Gas Workers' and General Labourers' Union, and both called in the services of Will Dobbie who said, at a public meeting organised by the GWGLU, that he hoped the day was not far off when no man in York would work for less than 6d. an hour. (32) The sand catchers were successful in obtaining their demands, but the carters resumed work on the old terms while Dobbie negotiated with the masters on their behalf. The negotiations dragged on, and the men reduced their demands to 24s. (33)

Reports of those negotiations said that many of the men had been receiving less than £1 a week (and overtime), and those who struck were mainly employees of Messrs Blundy and Messrs J.H. Walker of Layerthorpe Bridge. At the height of the strike it was reckoned that some 700 carters were involved, and when Dobbie formulated their original demands they were for '6d. per hour for ordinary time; time and a quarter for overtime; time and a quarter for Sunday stable duty; double time for ordinary work on Sunday ... [with the] working day [to] consist of the following hours: 6 a.m. till 5 p.m., and on Saturday 6 a.m. till 1 p.m.' The settlement finally arrived at seems to have been for a wage of 21s. This was revealed during the November municipal elections when Will Dobbie said that it had taken Robert Richardson, a Tory candidate, 'six weeks to give the carters of the city a minimum wage of 21s. per week.' Richardson had 'presided over the gatherings of the masters, because he was invited to do so', but denied Dobbie's allegations. His wages book showed that his men averaged £1.11s.11d. per week per man, which was very good 'for this class of labour' he said. This totally missed the point, surely, as it probably included higher grades and overtime. Dobbie said 21s. was the minimum, and if that is what the men got, they were very poorly paid.

The glassworks was another major employer of labour in York and at the meeting at which Dobbie made his remark about 6d. an hour G.P. Richardson, and Reilly the chairman and secretary of the York Gas Workers' Union, urged the glass workers to take action. They did, and not before time if some of the reports that went round the city were true (and it is clear they were). Some of the men said that able bodied workers were sometimes leaving the glass works with only 13s.11d. and these, believe it or not, still often continued to work during the dispute - going in to cries of there go 'the "Thirteen and eleven penny men"'. (34) Later Dobbie said that the glass workers 'had been goaded on to desperation' and Reilly painted a dreadful picture of conditions there. There were men at the works, he said, 'who ought to be receiving 33s. per week as a standard wage for 54 hours work [who] were actually working from about five o'clock in the morning until nearly nine o'clock in the evening for a *paltry 17s.3d. Those were men who had actually served a seven years' apprenticeship to their particular business.' (35)*

G. Wilson Clarke and W.W. Langwell, joint managers of the glass works, wrote a letter to the press which must rank with that of Edith Milner about the scouts for weirdness. After saying they would have no union recognition and that the teasers (the furnacemen) got extra pay Clarke and Langwell said that 'It should also be stated that washing bottles by piecework has enabled good workers to earn 11s. to 12s. a week.' (36) This is incredible, unless they meant 11s. to 12s. *extra*, and one once again wonders why there were not more strikes much earlier (and is forced to the same conclusions mentioned earlier about fear and unemployment).

Leetham's had been a prosperous firm for some years, as has been noted, but the York Glass Company had been going through a lean period. For five years, J. Tatham Ware pointed out, shareholders had received no dividends, then last year received $1\frac{1}{4}$ per cent and this year $1\frac{1}{2}$ per cent. (37) Perhaps the 'Thirteen and eleven penny men' were on short time or on badly paid piece work, and no doubt the firm said it could not afford increases, but what were the 'official' rates there ? According to one report the teasers received 31s. for alternate weeks of 84 and 72 hours; order-getters got 24s.; coopers £1; packers 18s.; bottle sorters £1; and women *6s. to 7s. a week*! (38) The men demanded wage rates of 5d. to 6d. an hour; the abolition of piece work (not surprisingly); double time for Sunday work; and a 53 hour week.

The chairman of York Glass was Sir Joseph Sykes Rymer, the Tory council member who had said he would never present another increased rate demand, and within a day or so of the strike starting it was reported that 200 of his men had joined the Gasworkers' Union. The strike was less than complete (one report said that at one stage only 50 to 60 workers were out) and it was marked by some violence and the court appearance of three workers. These were Fred Sharp, John Benson and William Barnwell, and they were prosecuted under Section Two of the Trades Disputes Act for what Norman Crombie called '"peaceful picketing" in connection with the Glass Workers' strike'. (39) They had gone into the works and forced William Lowther, a furnace man, to leave work. He was taken back in by G.W. Clarke, who along with Langwell and others had organised a picket of the pickets. Sharp was eventually bound over for six months and ordered to pay costs, and all three defendants lost their jobs.

The glassworkers, the sand catchers, the millers and the carters were not the only groups to take industrial action in 1911. 'The uneasiness which ... prevailed in the industrial world' also 'infected the tramway employes of the City Corporation' it was reported in August, and the men met to consider forming a branch of the Amalgamated Society of Tramway Workers. (40) A little later the schoolboys of York (or some of them) struck (and got struck).

The schoolchildren's strike of 1911 is fairly well-known and quite recently (1990) formed the subject of a BBC radio documentary. Throughout the country children emulated their parents and struck - for less homework, half holidays, cushioned seats, for fewer beatings, and in some places for pay. (41) In York the 'movement' was nipped in the bud. Elsewhere there was violence and window breaking. In Stoke police were on duty at some of the schoools.

In early September some 30 children at Queen's Street School struck during the lunch break. It was said they were encouraged to do so by some who had left school, and most of them went and played football. During the afternoon a *Press* reporter visited the school and found that there were only eight out of 20 attending one class, and only ten out of 46 in the woodworking class. While he was there a parent called and said ' ... "They [the strikers] say they want less work and less cane."' '"They will probably get more of both," was Mr Gent's [the headmaster's] grim reply. "I shall have my work set out for tomorrow."' A similar demonstration of militancy was rapidly quelled at the English Martyrs school. (42)

The local newspaper reporters had a marvellous time reporting the schoolboys' strike, and their reports showed that pupil power was not even a cloud on the horizon. The trouble at Queen Street threw up no natural leader - which is a pity. 'Some carried big sticks', it was recorded, 'but there were no flags and no speeches.'

In discussing the position Mr. Gent propounded a reason for the strike. Asked how the trouble had arisen, he replied: "I blame the newspapers for it. My boys know all about the strikes at Leeds, Hull and even Llanelly. (43) I especially blame a London daily, and I think the reports circulated are outrageous. They simply fire these children with a desire to go out truanting, or striking as they call it."

"I do not think," continued the headmaster, "that my boys would have gone but for the organised attempt made by others who are older. The worst of it is that the boys will suffer. I shall withdraw them from the shorthand class and from the libraries until Christmas, and, if I can gain the consent of the Education Committee, I shall not allow them to compete for the silver medals offered for swimming. Then there is the football club. Nineteen of this afternoon's absentees are in the football club, and I have ordered my teachers to send the ball back, and to withdraw from the Schools League. They must be punished in some way, because it is serious, from a monetary and disciplinary view, and also the effect it will have on the boys so far as I am concerned personally as the headmaster.

The following day the *Press* reported that all 65 strikers had gone back to Queen Street school. 'One of the older boys, when asked why they had come out on "strike", replied, "Oh, we wanted a holiday, and we got one. We also got ten strokes with the cane, too," ... ' The punishment which 'had been inflicted ... had [had] the desired effect', it was reported, 'as the boys stated they had no intention of coming out on "strike" again.' Mr Gent had methods of bringing his strike to an end that were not available to the likes of Sykes Rymer, Robinson and Clarke.

The York strikes were stimulated by what was going on nationally and conditions, not reason, pushed men towards militancy and unionism. It would be seen whether the unions that were created would last, but the older established organisations had also increased in strength. Will Dobbie was a member of the General Railway Workers' Union (Bermingham's union) and he said that his York branch had grown enormously from having 200 members at the start of the year, to 1,800 in August. (44) Perhaps the influx came in the summer when the strikes occurred, or perhaps Bermingham's pleas had at last had an effect. It is not known, but the General Railway Workers' Union was involved in the most sensational of the York disputes of 1911 - one which led one paper to carry a headline alleging there had been 'MOB LAW IN YORK'. (45)

Trouble had been simmering on the railways for the whole of the year, and it came to a head in the summer, but this time the York railwaymen were caught up in a national movement. The earlier strikes described in this work - including that of Shunter Goodchild for instance - had been NER troubles. In 1911 'England found herself for the first time in the throes of a general railway strike.'

The troubles of 1911 went back to a Board of Trade conciliation scheme set up five years earlier. This was generally reckoned to have been a confidence trick perpetrated on the workers and 'specifically did not allow for union recognition and was only acceptable to the companies in that form.' (46) This had caused tremendous resentment and the unions called a general strike to start at 8pm on 16 August. On the day the decision was made (15 August) troops had fired on striking dockers and two men were killed; it was a strike in which railway porters had struck in sympathy with the dockers. Asquith's last minute attempts to avert the railway strike failed.

The interesting fact about 1911 as far as the north east is concerned, is that the NER had actually recognised the unions - though that recognition was perhaps more apparent than real. So the men who came out in York and the rest of the NER's area did so in sympathy with their colleagues elsewhere. That is frequently said, and is partially true, but only partially. Whatever the constitutional system was, conditions on the railways were bad for many with low wages, (47) short time and frequent harsh management decisions. Bermingham and others demonstrated that, and whatever the ostensible reason for the strike of 1911 was, the reality was that the men were protesting as well against what, for many, if not all of them, were dreadful conditions. During the troubles in York there were stories of take-home wages as low as 17s.

The York newspapers were full of the events in the run-up to the railway strike and the day before its commencement the ASRS resolved not to handle any black legged traffic and a day later it was reported that 'railway business in the Minster City ... is paralysed, and [that] absolute chaos' reigned. On that day also pickets, distinguished with white ribbons, were evident in places like Holgate Road and in front of the station a porter was stoned, and 5,000 railwaymen were said to be out. On 19 August the whole of the most important news page of the *Press* (for example) was given over to the strike and there were descriptions of trains being stoned, while troops of the York and Lancaster Regiment patrolled the streets and guarded sensitive areas. J.F. Glew and J.H. Hartley had taken control in York, and they were said to dominate the city. Terry's factory had had to close 'in consequence of their inability to despatch consignments of goods to customers because of the strike', and the magistrates were ready to read the Riot Act. This was the day when the press recorded there was 'MOB LAW IN YORK', and this was also the day when a *Times* report drew attention to the strange fact that whereas the strike was supposed to be over union recognition, things were at their very worse in the one area where that principle had been established - the north east.

Trouble got worse in York as the railway strike went on. There was more stoning of trains that were running, and incidents were reported from outlying places like Earswick and more troops were brought in (48) - leading one newspaper to say that the scenes at York station when they arrived were reminiscent of those of a decade earlier when troops were departing for South Africa. But nationally the strike was over quite rapidly. Asquith handed over the task of negotiating with the strikers to Lloyd George and a Royal Commission was set up to examine grievances.

The strike ended nationally, but the men at York, who were not involved in the demand for 'recognition', stayed out, and 5,000 strikers and as many onlookers assembled on the Knavesmire to hear Glew and others demand a pledge from the company of 'no victimisation'. Two days later Hartley, Dobbie and others announced that assurances on this score had been given, and the dispute was officially over. Glew gave it as his opinion that the unions elsewhere had been beaten; Dobbie publicly spoke of the next strike.

The North Eastern Railway Company had been very adept at forestalling unionism and wage demands - and James Bermingham had spelled it all out. In 1911 they used a ploy which, it is said, they used again in 1926. (49) They rewarded (quite handsomely) those who did not strike - or who remained 'loyal' - and they were not alone in doing so. At the height of the dispute the London and North Western, the Great Northern and the Midland announced that double pay would be given 'to all those men connected with the movement and handling of traffic, [who] have remained loyal'. (50) The NER waited a little longer (it seems), but they did the same. '£20,000 is being distributed among the employes who remained at work during the recent strike', it was reported in September, 'and who rendered special services to the company on that occasion.' (51) Several hundred York clerks (who acted as porters) and others were said to be among those receiving payments.

A spin-off of the wave of York strikes in 1911 was the creation of a trader's association - the creators of which were all clearly tariff reformers. It was an organisation which, perhaps, the city's Tories looked askance at, as it quite clearly could become a force agitating along the lines of the ratepayer's association which was being spoken of at the time. Sykes Rymer's presence at the inaugural meeting would have added to those suspicions. He complained, again, about the level of the York rates and deplored the fact that income tax was now levied at 1s.2d. in the pound. Other figures prominent in the creation of the trader's association were Rhodes Brown and Councillor D. Dickinson, who admitted from the platform that men in York were receiving wages as low as 20s. a week.

During that summer of 1911, while the men (and boys) were striking, a York Tariff Reform League came into being and began to hold public meetings. This contributed to the intense political feeling that prevailed at the time. Then some municipal elections became due and these, too, added to the excitement. (52) They also gave Labour a chance to test the water. Had their fortunes revived ? Had the considerable skills of Dobbie as a strike leader and union negotiator produced a favourable swing in their favour ? How would they fare (always bearing in mind that the electorate was still a restricted one) ?

In May, before the industrial troubles really got under way, J.F. Glew, the railwayman, had failed to secure a seat for Micklegate. Then right in the middle of the disputes, Councillor Walker was made an Alderman, and an election to replace him became due. James Botterill Clarke, a solicitor, was chosen almost immediately by the Tories, and he campaigned for a fair wage clause for Council employees and better housing. His posters demanded 'A businessman for a business ward' and advocated 'Progress without extravagance.' The Tory situation at that stage can be seen in Clarke's programme. Fair wages and better housing were popular Progressive demands, and the plea implicit in the second slogan quoted might indicate how touchy the electorate was on the question of rates. The Liberals chose Charles Augustus Streicher, a bookseller, as their representative - a man who was well-known in the Hungate area for his work at a local Mission. Streicher went on record as saying that nearly all the men who had been on strike had joined a trade union.

The Guildhall election was to be a three cornered one - no doubt to the considerable annoyance of J.M. Hogge. (53) Who was to be Labour's candidate ? The choice looks like an obvious one - it was Will Dobbie.

Dobbie stood on the usual municipal Labour/Progressive platform and, of course, split the anti Tory vote. During his campaign one of his supporters made a powerful speech about the Hungate area, using, no doubt, statistics from the Health and Housing Reform Association which was still in existence - and still had plenty of work to do. There 'were 50 houses to the acre' there, the speaker said, compared with 44 for any other ward. There were 284 people living to the acre in Hungate, compared with 21 [sic] for the remainder of the city. (54)   In Hungate the death-rate was 28.9, 'whilst for the rest of the city it was 16.2.' All this was true, but many of those living in such dreadful conditions did not have the vote. Dobbie, nevertheless, scented victory. They had won in the Leetham's dispute, he said, and they had won a victory for the sand carters. Now they could win Guildhall, he thought, but he was wrong. In one of the smallest polls ever recorded in York, in which only 344 out of an electorate of 1,140 voted, Clarke won. (55) Perhaps the result signified that growing dissatisfaction with the Tories and their high rates. Perhaps their supporters simply stayed away.

Dobbie had really arrived on the York political scene, and in September the Gas Workers' Union decided to nominate him as a candidate for Walmgate at the November elections. These had to be more than usually interesting because the Liberals really were within striking distance of obtaining power locally. But would Labour, cock-a-hoop at the successes in the summer, spoil things ? For the first time in many years there would be contests in every ward. It would be like the early days of George Hudson's career all over again.

Labour ran only one other candidate along with Dobbie - which is perhaps surprising. Perhaps they tempered their new enthusiasm with a degree of realism - or perhaps, even now, there was an arrangement with the Liberals. Rather more likely the two sides simply recognised the facts of life and gave each other what they thought was a fair crack of the whip. Anyway, Glew was put up by Labour for Micklegate, with only one Liberal against him - J.B. Morrell. Dobbie also 'ran' with only one Liberal - the sitting Councillor William Henry Birch. What happened ? In Walmgate Dobbie and Birch were easily returned (56) and in Micklegate, where polling took place at that Queen Street School so recently the scenes of juvenile militancy (and where 2,744 out of 3,461 voted), J.F. Glew topped the poll, well ahead of Morrell, the second successful candidate. (57) O.F. Rowntree was returned again, (58) and in Bootham a sitting councillor was defeated by William Haughton Sessions and Dennis Vivian Scott in the highest municipal poll ever recorded. (59) What was the result of the elections ? Labour gained two seats; the Liberals gained one; and the Tories and the Liberals were thereafter equal in number on the Council. This election, incidentally (still fought on a very restricted register), saw women candidates at places like Carlisle and West Hartlepool, but none ran in York. At places like Bath and Birmingham women had been returned.

The gains of November 1911 were small but very significant. A prolonged period of Tory government had at last come to an end. J.M. Hogge and K.E.T. Wilkinson were generally reckoned to be the most influential among the Liberal councillors, and the way they had pushed municipalisation was remarkable. However, it looked as if York might be about to see the last of Hogge, as he was selected by the Liberals to fight the by election in Edinburgh East, caused by the death of Sir James Gibson. (60) The contest was to be as exciting as most things Hogge was involved in were.

Hogge had one opponent in Edinburgh - J. Gordon Jameson, a Tory. This time Hogge was supported by the National Union of Women's Suffrage Societies, as he deserved to be, and his opponents made a great deal of the fact that he was not enthusiastically welcomed as a prospective colleague by the hierarchy of the Liberal party. Whereas Jameson had been publicly endorsed by Bonar Law, Asquith and others had said nothing to the same effect on behalf of Hogge, the papers pointed out. Eventually Lloyd George went some way to remedying this apparent snub and Arnold Rowntree went up to Edinburgh to speak on Hogge's behalf. The campaign was particularly notable, however, for the York man's past being dragged up. He was reminded of his 'dream' speech of 1909, which the Dean of York had said was blasphemous. Hogge was questioned about the occasion when he gloated over the defeat of the 'anti-municipalisers' in the tramways election. Did he really give that speech a questioner asked ? No, replied Hogge, he did not. This was a bit much and the *Scotsman*, the *Herald*, the *Press* and other papers reprinted the text of Hogge's booboo (and pointed out that he had not denied giving it at the time). Where had his tormentor(s) got the story about his speech from, Hogge asked. From that Dr Kemp of York (sometimes rendered Kempe) he had had a little trouble with in the past he said. Kemp, it will be recalled, had given voice to a conspiracy theory about the Progressives' desire for a municipal tramway system in York. The Rowntrees - for whom Hogge was a mouthpiece, he said - wanted the trams to go out to New Earswick for the prime purpose of putting up the price of land there. This was preposterous, as the model village had nothing to do with the company, as Hogge pointed out, but Kemp was nevertheless taken to court for libel and lost the case that was heard in Leeds.

Rowntrees magnanimously waived any claim to damages, but in the 1910 municipal elections Kemp had contested Castlegate against Hogge - and lost quite impressively.

Hogge lied when he denied giving the 'dream' speech, (61) and the man who prompted the lie with a question wrote to the *Press* to say so. He also denied that he had ever heard of Kemp, and the latter's lawyers wrote to the press to say that James Myers had also got the details of the libel case wrong. Did these revelations harm the Hogge cause? Well they did, but he was returned nevertheless, with a reduced Liberal majority (but with a greater one than Gibson had had in his first election). (62)

The Edinburgh election saw Hogge getting the kind of treatment he had frequently dished out to others, and his past was dissected mercilessly. He was being pilloried because he was a working class lad whose father had been a working tailor, Hogge lamented, and he also had to answer for his actions a decade earlier. While Jameson was at the front with the 19th Company of the Imperial Yeomanry, Hogge was organising pro-Boer meetings, it was contended. Hogge was also repeatedly questioned about the new National Insurance Act, and frequently got the details about it wrong according to his critics. This was a measure which had caused immense hostility everywhere, with protests about it being as vehement, as unjustified, and as patronising in York as anywhere. (63) An example of this appeared in a letter which appeared in a local paper. It is a fair indication of the hostility and the level of argument marshalled to oppose a revolutionary reform. The letter was signed 'A Mistress, Haxby' and appeared in the *Press* on 23 November 1911. The headline declared 'INSURANCE BILL TYRANNY: MISTRESS AND SERVANTS.'

> Do you think [it asked] that the mistresses and maids of York and district fully realise the meaning of Mr. Lloyd George's mad and mischievous Insurance Bill? Do they understand that mistresses are told by him to rob their servants every month of 1s., also to pay 1s. themselves, and obtain stamps for the insurance card? ... Will not some influential ladies of York, and ... every town and village in the United Kingdom organise a house-to-house call for the purpose of obtaining signatures to both mistresses and maids who do not intend to be oppressed by Mr Lloyd George and his tyranny. ... railway men, miners, dockers, etc., strike and get what they want, therefore women of England must do likewise, and positively refuse to pay this unjust servant stamp tax.

Hogge made a triumphal return to York, and the arguments over the 'dream' speech ran and ran. The new MP announced that his victory had pleased everyone - that he had got in pleased the Liberals; that he had a reduced majority pleased the likes of Butcher. Would he now disappear from York, just as the control of the Council seemed about to be taken from the Tories? He would devote as much time as he could to municipal politics, he declared, and would at least see out his term of office. He would be present at the next meeting of the Council, he said. At that meeting he received what were patently insincere congratulations from many on his recent electoral success and took a prominent part, as always, in the deliberations. The most important decision made that day was to oppose a bill put before parliament by the York United Gas Company, which wanted to extend its area of operations. On his return to York (when Mrs Hogge declared that she was delighted with her husband's recent success at Glasgow!) Hogge had said that he would be representing York as well as Edinburgh, and that one of the things he could do was to 'block' bills there. Perhaps he had the Gas Company's legislation in mind. At that same Council meeting of February 1912 the wind of change which the likes of Hogge hoped to see blow through the corporation's dealings might perhaps be seen in a decision about the payments to be made to temporary workers employed in clearing the streets of snow. Both Labour and the Liberals had for long agitated for a 'fair wages' deal for Council employees, and during the great strikes of the summer Dobbie had said that no man should work in York for less than 6d. an hour. In February he supported that figure for the snow clearers and it was accepted. (64)

After many years in power, during which they adopted many opposition policies, the Tories had now to accept a different political situation, and in February they made what looks like an overtly political move when the Licensing bench of magistrates was chosen by their colleagues. Hitherto the licensing justices had always contained prominent Liberals and even prominent temperance men in their ranks, but in 1912 all those chosen were Tories, and all but one of them were churchmen. What would be their attitude to the pressing local issues a correspondent to the press wondered ? (65) The question of a pub or club (or pub and club) in the Bishopthorpe Road area was coming up yet again, a correspondent to the *Press* said. Canon Argles, he went on, should be on the *qui vive*. Just after this, incidentally, the very first working man was appointed to the York bench of magistrates. He was that Andrew Pattison Mawson, of Fulford Road, who had been one of the early Labour members of the Corporation. He worked for the York Glass Company, and for years had been a member of the Flint Glassmakers' Society and prominent as a York trades unionist. (66) (In August 1911 the first lady lawyer had appeared in the court Mawson was to grace.)

At just about the time Mawson was appointed to the bench a young lad appeared in court charged with stealing some empty beer bottles - and was birched for doing so (it was not his first offence). He had also been punished by his father, who told the court that his son had probably committed his terrible crime to get money to go to 'the pictures' and their effect on the young had concerned and was to continue to concern many people for many years. In York, not long before the lad swiped beer bottles to raise money to go to see the exploits of Rin Tin Tin (or something), the first purpose-built picture house had opened there

In Fossgate it had been planned to build two shops, but the developers encountered problems with subsoil water at a depth of about a foot and the work was abandoned. In place of the shops, National Theatres Ltd built a cinema called the York Electric Theatre. It was 125 feet wide; it had a screen made of 'cement plaster' which measured 21 feet by 14 feet; and it claimed to be 'The Finest and Most Luxurious and Up-to-Date Theatre in Yorkshire.' Admission to the Electric cost 3d., 6d., or 1s. (reserved seats), and children could gain entry for 2d., 3d., or 6d. It opened in June 1911, providing a balanced programme - part of which does not look as if it was worth getting birched for. (67) The *Press*, however, said the patrons were well pleased.

> The Electric Theatre, Fossgate, was filled last night, and its patrons appeared to be well satisfied by the films which were shown. The pictures, which were reproduced with wonderful clarity there being hardly a flicker, included a good variety of comics and dramas. "His first patient" depicted a doctor in love with a nurse, and after various complications the episode ends happily for all concerned. The comics included "Baby's Fall," "Scroggins goes in for chemistry," and "The tenor's lovely head of hair." Other dramatic films were "Priscilla and the Pequot," a story of the early Puritan settlement in New England; "Boniface," an historical play concerning the love affairs of the Pope's (Boniface's) niece and Sciarra Colonna, who ultimately separate owing to Colonna's treachery towards the Pope.

With the appearance of the Electric York had no less than four places showing films regularly, and the proprietors vied for custom with each other. Bert Rutter at the Victoria Hall, where there was a fire two days after the Electric opened, (68) one of many serious outbreaks in the city at that time, (69) was perhaps the most enterprising of them. He ran the controversial 'Sins of Utah' which managed to offend the local Mormons, and in November 1911 Rutter had introduced kinemacolour films to the city, obtaining them straight from the Scala Theatre, London. Moving pictures coloured by hand had been seen in Old Ebor before, the *Press* said, but this new invention by Charles Urban and G. Albert Smith would 'alter the whole aspect of cinematograph performances.' One of the first of the coloured films to be shown was a news reel of the unveiling of the Queen Victoria Memorial by King George V. (70) Another interesting development in the local film world took place in August 1911 when Debenhams, a local firm, set up a 'cinematograph department' to make films of local interest. One of its first ventures was to make a 500 feet long film of the Ebor Handicap. The race took place at 3.30 pm on the 30th of the month and was showing at the Empire and the Electric before 8.30 that evening.

The great counter-attraction to the flickers had been the two roller skating rinks in the city. What had happened to them ? Was the 'craze' for skating as short lived in York as it is generally said to have been in most places ?

The Sycamore Skating Rink had a short and troubled life and it closed on 3 June 1910. At the annual meeting of the York Skating Rink Company, held four months later, the secretary (H. Appleton) had a gloomy tale to tell. They had had an extremely unsatisfactory year, with 'trade' being good for only the first few months, he said. As winter approached attendances had fallen and the rink (which was built on land leased for five years) had been run at a loss. The directors had given up taking salaries, but a net loss had to be recorded for the period 17 July 1909 to 31 July 1910. A.E.Wynne, the chairman, told shareholders that 'The time had gone for making money out of skating rinks', and said they had tried to get a cinematograph company to take them over. (71)

Despite A.E. Wynn's statement that the skating boom had ended the Sycamore Rink was taken over by the Victoria Pier Syndicate - the owners of seven rinks - and reopened for business (charging less) in late October. (72) It was a bad deal, however, and on 3 April a winding up order was made, with stated liabilities of £190. (73)

One of the reasons given for the Sycamore Rink's failure was that it was too far out of town, and, of course, it had a competitor. The rink in Fishergate, however, was also in difficulties. It might have been expected that the demise of its competitor would help it. Maybe it did, but it was not enough, and in July 1911 it was announced that the parent company was going to be wound up under clauses of the Companies Consolidation Act of 1895. (74)

There had been hints in the press that all was not well with the City Roller Skating Palace, and in June 1910, just as its rival was folding up for the first time, an application was made for a licence 'to enable musical entertainments to be held there in place of roller skating.' (75) Despite this it reopened in September with accommodation for 700-800 skaters and 5,000 spectators. (76) It clearly was not doing well, however, and a month later it was reported that 'Kardoc the Handcuff King and Jail-breaker' was appearing there. (77) The likes of Kardoc, however, clearly did not help matters and when the decision to wind up the project was made there was but £8 in the kitty.

In October 1910, in the Burnley County Court, a public examination was held into the bankruptcy of Herbert Whitaker and William Greenwood, both of Padiham. These two and another had put £500 into the York venture and six others had put up £250. They had built the rink, but had then sold it to the City Roller Skating Palace Company, which, it will be recalled, had been formed to get a 'footage in Fishergate'. The sale price had been £6,750 and it seems that Whitaker - an undisclosed bankrupt, had stayed on as company secretary. (78)

Like the Sycamore Rink, however, the Palace was to get a new lease of life, and it was purchased from the liquidator and reopened under new management in the late summer of 1911. (79) It seemed to boom and once again the papers became full of the

221

build ups to, and descriptions of rink hockey matches. In December York played Putney, undeafeated in two years, with Leslie Stephens one of its stars. York's star at that time was J.W. Duxbury - 'considered ... the finest player in the world.' (80)

Another interesting development at about this time in the local world of entertainment occurred when Bert Rutter, Hogge, Forster Todd and others decided to set up a York Association Football Club as a limited liability company with a capital of £1,000 to be raised in 5s. shares. (81) Why was this ? The Lord Mayor said it was to raise the standard of the game in the city. They had no intentions of competing with the Rugby League side, it was emphasised, but although there were football teams in abundance in York 'there was not one which rose to the position of respectable mediocrity.' The intention was to seek entry to the Midland League and look for a ground on a tramway route. A Mr Biscomb waxed eloquent about what this new venture meant. He said that

> If managed by a committee of business men it was bound to succeed. Up to now York had not been able to boast of a sporting team worthy of the name of the city, but he hoped that night they would lay the foundation of a team that would bring credit and honour to the city. He went on to speak of the good moral effect which clean sport had on any town, and said that investigation had proved that where they ran big football teams there was less drunkeness when matches were played at home than when there were not.

The launching of the York professional football club got off to a slow start. In June the prospectus of the new organisation appeared. By now it had been decided to raise capital of £2,000 in 5s. shares, and a public meeting was held in June to hurry things along, as only £180 had been raised at that stage. (82) The directors announced that they would not proceed to an allotment until they had got 2,000 subscriptions, and their pleas did seem to have an affect, as the number of shareholders increased dramatically in the following week. (83)   A football ground which had hitherto been used by St Peter's School had been obtained in Burton Stone Lane, it was reported, and a tenancy of five years. Furthermore the club had been offered one of seven vacancies in the Midland League, and one of the speakers rather ambiguously announced that there was every reason for expecting that if the project succeeded, English Cup games would be seen in York before long. (By this he really seems to have meant that cup semi-finals could be played on the new ground.) Bert Rutter revealed that Peter Boyle, an Irish international full back, who had played for Sunderland, Sheffield United, Motherwell and Albion Rovers, had been appointed as player manager. 'The prospects of a high grade Association game in York are now very bright', said the *Press*, as enthusiastic as Mr Biscombe, 'and next season can be looked forward to with avidity by all Soccer devotees'.

The Burton Stone Lane ground (Field View) was renovated in rapid time, and the papers followed the signings of the club with great interest. The pitch had needed levelling and draining, work done by the firm of Backhouse, and a stand to hold 1,100 was designed by G.H. Pegg of New Street. In addition to this two stands erected by the old York City Football Club at Holgate were bought and rebuilt on the new site and the rest of the ground was terraced. The second hand stands held 650 and the ground capacity was 10,000.

Councillor J.B. Clarke was an active supporter of the new club and at the first annual meeting he said 'They had a winning team; in fact, if the team that they had could not beat anything that they met in the Midland League, then they would be disappointed by them.' Clarke was an optimist and the club did indeed win its first game against Rotherham. On that day the *Herald* printed a splendid picture of the Lord Mayor starting the game off with a kick which looks as if it might have deposited the ball in the Ouse. It also published a picture of Tiny Tim, the club's mascot. Tiny was a small white dog who was photographed balancing on a perimeter rail and smoking a pipe! Tiny's team did quite well in the FA cup that year beating Mexborough in extra time after three goes and drawing Grimsby St Johns in the subsequent round. At that time, however, the 'Citizens' as the York team were known initially, were third from the bottom of the League.

The moves among the soccer devotees produced a response in the ranks of the much longer established Rugby League Club. When the soccer ground was being renovated, the rugby club was losing its most famous player (Tot Moore, who had gone to Australia) and was about to discuss turning itself into a limited liability company. This was an idea floated at about the same time as Bert Rutter and the others held their first meeting about a professional FA club, but it got nowhere. He had sent out 400 reply paid post cards a Mr F. Wilson reported, and had received only 135 back - with 91 against the new scheme. The few replies showed, Wilson said, 'that the general members had no interest' in the club, 'but it had always been the taint in all sport in York'. (84) That could not have been good news (if it was true) for investors in the York FA Club.

Between the turn of the century and 1912 the entertainment facilities in York had expanded enormously, but there were still many - despite the recent strikes and the considerable efforts of people like Glew, Hartley and Dobbie - who would have been very hard put indeed to have afforded entrance to the cinema, the soccer ground or the theatre. Just a month before the new football venture was launched Seebohm Rowntree updated his findings of a few years earlier and in a lecture at the National Liberal Club told his audience what he, then, considered was a living wage. (85). Twelve years earlier, he reminded his listeners, he had done his famous investigation in York and, 'taking a dietary more stringent than that of workhouses', had concluded that '12s.9d. a week was absolutely necessary to feed a family of five'. To that figure had to be added an amount for rents (86) and clothes, meaning that, now, 23s.8d. was an absolute minimum for a similar family 'without allowing a penny for papers or trades unions, for trains or trams or recreation.' That was much more than many received in York, as any number of examples could show. Wage rates have been frequently quoted and, by Rowntree's calculations, many in the city would have been below his line of subsistence. Will Dobbie and Hartley were still trying to get the Corporation to accept a minimum wage for all their workers (of 6d. an hour) and in June 1912 it was revealed that road sweepers received 24s. a week. (87) Earlier, in April, also at a Council meeting, it was revealed that some clerks employed by the Corporation were getting only £1 or £1.2s. a week (88) and in that same week it was revealed in a speech by a Mr Barnett at the Opera House that some railwaymen's wages were still just £1. (89) In February 1912 a letter to the press from an unemployed man complained of favouritism at York's new Labour Exchange where, he said, he had not been offered even the jobs that were going at 4^1/2d. an hour. (90) Once more it must be recorded that better paid workers like the joiners, who were getting 8d. an hour, (91) would be in severe trouble if and when the weather or trade depression put them on short-time or made them temporarily unemployed (even if they got a union payment). In 1912 there was a coal strike which caused severe disruption throughout the country and did so in York. During it Rowntrees went on short time, though it does not seem that workers there lost wages. Elsewhere in the city other establishments closed down, and it is very unlikely that the employers there were as generous as were those at the cocoa works. (92) In April 1912 the Salvation Army's soup kitchen was as busy as it had ever been, and Adjutant Oliver Chalker said that, then, 'distress [was] increasingly prevalent at York'. (93) In March, perhaps this is a sure indication of hard times for many, 222 residents were prosecuted for non payment of rates. (94) In July 1912 the bankruptcy hearing of William Henry Smith, an auctioneer of Gillygate, was heard and he said conditions then were the worst he had ever experienced. 'He had never known trade to be so flat as it had been since January, 1911' said the hapless Smith. (95)

Things were as bad in York for those at the lower end of society as they had been since the end of the South African war. The Corporation had tried to attract new industries to the city as had their forebears in the 1820s, and with as little success. What cures for the current problems were there ? People like Seebohm Rowntree (who was made a York magistrate in August 1912) still spoke in general terms about land reform and charity, but remained locked into a rigid belief in free trade. The only positive alternative was tariff reform, but that had been rejected at the two elections of 1910. Nevertheless the ideas of the reformers were continually put forward, and in York the Tariff Reform League held regular meetings throughout the city. At one of these H. Henshall did a splendid job on Seebohm Rowntree and his alleged useless 'cures'. (96) J.G. Butcher also spoke regularly about tariff reform as the only remedy for unemployment, and so did his new colleague Sir Cornthwaite Hector Rason, who had been chosen in April 1912 to replace Riley-Smith and stand with Butcher whenever the next general election was called. (97)

Rason had been born in 1858, the son of a medical officer in the Royal Navy. He worked on the engineering staff of the North Eastern Railway for a time and in 1883 married Mary Evelina Terry, the niece of Sir Joseph Terry, of the York confectionery firm. Rason went to Australia to work on railway construction and in a very short time became an MP for Western Australia, and eventually its Premier. He then returned to Britain and between 1906 and 1909 was Agent General for Western Australia in London.

York's suffragettes were delighted with the Tory's choice of a second candidate - Australia had long since conceded the vote to women - and it seemed reasonable to expect that Rason would be an ally. They were right. The York branch of the National Union of Women's Suffrage Societies had continued in existence alongside its more (much more) militant contemporary, and in May 1912 it lobbied Rason. The deputation contained Mrs Alymra Gray, and the wives of K.E.T. Wilkinson and Sebastian Meyer, the two prominent and influential Liberal councillors. The arguments for the vote were rehearsed for Rason's benefit and a splendid (and perhaps surprising) debating point was made by the ladies when they told Sir Cornthwaite Hector that the executive of the York Tory party had declared for women's suffrage. (98) He agreed with them, but, sensibly, would not pledge himself to particular tactics.

Mrs Gray and her colleagues must have been elated at the response they got from Rason. J.G. Butcher was still very much against them, but there can have been few Tory candidates who were as unequivocally for them as was Rason. Not only that, but in their own city a York Men's Committee for Women's Suffrage had been formed. Little can be discovered about this group, (99) but in all probability it consisted of people like J.F. Glew. He had been active on the public platforms of the York WSPU branch, as had a Mr E.P. Holmes of 55 Wentworth Road, a railway clerk who, surprisingly, was a Tory - one of those who signed Butcher's nomination papers for one of the 1910 general elections. (Perhaps it was Holmes who had converted the Tory executive committee to supporting 'votes for women'.)

The WSPU had campaigned in York less militantly than it had elsewhere but what the Union stood for was never left in any doubt by prominent speakers invited to the city. In September Mrs Pethick Lawrence was a visitor, for example. (She was a socialist and the WSPU was shortly to declare 'war' on the Labour party.) The Union took a low profile in 1910, but in the following year began to hold regular weekly meetings at which no punches were pulled. In November, for example, Miss Annie Williams of Huddersfield and Miss Violet Key Jones of York were the main speakers and the latter urged her listeners to adopt militant tactics. (100) Later in the year, in Exhibition Square, Dr Helena Jones gave what must have been one of the most militant speeches heard in the city since Chartist times. A woman, Helena said, 'had a moral right to break every law in the land because she was not concerned in the making of them. The franchise', she went on 'had never been got in any other way.' This was true. 'Hers was the militant suffragist's society,' she concluded, 'and she was one of the representatives of the women who broke windows and got locked up.' (101) No windows had been broken in York as yet in the interests of female suffrage (though many were regularly broken because of John Barleycorn), but the suffragettes had a good time in March when they broke up a meeting presided over by Edith Milner, who has been absent from these pages for long enough. Edith must have been loathed by the likes of Mrs Gray and Violet Key Jones, and the reaction of those like them when they turned up at a meeting of the National League for Opposing Women's Suffrage must have been wonderful to behold. Edith presided and told her audience that 'There was no more beautiful work for women to do than to attend to the expansion of their own home life, which was real Home Rule.' The principal speaker that evening was a Mrs Harold Norris who trotted out fatuous arguments about female suffrage that might have pleased Mr Norris but which infuriated some of the York ladies. They broke the meeting up, passed resolutions of their own, and Edith, of course, wrote letters to the press complaining about them. She, leading from behind like the Duke of Plaza-Toro, had been a tremendous help to her brother in his political career, she said, and her critics should be satisfied to do the same. She would have thoroughly approved of the political attitudes of J.G. Butcher, who was, of course, against votes for women, (102) Home Rule, free trade, the land tax ('land robbery'), the Parliament Bill ('a huge fraud'), and the Insurance Act. What she made of Rason is not recorded.

In the autumn of 1912 the city of York was visited by a group of suffragettes who were marching from Edinburgh to London, where they intended to present a petition to Asquith. The ladies, one of whom (a Miss Beck) was 66 years of age, marched from Easingwold to York as one of their stages, and were met at the city boundary by supporters and a brass band. (103) Copies of their petition were left at the headquarters of the two York suffrage organisations, and in the evening they held a meeting in Exhibition Square where they made it clear that as a first step they were demanding householders and not 'womanhood suffrage'. Their meeting was chaired by an old supporter - Richard Westrope. (104) He, a socialist, and an extremely active conscientious objector (against the education rate it will be recalled), had now calmed down and was devoting his energies to running the York St Mary's [Educational] Settlement. A recent visiting lecturer to that splended establishment had been Isabella Ford, from Leeds, a well-known fighter for women's rights. (105)

The suffragette demonstrators must have been heartened by their reception in York where a large number of prominent men signed their petition. Many of these were Liberals, like K.E.T. Wilkinson and Hogge, but the ladies would have been reminded that not all Liberals were as liberal on the question of the vote as were Hogge and Wilkinson. When they got to London the marchers found that Asquith was not prepared to meet them, and Violet Key Jones, the York WSPU organiser, found that she was not welcome at a party meeting in York. John Redmond, the Irish leader, was invited to York and he addressed a meeting on Home Rule, along with Arnold

Rowntree and J.M. Hogge. Violet paid sixpence to get in, but was recognised and thrown out. She threatened to start an action alleging an assault and demanded her money back, and later she lobbied Rowntree. He was a supporter of women's rights but told Violet that he would do no more than he had been doing in the past, saying that he feared that Asquith would resign if MPs pressurised him. (106)

Just before the suffragette marchers set off from Edinburgh the York Tory candidate who supported them resigned. In mid October C.F. Elmhirst announced to his party that Rason had withdrawn his name, and that they would be looking for a replacement for him. (107) The reason was all to do with money, however. Rason had not been as careful with his finances as he should have been, a point he had to make to the London Bankruptcy Court in October 1912. (108)

A bankruptcy petition against Rason had been issued on 7 May 1912, about a month after he had been adopted for York. The court heard that he had had a bank balance of £400 when he stopped working as Agent General (in September 1909) but that he had then lost £2,000 helping friends out of difficulties. He had something like £1,200 a year from various directorships, but had resorted to moneylenders and had liabilities of £8,000.

A Tory general election campaign with Rason and Butcher running in tandem would have been a fascinating affair, and no doubt the likes of Violet Key Jones would have had a field day pointing out the differences between the two. Who was to replace Rason? In the autumn of 1911 a party hopeful attended a dinner of the Fulford Conservative party, and at the end of the month he was chosen to replace Rason. He was Urban H. Broughton. (109)

Broughton was 55 years of age, a qualified engineer, who had been educated at London University. Between 1887 and 1912 he had worked in the USA as a mining engineer and in railway management. His experiences there, his supporters said, taught him the benefits of living in a protected country and he presented himself as an ardent tariff reformer, with tariff reform, naturally, as the only real remedy for unemployment, under employment and low wages. Broughton presented an awful picture of the state of the country at his adoption meeting. '... what was the state of affairs today?' he asked rhetorically. The majority of the working class, he went on,

> received wages inadequate to the cost of living, and a large percentage
> were actually underfed. Trades disputes had increased; agriculture, the
> leading home productive industry, had greatly diminished; emigration
> had increased; the cost of living had increased in a much greater ratio
> than wages; the leading Government and other British securities had
> declined; and British capital sought foreign rather than home investment.

The Tory party made a great deal of the fact that at Broughton's adoption meeting there were 'Labour representatives' and one of these, a Mr Warriner, said that he thought 'Tariff Reform was the only solution for unemployment.' That was still, however, not acceptable to the Labour movement, though the arguments put forward by people like Broughton and Butcher must have caused some to wonder whether the old doctrines of free trade were able to remedy the problems of low wages and unemployment. 'As to the effect of a tariff on wages,' Broughton said

> he was well within the mark in stating that American wages were 125 per cent. higher than in Great Britain, and that the cost of food, housing, and clothing was not more than 60 per cent higher than in Great Britain. Moreover the worker's food in America was more varied and liberal than in Great Britain.

Labour organisations in York had made some considerable strides in the strikes of 1911. They had thrown up local leaders like Glew and Dobbie and, with a general election apparently not all that far away, it was perhaps inevitable that another socialist candidate was produced for York. The choosing of first Rason then Broughton may have hastened the process - it probably did - as would a desire to get in before the Liberals chose a second man. This time there would be no chance of a deal with them - Labour had become too disillusioned with the Liberals for that, but if they got in first, the York socialists would have reasoned, the Liberals might be forced to recognise political realities and run only one man. They were almost certainly right and they started to put their organisation into some kind of order (again). In April 1912 there was talk reported in the press about a Labour candidate, and a Micklegate Labour Association was formed. (110) Clearly the organisation which had promised so much in 1906 had collapsed or become moribund but the Trades Council was still strong and active and the new unions formed during the troubles of 1911 seemed to be flourishing. (111) In May there was a demonstration on St George's Field at which Dobbie was a speaker, and there once more, a Labour candidate was spoken of, (112) while R.C. Wallhead made some telling points about what had happened to steerage passengers on the *Titanic*. In May there was a meeting held to present an illuminated address to Fred Boaler, an ex-secretary of the Trades Council who, it was claimed, had been forced out of York by angry employers. (113) At that meeting G.H. Stuart was present. Was he going to stand again in York ? When asked he denied he had any intention of doing so. Three weeks later, at a conference attended by Arthur Henderson and 65 delegates, Stuart was chosen to fight York again.

Stuart, when he was re-selected, was general secretary of the Postmen's Federation, and he was a seasoned campaigner, having fought two contests since his appearance in York in 1906, one of them perhaps the best known by election in British history. This was at Dundee in March 1908. Winston Churchill had lost a by election at Manchester - an event celebrated in York, it will be recalled, in some verses by Clifford Segler -

(114) but within 'five or six minutes', in his own words had received 'the unanimous invitation of the Liberals of [Dundee] that I should become their candidate in succession to the sitting member.' (115) At Dundee the future Prime Minister was opposed by a Liberal Unionist (Conservative) and Edwin Scrymgeour a prohibitionist 'who pleaded for the Kingdom of God upon earth with special reference to the evils of alcohol' who also fought Churchill again in January 1910. The Labour candidate (and Dundee's other MP was Labour) was G.H. Stuart. All Churchill's biographers agree he was a formidable opponent. Churchill won the Dundee election, of course, and in 1910 Stuart stood for the Eccles division in South East Lancashire, where he came bottom of the poll. (Sir G.H. Pollard, Liberal 7,093; G.F. Assinder, Conservative 6,682; Stuart 3,511.) Stuart's predecessor as Labour candidate for Eccles had been the famous dockers' leader Ben Tillett (who had also lost to Pollard). Stuart's selection made it certain that there would be at least four candidates for York when an election was called.

Broughton looked a better candidate to run with Butcher than did Rason, and the two of them must, at the time of his selection, have thought that they stood a very good chance of obtaining both York seats. Nationally the Liberals were getting a dreadful hammering over Home Rule and (very unfairly) national insurance and Labour was quite disillusioned with them. So, nationally, their fortunes seemed in the ascendant with by election results going their way. On a local level in York, however, the split between Liberals and Labour was not yet serious and the likes of Glew and Dobbie were enthusiastic about what the Liberals were doing in their first year of municipal power. Local government in the city certainly had an atmosphere of energy about it that had been lacking for long enough. What had been going on since the Liberals gained power in November 1911 ? Just before the Council elections of November 1912 the Tory *Yorkshire Evening Press* carried an advertisement in two parts saying what the 'Progressive party' had done, and what it intended to do in the future. (116) It had grown from six to 17 in seven years, and, it was claimed, had been responsible for municipalising the trams. This might well be a justifiable claim - the Liberals had produced all the arguments and most of the enthusiasm for a local authority tram system, but it remained a fact that when the take-over was accomplished the Tories were in power, a fact people like Vernon Wragge quickly, and justifiably pointed out. More recently, the publicity went on, the Liberals had: done what Dobbie and Hartley had demanded for so long and established standard, fair wages for council workmen; created a school meals service; and set up an education ladder, on which bright children could progress to better things.

The Liberals had achieved much (by local standards) in a short time, but the list was not complete. There were other things, perhaps of a minor nature, and for some of these they needed to raise loans (that would maybe put up the rates and cause criticism). Enquiries had to be held at which applications to borrow had to be considered, and at these enquiries, always, detailed descriptions of what York was like were given. In

November 1912, for example, an application was made to borrow £2,350 to complete a street from Pavement to Piccadilly (which had caused some controversy) (117) and two months earlier the Council had asked to be allowed to raise a loan of £3,030. (118) This was to enable a site of some eight and a half acres of land at Bull Lane, Heworth to be purchased from a Miss Leake, who had offered it at a bargain price. People in the locality had petitioned the Corporation, and it was intended to get the ground partly for public works, but mainly to lay it out as a children's playground. During the hearing the city treasurer, James Davison, said that

> the area of the city was 3,692 acres. The population at last census was 82,279, and was now estimated at 82,863. The annual assessable value was £329,511, and a penny rate produced £1,635.9s.3d. The annual rateable value was £417,121, a penny rate producing £1,728.11s.10d. The outstanding loans under Public Health and Sanitary Acts amounted to £316,356, and the borrowing powers sanctioned under those Acts amounted to £564,213, while the unexercised loans were £73,525. The outstanding loans under local Acts were as follows:- District £54,794, city £8,976, bridge £24,723, Foss £2,631, total £91,124. The borrowing powers sanctioned under local Acts amounted to £189,492, and the unexercised loans totalled £4,680. The total city debts (loans and bank) totalled £777,463, and the bank overdraft on capital account at March 31st, 1912, was £7,188. The rates of the city amounted to 8s. in the £.

More money was being spent in the city and the corporation was using some of it (creating play spaces and recreational areas) on the kind of projects which had hitherto been left mainly to private munificence (usually from the Rowntrees). The party in power also had grand schemes for the future, and these were outlined in the aforementioned *Press* announcements. They would, they said: create that municipal cemetery which they had been demanding since the days of the Boer War; they would consolidate the York charities; they would make sure that something like proportional representation happened when the Aldermanic bench was chosen; they would municipalise the York waterworks; and similarly take over the city's gas supply industry. It was an impressive programme and the Tories sprang to the defence of their record. K.E.T. Wilkinson (in particular) had said that the city had been neglected under those long years of Conservative domination. Had it been neglected ? No way, the *Press* said. Its favoured politicians had: taken over the trams on very good terms; had extended the cattle market; and built six schools, the courts of justice, the sewerage works, and the municipal girls school. Of course it was not mentioned that some of these improvements were the result of government directives rather than local pride or iniative. The Tories might also have said that they had been responsible for the municipal electricity supply works, but the electricity undertaking, then, was not the most profitable concern in the world and claiming credit for it might not have seemed to have been worthwhile. (What the Tories did do was draw attention - justifiably - to the fact that in their first year in power the Liberals had wiped out the electricity 'reserve fund'.)

The question of whether or not the gas undertaking should be municipalised had been more or less decided shortly after the Liberal take-over of November 1911. The York United Gas Company was the result of an amalgamation in the 1840s of two early companies, and in 1912 it promoted a bill in Parliament asking for powers to expand some seven miles beyond its present supply area and raise more capital. (119) In April it was before a Lords Select Committee, and there the York Corporation's objections to it were revealed. What were they ? The councillors maintained that if the Bill was passed it would enhance the value of the company and would therefore cost the council more if and when it was taken over. (120) Arnold Rowntree opposed the Bill on the same grounds (and had to take some stick because his firm was a major consumer).

At the end of April the Council debated the issue of whether to take over the gas company, and decided almost unanimously that it would. (121)   It was debated a second time in June, when more details of what was involved were described by officials and committee chairmen, and before the Company's bill went to the Commons. Sebastian Meyer was the spokesman for the ruling party, and he made a number of interesting points. (122)   The gas company's bill provided for the candle power in York to be reduced, Meyer said, and this could (would) reduce costs by something like £2,700 a year. Dividends currently being paid were four per cent and revenue last year amounted to £18,700.   The company had £420,000 capital, excluding debentures, Meyer went on, and he thought it might possibly be bought at par over 35 years. What about the contention that purchasing the company would put up the rates ? Meyer said that the rates could be reduced and made the obvious point that control of the gas company would give the corporation control of the streets (many of which were then at last being macadamized). (123) Then, as now, complaints rained in to the council about the continual opening of York's thoroughfares. Voting at the end of the June debate showed an increase in the dissident vote: for purchase 24; against ten; neutral four. Within a day or so of the vote a by election was held in Castlegate in which the Tories lost a seat to G.H. Mennell. (124)

The most vociferous opponents of municipalising the gas supply in York were Rhodes Brown and the tetchy Hibbett, both of whom always took an extreme right wing attitude to any question, and they were supported by R.H. Vernon Wragge. But there was an overwhelming majority in favour of purchase, and negotiations began with the gas company. A clause enabling the purchase was put into the bill and a price of £400,000 was spoken of. (125)

The question of purchasing the gas company - and whether it would be a bargain - was to be an issue at the municipal elections of 1912, though the Liberals might well have thought that the issue was then over and decided. The Tories were split over the matter, as they had been over the tramways, and notable among those who were unequivocally for the latest dose of municipal socialism was Councillor George Sharp. He was a member for the Liberal ward of Micklegate, and on the stump he declared that he was decidedly for an 'amicable purchase.' (126) Sharp had earlier supported a demand by another Tory J.T. Clark (who sat for Guildhall) for a concrete bridge to be built at a cost of £10,000 that would link Leeman Road to Poppleton Road, a demand which received the support of Alderman Meyer. (127)

Sharp also addressed himself to the question of the composition of the York Aldermanic bench during his election campaign, and he came up with a nice explanation of why the Tories were in the majority there. It was general practice to make ex-sheriffs into aldermen, he said, but the Liberals over the years had resolutely refused (as a general rule) to take that office. In the last half dozen years five of the city's sheriffs had been Tories, and all of them had been elevated. It was the Liberals own fault then, that the senior part of the Council was Tory dominated. It was a good argument, and perhaps one would be justified in wondering why, then, the Liberals had not protested against choosing the aldermen from the sheriffs.

The Liberals had difficulty in finding not just a sheriff for 1912-13, but also in finding a Lord Mayor. The general impression one gets from the 1980s and 90s is that there is never any trouble in finding someone willing to deck himself out in the idiotic cap and gown which York demands that its first citizen wears, but in the autumn of 1912 there seemed to be no takers. The three aldermen who had 'not passed the chair' refused, and so did Councillor J.M. Hogge. (128) (A year with Hogge as Lord Mayor might well have been an entertaining one.) Eventually Sir Joseph Sykes Rymer was prevailed upon to take office - for the fourth time. Rymer, it will be recalled, was the Tory finance committee chairman who had said he would never again preside over deliberations that led to a rate increase. Rymer, a prominent Wesleyan, had been elected as a councillor for Monk in 1867, and made an alderman in November 1885. He had served as York's 500th Lord Mayor three years later.

Perhaps the Liberals in 1912 were determined to get a Tory council member as Lord Mayor to strengthen their hands (129), and putting Sykes Rymer into a non political seat certainly took a powerful opponent out of their way. There would be much of a contentious nature in his year of office that he, now, could not comment on. (That is unless he turned out to be another George Hudson, but that was very unlikely.)

The Liberals' first year in office had been a remarkable one. They had done all the things K.E.T. Wilkinson mentioned and had set about improving the city in a way that was long overdue. They had started to provide housing for the workers (at last); they had stepped up the improvement of the city's streets; and they had begun to provide more leisure areas. But all these things would raise the city's debt and could raise the rates, as a letter writer complained with awful predictability. (130) What would happen at the elections of November? Had the new party gone too far too quickly? There were contests in five out of the six wards. (131)

Perhaps the most interesting fight of 1912 was in Micklegate where George Sharp, the Tory supporter of municipalising gas, was defending his seat. There the Liberals gave Labour a free hand, and that party put up the well-known J.H. Hartley and C.W. Shipley, who had come to prominence in the trade disputes of 1911. Sharp did extraordinarily well to gain election with Hartley. In Walmgate there was a four cornered contest for the two seats and there, a splendid result for them, Labour topped the poll with Will Horsman ahead of K.E.T. Wilkinson. (132) Councillor S.H. Davies, another prominent municipaliser got in in Castlegate, and in the one ward where there was no fight (Bootham) another member of the Rowntree family (Theodore Hotham) was returned. After the elections the situation among the councillors was said to be: Liberals 21; Tories 21; Labour four; Independents two.

It seems surprising that in the hectic political atmosphere of 1912 again no women candidates came forward. Violet Key Jones, or someone like her, might have been expected to stand, but no-one did. In the immediate aftermath of the polls, however, the council debated women's suffrage and declared its support for it. R.H. Vernon Wragge, despite his party's alleged support for the idea, declared himself against, sugaring the pill a little, perhaps, by making much of the fact that he thought votes for women was not really 'council business'. (133)

It has been mentioned repeatedly in these pages that the still restricted electorate was a factor very much against the progress of labour. Obtaining candidates who could afford to devote the time to corporation work also limited them effectively to using Rowntree or NER employees, and the cost of an election campaign also had to be taken into account. In 1912, most unusually, a return of candidates' expenses incurred in their campaigns was published in the press. (134). It makes interesting reading and is self explanatory. It included the following.

	Party	Expenses in £	Votes	Average cost per vote (pence)
Castlegate				
F.W. Birch	Cons	24.6.5	1,003	$5^3/_4$
S.H. Davies	Lib	31.9.4	751	10
T. Betchetti	Ind	11.7.6	671	4
Micklegate				
J.H. Hartley	Lab	8.10.7	1,392	$1^1/_2$
G. Sharp	Cons	46.15.8	1,334	$8^1/_3$
C.W. Shipley	Lab	8.10.7	1,292	$1^1/_2+$
Walmgate				
W. Horsman	Lab	17.10.8	992	$4^1/_4-$
K.E.T. Wilkinson	Lib	25.10.5	916	$6^3/_4$
T. Morris	Lib	25.10.5	880	7
J.E. Gibbs	Cons	32.18.5	866	$9^1/_3$

The council just gave itself time to declare itself in favour of the aims of the suffragettes before it turned its attention to the gas question again. Early in December a special meeting was called to consider a corporation bill enabling purchase to be made. (135) Lumped in with the provision regarding the gas works were to be four other powers enabling: the Skeldergate Bridge to be freed of tolls; an extension of the period the council could repay loans it had raised for its asylum; land to be acquired for the electricity undertaking; and the purchase of land to enable a foot bridge to be built from Piccadilly 'to give access to St. Margaret's School.' Voting was overwhelmingly in favour (31 for; 19 against; four neutral), but among the opponents again were Rhodes Brown and Hibbett. What would municipalising mean ? Rhodes Brown said that it would put 5d. on the rates and that the price of gas would go up to a half a crown per 1,000 cubic feet (from 2s.0p.)

Rhodes Brown, who had been relatively quiet on the issue during the election, started a campaign against taking over the gas company. At a meeting of the Micklegate Conservatives he said that York would eventually be lumbered with a debt of £1 million if the ruling party took over both gas and water. (136) He addressed open air lunch time meetings on the subject and maintained that Meyer and others had got their calculations wrong and had misled the council and the city. (137) The company was old and broken down, he said, and its market price was an inflated £378,000, while Meyer and his mates were prepared to pay £435,000. The usual kind of press and platform arguments ensued with Meyer and Hartley doing a nice hatchet job on Rhodes Brown, by challenging his figures, and likening the arguments he was putting forward to those that had been used to try and stop the tram take-over. In the middle of January Brown presented a petition to the council, demanding a poll on the question of a gas take-over. It was signed by 120 persons (including Wragge, Canon Argles, Whitby C. Oliver and Hibbett) and was drawn up in accordance with the provisions of the Borough Funds Acts of 1872 and 1903. The petition was accepted (as it had to be) and the poll was fixed for Friday 31 January 1913.

Between the presenting of the petition and the poll a hectic campaign was waged by both supporters and opponents of York's latest move towards 'municipal socialism' (a phrase which seems to have disappeared totally by 1913). The outcome was sensational.

Who could vote in the 1913 poll ? '... all persons on the parochial register' was the answer 'i.e. those people who have votes at a guardian's election are entitled to say "Aye" or "Nay" on the question of the York Gas Bill.' (138) This meant parliamentary and municipal electors, married women carrying on businesses on their own account, owners of property, lodgers and single freemen who were not householders. The electorate amounted to 8.629 persons, and they were to be enabled to vote at 27 polling booths in various parts of the city.

Wragge and Brown were the main speakers for the anti municipalisers, and Wragge wrote a powerful letter to the press outlining his case, which was already well known it must be said. (139) J.H. Hartley had got very angry somewhat earlier about the gas company's slot meters which he called 'thieving machines' and which, he contended, were unfair to the poor as they charged a higher rate than the ordinary meters. Wragge had a great time pointing out that if Hartley had his way the Corporation would become the owners of the 'thieving machines' and he also elaborated on his and Brown's contention that the gas company was in a rotten state and that if it was taken over huge sums would have to be spent on new equipment and mains (at the city's expense). 'We are asked by Councillor Hartley and those associated with him to give some £500,000 (half a million of good money) for all this defective, worn-out, and obsolete plant, machinery, cookers, and meters', Wragge wrote. He called the prospective take over a 'gigantic blunder', one that would put prices up, and put 'an end to a most desirable competition between gas and electricity'.

Meyer was chief spokesman for the advocates of the take-over, and, like Rhodes Brown earlier, he addressed open-air, lunchtime meetings of working people. At Holgate Beck he told railwaymen that the likes of Wragge were against the Corporation owning anything (maybe forgetting Wragge's attitude to the trams), whereas he and his colleagues 'thought that those great monopolies should be run by the town, and not by private firms'. They would take over both gas and water, he went on, and he estimated that there would be a revenue income of £26,000 a year, with a surplus of £4,500 which cou¹d go to lowering the rates, or keeping them down.

The campaign of January 1913 built up to a splendid climax. On the eve of the poll the 120 petitioners took whole page press advertisements to state their case ('The lights will be worse, the price more') and the Labour party tried to organise a public debate in the Exhibition Buildings. Rhodes Brown and ex-Councillor H. Hopkins were put up against Hartley and Glew, but for some reason the Liberals had not agreed to take part. (140) This was almost certainly due to an oversight (though of course the others did not agree that that was the reason) and the evening ended with the undignified spectacle of K.E.T. Wilkinson and Sebastian Meyer arriving late and trying to harangue the assembled - two irate Liberal gentlemen re-enacting scenes from the days of George Hudson. The proceedings ended in total disorder with - appropriately enough - the lights being turned off.

The poll was held on Friday 31 January and the result was announced to the city at 9.45 pm, with an overwhelming rejection for municipal ownership of York's gas supply. About half those qualified voted.

Against	5,346
For	3,279
Majority	2,067

When the Tories, the anti municipalisers, had been in power the city had voted to take over the trams; when the Liberals were in power the city had voted against public ownership of gas (and by implication water). One reason might be that the arguing about whether or not the trams were profitable that went on and on had convinced many that perhaps the 'Progressives' were not right about the profitability (or the potential profitability) of the things they wanted to take over. Following from that, people were perhaps persuaded by that old old argument about the rates (to the working people this meant higher rents). Lastly there was a great distrust of the people like the Rowntrees and Sessions - employers of labour - and men like S.H. Davies and Hogge who worked for them. Their business methods (as councillors) were looked at with great suspicion. Rhodes Brown and Wragge, for example, had made much of the fact that the reserve fund for the electricity undertaking had been scrapped. Surely this was wrong? Not at all. Hogge had declared at an eve of the poll meeting that it was common business practice!

The poll result of 1913 was a bitter blow to the Liberals with their great hopes that their plans for the city would go through and be popular, and that if the rates went up people would think nothing of it. Just after the poll the committee set up to look into obtaining land for a municipal cemetery reported, recommending the purchase of three acres of land in Acomb at £100 an acre. (141) That must have underlined how expensive progressive policies might be (if the Wragges were right) and also, at about the same time, there was a demonstration that maybe private enterprise could deliver the goods. Before the middle of February the York Gas Company announced reductions in its prices. (142) Ordinary customers with standard meters would pay 1d. per 1,000 cubic feet less than hitherto; slot meter charges would be reduced by 1d. in every 2s. (or 1d. per 1,000 cubic feet of gas consumed.) Why was this being done ? For political reasons without doubt, but the *Press* hazarded a guess that an increased dividend was contemplated, and the company was prohibited from paying a higher return to its shareholders unless it was accompanied by a price reduction. At its annual general meeting in February the gas company announced that it was considering a co-partnership scheme, in which management and workers could participate. (143)

The gas company's action could not have made the Liberal party's local prospects look much better, and neither could the announcement of March that the rates would indeed go up. The level would henceforth be 8s.1½d. in the £, within a halfpenny of the figure which had led the sitting Lord Mayor to declare that he would never preside over setting a higher rate back in 1905.

The council had been helped in setting the rate for 1913 by the fact that the guardians had decreased the demand for the poor rate by 2d. In April the guardians' elections were held, and one of the new candidates (who was successful) was R. Wilfrid Crosland of the York St Mary's Educational Settlement. (144) Much was to be heard in York of the activities of the much loved Wilfrid Crosland in a few years time, but he made his way slowly in the affairs of the guardians. Women stood and got in in those elections, making their absence in November at the municipal contests look like a missed opportunity. The deliberations of the guardians had been hectic during the life of the last board - and they got off in the same way with a splendid row at the first meeting of the new lot. The leading figure in most of the arguments of the past had been Will Horsman; it was he who made the initial meeting of the new board a memorable one. (145)

On the day the guardian election results were declared some people directly, and everyone indirectly, got a lesson on the fact that Progressive government might be dear government. On that day hearings were held in the city magistrate's court on objections to the bills the corporation had sent out to citizens demanding a part of the cost for street improvements. By an odd coincidence two of the three magistrates on duty in the cases were prominent believers in municipalisation - Harry Miles (very active in the campaign to take over the gas company) and Seebohm Rowntree (and the third was a very prominent Liberal). (146) Miles had been appointed to the bench at the same time as Rowntree in what was clearly a determined attempt to make that august body of citizens more representative, and it is a fact that by 1913 they were that. (147) Andrew Pattison Mawson had been appointed as the first York working man to sit on the bench and he was joined there later by C.W. Shipley and J.H. Hartley, soon to be spoken of as a possible Lord Mayor. (148) Hartley, like Thomas Anderson before him, had in 1912 made an attempt to get out of politics - or rather he applied for a job on the council that would have made him drop out of politics. In May he was an applicant for the post of secretary of the York Labour Bureau - a job paying from £160 to £200 a year. (149) He did not get it, which is perhaps not surprising.

The loss of the citizen's poll was a blow to the Liberals, and at the first council meeting after the declaration there were some extremely nasty insinuations made against the leading party and the city's leading Liberals. In the not very distant future the Council was going to apply for yet another loan to enable expansion of the electricity works. Why did this have to be done? At least partly to meet additional demands from Rowntree and Company it was revealed. What arrangements had the council come to with the cocoa works the Tories asked? Incredibly they were not told. The deals' details were a secret. Why? The most obvious and most unjust conclusions were hinted at. Why on earth the Liberals adopted the attitude they did over the Rowntree contract is impossible to understand. (150) With two members of the family among the ruling councillors and with people like S.H. Davies employees of the firm it was a stupid thing to do. That skilled and competent politicians like Meyer and Wilkinson could be party to such a daft thing when their popularity was clearly beginning to wane is simply amazing.

It looked like the Liberals were courting trouble over the Rowntree/electricity affair. They also raised up immense opposition, quite unnecessarily, over another issue; one that can cause tempers to fray even now, in the 1990s.

In April 1913 the council met and Will Dobbie, having got it to agree to fair wages earlier on (6d. an hour for Council workmen at least) persuaded it not to accept tenders from firms paying less. But Swaby, Mellor, and Scaife, Dobbie said, were paying carters only 21s. a week, less than a living wage, and it had done work for the Corporation. Meyer seemed genuinely surprised that men were getting so little and recalled the carters' strike of 1911 which Dobbie had taken control of. Why, if it was not a living wage, had the men agreed to that rate (it had earlier been 18s.) he asked? '... because they were so miserably poor then that they could not afford to do otherwise', replied Dobbie, and many were not getting even that agreed amount. 'Eighteen shillings a week was not the minimum sum,' Dobbie went on, 'as many were receiving as small a wage as 15s. per week.' Once more attention had been drawn to the existence of an appallingly badly paid lower strata in York society. The same kind of story was told at a guardians' meeting reported in the *Press* of 12 June. Then Will Horsman was trying to get his colleagues to put up a night porter's wages from 22s. to 26s. a week. Many of them agreed that the higher figure was necessary (but decided on 24s.), and a Mr De Camps said that he also knew of fully grown men in York receiving 15s. a week!

To its everlasting credit the council supported Dobbie, then engaged in some unbelievably rash action (when all but a handful of the Tories went along with the ruling party). A deputation led by J.A. Shaftoe lobbied and addressed the Councillors and Aldermen, and presented a petition signed by 1,187 persons. What did they want ? Who were they ? They were sabbatarians, and they wanted the council to act on a resolution it had passed in 1902 - and totally ignored thereafter - that shops should be closed on Sundays, and that malefactors should be prosecuted. Shaftoe was supported by John Howard and others and they achieved a remarkable success. The council agreed with them by an overwhelming majority (31:five) and, as the *Herald* said, 'The amendment for the enforcement of the Lord's Day Observance Act was therefore carried, and Sunday closing of all shops will become operative in the city!' (151) The decision was greeted with incredulity. It could (with some justification) be presented as an anti-working class move, and it was. It brought immense trouble for the Liberals but some of them had logical reasons for turning York into an even deader place than it already was on Sundays. What were the reasons for this move backwards ?

John Howard, one of those who lobbied the council, represented the Sunday School movement in York, and he took a simplistic view about Sunday trading. The Sabbath should be a day of rest; trading then was sinful. 'It was demoralising to allow the children to spend their pence on Sunday', Howard said. Religious considerations of that kind were clearly attractive to those councillors closely connected with groups like the Wesleyans and Quakers (Meyer, Morrell and Theodore Rowntree for example), but one or two justified Sunday closing on other grounds. Glew, for example, said that he wanted to close the shops to ensure that workers did in fact get a day of rest. There were indeed shop assistants who were employed on Sundays, as Glew suggested, but there must have been relatively few. The vast majority of the 'Sunday' shops were tiny little places run by the owner himself or herself, and Glew's attitude as far as they were concerned was simply ridiculous.

Glew was a Labour member of the council, and no doubt people would have said that he (a Rowntree employee) went along with his bosses and managers. Dobbie and Hartley, however, voted in the tiny minority (152) against activating a antiquated act. What did they maintain had happened ? They had a conspiracy theory. Closing the shops on Sundays represented a movement of the larger shopkeepers against the small people, they maintained. They insisted that if the legislation was to be implemented it should be implemented in full. (153) They did this at one of the many protest meetings held in the city. (A Wesleyan preacher added fuel to a mounting controversy by announcing that 'Sunday openers were nothing more nor less than blacklegs.')

It seems very unlikely that Dobbie's conspiracy theory was correct, though maybe the larger shopkeepers did nothing to stop Shaftoe and his mates once they had started. What really happened in all probability is that the councillors and aldermen simply voted impulsively and rashly - in accordance with their own prejudices certainly - and lived to rue the day. Had any of them had a sense of history they might have remembered that sabbatarian arguments of the kind which were to shortly engulf the city were trotted out in George Hudson's time (over the running of Sunday trains). Then George had devastated the advocates of a dismal Sunday for all for their illogical attitudes, just as they were to be devastated in 1913.

Protest meetings about Sunday closing in York began to be held regularly, and the *Herald* and the *Press* began conducting regular interviews with small tradespeople who would be affected, like Mrs Chapman, of Earlsborough Terrace, who, perhaps predictably, wanted a citizen's poll. (154) How many shops did open on the Sabbath? The Chief Constable (who retired in June) (155) reckoned there were 154 when he compiled a report dated 26 January (156), but at a traders' meeting in May the figure was estimated as 168. (157) At meetings like that one a great deal was said about the fact that many workers did not get paid until late Saturday night, and that, of necessity, they and their families bought on Sundays in very small quantities. A Mr W. Taylor asked 'how many of the city councillors knew what it was to provide for a household on £1 a week. In his district, Leeman-road,' he went on, 'there was a great demand for very small orders.'

The small shopkeepers maintained that many workers needed their shops open on Sundays because of the practice of paying wages late on Saturdays, and many claimed that Sunday trade was essential for them to survive. All this had no effect, however. The Council had instructed the Watch Committee to order the police to bring prosecutions - and this they did. Nineteen cases were brought, under section one of the Sunday Observance Act of 1677 regulated by the Sunday Observance Prosecutions Act of 1871. Chief Constable James Burrow must have wondered why on earth he had opted to stay on for two years beyond his retirement age.

An interesting fact about the first 'Sunday' prosecutions is that one of the chief opponents of the council's act - a councillor - was a member of the bench which deliberated on them. The JP was J.H. Hartley, and he was but the first of people intimately concerned with the council's act to sit in deliberation on those who ignored the new trading rules. It would never happen today.

One of the people proceeded against in June for the terrible crime of opening a shop on a Sunday was Peter Flynn. He was secretary of the York Small Traders' Association, and kept a refreshment shop in Fulford Road, opposite the barracks. Walter Hawkins, a tobacconist of Tower Street, was another, and these two, and other defendants were represented by Robert Brighouse of Stockport, 'the small traders' champion'. The bench decided to dismiss the cases under the Probationer's Act, and they told the Chief Constable to hold his hand. (158) A suggestion was made that the entire bench should, sometime in the future, sit on what would amount to a test case.

Inspector Pinkney of the York city police was ordered to select two cases of shopkeepers breaking the law on 8 June, and this he did. The first offender was that same Walter Hawkins who had been done just a couple of days earlier. Wally had sold some tobacco on the fatal 8 June - which is not altogether surprising as he was a tobacconist - and he told the court that he had deliberately ignored the law. Why ? 'My only reason', he said, 'is that I think it very unfair that I should be brought here for selling tobacco when 300 public-houses and 70 off-beer licences are allowed to sell it'. Wally was only half right, as the Chief Constable pointed out. The pubs may well have been selling the foul stuff, but they were doing so illegally! Charles Robinson of Walmgate was proceeded against for selling bread and vegetables. Charlie thought that it was all wrong that petrol could be sold on the Sabbath. 'If we have to stop feeding Christians on Sunday,' he said, 'surely we aught to stop feeding motor cars ?' He had a point, but, like Wally, he was fined 5s.

The humiliation of Walter Hawkins and Charlie Robinson was not an end of the matter of Sunday trading - quite clearly people like them had no intention of shutting their premises on the one day some of them could make a shilling or two, and the police set about collecting evidence on such as they over the following week-end. While they went about doing so, the *Press* noted, the labourers laying junction rails for the tram system and the skilled men who were called in to weld the joints, went about their business unmolested. (159) They were working for the Corporation, of course, so, the *Press* said on 23 June, 'There was the unedifying spectacle of the City Council who are responsible for the extension of the tramways employing 100 men to work on Sunday, while the same body had the police out inspecting, watching, and harassing about 100 small shopkeepers ... for keeping their shops open. Many people ... made the suggestion that the workmen and officials should be prosecuted for following their ordinary calling on Sunday ...' These people were not far off the mark. While the police were collecting evidence, so were the small traders. They were also out looking for people who were following their normal calling on the Sabbath and they announced that for every summons the Council brought, they would bring another themselves. They reckoned they already had enough evidence to proceed against 100, and among them were the foreman of the navvies working in Queen Street; an Alderman; and two JPs with labour sympathies. One of these, they said, might be charged 'on the ground that he did not publicly or privately exercise himself in religious observance as expressly stipulated in the Act of Charles II.' One hopes that this refers to either Mawson or Shipley as Hartley was against all these idiotic proceedings.

The next batch of prosecutions appeared before the York bench, and this time Robert Brighouse (absent when Walter was fined) appeared again on behalf of the small traders, some 38 in all. All the first offenders were fined and those who had been up before got clobbered for costs as well, to the accompaniment of a ponderous declaration from the bench that they had to 'uphold the law'. Then Brighouse applied for his summonses, and provoked Meyer into some very undignified wrangling with him. Who were to be prosecuted by the small traders ? Peter Flynn charged a bookie, Walter Langstaffe, with playing golf - an offence which rendered him liable to a spell in the stocks. Captain Grace of the SS *River King* (the boat which took Edith Milner and the Primrose League on outings) and Frank Day of the SS *Graphic* were to be charged, and George Coverdale, York's best known chemist, was alleged to have sold soap. J.J. Hunt, the JP and brewer of Aldwark was to be done, as was B.S. Wales, another JP, who sold a spanner. Forster Todd was to be charged with selling cigarettes and John Joseph Deighton summoned the Lord Mayor, the Aldermen and the burgesses for selling a tiny piece of soap at the Yearsley Swimming Baths. Robert Stokes a park attendant, and others, completed an impressive list.

Brighouse's riposte to the Council's prosecutions demonstrates better than anything, perhaps, how stupid the Corporation had been - and echoes of the controversy can still be heard. (In February 1989 *The Sunday Times* alleged that 15 Anglican Cathedrals were 'breaking the law on Sunday trading'.) (160) The Sunday Observance Acts were inconsistent, out of date, discredited. It was inevitable that people like Dobbie and Hartley would point out, as George Hudson had, that transport ran on Sundays and that people like Walter Langstaffe played golf. The Liberals, with trouble over the gas take-over, were stupid to jeopardise their chances of staying in power. Councils in those days had no time to work at their programmes and hope that the citizens would see that increased facilities were worth the increased rates. In those days they were held to account annually, and reformers in a hurry ran the chance of a set-back each November. That makes the idiocy of the campaign against Sunday traders look all the more ridiculous. It would be vain to protest that the Tory opposition had gone along with them. The party in power would have to take the blame - and quite right too.

While the small shopkeepers were being harassed the suffragettes had become very active, and York got its first martyr to the women's cause. Mrs Pankhurst had hotted up the campaign for votes for women and 1913 was a year in which accounts of women window breaking, attacking property, being forcibly fed, and tried, filled the papers. In January a deputation from the York WSPU went to London to attend a suffrage conference, (161) and among them was a Mrs Pearson. She was a Liberal who had left the party because of the incidents at the Redmond meeting when Violet Key Jones was ejected, and at the end of the month she was given 14 days in London for not paying a fine. (162) She was let out when her husband, against her wishes, paid up on her behalf. (163) The same York paper that reported her incarceration recorded that suffragettes had destroyed some mail in York by posting letters containing vitriol (and carrying slogans saying 'Votes for Women'). Two postmen had suffered minor burns. In April, early one Sunday morning, a bomb - 'an infernal machine' - was found in the doorway of the offices of the *Yorkshire Evening Press* in Coney Street. It was a timed device, consisting of an accumulator and gun cotton, and was similar to those planted on the railings of the Bank of England in London. It was intended to cause a fair old explosion and represented the first attack on property in York by the followers of Mrs Pankhurst. The bomb was doused by a viligant policeman but a serious incident was 'unquestionably planned by feminine vote-seekers' said the *Press*. (164) Violet Key

Jones wrote a letter to the papers just before this incident justifying militancy 'against property, not persons.' (165)

The small shopkeepers, however, were causing more concern to the authorities than the suffragettes in the summer of 1913 and in July their counter prosecutions were heard. One of the best ways of dealing with a ludicrous situation, perhaps, is to point to its inconsistencies and poke fun at it. Brighouse did that superbly and was responsible for what must have been one of the most entertaining days ever held in the York Magistrates' court. The prosecutions, Brighouse said, were brought under an Act of Parliament which spoke of the stocks, bull baiting, and waggoning, (166) and it was being used by the council against only the poorest section of the trading community. Forster Todd was being charged because he had sold cigarettes on a Sunday, but why had he been left alone by the Corporation ? What he did he did openly. He was not proceeded against - but Mary Nicholson was. Mary had a little shop at Lendal Bridge from which she had sold some tobacco, and for which she was fined five shillings. Surely, Brighouse contended, with unanswerable logic, 'if it is wrong for Miss Nicholson to sell cigarettes at Lendal Bridge on a Sunday, it is equally wrong for Mr. Todd to do so ...'. J.J. Deighton had been picked on, like Mary Nicholson, and the summonses against the Yearsley bath attendant was in his name. Brighouse's sarcastic introduction ended by referring to it.

> Then we have the worst offence of all... . One can understand ordinary private individuals committing ... offences through ignorance of the law, but here we have the Lord Mayor and Aldermen, represented by their clerk there, and they have themselves been committing a very serious offence indeed, for they had sold at the baths a penny packet of soap. Could anyone imagine a worse offence than that ? It was done through their agent, Mr. Wilfrid Betchetti ... The Corporation were responsible for the action of their servants. What was sauce for the goose was sauce for the gander, and as the magistrates had started on making York a holy city the small traders wanted to make it holier than the magistrates had intended to.

In addition to Forster Todd (167) and the Corporation J.J. Hunt was proceeded against. His crime ? He had allegedly sold cigarettes as licencee of the Ebor Hotel Vaults. What happened? Hunt, it was shown, was not the licencee of the Vaults and his case was dismissed with costs, and the magistrates decided *en passant* that a licensed victualler was not a trader. The unfortunate bath attendant, it was decided, was performing an act of necessity when selling his piece of soap, and that made it fall within the permissive clauses of the Act and his case was dismissed. Matters were adjourned for a day, at the half way stage, and the *Press* summed up the state of play. 'The Bench', it said (168) gave an important decision when, in the retaliatory cases, they said the licensed victuallers were not traders under the Act of 1667, and the summonses were dismissed. The Bench also decided, in effect, in other cases that a Corporation may sell on Sundays which private individuals may not.

When battle recommenced the man in the firing line was J.W. Clayton, Rowntree's gas foreman. He had been at work on a Sunday and Brighouse, who agreed that unless the boilers at Rowntrees were looked after some 2,600 would be unable to work on the Monday, agreed that this case was on the border line of 'necessity'. However under Charles II's Act 'all that was allowed to be done was to do such things as would keep body and soul together', and so Clayton was prosecuted. The nominal persecutor of Clayton was asked why the case had been brought, and his answer revealed who he thought was responsible for the wave of prosecutions. Clayton had been prosecuted, he said, 'Because I have been brought here myself, and *because Rowntrees brought it against us at the City Council*, and yet they continue to do what they are stopping us doing.' (169) Rowntrees protested that they were in no way responsible for what was going on, but the presence of many of the family, and works employees on the council, led many to believe that York was a company town. There were always suspicions about Rowntree influence in York; suspicions which seem unbelievably unfair, but that distrust of the city's first family reached amazing proportions in the 1914 war when they were presented as pro-German and enemies of the state.

The case against Clayton was dismissed, as was that against the captain of the *SS Graphic*. The Observance Act forbade travel by boat or barge without the permission of a magistrate, but the *Graphic* case was thrown out for lack of evidence! The popular Captain Grace of the *River King*, however, was found guilty and fined - and he rapidly announced that there would be trips the following Sunday. Did he consider river excursions a necessity, Grace was asked? Yes he did, he replied. The people he took on outings had but one day of leisure a week, and many of them would never go anywhere unless they went with him on a Sunday. (Grace's photograph eventually appeared in the press with a caption which said he was 'one of the victims of "King Charles II" and the York Corporation'.) Frank Wasling, of Blake Street, was fined for selling a bike pump to Peter Flynn, and George Coverdale and Benjamin S. Wales got similar treatment. The case against Wally Langstaffe for playing golf was found not proved, and Brighouse immediately asked for a stated case.

By the time Clayton and Coverdale were prosecuted the small traders had begun to organise themselves. A huge petition that made that of Shaftoe look puny in the extreme was organised and funds were collected - with the Irish Nationalist Party pledging its support. The *Herald* took up the cause of the small traders, and they talked of running municipal candidates when the opportunity arose and began to demand the appointment of a stipendiary magistrate for York. Why? Because, they said, 'their interests are not safe in the hands of the magistrates because many of them are also members of the City Council'. Ridicule was still one of the strongest weapons used by the traders, however, and the long suffering Wally Wright displayed his summonses in the window of his shop (which was aptly named The Bow Wow). Wally also had a banner draped across his shop front which read. (170)

"YORK THE HOLY CITY"
SUNDAY TRADING PROSECUTIONS.
FOSSILISED ACT OF 1677 ENFORCED.
AT THE INSTIGATION OF A FEW
BUSY BODIES
LET THE CORPORATION PRACTICE
WHAT THEY PREACH.

Just after the first prosecutions for Sunday trading were completed, two by elections became due. Aldermen James Birch and Lancelot Foster died and it was almost certain that they would be replaced by two councillors. The Sunday traders announced that they would put up candidates for their seats, (171) and this necessitated some careful manoeuvring by the party in power. Clearly some wheeling and dealing was engaged in and eventually J.H. Hartley and W.H. Birch were elected - Hartley becoming the first ever Labour alderman - in a four cornered 'contest'. (The two other candidates were the ultra conservative Hibbett, Rhodes Brown's political ally, and W. Page.) (172) Voting for the new aldermen was extremely low. (173)

The aldermanic elections represented, in effect, one Liberal gain and undoubtedly represented the ruling party's determination to break the long Tory monopoly of the bench. James Birch had been a Liberal, and so, too, in his early days, had been Lancelot Foster, but his allegiances had slipped and in 1913 he had to be counted among the Tories. He 'was for a long time associated with the Liberal party', the *Herald*'s obituary said on 19 June, 'but in recent years he ... avoided political affairs and was understood to have a leaning to the Unionist Party'.

At the council meeting that saw the elevation of Hartley that body heard representations (again) from those for and against Sunday trading. Shaftoe, who was a shop assistant, urged the Council to carry on hounding the Sunday openers in a memorial which was signed by clerics as well as by three prominent members of the Trades Council (George W. Halliday, George Ward and W.R. Leason). W.P. Leavis (who had replaced Flynn as the 'trader's' leader) maintained cleverly that 13 York shops would remain open whatever the council did - paying the fines which (at the rate that could be levied) meant nothing to them. However, Leavis said, the Wally Wrights would eventually be forced out of business and the Council would have created a monopoly for the larger concerns. (174) This was clearly the reasoning used by Will Dobbie when he said there was a conspiracy among the bigger traders.

The traders were referred to the Watch Committee (a member of which was Hartley) and there the two sides came to an agreement embodied in a compromise which said that grocers and others should close at 1 p.m. on Sundays (if they opened at all) and could trade between 5 and 6 p.m.; tobacco sellers, ice cream and sweet sellers, confectioners and so on could open from 1 to 10 p.m. (175) Later this went before the Council where a revised version of the deal (proposed by K.E.T. Wilkinson) was carried by a majority of five (18 to 13). During the convoluted debate on the matter Hartley spoke nothing but the truth when he said 'you are winking at the trade done by the big people and crushing the trade of the small people' and a proposition of the Lord Mayor was carried which said the Chief Constable should not prosecute those who opened during what would now be called 'permitted hours'. Wragge, however, pointed out the utter stupidity of what was being proposed. They were acting *ultra vires*, he said; they had no powers to alter the old Act. The York bench had made absurd decisions Wragge claimed - 'The magistrates had not only made a new law, but now the Council were to make a new Act'. (Presumably what Vernon meant by his first contention was the declaration that the Corporation could trade on Sundays, though he may well also have challenged the decision that licensed victuallers were not traders.)

The prosecutions went on - the Chief Constable having been told not to prosecute people who only opened during the hours the Council had stipulated. Early in August Peter Flynn (whose refreshment license meant he could sell for consumption on, but not off, his premises), Walter Hawkins (of The Bow Wow) and Charles Robinson were taken to court again for offences committed on the 3rd. (176) All charges were dismissed as being trivial. (177) Later in the month 16 more small traders were taken to court, their cases being, in Norman Crombie's words, so paltry that it was a waste of time dealing with them. He also told the court that the bench in Southport had said that unless the Charles II Act was implemented in full there they would not convict. (178) These cases, too, were dismissed by a majority decision of the bench. Early in September Louis Frankie appeared for selling a halfpenny ice cream on a Sunday (with a dozen others including Wally and Charlie). This time Crombie got an adjournment on a point of law, (179) but when heard the cases were dismissed. (180) The varying decisions and the obvious differences of opinion among the magistrates made the administration of law in York look foolish. 'SEE-SAW LAW AT YORK. DIFFERENT DECISIONS DAY BY DAY' was a typical press headline. (181) The Lord Mayor actually spoke of 'OBJECTIONABLE PROCEEDINGS' from the bench. (182)

At this stage the two by elections became due, and the small traders' threat to run candidates must have worried the Liberals - so they did a deal, at least according to the tetchy, Charles A. Thompson of St Pauls Square, and he was almost certainly right. Labour had differing views on Sunday trading, with Glew and Hartley adopting very different attitudes, and the deal was that there would be no Labour candidates in Walmgate and no Liberal would stand in Micklegate. (183) In Walmgate in November Labour had made a sensational gain when Will Horsman topped the poll and was returned with K.E.T. Wilkinson. The Tories decided not to stand there and the Liberals ran their second man of November - Thomas Morris. Meetings were held on his behalf (the Tories' intentions were not known) and Birch boasted, justifiably, of the fact that the council had just increased its basic wage for labourers by a halfpenny an hour. Wilkinson spoke of 'the bright prospects of the Progressive Party, who were now in a majority, and were able to carry out the things on which they had set their hearts'. (184) What about the Sunday traders ? Wilkinson said he was against prosecuting them, yet it was he who had suggested the recent Council compromise. (Everyone assumed that that meant traders could open in 'permitted hours' and would get done if they stayed open longer.) Morris also declared he was against prosecuting the likes of Wally Wright through what he called a 'musty old Act of Parliament.' (185)

In Micklegate Labour ran C.W. Shipley, one of the new JPs who had also run unsuccessfully in November. He was opposed by a formidable Tory, Edward Relton, the builder. The Liberals were just then unfolding their latest reform schemes. and Relton went for them all, referring to them as 'mad cap'. The new cemetery would cost the product of a halfpenny rate, he said, and 'as the Tories were being pushed out the rates were advancing'. (186) In Piccadilly the Liberals had been responsible for pulling down 30 cottages which had been let for 5s. a week and replaced them with new ones letting for 7s. In Relton's eyes (he was accused of being a 'jerrybuilder' himself) this was dreadful, but what was his attitude towards the prosecution of Sunday traders ? Relton made much of his poor childhood, said he sympathised with those who believed in the need for a day of rest - and those who needed the shops to buy their small purchases - and came up with a compromise. (Compromises were in the air.) He demanded that only shops of £14 to £15 rental should be allowed to open, and that no assistants should be employed. (187)

Relton had an uphill task in Micklegate, but his attitude over Sunday opening (and therefore prosecutions) would not have helped his chances, and Shipley was returned. (Shipley 1,161 votes, Relton 957). (188) What would happen now ? Labour councillors had emerged as champions of the small traders and the Liberal/Labour hold on the council had been strengthened. Could the prosecutions be dropped before the annual municipal elections, or would the populace hold the handling of the traders against them and bring the short period of Liberal rule to an end ? There was also that new package of reforms to be unveiled, analysed and argued about. Would this restore Liberal fortunes (if they needed restoring), or would the citizens decide, as they did so often, that much needed and beneficial reforms were not worth higher rates ?

1. The Square and Compass, the Wheatsheaf, the Sportsman, the Garden Gate and the Bricklayers Arms.
2. The Square and Compass (Albion) and the Sportsman.
3. For the 1911 Brewster Sessions see *Press* 8 February and 8 March 1911.
4. There were three candidates for Lord Mayor for 1910-11: Alderman Birch, the incumbent; Carter, the senior Alderman who had not then served; and Riley-Smith. Riley-Smith had been proposed a year earlier when Carter waived his claim.

5. 180 full licenses, 32 beer houses; 25 properties licensed to sell wines and spirits; 75 'off' beer houses.
6. *Press* 10 March 1911
7. *Ibid* 25 May 1911
8. *Ibid* 7 April 1911
9. *Herald* 2 May 1911
10. Since the general election of 1906 York's rates had gone up thus: 7s.10d. (1906); 7s.5d. (1907); 7s.8d. (1908); 7s.11d. (1909).
11. See the letter in *Press* 10 May 1911 making precisely this point.
12. *Ibid* 8 May 1911
13. *Ibid* 3 May 1911
14. Increased naval expenditure in the last years before the Great War was a constant concern of such as Hogge
15. *Press* 28 February and 1 March 1911
16. *Ibid* 25 March 1911
17. *Herald* 2 May 1911
18. *Press* 10 May 1911
19. *Ibid* 4 May 1911. It was frequently said that the coronation festivities for Edward VII were a fiasco. See eg the letter in *Ibid*.
20. *Ibid* 8 May 1911
21. *Ibid* 11 May 1911. Councillor Hibbett was the person referred to
22. *Ibid* 22 August 1911, editorial. The weather had just then broken
23. 'The Agadir Crisis'.
24. Ensor *op cit* p. 437
25. Gretton *op cit* p 44
26. *Press* 10 and 12 July 1911
27. *Ibid* 10 July 1911
28. *Ibid* 13 and 14 July 1911
29. *Ibid* 19 July 1911
30. *Ibid* 28 August 1911. The Trades Council had also made a donation.
31. For the sand catchers' strike see *Ibid* issues from 2 to 10 August 1911
32. *Ibid* 5 August 1911
33. *Ibid* 28 and 29 August, 1 September and 11 October 1911
34. *Ibid* 29 August 1911
35. *Ibid* 11 September 1911. My italics.
36. *Ibid* 12 September 1911
37. *Ibid* 28 August 1911
38. *Ibid* 12 September 1911
39. *Ibid* 30 August and 4 September 1911
40. *Ibid* 10 August 1911
41. The schoolboys' strikes are briefly mentioned in the *Annual Register*
42. *Press* 14 September 1911
43. At Llanelly there had been very serious incidents during a rail strike (see later) when a train had been held up and burned; soldiers stoned; a magistrate's house attacked; and eight men killed and many injured.
44. *Press* 5 August 1911. Speech at a public meeting.
45. *Ibid* 19 August 1911. The railwaymen's dispute is fully covered in all the York papers from about 16 August.
46. Irving *op cit* p.67
47. *Press* 19 August 1911. It should be said, in fairness to the NER, that it made many concessions in July. Details in *Ibid* 11 July 1911. With the new rates carriage builders would now get 31s.; labourers got rises which meant they now got 19s. at York; rough painters were to get 21s.; strikers 21s. Piece rates were not increased.
48. Later labour leaders criticised the Lord Mayor for calling in the troops to deal with the York strike. It was very correctly pointed out that he did not do this, and that the troops were in York to be distributed elsewhere in the north east if needed.
49. No victimisation was a condition agreed to at the end of the General Strike. It is said that in York railway employers honoured this. They did not mark the records of those who left work in any way.

248

They did, however, mark those of the people who stayed at work!

50. *Press* 19 August 1911. The quotation actually refers to the LNW.
51. *Ibid* 25 September 1911
52. For the elections see *Ibid*, issues of 9 to 18 August 1911
53. Earlier in the year, in July, R.B. Lambert had relinquished a Guilhall seat and been replaced, without a contest, by Edward Allen, a taxidermist.
54. *Press* 10 August 1911
55. *Herald* 19 August 1911. Result Clarke 417; Dobbie 233; Streicher 89.
56. Birch 1,306; Dobbie 945: F.W. Chapman (Tory) 861; Robert Richardson 845.
57. Glew 1,428; Morrell 1,186; David Sanderson Long (Tory) 1,003
58. Rowntree 1,021; Edward Tate (Tory) 1,006; George Henry Mennell (Liberal) 884
59. Sessions 1,480; Scott 1,398; Henry Hopkins (Tory) 1,230
60. The Hogge election (he carried out a fortnight's campaign) can be followed in the newspapers from about 19 January 1912
61. *Press* 30 January 1912
62. Hogge 5,064; Jameson 5,139
63. The National Insurance Bill was introduced while the Parliament Bill was still going through the parliamentary stages in the Commons. It established a contributory system of national insurance modelled on a German system of 1889.
64. In November, just before the municipal elections, the Corporation had also awarded wage rises to the tram workers - who had recently formed a union branch. By this agreement motormen were to be paid 6d. an hour rising to 6d. after a year; conductors were to get a top rate of $6^1/2$d.; and hours were reduced from 60 to 54 a week. *Press* 8 November 1911.
65. *Ibid* 6 and 7 February 1912
66. *Ibid* 10 February 1912. The first lady was a Miss Escreet who appeared in a case in which the York Hygienic Laundries Ltd. were prosecuted under Section 26 of the Factories Act and were found guilty of allowing (or making) girls work longer than permitted hours. *Ibid* 24 August 1911
67. *Ibid* 3 and 6 June 1911
68. *Ibid* 5 June 1911
69. There had been a blaze in the Gas Company's premises in Little Stonegate, Boyes' Stores on Ouse Bridge had also burnt down, and there had been a serious outbreak at a mill in Skeldergate. In addition to this, in 1912, the clock tower of Boyes' property fell, killing a member of the Bowman family. See eg *Ibid* 8 December 1910 and 21 June 1911. In 1912 there was a serious fire behind St Deny's Street, in property occupied by the Sheppee Motor Company, once owned by the Criterion Cocoa Factory. *Ibid* 10 June 1912
70. *Ibid* 1, 7 and 14 November 1911. The Debenham's films venture is reported in *Ibid* 8 and 31 August 1911. Kinemacolour did not last long. See *Ibid*. The 'Sins of Utah' seemingly depicted the conning of young girls who were taken off to Utah to take part in polygamous marriages. Elder Patrick and Elder Waters led deputations to the Victoria Hall in protest. Bert Rutter, however, stuck to his guns and showed the films (and did handsomely). *Ibid* 12 March 1912. The 'Sins of Utah' had done well in London.
71. *Ibid* 6 October 1910
72. *Ibid* 1 November 1910
73. *Ibid* 21 April 1911
74. *Ibid* 11 July 1911
75. *Ibid* 13 June 1910
76. *Ibid* 8 September 1910
77. *Ibid* 8 November 1910. See also *Ibid* 21 June 1910
78. *Ibid* 29 October 1910
79. *Ibid* 28 September 1911
80. *Ibid* 1 December 1911
81. *Ibid* 20 April 1912
82. *Ibid* 15 June 1912
83. *Ibid* 18 June, 13 July 1912
84. *Ibid* The description of the ground renovations and opening games from *Ibid* 23 and 24 August 1912 and *Herald* 9 September 1912
85. *Press* 5 March 1912
86. Rents in the Bishopthorpe Road are a were said, at the Brewster Sessions of 1912, to be 5s.

or 6s.

87. *Press* 4 June 1912
88. *Ibid* 2 April 1912
89. *Ibid* 6 April 1912
90. *Ibid* 27 February 1912
91. *Ibid* 19 March 1912
92. The effect of the coal strike can be followed in the local papers from about the third week of February. The *Herald* carried some impressive photographs showing the effects of the strike
93. *Press* 6 April 1912
94. *Ibid* 20 March 1912
95. *Ibid* 5 July 1912
96. *Ibid* 8 June 1912
97. *Herald* 6 April 1912. The following biographical details about Cornthwaite arefrom this source
98. *Press* 4 May 1912. See also letter from Caroline Wilkinson in *Ibid* 1 April 1912
99. About which 'branch' of the womens movement it supported
100. *Press* 28 November 1911
101. *Ibid* 11 September 1912
102. *Ibid* 30 March 1912
103. *Ibid* 28 and 29 October 1912
104. Wrongly called William in the *Press*'s account
105. The Settlement ran a 'current affairs' series of lectures in which she took part. Other participants were Sebastian Meyer and the well-known Ben Turner from the West Riding. Another lecturer taking a full lecture course at the centre was Arthur Greenwood, destined to become a Labour cabinet minister. See Ibid 28 September 1912
106. *Ibid* 18 November 1912
107. *Ibid* 12 October 1912
108. *Ibid* 3 October 1912
109. *Ibid* 23 and 28 November and 7 December 1912. There is a photograph of Broughton in the issue of 7 December
110. *Ibid* 13 April 1912
111. See eg the account of the first annual meeting of the Gas and General Workers' Union in *Ibid* 24 June 1912
112. *Ibid* 6 May 1912
113. *Ibid* 27 May 1912
114. See earlier, chapter 4
115. Quoted P. de Mendelssohn, *The Age of Churchill* (1961) pp 342-43. Also R.Churchill, *Winston S. Churchill* Vol 2 (1967) pp 261-65
116. *Press* 31 October 1912
117. *Ibid* 27 November 1912. See also fn 13 for loans for street improvements and house building
118. *Herald* 6 and 7 September 1912
119. *Press* 5 July 1912
120. *Ibid* 25 April 1912. There is quite a good history of the company in the account of the bill before the Commons.
121. *Ibid* 30 April 1912
122. *Ibid* 11 June 1912
123. This was another Liberal initiative for which the Corporation applied for a loan of £5,575. See *Ibid* 23 February 1912 for an account of the usual enquiry. The Corporation wanted to tarmac over cobbles in 86 back streets. In fairness to the earlier administration it might be pointed out that evidence was given that in the previous year 21,920 square yards had been covered. O.F. Rowntree was particularly concerned with these works, his main considerations being those of the health hazards caused by the old roads. Earlier the council had applied for permission to borrow £8,977 to erect houses in Alma Terrace etc.
124. It had been caused by the death of Councillor Tate. At the election Labour was at odds with the Liberals, and during the campaign the gas question was, naturally, of importance. The result was: Mennell 1,735; T.J. Betchetti 662. On the election eg *Ibid* 15 May, 11 and 12 June 1912
125. *Ibid* 24 June and 5 July 1912
126. *Ibid* 30 October 1912
127. Meyer put the matter to the Streets and Buildings committee. *Ibid* 3 September 1912

128. *Ibid* 29 October 1912
129. The Lord Mayor did not have to be a council member, of course. It has already been mentioned that Riley-Smith had been approached when he was connected with the city
130. *Press* 14 September 1912
131. *Ibid* 1 and 2 November 1912
132. Horsman 992; Wilkinson 916; T. Morris (Lib) 880; J.E. Gibbs (Tory) 866.
133. *Press* 3 December 1912.
134. *Ibid* 4 December 1912
135. *Ibid* 10 December 1912
136. *Ibid* 20 December 1912
137. *Ibid* 7 January 1913
138. *Ibid* 30 January 1913
139. *Ibid* 22 January 1913
140. *Ibid* 30 January 1913
141. *Ibid* 30 May 1913
142. *Ibid* 11 February 1913
143. *Ibid* 21 February 1913
144. *Ibid* 7 and 8 April 1913
145. *Ibid* 17 April 1913
146. The third member of the bench was B.S. Wales
147. *Press* 14 August 1912
148. A dozen new magistrates were elected at this time - nine of whom were either Liberals or Labour supporters. Robert Kay, who was to become well-known for his activities in 1914-18, was another of the Liberals. J.M. Hogge said that prior to this influx the bench had been entirely Tory, which does not seem to be absolutely true
149. *Press* 16 and 18 May 1912. The successful applicant was 39 year old Walter Middlewood Temple, a school teacher
150. *Ibid* 4 February 1913
151. *Herald* 8 April 1913
152. The other three dissentients were Councillors Robinson, Benson and Hardgrave
153. *Press* 22 May 1913. The Wesleyan mentioned in this paragraph is the Rev Stanley Parker who made the remarks quoted from the pulpit of Wesley Chapel. Canon Argles was of similar views
154. *Herald* 10 April 1913
155. *Ibid* 11 and 12 June 1913
156. *Ibid* 10 April 1913
157. *Ibid* 3 May 1913
158. *Ibid* 6 June 1913
159. *Ibid* 23 and 28 June 1913
160. *Sunday Times* 19 February 1989. It should be said that the breaches reported then were of the 1950 Shops Act.
161. *Press* 22 January 1913
162. *Ibid* 30 January 1913
163. *Ibid* 7 February 1913
164. *Ibid* 21 April 1913. There is a photograph of the 'infernal machine' in *Ibid* 22 April 1913.
165. *Ibid* 16 April 1913
166. *Ibid* 7 and 8 July 1913. Also Ibid 30 June 1913
167. What happened to Forster Todd is not clear.
168. *Press* 8 July 1913
169. My italics.
170. *Herald* 7 July 1913
171. *Press* 10 July 1913
172. Hibbett died shortly afterwards - before the November elections. He was 66. For an obituary see *Ibid* 6 October 1913.
173. Voting was Birch 25; Hartley 20; Hibbett ten; Page five
174. *Herald* 15 July 1913
175. *Ibid* 26 and 29 July 1913
176. *Press* 11 August 1913
177. At about this time the first York prosecution for a breach of the Shops Closing Act of 1912 was

brought. This was adopted by the Council which, in an order dated 18 January 1913, made Wednesday a half holiday for shop assistants. The offender was one William Firbank, his fine was 1s. See *Ibid* 21 August 1913. See also *Ibid* 1 September 1913 - a prosecution of a shopkeeper who kept open on a Wednesday race day.

178. *Ibid* 21 and 28 August 1913
179. The Chief Constable had brought the charges then sent Superintendent Woolnough to prosecute. This was not permitted - 'no person could appear for somebody else'.
180. *Press* 4 and 18 September 1913
181. *Ibid* 4 September 1913
182. *Herald* supplement 19 July 1913
183. Letter from C.A. Thompson in *Press* 28 July 1913
184. *Herald* 21 July 1913
185. *Ibid* 22 July 1913 wrongly refers to Morris as a Labour candidate. Tom lived in Escrick Terrace, and was a plasterer contractor. There had been some suggestions that a James Wilkinson would also stand as an 'Independent Liberal'. *Ibid* 22 and 23 July 1913
186. *Press* 30 July 1913
187. *Herald* 22 July 1913
188. There were 3,541 electors, of whom 2,122 voted.

CHAPTER 8

'NO SHUNTER LORD MAYOR FOR YORK'

The Liberals had retained their seat in Walmgate in 1913, and got a sympathiser for their basic programme returned for Micklegate, and the prosecutions for Sunday trading went on. Then a change occurred. The Watch Committee, in October, decided that they should stop until the whole Council had deliberated again and decided otherwise. (1) They, the police, the magistrates, and the Council, had been made to look foolish and partisan and a change of mind looked the sensible thing to do. But how would the populace regard the change of heart ? Would they think it genuine, or would they think that if the Liberals were returned in increased numbers they might start the whole stupid business again ? Not only that, but a pressure group had come into existence which kept the issue alive and did the Liberals no good whatsoever.

Towards the end of September, just as the opening moves in the year's municipal contests were starting, the York Lord's Day Observance Association was reformed and began to organise a campaign to persuade the Council to continue the persecution of the small traders. Among the sympathisers, and appearing on its platforms, were a number of well-known Liberals and Liberal councillors (and Glew). J.T. Clarke was one of them, Charles T. Hutchinson was another. J.A. Shaftoe was also a member and so was that Rev Stanley Parker who had called Sunday openers 'blacklegs'. Canon Argles was, predictably, a supporter, and so was W.J. Henderson. He gave figures at the Association's first public meeting about the number of prosecutions in York. There had been up to that date, Henderson said, 177 cases brought, in which 92 fines had been imposed and 85 cases had been dismissed. Thirty nine magistrates had fined the 92, and 15 had dismissed the 85. (2) Harry Miles was one of the JPs who were resolutely in favour of continuing to harass the small shopkeepers, and he was prominent on the platforms of the Observance Association.

The Lord's Day Observance Association got a dreadful reception in the city. A. Dearlove, president of the Free Church Council (not Arthur Dearlove, the conscientious objector) advocated supporting only candidates who would continue to clamp down on the traders, and the Rev Russell Smith denounced 'Sunday in York under the Corporation' from the pulpit of the Priory Street Baptist Church. Anything but an updated and even more dreary version of the Victorian Sunday was not good enough for Smith. He revealed that he had been a prime mover in the initial approaches to the Corporation. They had gone to the Council, he said, and asked them 'to protect the whole community against the action of some who kept neither the law of God nor the law of England, and ... by so doing, were robbing the law and God-fearing citizens of their living and seducing children from the path of God.' (3) How were they doing that?

The Council's opponents made much of the fact that it was selective in its targets and hypocritical in its attitude by prosecuting some and not others and not going the whole hog with the Act. Smith used the same arguments and campaigned to stop the band concerts which brought a little pleasure to dreary lives on that dreary day. Smith, with a captive audience, piled on the rhetoric. "'They are piping to the young people of our city", he exclaimed, "when we are attempting to win them for God. It is not fair of them ... this is a deliberate enticement which will make the work of the churches even harder". The Corporation had put a stumbling block in the way of those who sought to return to God.'

Russell Smith no doubt was well received amongst the Baptists assembled in Priory Street, but he was howled down when he addressed open air meetings of the Lord's Day Observance Association. The crowds greatest anger, however, was directed at Harry Miles, that JP who had been a prominent pro-Boer and several times an unsuccessful candidate for municipal office. Harry's sense of judicial discretion went to the winds when he 'declared that he "would fine the whole lot of Sunday openers"', but he looks an unlikely colleague of Shaftoe (who was connected with the Sunday Closing Association), John Howard and the likes of Russell Smith, Argles and the Reverends Brightling and Gregg. Miles put forward his objections in a socialist fashion (if Sunday labour became general, he said, 'the capitalists would demand that the workers should do seven day's work for six day's pay'), (4) but the populace chose to regard him as a bigoted Sabbatarian pure and simple. Just before the municipal elections he, bravely, shared a platform with the Rev Stanley Parker. The question they were discussing Parker told the crowd, was of far greater importance than Home Rule or anything else that was before this country. Parker may well have believed that silly remark to be true, but he was howled down, then followed by Miles. Harry had just got nicely started when an interrupter who was presumably not a member of the Priory Street Baptist congregation twisted his earlier remarks and shouted - "'Mr Stanley Parker does one day's work in seven and has six day's rest, but he gets seven day's pay".' Miles was asked if he thought he was 'a fit man to try Sunday traders ? It is about time we had a stipendiary magistrate', the interrupter went on, 'and did away with the likes of you.' (5)

The city of York was building up to the most exiting (and important) municipal elections for a century or more, and the issue of Sunday trading was perhaps the most important fact making it so. But there were other issues - all of which must have made the Liberals' task that year a formidable one.

The ruling party had taken a severe blow when Wragge, Hibbert and Rhodes Brown, who took part in the Sunday trading dispute, obtained the citizens poll over the municipalisation of gas. They behaved stupidly over Sunday trading, but were determined to press on with their programme of reforms - and K.E.T. Wilkinson seems to have reasoned that the package they had to offer would restore their fortunes.

Winning in the Micklegate by election in the summer would have revived their spirits somewhat, and in October they produced their biggest package of reforms ever. It was impressive. They asked the Council to consider (among other things): a suggestion for a covered market; a recreation area on the Knavesmire; essential repairs to Monk Bar; a recreation ground at Heworth (for which the land had already been obtained); a Leeman Road/Clifton bridge which would cost £33,000; new offices for the Weights and Measures Department which would cost £2,500; and a municipal cemetery at the junction of Poppleton Road and Beckfield Lane. (6) These new proposals were not surprises - many of them had been spoken of for a long time - but they were the subject of great discussions during the campaign leading to the November election. Relton, who stood again in Micklegate, was one of the Tories who put these latest Liberal proposals (and others) under close scrutiny. What were his verdicts ? The education system in York, he said, was too expensive and 'more time' should be 'devoted to the three R's and night schools for future study made compulsory.' He was against the Clifton Bridge proposals, and against the cemetery proposals (a frequent criticism was that it was too far from some parts of the city).The proposals to amalgamate the city's charities were 'plunder'. Relton unequivocally said he was against the prosecution of Sunday traders. (7)

That last issue came before the Council once more before the elections - at that same meeting when that huge package of reforms was discussed. Councillors had to discuss the Watch Committee's recommendation that the prosecutions (the persecutions) should be stopped. The debate produced enough bigotry for a lifetime and again showed up serious splits between colleagues. K.E.T. Wilkinson revealed that the compromise that he had suggested was totally ignored and J.B. Inglis, a jeweller, said that he had toured the city and established beyond all doubt that very very few shop assistants were employed on Sundays. G.H. Mennell said that Sunday opening was undoubtedly on the increase and Theodore Rowntree told the Council that he had changed his mind on the issue. He had voted twice for continuing the prosecutions, Rowntree said; now he would vote differently. Alderman Birch said that the people who were changing their minds were probably afraid of their seats. By this he perhaps meant the Tory Inglis - Rowntree was not standing for re-election. If there had to be a prize for the most bigoted and idiotic contribution to this debate, however, it would go to Labour's G.F. Glew. 'It was a most deplorable thing to see children running for sweets and seeing them sucking them on Sundays', said Glew. J.H. Hartley then poked fun at his colleague by saying that Glew himself broke the law every Sunday when he did paid work for his trade union. Glew had proposed that the prosecutions should carry on, and his proposal was carried by one vote (19 to 18). Then a strange alliance (Hartley and Wragge) resorted to (justified) ridicule and proposed that Charles II's act should be 'put into force in its entirety', and was defeated (20 to 14). The Small Trader's Association afterwards issued a hit list of people it urged voters not to support. They were: William Page, a corn merchant of Holgate House, a Liberal; Robert Varey, colliery agent, also a Liberal and, like Page, a candidate in Castlegate; John Thomas

Clarke, manufacturer, a retiring councillor who was standing in Micklegate; Arthur Wilkinson, a works manager, another Liberal standing in Micklegate; and Francis Edward Pollard, a councillor and a schoolmaster, standing as a Liberal in Bootham.

None of the Tories who had adopted the 'prosecute the small trader' policy were standing in 1913 and neither was Glew, so if Sunday trading was going to be an issue at the election (and it was) the Liberals had real problems. There was another local government issue that was also causing concern at that time, and although not a strict party question it also caused tempers to rise. It had to do with who was to be the next Lord Mayor, and it revealed some very interesting attitudes and assumptions.

York frequently had difficulties in finding a Lord Mayor, and some of the occasions when this happened have been mentioned. Alderman Agar, for example, stepped in and took office with only minutes to go in the words of the *Press*, and although people refusing could be fined, this did not persuade many to change their minds. The post usually went to an alderman and this year, of course, there were two new members of the bench who, because of the ways things went, were considered for office.

The search for a Lord Mayor began shortly after Hartley and Birch were made aldermen. In September a Council sub committee was set up to interview people for the office of first magistrate - it was the Liberals turn, but despite that Sir Joseph Sykes Rymer, the sitting Tory, was asked to serve. He refused as did Aldermen Meyer, Forster Todd, and Walker. Meyer, who had distinguished himself by engaging in those indiscreet slanging matches over Sunday trading, would seem to have been an extremely bad choice at that time, but he was asked a second time, and refused a second time. At this stage in the proceedings the names of Arnold Rowntree, Councillor William Page and Harry Hartley were put forward. (8)

For a month the possibility of Hartley becoming York's first workingman Lord Mayor was discussed, with the idea finding favour in some circles (like the ILP), (9) and not in others - naturally. Early in October he accepted nomination, but then the question arose about whether he would want a salary. Labour had put forward a proposal that he be selected, but this was withdrawn and Birch was asked if he would stand. He declined, but announced that he would like to be offered the post again at some stage, and declared himself a determined opponent of paying the Lord Mayor a salary. 'The Lord Mayor ought to have sufficient means to keep up the dignity of the office', he said. With this refusal Hartley was chosen, and a most unpleasant episode in York's history got under way.

Hartley approved of the municipal policies of people like Meyer, but he, more than anyone, had led the campaign of the small traders and exposed the differences in the Liberal ranks, yet the Liberals could not be seen to oppose him (openly anyway). So they supported him when all the other Mayoral candidates refused to serve. Hartley accepted their offer, but made it quite clear that on a railway shunter's pay he could not offer hospitality at the Mansion House. That residence would probably remain closed during his mayoralty. It is a shock to realise 'that ... the old traditions of the Mansion House, which have been observed since that building was erected about 1730, are in danger of being abrogated' wrote the *Press*. (10) Later Hartley said he would live in the official residence if the Corporation would pay and feed the staff, but the Estates Committee were said to be in favour of letting Harry work from home and closing the place down. (Many years later a much loved Lord Mayor adopted the same attitude as Harry Hartley and lived at home during his term of office.) (11)

A furious and very unpleasant series of letters began to appear in the papers about the merits of Harry Hartley as a Lord Mayor. One of the nastiest was signed 'Ichabod' and he reminded his readers that quite a lot of people did rather well during the reign of a generous and wealthy Lord Mayor. (In York's history George Hudson was number one in that respect without a doubt.) A Hartley term of office, Ichabod said, would kill 'trade for the whole year.' He then got mixed up a bit. 'All social functions are stopped; dressmakers are thrown out of work; no catering, hence waiters, female attendants are not wanted, no engaging of rooms curtails the use of gas, electric light. Catering gives works to poulterers and other trades, likewise cabmen. Motor-men have part of their livelihood stopped, and many others who during the year have expenses to meet , rent to pay, rates ditto.' (12) Disaster could hit the city according to Ichabod - others were more unpleasant. 'Progress' excelled himself. (13) If Harry was made Lord Mayor, he said, the results would be ludicrous. Should Mr Hartley be finally elected, accept, and still follow his occupation as a shunter, could anything be more ludicrous and undignified than his Lordship leaving the station yard and returning 'to the Mansion House in the uniform of a N.E.R. shunter, accompanied by his bread basket and tea can? The whole thing is too monstrous for words. What a harvest would the comic artists reap.' Another letter in the same paper that Ichabod's missive graced said that Harry Hartley had been a councillor, alderman, Labour leader, Justice and 'an applicant for paid office'. Now, he went on, he was 'to be Lord Mayor, ... [and a] candidate for Parliament'. It looks, he went on, as if he had '"come into his own" very well. Has he ambitions to be archbishop also ?' (14)

That the local papers allowed letters like that from 'Ichabod' to appear is deplorable, and it is a wonder that someone did not rake up the allegations about Harry's expenses fiddle of a few years earlier. The paid job that he had applied for has been mentioned, but had he parliamentary ambitions ? The answer is that he had.

G.H. Stuart had been selected as York's next Labour candidate, and an extremely good candidate he would have been. For some reason, however, he dropped out, and in March 1913 the party held a selection conference to replace him. The event caused a great stir in York and the short list contained three names. The first was that of H.H. Schloesser, a barrister and standing counsel to the Labour party; the second was J.

Bromley, an organising secretary of one of the railway unions; and the third was Hartley. Schloesser was selected. (15)

The scene was set for an exciting series of municipal contests in January 1913. There had been industrial troubles in the city again (of which more later) and they had heightened political feeling. So too had the Sunday prosecutions and the big package of reforms (costly reforms) which had been formally sprung on the Council late in the municipal year. Finally the question of whether the city wanted a Labour Lord Mayor was an issue. If the Liberals were still in a majority after the polls it would be Harry Hartley for sure - Harry who not long before had protested against militarism in schools, the present to J.G. Butcher, the spending of corporation money on junketing (while possibly going to those junkets himself) and much more.

Who were the most important candidates of November 1913, and what had they to say ? There will be no surprises regarding the latter, but one man was conspicuous by his absence. J.M. Hogge's term of office had come to an end, and he did not seek re-election, presumably on the grounds that being a Scottish M.P. left him no time to slug it out in York with the likes of Vernon Wragge. The five Liberal pro-Sunday prosecutors (Varey, Pollard, Page, Wilkinson and Clarke) have been mentioned. They seem to have kept off the Sunday issue and Varey and Pollard (Varey was standing for Hogge's old seat) made much of the Liberals' record over electricity and the trams, demanded the opening up of Leeman Road and the incorporation of Acomb, Fulford and Heworth into York. (16) Pollard spoke up for small council house estates (17) (a big meeting had recently been called by the Council to explain their plans for town planning). Clarke and Arthur Wilkinson, retiring councillors for Micklegate, made much of the plans for a new cemetery and the need for better access to Leeman Road. Clarke, to his credit, did make his attitude clear on Sunday traders. Continuing doing them was his policy. (18)

The only other prominent Liberal standing in 1913 (for Monk) was Cuthbert Morrell, the retiring councillor. He was to get into a nice little controversy during the campaign.

The Tories who were retiring were Rhodes Brown and J.B. Inglis. The former had taken no part whatsoever in the Sunday trading disputes, but Inglis had proved to be a powerful opponent of the prosecutions. He had shared platforms with Hartley and Tom Morris and layed about him in fine style. Like Morris he had presented some of the persecutors as hypocrites. Forster Todd and J.T. Clarke, he pointed out, were members of the bands committee of the council, and of course that committee brought bands to York which played on Sundays, and at their concerts programmes were sold and chairs were hired out. (19) The Rev Russell Smith would have had difficulty in defining his attitude to these two, presumably; two men who hired bands and sold programmes yet prosecuted (or approved of the prosecuting of) people who sold apples. Is it 'not strange', Inglis asked, 'that we should be instrumental in prosecuting poor people who have the greatest difficulty' in getting the necessities of life ? It was not at all surprising. Inglis had answered his own question earlier. The persecutors were hypocrites.

Inglis and Brown were unopposed in Guildhall (20) and the most prominent Tory to stand with them in 1913 was that Edward Relton, who had fought the Micklegate by election earlier in the year. It was he who got into a row with Cuthbert Morrell. Relton was a builder (who paid union rates) who had put up many of the houses on the South Bank area - that area that Canon Argles and others had successfully deprived of a pub it will be recalled. Relton said that the Holgate Gardens Estate Society Ltd had had preferential treatment from the Council - and this was a project with which both Cuthbert Morrell and the harassed Sebastian Meyer were connected. Meyer and Morrell, Relton said, had 'dismally failed to provide houses for the workers at a rent they can afford to pay, and although not wanting profits the [Holgate Gardens] company to which they belonged is in liquidation.' Men like himself, who built for profit, were at a disadvantage, Relton went on, 'yet our City Progressives insist upon trying their 'prentice hand to solve the problem "How to house the workers."' York had spent £1,600 on this failed venture Relton concluded, and he got a writ slapped on him for slander. Morrell issued it, and he said that £1,300 had indeed been spent on sewer and street works, but that bondsmen had agreed to pay it back with interest in ten years. Five years had elapsed since then, Relton pointed out, and the sum involved amounted to the equivalent of a penny rate. (21) It was all good knockabout stuff, and it did Relton no harm whatsoever.

Labour put up a number of candidates in 1913 - none of whom adopted the attitudes of Glew. In Micklegate Robert Thomas Mackereth, an engine driver, and John Noble Mercer, a plumber stood. In Walmgate the veteran A.P. Mawson, the retired glassmaker and magistrate stood. There were again no women candidates, but a number of ladies signed proposal forms for various candidates. Lydia Skelton and Elizabeth Sharp, for example, sponsored Rhodes Brown and Elizabeth Richardson Petty and Emma Workman proposed Cuthbert Morrell. Mary G. Swanson and the splendidly named Emily Eupotoria Barry nominated Benjamin Dodsworth, solicitor, for Bootham.

What happened at the municipal elections of 1913 ? The Liberals had put forward a huge programme of reforms and were talking of implementing town planning schemes. The Tories stressed the cost. The Liberals were blamed (rightly) for the harassment of small shopkeepers and were running five candidates who thought it should continue. The Tories had no-one associated with the persecution of the shopkeepers, but many like Inglis, were against it. Relton had hinted at some sharp practice, and the Tories won sensationally. All but one of those on the small traders' hit list were defeated, and Cuthbert Morrell was ousted from Monk. (One of those on the hit list had to get in as a glance at the list for Castlegate will show). In Micklegate Relton was returned with a tremendous majority and Mawson failed in Walmgate. The full results in this momentous election were as follows (retiring councillors marked *). The top two in each ward were returned.

Bootham.

Benjamin Dodsworth, * solicitor,	Conservative	1,635
Clarence Cecil Lucas, solicitor,	Conservative	1,547
Alfred Verrell Iredale, clerk,	Labour	949
Francis Edward Pollard,* schoolmaster,	Liberal	884

Castlegate.

Alfred Wiseman, farmer,	Conservative	1,091
Robert Varey, colliery agent,	Liberal	695
William Page, * corn merchant.		650

Guildhall (no contest).

James Brown Inglis, * jeweller,	Conservative
Henry Rhodes Brown, * merchant,	Conservative

Micklegate.

Edward Relton, builder,	Conservative	1,242
John Noble Mercer, plumber,	Labour	1,152
Robert Thomas Mackereth, locomotive driver	Labour	1,109
Arthur Wilkinson, * works manager,	Liberal	647
John Thomas Clarke, * manufacturer,	Liberal	530

Monk.

Charles Benson, * gentleman,	Conservative	1,130
Charles Arthur Bury, barrister,	Conservative	1,049
Cuthbert Morrell, * gentleman,	Liberal	561

Walmgate.

Joseph Hardgrave, * slating contractor,	Conservative	1,099
John Edward Gibbs, consulting engineer,	Conservative	940
Andrew Pattison Mawson, retired glassmaker	Labour	813
Hugh McGargle, machinery beltmaker,	Liberal	729
Albert Till, marker gardener, non party		371

The elections (which had been held on a Saturday, which was reckoned to be a good day for Labour) had ended with a Tory at the head of the poll in each ward, and with the defeat of five retiring Liberal councillors - one of whom had been on the council for 22 years. 'It is doubtful if ever in the history of the municipal politics of York the Progressives were so completely routed' commented the *Press*. The situation on the Council now was that, once more, the Tories had a majority (26 to 22). The Aldermen numbered one Labour, four Liberal and seven Conservatives. The Councillors were 12 Liberal, five Labour and 19 Conservatives. Quite clearly the Liberals had been beaten because of the prosecution of the Sunday traders and a fear of the cost of their proposed reforms. The *Press* got it right. (22) 'The Liberal party', it said, at last calling it by that name

> have in season and out supported the prosecution of small struggling shopkeepers who supply a real need in the poorer parts of the city by opening on Sunday. ... It is expected that one of the first acts of the newly-constituted Corporation will be to rescind the resolution directing the prosecution of small traders. ... The result of the election is also a severe condemnation of the extravagant schemes promoted by the Progressives, and is in every sense a vote of no confidence in that party.

The risking of their control of York by the Liberals through that appallingly stupid policy of trying to implement a centuries-old act which defied logical interpretation in the conditions of 1913 is simply amazing. For years they had been shut out of power, but impulsively, and with an incredible ignorance of what had to be the consequences, they went along with bigots like Shaftoe, Argles and Parker. In doing so they jeopardised their chances of implementing the measures K.E.T. Wilkinson said they set so much store by. Maybe the cost of those improvements would have weighed against them anyway, but to risk them by implementing out-dated Sabbatarian laws in a totally inconsistent way was simply daft. People like Wilkinson, Meyer, Davies and the Rowntrees might have been expected to be a little less naive than they were. They persisted in their folly right up to the eve of the election and caused allies like Hartley to urge voters not to support people like Clarke. To say that the ruling parties were 'divided' in 1913 would be a monumental understatement. Hartley had been in the West Riding addressing meetings at which he had made remarks that when reported amounted to a declaration that he would happily see the Mansion House plate melted down, and he certainly gave the impression that he would not wear the regalia which York still insists on making its first citizens look ridiculous in. All this was used against him, of course, leading a London evening paper to carry a story headed 'No shunter Lord Mayor for York' (23) and on 6 November 40 out of the 48 members on the council met in committee to reconsider their invitation to Hartley to become the next Lord Mayor. (24) Inglis, the Tory, and Mennell, the Liberal, proposed that the invitation be withdrawn, and their proposal was carried (25 for, 12 against, three neutral). The debate became heated, with Hartley singling out Norman Green for particular attack, and C.A.Bury contending that whether or not to have shunter Hartley as Mayor was the single most important factor at the recent elections. The selection of York's Lord Mayor in 1913, the *Press* said, on 7 November, had 'gained world-wide notice.'

Who was to replace Hartley (or rather Sykes Rymer)? It was the Liberals 'turn' to nominate the Lord Mayor, but there was no way in the aftermath of the November election rout that the Tories would allow that to happen, and Rhodes Brown was chosen by a thumping majority. The Liberals, it will be recalled, had every intention of altering the composition of the Aldermanic bench when half that body came to the end of their terms of office in November 1913. That way they could have increased their hold on the Council, but they were now no longer in a position to do that. At a special meeting at which Rhodes Brown was chosen to replace Hartley, the Aldermanic bench was simply re-elected.

Labour would not accept what the special committee had done and Hartley announced that his name would go forward to the full council. It did, and York had a contested election for Lord Mayor (the outcome of which was never in any doubt whatsoever). Alderman J. Agar and Councillor W. Robie Robinson - the senior councillor - duly nominated Rhodes Brown, while Dobbie and Glew put forward Hartley. The latter maintained that the only objections to Hartley were that he was a working man, but they got little support. (25) Twenty six persons voted for Brown; 15 councillors voted for Hartley (amongst whom were Sessions, Davies, Oscar and Theodore Rowntree, and of course the Labour men). In his acceptance speech Brown stressed his own working class background (he had come from an even less privileged background than Hartley he said) and showed a considerable amount of political acumen when he said that he and the Lady Mayoress would not carry out any civic duties on Sundays. Brown probably had the likes of the Rev Russell Smith in mind when he made this decision.

The first meeting of the council after Brown's election received a letter from Smith, that great advocate of the dreary Sabbath. Smith was anti Sunday trading, and anti Sunday band concerts. He scaled down his demands in the light of the election results and asked the corporation to arrange the concerts so that they did not conflict with divine service. (26) The Watch Committee had decided to hold its hand until after a council debate (27) and that debate was duly held at the first opportunity - and the persecution of the small shopkeepers was ended. But not until after Glew and Petty had trotted out their dismal demands once more (with some of them stressing the 'rest for the workers' argument against the religious one). Glew wanted the prosecutions to go on, and Petty took some hefty swipes at the York justices, having, no doubt, Harry Miles in mind as well as the troubled person he mentioned by name. '... the action of the magistrates', Petty said, 'called for strong protest. He objected to magistrates like Alderman Hartley standing at one street corner and telling defendants before they were tried that he was going to let them off, and another magistrate at another street corner saying he should fine them.' Quite right too; the York magistrates (or some of them) had entered openly into politics in a way that was reprehensible. 'The whole thing was a humbug, and a travesty of the word justice', Petty concluded. A decision to leave the traders alone was passed with a large majority (27 to nine).

The Liberals used to accuse the Tories of doing nothing - or next to nothing - in the days of their supremacy. They showed a predictable burst of activity in their first couple of weeks back in power in 1913, however, dismantling what there was of the Liberals' reform programme. A.P. Dale and Councillor C. Lucas told Bootham Conservatives at their victory concert what had been achieved in less than two weeks. Lucas had been moved in to Bootham as a last minute replacement for Hibbett, and he told his audience that 'He thought they had done something in the last fortnight.' He was right, and he gave details. (28) The Clifton bridge scheme had been buried, the cemetery scheme had been referred back, the trams were not going into Acomb, and the Corporation Bill had been amended to obtain power to run trolley 'buses down Burton-lane.

York local government must have been at its most entertaining ever in 1913, and crowds attended to hear the final rounds fought in the Rhodes Brown/Shunter Hartley fracas. This was good, cheap entertainment. How had the provision of professional entertainment changed since the revival of the Fishergate skating rink ? Had it survived, or was the roller skating craze as short lived in York as it was elsewhere?

The City Roller Skating Palace was reopened in the late summer of 1911, but it did not prosper, and eventually the rink was dismantled and the building put to different use. '... it will be remembered', a press report said, that the place was used 'for some time as a skating rink, but now that the boom [for skating] has gone it had been utilised for another purpose.' (29 It had been turned into a cinema - the City Picture Palace.

The City Picture Palace was another 'luxury' cinema (all tip up seats) to add to the already impressive list of those places in York. Reconstruction (by the City Picture Palace Company, York, Ltd) had cost £2,000 and it could accommodate 1,000 patrons. It opened with much ceremony in August 1913, and one of its first features was a local Debenham's film of the recent Military Sunday in the city. (30) Along with this newsreel were shown classics like 'Bronco Billy's Girl', 'Tweddeldum stuck to the Saddle', 'The Terrible Turk', and 'A Dollar Did it'. It looks as if the last title should have aroused the interest of such as Canon Argles and the Rev Stanley Parker.

The demand for seats at the cinema seemed inexhaustable, and the picture houses in York (and everywhere else) vied with one another to bring 'the greatest epic ever made' to the city each week. The Electric, for example, in March 1912, began to employ a violinist as well as a pianist, (31) and a month later it showed film of the huge Belfast demonstration against Home Rule. (32) (Perhaps the role of the cinema in giving the ordinary man in the street some knowledge of politics and international affairs has been underestimated.) Also in April 'The Titanic on her fatal voyage' was showing at the Victoria Hall, (33) and the following month Bert Rutter showed a feature on the Crimean War and once more invited the city's veterans to attend. (34) Later in the year the Electric showed film of the signing of the Ulster Covenant (as well as the 'Relief of Lucknow'), (35) while early in 1913 the Victoria Hall obtained a series of ragtime dancing films. These featured the famous Joe Bisset and Enid Sellers and a novel way of synchronising music with the action. Seemingly the films showed a conductor in an unobtrusive part of each frame and the house pianist was able to follow his baton while playing (one hopes) the immortal compositions of Scott Joplin and James Lamb. (36) (What the Rev Stanley Parker made of the bordello based music of Joplin and Lamb is not recorded.) In May 1913 another local feature was played at the Victoria Hall when film of the York City/Rotherham football match was shown (with shots of Tiny Tim it is hoped), (37) and later visitors to the same place saw film of the most famous ever Derby, the day after it was run. (38)

Rutter specialised in getting films of sporting events and was invariably first with such things. The fights of Bombadier Billy Wells (against Colin Bell, for example) were regularly shown there, and in July the film of Georges Carpentier's battle with Gunboat Smith for what was called the white heavyweight championship of the world caused a considerable stir. (The black heavyweight Jack Johnson was the official title holder at that time.) Gunboat was beaten by Carpentier, but some reporters said that the Frenchman had been staggered at one stage during the proceedings. The Victoria Hall played the footage through at slow speed to enable the citizens of York to make up their own minds on the matter. Just a month after this it was reported that Carpentier would not fulfil his next engagement against Young Ahearn. Why not ? War had broken out and Carpentier had joined up.

Ragtime dancing was featured on the screen at the Victoria Hall, and ragtime piano playing was heard at the Opera House in November 1913 when Joe Thompson appeared there. (39) Joe's playing in that glorious style was incidental, however, since he had been booked there as a dancer with Wilmot Karkeek to demonstrate the latest dance craze to York. This was the tango and the Opera House decided to combine a demonstration of it with another attraction (as well as Joe Thompson's ragtime playing). A 'Tango Tea and Dress Parade' was advertised. What was it like ? Well the dancing was only passable according to the press, but the dress parade (or at least a part of it) was something else. 'A.E.P.' wrote to the papers to say that he went and stayed up to Item 13 'when four or five ladies appeared in white corsets over black underclothing [and] I thought it time to depart.' (40) The tango, ragtime, and ladies in their underwear! One imagines that the likes of Glew, Stanley Parker and Russell Smith would certainly not have approved.

With the Opera House showing films regularly as a part of its bills and with the emergence of the City Picture Palace one would have thought that the filmgoers of York were more than well catered for. The likes of Bert Rutter thought so, too, and they eventually appeared as objectors to two more cinemas planned for York. They objected on the grounds of 'redundancy', which seems an odd expression for a place yet to be built.

On 1 April 1914 the *Press* published a report saying that a memorandum and articles of association of the York Picture House Ltd had been filed and a certificate of incorporation issued. The Company was to have £16,000 share capital, to be raised by the issue of 24,000 cumulative preference shares of 10s. each, and 80,000 deferred shares of 1s. each. The Company was to purchase numbers 25, 25a and 26, Coney Street and build a large cinema there with some 1,200 seats and a restaurant facility. William Henry Waddington, a York piano manufacturer, and Councillor George Sharp were prominent among the instigators of the new scheme. The prospectus of the company appeared in the papers of 5 May.

Plans for the new cinema were approved by the City Council and the *Press* of 28 July recorded that an application for a licence was considered by the Corporation's Cinematograph Committee. There it was revealed that the new picture house would seat 1,250 and cost £1,700 to build, but no such details were given for a second place to be put up in Skeldergate. This was simply referred to as the 'Skeldergate Hall' and the joint proprietors of it were John Blackburn and C.W. Gilbertson. Norman Crombie appeared before the committee on behalf of Rutter and the other York city cinema interests. Their arguments were that they could be put out of business if two more competitors appeared, but the committee deferred making a decision. It had not declared its final intention when the Great War broke out.

At about the time the City Picture Palace opened, the professional York City Football Club was about to enter its second year in the Midland League. How had it fared ? At the end of its first season - and after a dreadful start - the club had finished in tenth position, and heavily in debt. At the annual general meeting of the club held in June it was revealed that £2,000 had been spent 'on the field'. (41) Nothing like the whole of the share capital had been taken up and expenditure (£2,224) had exceeded income by £627. One of the major items of expenditure had been 'wages and staff' (£1,328) and this had been inflated because the club had been unable to find many of the players the jobs they had been promised and so had been forced to pay them an extra £1 per week. The club had also made a mistake in employing 'several players, who were colloquially known as "good old has-beens".' It also had problems that have a modern ring about them, and had sacked the manager (and others) after a relatively short stay. (The Rugby League Club, when the Association club was taking stock, was looking forward to the return of Tot Moore its star player.)

York, a civic dignitary had once said, was always late in getting the latest 'thing' (like a skating rink), and it was late in being visited by the flyers - the aeronauts - who were making the headlines in the last years before the Great War. There had been many rumours that the city would be visited or flown over, but it was not until February 1913 (when the country was riddled with stories of mysterious airships being seen anywhere and everywhere) that that happened. (42) In July 1911 B.C. Hucks, of the Blackburn Monoplane Company of Leeds (which was in the process of moving from Filey to a site between Leeds and Wakefield) was scheduled to fly over York en route to Lofthouse Park, a distance of 68 miles. (43) Hucks, the first man to 'loop the loop' 100 times, was planning to follow the railway lines in a plane powered by a 70 hp, seven cylinder engine and crowds assembled to see him. They were disappointed. A little later Hucks' flight was re-scheduled and his journey was going to be broken this time with a landing on the Knavesmire. Again crowds assembled, and again they were disappointed - Hucks developed a fault and had to land at Weaverthorpe. (44)

Almost two years went by before a plane did land in York, piloted by Captain C.A.H. Langcroft of the Welsh Regiment, attached to the Royal Flying Corps. Langcroft was flying a Bee biplane from Farnborough to Montrose and he took off for York from Newark, a distance of 70 miles which he completed in a time of one hour ten minutes. Sometime after Langcroft arrived two more Farman biplanes piloted by Lt Herbert and Capt Waldron landed. A couple of days later Captain Dawes and Captain Becke flying a Farman and a Bee arrived in York to be greeted on the Knavesmire by Lt Gen Plumer, GOC Northern Command, a famous figure in the First World War. (45)

After the sensational visit of Captain Langcroft and his colleagues the appearance of planes on the Knavesmire (there to be refuelled by the Anglo-American Oil Company Ltd of York) became a regular occurrence. In May, for example, Captain Beck flying a Bleriot Biplane 212 and a Major Burke arrived. (46) Early in 1914 Captain Dawes and a Lt Kelly were forced down on the Knavesmire en route from Farnborough to Montrose. They were flying the Farman machine which won a £1,000 prize in the military trials held on Salisbury Plain in 1913 and, through 'meatearological conditions' in the words of the *Press*, were forced to stay in York for a period (before going on and being forced down at Whitley Bay). (47) By this time the Blackburn Company had built a hangar near the Knavesmire, and in February one of the Company's monoplanes crashed on take-off - another York first. (48) Captain Dawes and two other pilots were back in York (again en route for Montrose) in March 1914. These airmen were taken to their hearts by York citizens and their subsequent exploits followed with great interest. The first trips made by York people from the Knavesmire seem to have been in September 1913 when the famous flyer Salmet took people up. (49)

During the months when the airmen were expected in York for the first time, industrial unrest had started again. There were always rumours that discontent on the NER would end in strike action, and in May there were strikes among the tram workers making the new route to South Bank, and among the slaters. The tramway workers' dispute is an interesting one because it took place among the private contractors' men who were receiving 6d. an hour - a halfpenny less than the Corporation men working alongside them and benefiting from the Liberals' fair wage policy. (50) The slaters struck for an extra penny an hour (9d. to 10d.) and the employers offered only half that. The slaters' dispute reached the stage it did, it was recorded, because they were the only group of building workers in York who did not have a conciliation board. (51) In July there was a shortlived strike at the Glass Works, during which a quarter of the work force downed tools (52) and later another at Leetham's. The background to these small yet significant disputes (53) was continuing price rises, and at about that time a Board of Trade enquiry showed their extent. Retail prices of food and coal had shown an increase of 13 per cent since 1905, it stated, and rent and retail prices together had gone up by 10.3 per cent in the same period. (54) Bacon had increased in price by 32.1 per cent between 1905 and 1912; eggs by 12.6 per cent; cheese by over 18 per cent; and bread by 15.3 per cent.

Of much more interest than the slaters' strike was that involving nearly all the female laundry workers in York. It started in the summer of 1913.

Conditions in York's laundries were by no means ideal in 1913, and several prosecutions for employing girls for too many hours have been mentioned. In June Hartley, Dobbie and a Miss Airey of the Yorkshire district of the National Federation of Women Workers drew attention to the sweated labour in York laundries. Girls were employed by professing christians from six o'clock to six o'clock for from 5s. to 12s. a week it was claimed. (55) Shortly after this a Mrs Franks, an attractive lady who had joined the union, was dismissed and a dispute took place at premises in Layerthorpe. (56) It was remarkably successful. Mrs Franks was reinstated, the union was recognised, and the members who had come out decided to join the local branch of the Gas Workers' organisation. (57)

The National Federation of Women Workers was responsible for putting demands to the employers and in the two months after Mrs Franks' reinstatement, a recruitment drive started, and in September a strike began at the premises of the York County Hygienic Laundries Ltd at Foss Islands. A deputation headed by Miss Airey (who came from Sheffield) waited on Mr H.A. Clark, the manager, who agreed to implement shorter hours, but refused to grant any wage increases. At lunch time on 24 September the workers struck (without the agreement of Miss Airey it seems) and the situation turned ugly in the afternoon when office workers had to be taken into work with a police escort. (58)

On the day following the beginning of the dispute at Foss Islands a conference was held to discuss it in York. Representatives included J.W. Stark, the secretary of the National Federation of Laundry Workers' Associations, Will Dobbie, representing the Gas Workers, Miss Airey and delegates from the National Federation of Laundry Associations, the employers' organisation. At this meeting the strikers' demands were formulated. They were for an eleven (as against a 12) hour day with one and a half hours for meals, and a rise of 2s. a week.

Outside the conference things took a very nasty turn. H.A. Clark was 'badly handled by a large crowd' and he had to take refuge in the *Herald* offices and be spirited away, across the Ouse , just as George Hudson had during the heady days of the Reform Bill struggle in the 1830s. A Miss Dickman, the forewoman in Clark's ironing department, was also mobbed. She left Clark's house to go home at about ten o'clock at night and was quickly surrounded by a crowd that grew to between 200 and 300. She had to be escorted by the police, and she told a *Press* reporter what happened and why. (She did not say what the crowd shouted, but it is not difficult to guess at certain possibilities.)

"As we went long," she said, "the crowd shouted and behaved in a most unseemly manner. They threw all kinds of things at me, and something hard hit me on the back. The policemen who were with me had great difficulty in keeping them back, and it was only by swinging at them with their capes that they were able to do so, ... "Why did the people attack you?" asked our representative. ... "Because", said Miss Dickman, "they thought I was sticking up for Mr. Clark. They thought I was working in the laundry, but they were mistaken." ...[Why had the women struck the reporter asked.] "They won't say anything except that they want shorter hours and more wages. I have had a long experience in laundry work in the North of England, and I can say that the wages, at any rate ... in the ironing room, are quite as good as at any laundry I have known ... "

On the following day Miss Dickman and three clerks were again abused in the streets, then, after a couple of days, the strike took 'on a more serious aspect'. It spread and employees of the Yorkshire Laundry in Peaseholme Green and the Wanted Laundry, Picadilly, were forced to stop work. Charles Grainger, the general manager of the Yorkshire complained bitterly that his workers worked fewer hours than at other places, but a crowd accompanied by Dobbie and Miss Airey (and 'a crowd of hooligans from the district') nevertheless stopped his workers at the gates. The crowd then announced that they intended to close down the Wenlock Laundry.

The Wenlock Laundry, Ambrose Street, received the attentions of the lady strikers and early next morning many went out on the trams to picket the York and Ainsty establishment at Fulford. Eventually the whole of the city was affected and the streets echoed to the chants of 'We came out like ladies, and not like hooligans and we shall stop out until justice is done', 'How would you like to work for 5s. a week ?' and 'We are striking for a living wage. A woman cannot live decently upon 10s. a week.' At least one woman was beaten up and after a few days another conference was held which brought the dispute to an end. This time the workers were represented by Dobbie, Miss Airey, Walter Shilleto of the Gas Workers and Schloesser, the Labour candidate. A five per cent rise was negotiated and a sliding scale of wages adopted rising from 6s. at 16 years to 12s. at 21 years! This was 'accepted ... as a minimum basic standard wage for the whole of the city, on a basis of a 55 hours' week.' Piece work rates were to be as they were before the strike (most of the women were on piece work) and basic overtime pay was to be one and a quarter. No victimisation was a part of the deal.

The laundry strike, short though it was, was extremely bitter and the workers do not seem to have been anything other than appallingly underpaid at the end of it. Frequently during the dispute confusion reigned about what the women actually took home, and great hostility was shown to the local press. Grainger, (who made the remark about hooligans) for example, was greeted in the streets with shouts of '"We are not hooligans, we are decent working women. Put that in the 'Press' and be fair." "How would you like to work for 5s. a week?" etc, etc.' At this stage they were saying, some of them, that they wanted 10s. a week and a reporter said he had heard that they got 22s. Their reply was that they had no idea how their wages were made up. One striker said '"I have worked for the Hygenic for seven years and I don't know how the wage bills are made up."' She went on - and this is dreadful - '"If we had 10s. per week regularly we should think we were millionaires, and some of us are widows with young children to keep."' Several women agreed, and one of them remarked, '"We are striking to get what we actually earn for the 55 hours per week we work".' During the dispute the laundry owners were said to have declared 'we're not going to be bluffed by a lot of lasses' and this drove Will Dobbie to distraction. He attacked 'the capitalistic' party at a meeting attended by some 3,000 in the Market Place. 'The bald facts, as to the conditions of the life of the laundry girls in York', he said (the report is from the *Herald* of 1 October)

> until a week or two ago, were generally unknown to the people of the City. No one gave a thought to the lives of the girls who washed the shirts - (laughter) - and starched the cuffs and collars of the various "knuts" who promenaded Coney-street and elsewhere. (Loud laughter). Probably they would all have read the "Yorkshire Evening Press", and read there the account of the various hooligans who had stood about the laundry gates. (Laughter.) These were the arguments of the capitalistic party. (Laughter and applause.)   "The reply of the trades union movement," added the speaker, "is that the industries in York, and in the country, which cannot give humane conditions of labour, and wages which will allow the working classes to live a full life, ought to be driven out of the country and out of the city. (Applause.) And if these people are not fit to run their businesses on lines that will allow of these conditions, then the sooner the nation takes over the concerns the better it will be for all". (Applause)

Dobbie's campaign on behalf of the laundry girls was brave and long overdue. Great credit must be given to him and the likes of Miss Airey for first highlighting the existence of sweated labour in York, then doing something about it. The dispute, once more, highlighted the fact that conditions for many in pre-war Britain were absolutely appalling. Once again one feels bound to say that wages of the kind the laundry girls got, or short time, meant appalling misery and grinding poverty (for a 55 hour week).

A group of workers who had protection were the railwaymen, and at the end of 1913 the NER made concessions to them which look generous in the extreme when compared with the pittances the laundry girls got. Drivers and firemen, for example, had their shifts reduced from ten to nine hours, and all 12 hour signal box shifts were reduced to ten. Cleaners got a wage increase of 2s., and guards received increases of from 1s. to 4s. Platform porters' hours were reduced to ten per shift. Were these concessions acceptable ? Samuel Barrett chaired a meeting 'of a hostile character' which was called to discuss them. Councillor Glew was there and great hostility was shown to the working delegates who had been part of the negotiating procedure. They were criticised (with much justification) for not walking out when Vincent Raven, a chief mechanical engineer, said 'that he considered 21s. a week was sufficient for a working man'. Twenty one shillings was below the figure set by Seebohm Rowntree as a living wage years ago, and it looks as if Raven was both deficient in his knowledge of history, and current social conditions - to say nothing of public relations techniques. He would probably have been a success running a laundry, but such bluntness and stupidity were no qualification for running a trouble free railway. The men at York rejected the agreement and demanded the eight hour day which had been an objective of theirs for years. (59) 1914 looked as if it might see great trouble on the railways.

While the laundry strikes were taking place, what part, if any, did the city's suffrage movements take in them ? The answer is none whatsoever. Violet Key Jones was as noticeable by her absence from the fray as was the redoubtable Edith Milner (who would nevertheless come into her own when the war broke out). Not a word was said on the laundresses' behalf by either the militant or the constitutional wings of the suffrage movement in York. Neither was there any support for the likes of Mrs Franks from the latest local bi-sexual organisation demanding votes for women. This was the increasingly active Church League for Women's Suffrage and in November 1913 it was organising yet another petition. Prominent among its supporters was the rather unfortunately named Rev E.S. Hore. (60)

As the last peacetime Christmas approached there were signs in York of an increasing unease about world affairs. The York Settlement had always devoted some of its programme to a study of international affairs and in November 1913 a new group was set up following six lectures which had recently been given there on 'International Politics' by John Hilton and J.E. Raphael. Announcing its formation T.S. Lambert, the secretary, said that membership would 'not be confined to those in agreement with Norman Angell's thesis.' (61) At the same time the activities of the National Service League were stepped up, (62) and the York YMCA debated the question 'Should Military Service be Compulsory ? (63) Shortly afterwards J.R. Clynes, the famous Labour politician appeared in the city as part of what was 'described as a "No

Conscription" campaign.' (64) This issue was to cause tremendous dissension in the years to come.

1. *Press* 6 October 1913
2. *Ibid* 24 September 1913. Meeting at the Exhibition Buildings
3. *Ibid* 24 October 1913
4. *Ibid* 28 October 1913
5. *Ibid* 31 October 1913
6. *Ibid* 4 October 1913
7. *Ibid* 21 October 1913
8. *Ibid* 18 and 21 September 1913
9. *Ibid* 3 Oct 1913
10. *Ibid* 7 and 8 October 1913
11. This was Archie Kirk, a Labour Lord Mayor. There is a tape recording by Archie Kirk and another by his wife in the archives at Churchill College, Cambridge. Archie was severely wounded in the Battle of Arras, 1917, and the tapes are mainly about his war experiences.
12. *Press* 11 October 1913
13. *Ibid* 15 October 1913
14. *Ibid.* Letter signed C.T.
15. *Herald* 10 March 1913
16. *Press* 8 October 1913
17. *Ibid* 11 October 1913
18. *Ibid* 24 September 1913
19. *Ibid* 3 October 1913
20. Though T. Alison Booth had been reported as a candidate.
21. *Press* 28 October 1913
22. *Ibid* 3 November 1913
23. Quoted *Ibid* 5 November 1913
24. *Ibid* 7 November 1913
25. *Ibid* 10 November 1913
26. *Ibid*
27. *Ibid* 6 November 1913. Following comments from Glew and Petty from *Ibid* 18 November 1913
28. *Ibid* 22 November 1913.
29. *Ibid* 22 August 1913. The rink reopened in October 1912 for its last season devoting only three nights a week to skating and Tuesdays and Fridays to whist drives, and Thursdays to amateur boxing. *Ibid* 12 October 1912.
30. *Ibid* 23 and 26 August 1913
31. *Ibid* 16 March 1912
32. *Ibid* 17 April 1912
33. *Ibid* 25 April 1912
34. *Ibid* 27 and 29 May 1912. The veterans were James Kain, Patrick Crowe, James Addison and W. Noonan. There are pictures of them in the second of the papers just mentioned. There is a picture of Addison in uniform in *Ibid* 25 September 1913
35. *Ibid* 4 October 1912
36. *Ibid* 24 February 1913
37. *Ibid* 21 May 1913
38. *Ibid* 5 July 1913. This was the race during which Emily Davison Wilding threw herself under a horse at Tattenham Corner and was killed.
39. *Ibid* 19 and 24 November 1913
40. *Ibid* 24 November 1913
41. *Ibid* 28 June 1913
42. For airship 'sightings' and stories see eg *Ibid* 24, 25 and 26 February 1913.
43. *Ibid* 8 July 1911
44. *Ibid* 14 July 1911
45. *Ibid* 21 and 24 February 1913

46. *Ibid* 17 and 21 May 1913
47. *Ibid* 28, 29, 30 January, 3 February 1914
48. *Ibid* 4 February 1914
49. *Ibid* 18 September 1913 for Salmet's visit to York.
50. *Ibid* 1 and 2 May 1913
51. *Ibid* 2 and 15 May 1913. In 1912 there had been an interesting plasterers' dispute in the city. It had been over a change of work rules and was eventually referred to a conciliation board. For something over half a century the plasterers' day had 'begun' when they reached the city bars and they were paid for the time it took to walk from there to their jobs. They walked back in their own time. In 1912 the masters contended that modern transport had altered the situation and they wanted the limit to be extended to one mile beyond the bars (or to about the equivalent of the boundary of the city then). The union involved was the National Association of Operative Plasterers. See eg *Ibid* 2 May and 6 June 1912.
52. *Ibid* 31 July, 1 August 1913. On the Leetham's strike see *Ibid* 22 October 1913
53. Not that at the glass works, which was over the suspension of a worker.
54. Report mentioned in *Press* 13 August 1913. The survey related to the period 1905-1912.
55. *Ibid* 23 June 1913
56. *Herald* 17 and 18 July 1913
57. Which had a membership in York of 560 in 1912. *Press* 23 April 1912
58. The details of the laundry dispute can be followed in the papers from 23 September 1913. There is a short account of the founding of the Wenlock Laundry - one of those involved in the dispute - in V.C.M. Wilson, *The History of a Community* (York 1985)
59. *Press* 1 December 1913
60. *Ibid* 27 October, 11 November 1913
61. Norman Angell was an influential writer on international affairs.
62. See eg *Press* 18 December 1913
63. *Ibid* 13 November 1913
64. *Ibid* 22 November 1913

CHAPTER 9

WAR

1913 had been an incredible year in York's history. It had seen a reforming corporation throw away its chances of continuing in power and implementing its programme through going along with bigots who wanted to put the clock back, and it had seen the party which replaced it undo the reforms with almost indecent haste. It had seen militant feminism, and militant female industrial action. (1) The year had seen an exciting contest over the mayoralty, and the last of J.M. Hogge. It had seen Will Dobbie emerge as the most influential of the local Labour leaders and the magistrates 'descend' into street corner politicking in a most undignified way. New parliamentary candidates had been selected by the Tories and the socialists - and Edith Milner had been remarkably subdued. What had been achieved in the city since the turn of the century ? A modern transport system had been created, and some of the worst slums had gone. Some recreational areas had been created, and the motor car had become dominant in the streets. York in 1914 had an impressive number of places of entertainment and for some wages had increased (though prices had gone up) and hours (again for some) had been reduced. Old age pensions had started, and so had Lloyd George's national insurance scheme. The latter, however, was still bitterly resisted and prosecutions of employers who would not 'lick stamps' were not uncommon. Sad to say, though, grinding poverty still remained, the result often of that unemployment which the state seemed incapable of getting rid of. Low wages meant, for many, a life always below the 'necessary' levels suggested for the maintainance of health by Seebohm Rowntree, and short time frequently meant better off workers suffering privation when work was slack. Drunkeness and violence in the streets were as bad as they had been at the turn of the century, and the powers-that-be still thought it had something to do with the number of 'outlets' at which booze could be obtained. The process of reducing them was still going on.

The influx of that batch of Labour and Liberal magistrates on to the York bench did not produce any change of policy regarding the number of drink outlets in the area - and neither should it have done so, as it was still government policy to reduce and compensate. The Brewster Sessions, therefore, have a familiar look about them. In 1912 the Chief Constable gave figures for club membership in York (6,690 in 38 establishments) and the Lord Mayor, as before, said this membership 'was a matter which gave the licensing justices a considerable amount of concern' and went on to say that he and his colleagues wanted them to be brought 'more directly' under their control. (2) Yet again J.J. Hunt made an application (the twelfth) to be allowed to build a pub in the South Bank area (3) and yet again Canon Argles rehearsed his arguments against it - this time adding that 'one of the great objections to the public house was that it might be used by women.' As always, the application was turned down. In 1913 up it came again, with the usual result. This time John William Glew, who was to become the great Labour advocate of clobbering the small traders in a few weeks' time, appeared to support the application. (4) Getting a pub in the South Bank area must have cost more in time and legal fees than almost any other pub anywhere else.

The 1911 sessions had closed and compensated a number of York pubs; none had been chopped in 1912; but three were on the list a year later. These were the Glass Maker's Arms, Fawcett Street, the Prince of Wales, Skeldergate, and the Wellington, Goodramgate. All these were 'referred' for compensation, (5) and on 9 May the compensation authority met and effectively killed off these splendid places. (6)

The closing of pubs and the refusing of applications for new ones at least gave the appearance that *something* was being done about drunkeness in the streets, and incidentally it is interesting to note popular 'controversial' newspaper columnists writing in the late 1980s and early 90s as if drunkeness and drink related violence are products of the post 1939 war, or even the 1960s and 70s. (7) Even a cursory examination of the press of any large town (certainly York) would have revealed appalling levels of drink related street crime in the 1930s - and for that matter for any period earlier in the century. The York columnist noted in a footnote to this paragraph was at pains in 1989 to point out that those who contend that 'poverty makes people into criminals' are perpetrating 'a Lie'. He is certainly right if that is all people say, but to contend that poverty makes some people into criminals would surely be reasonable - and poverty, criminality and drunkeness went hand in hand in the poorer parts of York before (and after) the Great War.

The politicians and the magistrates of 1913 (without the benefit of that course in sociology which might have made them familiar with words like '"alienation", "underprivilege", "disadvantage" and other euphemisms') (8) thought they detected a causal relationship between crime, drink and poverty, and the closing of pubs has to be seen as a futile attempt to do something about it. The only positive 'remedy' for unemployment being put around in those days in reality was tariff reform, but that was a non starter after the elections of 1910. Given that, all that could be done was to try to lessen the impact of poverty through awarding pensions and closing places where hard earned wages could go on the old man's drink rather than on food for the family. That and private charity. Vernon Wragge hit on an idea for helping some of York's most accomplished drinkers. That great believer in free enterprise (except when York trams were involved) undoubtedly hoped that his idea would spread.

Wragge wrote to about 20 of York's 'habituals' who between them had some 200 convictions for drunkeness, and he offered them a sovereign each if they managed to complete a 'dry' year - by which, presumably, he meant a year in which they were not nicked for indulging themselves. If there were any who did not complete the course, Vernon said, he would give 'their' sovereigns to the County Hospital. (9) The whole city looked on to see what the effects Wragge's generous offer would be, and they did not have to wait long to see that it did not work as far William Kilmartin, a 33 year old of Speculation Street was concerned. The press announced that William, one of Wragge's 'quid men', had been found loaded near his house on 1 February. He was prosecuted, lost his chance of getting a reward, and complained bitterly in the magistrates court. 'I have never had a chance here yet', he said, 'Every time I have come here I have either to go to prison or pay a big fine.' (10)

Kilmartin must have been a big disappointment to Wragge, and at the end of the year the scheme's organiser had to report only a qualified success. Eight of the original 20 habituals had not been reconvicted during the year, Wragge reported, but one of those was in prison for a non drink related offence, and another was in hospital. The other six were to be given a tea party (and their quid), and the scheme was to go on. (11) Sad to relate one of those who enjoyed Alderman Wragge's tea party also turned out to be a broken reed. Arthur Dunbar, 'one of Alderman Wragge's 'quidders'" the *Press* reported on 27 January, had got drunk and was up in court again. He was fined half a crown and took his punishment with better grace than did Kilmartin before him.

It has been suggested above that poverty may well have been a contributory cause of crime, whatever present day newspaper columnists might say. Is there any definite evidence of the extent of that poverty and unemployment - anything to compare with the Rowntree findings of 1902 for example - for 1913/4? It has to be admitted that there is nothing comparable to *Poverty*, but there is plenty of evidence of a less definite kind. The free breakfasts for the poor children of Layerthorpe, were still being given and were still necessary. These were organised by the Layerthorpe Wesleyan Mission on Sunday mornings during the worst of the winter months, and from Christmas to the end of February, between 1,300 and 1,400 meals were provided. (12) The reports of the York Dispensary (13) and the Board of Guardians are also indicators of the state of many of the poor (there were 617 inmates in the workhouse in January 1914) and occasionally the appalling wages of people like laundry workers hit the headlines. Reports of court cases frequently contained information about the income and the plight of people living in places like Hungate and the Bedern.

Evidence about the health of York is much more easily obtained than facts that would enable a precise estimate of the standard of living to be made. Regular reports about the health of the city were published, and organisations like the Health and Housing Reform Association frequently highlighted the consequences of slum living. The health report for the week ending 31 January 1914, for example, showed that in that period there had been 28 births, equal to an annual rate of 17.4 per 1,000 of those living (the population was 83,802). Deaths of residents in the same week were 27, equalling an annual rate of 16.8 per 1,000. The average death rate for the 97 'great' towns was 18.4 per 1,000. (14) Later in the year a quarterly return recorded the number of cases of tuberculosis in York for the period ending 30 June. (15) There had been no less than 84 new patients, 1,237 re-attendances at the TB clinic at Castlegate, making an average weekly attendance of 101.

Tuberculosis was popularly associated with bad housing conditions and above it was stated that since the turn of the century a few of the worst slum areas had been improved. This is true, but the extent of that improvement was minimal, and a section of the superb part of the York *Victoria County History* written by Professor Eric Sigsworth gives some of the reasons why. As depression hit the city after the Boer War ended, the rate of private house building dropped rapidly - while the population was increasing. The fall in the rate of building was accelerated by a rise in the long term rate of interest and the shortage of houses caused by the rising population gave tailor made excuses for doing little or nothing about the slums. This is true, but the picture would not be complete were the number of *empty* houses that the slum dwellers could not afford ignored. (16) Another reason for the delay in slum clearance was the sheer complexity of the 1890 Housing Act. The Medical Officer of Health regularly recommended that Part III of the Act be used and its adoption was finally enforced as the Liberals were becoming stronger in 1909. In their short lived period in power they were talking of town planning but little *had* been achieved by the outbreak of the Great War. Professor Sigsworth summed up succinctly what little had been done. (17) (What people like Relton had been doing in areas like South Bank, of course, must not be ignored.)

> The net result of housing legislation between 1890 and 1914 was that 30 houses were built in 1912 for tenants displaced as a result of the construction of the new street of Piccadilly, and a further 28 for tramway employees in 1914. Otherwise the corporation remained content to deal with individual houses under Part II of the 1890 Act, though between 1901 and 1914 only 136 houses had thus been demolished.

It is only fair to point out that for most of the period Professor Sigsworth was writing about (indeed all of the period but for one year) the city was governed by the Tory party which ideologically was against municipal enterprise, and so had more than a little built-in reluctance to use legislation like the 1890 Housing Act. They no doubt would have pointed to the number of houses that did go up (and at every Brewster Sessions the figures for South Bank were trotted out), to which, with equal certainty, the Liberals would have replied that these were beyond the means of those who most needed rehousing. And they were right. The rents that were quoted for the new places in South Bank, for instance, were way beyond what the lowest paid railwayman with a family could afford for example

But now, in 1914, the Tories were back in power after that period of summer madness when the likes of Meyer and K.E.T. Wilkinson held the reins of power in York. They could repeal or drop most of the expensive projects their opponents had put forward - and say, quite rightly, that they had a mandate to do so. But they had to be careful. They could not totally ignore the things the Liberals showed needed to be done (and that private enterprise would not do). They had to do something, and if what

276

they chose to do was expensive they ran the risk of being regarded as no better than their predecessors, and in this situation (if the rates still went up) an opposition of the type which in latter times might have been called Poujardist might appear. A ratepayers' association opposed to both traditional parties might be brought into being which might break the traditional mould of York politics.

What would the Tories do ? They had fought their election campaign declaiming against the Liberals for being extravagant, bemoaning the inevitable rate increases that would occur, and supporting those who deplored the persecuting of Sunday traders. They had no difficulty in undoing the Liberal programme of 1913 as that speaker said at a victory concert held by the Bootham Conservatives in November 1913, just three weeks after the elections. (18) But after that what would they do ? The very first full council meeting of the new year had a long agenda, and it might be interesting to look at the major parts of it.

Rhodes Brown presided over the 1914 January Council meeting, and it was decided that illuminated addresses were to be given to Sykes Rymer and his wife and a letter was read from the Lord's Day Observance Society urging that municipal band concerts be held on week days rather than Sundays (the only day the working class could go to them and enjoy them). Relton then moved the adoption of the minutes of the Streets and Buildings Committee. They had got, he said, a 'nice scheme' for a footbridge at the Burton Stone Lane crossing and had written to the NER about it. Relton then raised some questions about the Holgate Gardens Estate - the matter which had got him a writ during the election, but was ruled out of order. (19)

Sebastian Meyer had been involved with the Holgate Gardens housing project, and he, like a good Progressive, moved a resolution urging an application to the Board of Trade under the powers of the Light Railway Act of 1896 extending the limit the Council could borrow by the York Light Railways Order of 1908 and the Extensions Order of 1912. Meyer wanted the limit to go up to £7,650 because money was required for carsheds, employees houses, and 'new offices for tramway and electricity purposes.' Meyer's proposals enabled the Tories to point, again, at the way their opponents happily increased the city's debts, and Wragge purported to be angry at the way important issues were sprung on them at the last minute. He might have thought that, given the Tory majority, this was perhaps the only way in which the likes of Meyer could get things through. (The decision to prosecute Sunday traders had got through because it was sprung on the Council in just this way.) They wanted 'something in black and white in their hands, so that they could consider the matter and have intelligent knowledge of what they were asked to vote on' said Wragge.

The *Evening Press*'s report of the January Council meeting had a paragraph heading saying 'SUFFERING FOSSGATE', which gave some insight into what York's streets were like in that last year before the Great War. It is not of major importance (though at the time some locals might have thought it was). Work was going to be done at a cost of £400 in Fossgate that was going to improve the road. Alderman Agar thought otherwise and objected to the recommendation that 'soft creosoted wood [should be] laid on [an already existing] cement floated bed' to replace the existing granite setts. What was wrong with them ? Councillor Inglis said they were 'an awful nuisance' and Tom Morris was more explicit. Fossgate, Morris said, would 'form as fine a skating rink as any in the North of England', and if the local RSPCA inspector 'did his duty he would take action against the owner of every horse driven along the road.' Councillor Wiseman spoke of the noise caused by the setts. 'As an illustration' of the difficulty of hearing one talk while traffic was passing, he said he went into a shop and 'asked for a pound and a half of sausages, and they gave him a penny duck.' Agar's amendment was lost.

The question of the amalgamation of the York charities came up again in January 1914. This had been recommended by the Charity Commissioners in April 1912, and in October 1913, just before the election, the Liberals had decided to make an amalgamation a part of their programme. This ensured that the Tories would be against it, and they looked at the scheme immediately after their return to power. In January 1914 they decided against it. Inglis had said that he was worried about the possibility of 'officialism' if the amalgamation went through.

The Watch Committee's minutes for the meeting of January 1914 raised the question of seditious literature being published in York. Was the Council aware, asked Alderman McKay, that leaflets had been published in Old Ebor 'asking for' recruits to fight against the Crown in Ulster ? What did they intend to do ? To this rhetorical question Inglis replied 'Join them', but the Town Clerk stated there was no case for proceedings to be instituted.

K.E.T. Wilkinson raised the question of how mentally defective children were being treated in York in that January assembly, (20) and the question of freeing Skeldergate Bridge of tolls cropped up. (21) This, the third York bridge over the Ouse, had been opened in March 1881, and had cost a total of just over £56,000. Alderman Green pointed out that the question of freeing the bridge had been before them for about a decade, and it was now recommended that it be free from 1 April next. But that move could be dangerous politically. Green had seen reports that the move would put a halfpenny on the rates, but they would go up by twice that amount he maintained. An attempt to stop the move going ahead was defeated by only two votes (23 to 21).

Councillor Glew in January moved an amendment to a committee's minutes suggesting that the city's street sweepers should have one Saturday night in four off duty for a trial period of three months. This was lost, but the new Council, it is pleasing to record, was still carrying out the policy of being a fair employer. The Streets and Buildings Committee in January had recommended wage rises and shorter hours for many of its workmen - rates which became a marker for other employers in the city. Men at the Works Department, it was decided, should work a week of 47 hours for 17 weeks in the year, and 53 hours for the rest; a half penny an hour rise was suggested for night men, a farthing an hour more for masons and flaggers, while paviors were to get 8d. instead of 7d. an hour. The new rates were implemented.

McKay's question about 'seditious literature' in York related to documents about Home Rule,and the Irish question had been aired on the streets. National political issues - with the suffragettes being relatively inactive - had not troubled York greatly since the second general election of 1910. The tariff reformers held occasional meetings, so did their opponents and so did the ILP (22) and the Fabian Society. (23) By the end of 1913, however, rebellion in Ireland looked a near certainty and in January 1914 a Unionist demonstration addressed by Urban Broughton and C.E. Elmhirst was held in the city. (24) In the next month Jim Larkin spoke on 'The truth about Dublin'. He was supported on the platform by J.H. Hartley, Glew and Dobbie (25) and launched into an out and out attack on capitalism, speaking of his knowledge 'that "in this town of York" there were hard-worked, ill-paid, ill-fed, ill-housed, ill-educated men and women.'

Larkin was right of course and, as has been said before, little was being done to house working people decently. The Liberals had announced that they intended to do something about real slum clearance before they fell from power, and in March, the new council decided it would do so. Again it must have looked like the situation as it had been a few years before - a Tory (local) government carrying out Liberal measures. Anyway a decision was made to purchase 47 acres of land belonging to the Ecclesiastical Commissioners situated in Heworth between the Derwent Valley Light Railway and Vicar Farm near Tang Hall Lane. The price was to be £125 an acre. Why did a Tory administration decide to embark on a programme of council house building ? The answer was quite simple. It has been given before and Alderman Carter gave it to the Council. The situation in the bad areas of York was so bad that 'something had to be done'. (The *Press* reporting the new moves spoke of the city's 'throttle-valve alleys that lead to sunless courts'.) The number of working class houses being built was the lowest since 1888 - and that was as far back as they had records. (26) Alderman Walker wondered whether even council house building could help. You might pull down 150 dreadful houses in Walmgate, he said, where people were living for 1s. 6d. a week, but could they afford the very reasonable 4s. 6d. that the new places would cost ? Wragge and Sykes Rymer were against the new proposals, but they were carried.

The elections of November 1913 were dominated by the Sunday trade issue but 'extravagant government' was almost as important and, without doubt, many York people expected the Tories to usher in an era of economy. Yet here they were, having abandoned some things, embarking on other schemes which looked as if they might be very expensive. And in addition to this, wage increases were being awarded which would put civic expenditure up. The rises given to men like the paviors have been mentioned, and teachers' rises were reckoned to amount to £1,000 to £1,100 a year. (27) This gave rise to concern that the rates might go up - with all that that would mean for the party in power.

The concern about the rates was justified, and as early as January 1914 rumours were going round that the increases would be as much as 3d. or 4d. The freeing of Skeldergate Bridge, definitely meant an extra halfpenny, the extra wages had to be found, there were the new schemes, and it was certain that the poor rate would increase. The guardian's were about to build new infant wards and the *Press* said they had depleted their once handsome balances in earlier efforts to keep the York rates down. They were definitely asking for 2d. in the £ more and press reports spoke of the rate being set at something like 8s.5¹/₂d. compared with the existing 8s.1¹/₂d. Rhodes Brown, the Lord Mayor, speaking at the annual dinner of the York Master Builders and Contractors Association, carried on alarmingly in the time honoured way about the effect high rates were having on York. He would, he said, when he left office, campaign from the floor of the council chamber for a fixed levy of 7s.6d. (28) Fixing a rigid ceiling on local government expenditure, which is what this would have meant, has a very modern ring about it.

The Finance Committee met and caused the various estimates from the council's committees to be revised. In March the papers were saying that they had got the proposed spending down - but that, nevertheless, there would be a levy of 8s. 3d., a rise of 1d. That could not have given the Tories who were up for re-election in 1914 any great cause for comfort.

Teachers' salaries were going to be a contributory factor of importance in any rate in 1914/15, but there was absolutely nothing the Council could do about that. At the beginning of March an employee of the education service in York retired, and his retirement had important consequences for York politics. The man who retired was William Thorpe who for 33 years had been York's school attendance officer. Who was to replace him ? A sub committee recommended to the full education committee that it should be a Mr J.W. Carrall, but then Dobbie and others put forward the name of Alderman J.H. Hartley. The voting was so close that it was decided to let both names go forward to a full council meeting. (29)

The papers printed many letters complaining about Hartley's apparent attempt to get himself a nice little number, some correspondents recalled that he had tried it on once before, (30) and many quoted the Rev Brightling - who had said that councillors would vote for the shunter because they wanted to get rid of him. After the lashings he had taken from Hartley during the Sunday trading controversy one cannot blame Brightling for going for his tormentor. The two candidates appeared before the full council in May and Hartley was duly chosen by such a handsome majority that one must consider at least the possibility that Brightling was right

Hartley had been a force to be reckoned with in York politics for many years - the Labour equivalent of J.M. Hogge. He had spoken out about things that needed speaking about, but had been reckless and not always a good advertisement for his party. His wining and dining at Corporation freebies had not gone unnoticed, and that business of his expenses fiddle could have caused more trouble than it did. His attempt earlier to get a council job had made him look like a self-seeker, and his successful attempt to do that in 1914 did not detract from that impression. One of the last things Harry Hartley did on the Council was to stop a married woman being appointed as the headmistress of a council school, and a month after that he had said that he wanted the Mansion House done away with as the Lord Mayor's residence. (31)

Hartley had to leave the Corporation, and his presence there would be clearly missed, though he was to continue to appear on Labour platforms elsewhere. The Labour party looked as if it could well lose another able campaigner when Will Dobbie was given notice to quit from the NER.

In May 1914 Vincent Raven, of the NER, the man who had angered members of the ASRS by saying a wage of 21s. was 'sufficient for a working man, gave Will Dobbie his notice. (32) Dobbie worked in the painting shop of the carriage works, and the company said he had used his job 'as a convenience for his own purposes as a general agitator in York, and elsewhere.' It had a good case. Dobbie, the NER pointed out, was on the Council and on 13 council committees. In addition to this he was a union representative, secretary of the local trades council, and a party to every industrial dispute that took place in York. Some weeks, the company said, Will only put in three a half hours at his place of work, and over all was absent 75 per cent of the time. Councillor Mercer, a plumber, was also warned.

Representations were made to the management on behalf of Dobbie and Mercer and the notice of dismissal was withdrawn. A condition to Dobbie and Mercer being kept on at work was that they had to promise 'faithfully to keep much better time in future'.

While Dobbie was being disciplined trouble, once more, was brewing on the railway. NER firemen and cleaners threatened to strike on 31 May, but this was averted by a promise of negotiations. (33) Trouble was still rumbling on, however, in June, and a union circular issued then once more drew attention to the appalling wages some workers were receiving. 'The cleaners' wage scales also requires [sic] some adjustment', it said, 'the minimum wage being one on which it is absolutely impossible for these lads to maintain an appearance of respectability or obtain the necessities of life.' (34)

The railwaymen nearly came out in the early months of 1914; the painters and paperhangers did. In March they gave notice that they wanted an extra $1^{1}/_{2}$d. an hour to bring up their rate to 9d. The masters offered a halfpenny immediately with another halfpenny in two years time. The men refused and announced that unless their demands were met they would strike on 1 April. (35)

The painters duly came out on 1 April, with the support of their union, the National Amalgamated Society of Operative House Builders and Ship Painters. It was a bad time for a strike as work was slack anyway, according to the employers, and after a couple of weeks, violence entered the dispute, which led to the appearance of six men in court. These were Albert George Barclay, John Moore, John Petler, Albert Edgar, William Morley and Thomas William Jarvis, and they were charged with 'unlawfully, wrongfully, and without legal authority' endeavouring to stop a number of men following their occupations. Evidence was given of 'marauding gangs' going round the streets of York 'in the name of peaceful pickets' and the non strikers were all seemingly employees of Messrs Bellerby working at Archbishop Holgate's Grammar School and Kilburn House, Fulford Road. One of Barclay's comments to one of the workers was given, as later reports of conversations said, with the expletives deleted. 'Hallo, you have crept back again have you? Barclay said, 'Come out you — blackleg'. He and his mates were bound over for six months and ordered to pay costs. (36)

On the same day that Barclay's court appearance was reported an announcement appeared that the painters' strike had been settled, though the gains the men had obtained were nil. They went back with the concessions the employers had offered them back in March - a halfpenny an hour more immediately with another halfpenny from April 1916.

The painters had gained nothing from their industrial activities, but their strike was studied in some depth in a report which makes extraordinarily interesting reading. Capt E.N. Mosley, the president of the York branch of the Christian Social Union revealed its contents in April. (37) York's wage rates, Mosley revealed, were lower than those anywhere else in the North of England, with the average weekly wage of a painter 23s. They had had no rise since 1900 - when hours were reduced from $53^1/_2$ to $49^1/_2$, and they were worse off than they were at the turn of the century. It would take an increase of a penny an hour to make the men as well off as they had been in 1900, the CSU concluded. They of course got half that.

Why did the painters fail to achieve anything in 1914? One reason was undoubtedly the fact that trade was slack, and there were as many unemployed painters waiting to fill vacancies as there were men anxious to fill strikers' shoes at the railway works. Another reason was the weakness of the men's union. All the union men struck, but the majority of the workforce was outside their their control. The painters simply did not have the power to succeed in 1914.

Had not the events of 1911 led to an increase of unionism in York? The answer is yes, but the growth had been patchy. Dobbie had been deeply involved in the 1911 dispute which had seen the creation of a branch of the National Union of Gasworkers and General Labourers and it reported a rapid growth (1,000 members) in January. (38) In June A.P. Mawson presided over a meeting to form a York branch of the National Amalgamated Sheet Metal Workers and Braziers' Society. (39)

Perhaps the painters' strike of 1914, however, had some effects. The local authority had awarded some wage increases, and so had the laundry masters and the NER. The laundry girls and the painters strikes had highlighted the plight of many workers (who had had stable wages for nearly 14 years) and shown that concessions might be in everyone's interest. Will Horsman, at that time, was highlighting what he said were the starvation wages paid to some of the guardian's employees, and in that atmosphere concessions were made to some groups. Quite clearly trouble was going to occur in the building trade unless something was done, and in May 1914 the local Conciliation Board awarded wage increases to the masons, the bricklayers, the joiners and the building labourers of either a halfpenny or a farthing an hour. The new rates meant that the bricklayers received an hourly wage of $9^3/4$d., the masons $9^1/2$d., the joiners 9d., and the labourers 7d. (40) In June the York Master Printers gave increases of 1s. a week from 1 April with an additional increase of 6d. from the beginning of April 1915. (41)

The whole of the country was in a turmoil in the early months of 1914, with trouble in Ireland, where the army mutinied at the Curragh, trouble in the industrial towns, where unskilled workers were frequently involved in industrial disputes, and trouble in many places where the suffragettes were active and violent. There were, however, only one or two minor incidents caused by the ladies of York in the little time that remained before war broke out. Violet Key Jones had been involved in some trouble at Doncaster, and she was probably behind a couple of incidents in York. In February a deputation of between 40 and 50 ladies concerned about the forcible feeding of women imprisoned for the suffrage cause called to see the Archbishop. This was on a Saturday and the following day 12 York WSPU members went to Bishopthorpe church. (42) Shortly after the Archbishop had read the second lesson they began chanting, 'O God, help and save the women who are being tortured in prison for conscience, sake, Amen'. Later the Theatre Royal was 'leafleted' from the balcony but this was tame stuff coming after attempts to bomb the *Herald* offices. Rather more serious was the firing of pillar boxes at various places in York with phosphorus. (43) The attacks coincided with the well publicised appearance of Lilian Lenton, a famous agitator, at the Leeds Assizes.

In July 1914 the by election caused by Hartley's resignation took place. Who replaced J.H. as an alderman ? It was the usual practice to elevate the Lord Mayor at such times, but Rhodes Brown was not toeing the line as a good party man. He had made those remarks about the rates and despite the the fact that Edith Milner pointed out that the Lord Mayor ought to be chosen, the Tories selected J.B. Inglis, the jeweller. Inglis was an extremely active councillor who had been prominent in the Sunday trading campaign.

The Tories had a comfortable majority on the council in 1914, and if they handled things 'correctly' over the aldermanic issue that could be increased. Naturally there were those who contended that Hartley should be replaced by a Labour man, but that was like asking for the moon. He was replaced by someone from the solidly Tory ward of Guildhall (for which Henry Rhodes Brown also sat). It was thought that the Labour party would not even try to run a candidate at the by election there. The assumption was correct.

There was danger looming up for Tories, however. On earlier occasions in the century there had been threats that a ratepayers association would be brought into being to try and break the mould of York politics. What could trigger this off? A significant rise in the rates could do that, and 1914 saw the York rates at the highest level ever. It looked as if the party in power was no more capable of running the city 'efficiently' than its predecessor, and no less a person than the Lord Mayor had been going on about the level of rates, and how he would campaign for them to be reduced when he left office. In May of 1914 10,000 leaflets were issued calling a meeting to set up a York Ratepayers Association. Rhodes Brown attended and he became the Association's first president. Apart from anything else, this alone would have ensured that he did not get that vacancy on the aldermanic bench.

An air of desperation crept into York politics as the Tories realised, first of all that they had to implement reform measures, and then that they would inevitably lead to the rate increases which could bring another opposition group into existence. What could they do? They very cleverly, and sensibly, set up an enquiry into York government, (43) dropped a scheme to build a municipal golf course, and it seems that they might then have done a good deal with the Ratepayers Association over the Guildhall election. G.W. Halliday, a large ratepayer himself, was spoken of as a Ratepayers candidate, but when the nominations went in he had dropped out, leaving just the Tory in the field. (44) He was Henry Hopkins, of 37, Petergate who was closely connected with the York Trader's Association and the Master Builders' Association. Hopkins, it will be recalled, was Rhodes Brown's closest ally in the successful campaign against municipalising the city's gas undertakings and someone clearly acceptable to the Ratepayer's Association. (45) Rhodes Brown, incidentally, boasted about 'his' victory over gas municipalisation (and much else involving himself) when he addressed a meeting of the International Municipal Congress at the Anglo-American Exposition at Shepherd's Bush in July. (46)

The Tories, it seems, had bought themselves some time by setting up the York Corporation enquiry and doing a deal with the Ratepayers' Association over the Guildhall by election. Would it be enough, or would things develop in such a way that they were taken on by a new political grouping in November? It might well have been that the municipal elections then would have turned out to be as fascinating as those of 1913. But something happened to change everything. War broke out, and with it came a party truce.

Another problem for the York City Council in 1914 was the bill it was promoting in Parliament. The Liberals had been promoting such a measure when they fell from power, and this was rapidly altered to one of some 121 sections which was comprehensive in nature and would have enabled the Corporation to make a new street, improve others, and run trolley and motor buses, and make provisions regarding the electricity undertakings, the markets and the tramways. (47) There were other provisions and the Council very reasonably called citizens meetings to discuss them. At one of these a move to pull down part of the city walls was defeated and Wragge and E.P. Holmes were largely responsible for lowering the intended library rate. (48) The Corporation accepted these decisions, but met with tremendous hostility from the Theatre Royal's lessee and the cinema owners (a touchy lot at that time) who claimed that municipal concerts would harm their trade. Other members of the public saw that the bill could mean rate rises and it undoubtedly had something to do with the appearance of the Ratepayer's Association. 'Ratepayer' (who else) wrote a long letter to the papers and his remarks nicely sum up an attitude prevailing in York then. (49) He agreed with the freeing of Skeldergate Bridge, he said, but could anyone justify the spending of £1,600 or £1,700 on the library ? 'There are plenty of volumes to satisfy every demand' in York, Ratepayer went on, achieving an impressive degree of silliness, 'unless it be a few selfish cranks who want a few specialities of an expensive character to bolster up some pet theory about the tomatoes grown in the "Stone Age", or the ancient history of the faggosites, which were supposed to have destroyed the bacillae in the early stages of the "milky way", before cocoa was discovered.' Ratepayer revealed that he had worked in the November elections and said he had naturally hoped that the new Council would 'sweep out all those absurdities of the Progressive-Socialist party and promote a more beneficial state of things for the ratepayers'. Someone calling himself "ANTI-FADDIST" had a letter published in the same paper that printed Ratepayer's arrogant effort. He pointed to clause 42 of the bill which regulated the keeping of pigeons. The bill, he said, was anti working class. 'The present conditions of life for the average working man and woman admit of very little pleasure or enjoyment' he concluded. Few could have honestly disagreed with that.

Ratepayer was clearly a Tory, one of those who thought his party was letting the city down, and one of those who may well have taken part in the creation of the new Association which could have proved to be a force to be reckoned with in November. The bill he hated so much was introduced into Parliament in February and was opposed there by the NER, the Theatre Royal lessee and the cinema owners. In June it was before a select committee. It had not completed all its stages by the beginning of August.

Throughout June the papers carried more and more news items about troubles in the Balkans and the movement of troops in and out of York. At the end of the month the West Riding RGA (Heavy Battery) arrived back in York after a fortnight's training in Forfarshire. (50) A member of this unit was a young solicitor who had been commissioned 'on April Fool's Day', who was soon to be in Flanders (and who later became the city's coroner). (51) In July a detachment of the 1st Battalion of the East Yorkshire Regiment left for Llanidloes and over the August Bank Holiday weekend many Territorial soldiers from the city were in camp on Scarborough race course. There was nothing unusual in that, but on 25 July the *Press* told its readers that 'War Confronts Europe' and five days later it recorded that a detachment of the East Yorkshire Regiment had been sent with ball cartridge to mount a special guard on oil tanks at Grimsby. The same paper reported rumours that the Royal Scots Greys, stationed at York, had received instructions to be ready for mobilisation at any moment. On 3 August the *Press* told its readers that: the Scots Greys were still in York; that the East Yorkshires had all left; that the 3rd and 4th West Yorkshires had been issued with rifles; that all subsidised horses had been called in; that 2,000 naval reservists had entrained at York for Chatham; and that the army reserves were being called up. Just one day of peace remained; just one more day before the old order changed for ever. Banner headlines on 5 August were succinct. 'WAR DECLARED ON GERMANY' they read.

(END OF VOLUME ONE)

1. What might have been the city's first Chinese laundry opened just after the laundry girls' strike. This was the Singlee at 81, Goodramgate. *Press* 5 January 1914
2. *Ibid* 13 February 1912
3. This time the same plans were submitted as were put in a decade earlier with the site, this time, the one usually put forward in Albermarle Road.
4. *Press* 12 February 1913
5. *Ibid* 12 February and 11 March 1913
6. Compensation Authority records *op. cit.* pp 101-6
7. For example Peter Mullen a columnist in the *Press*. He headed one of his contributions 'Beware of glib answers to violent questions', said he had been 'studying the crime figures from when he was young', and concluded that 'there wasn't the violent crime' then that there was when he was writing.
8. Another quote from a Peter Mullen column
9. *Press* 31 December 1912. There was great trouble at the County Hospital at this time. See eg *Ibid* 10 April 1913 for report of an enquiry into the running of the establishment.
10. *Ibid* 3 February 1913
11. *Ibid* 30 December 1913, 3 January 1914. (There is a photograph of Wragge in the latter.)
12. *Ibid* 7 January, 2 March 1914
13. Eg *Ibid* 26 February 1914
14. *Ibid* 6 and 13 February 1914
15. *Ibid* 24 July 1914. The Castlegate Dispensary was opened in 1913. *VCH op. cit. p* 47. Figures for the period January 1913 to January 1914 (of TB cases in the sanatorium) can be found in an account of a meeting of the York Insurance Committee *Press* 27 March 1914.
16. Figures of empty houses in York were given for the period when NER men were moved away from York. Similar figures for the period now under discussion (1913 and 1914) can be found in a report in *Press* 22 April 1914.
17. *VCH* op. cit. p 297.
18. *Press* 22 November 1913
19. *Ibid* 6 January 1914
20. Wilkinson raised the question of how many children had been excluded from the special school for mentally defective children, and was told five or six. He went on to say that the Council's powers were very limited until the Mental Deficiency Act of 1913 became operative. Shipley urged the Corporation to take 'early action in order that the ... Act ... may become operative in York on the 1st April, 1914.'

21. There is a potted history of the Skeldergate Bridge in the papers which reported the Estates and Bridges Committee's decision to recommend freeing it of toll. See eg *Press* 23 December 1913.
22. *Ibid* 13 March 1914
23. *Ibid* 9 February 1914. A report of a meeting at the Lantern Cafe on 'The Economic Aspect of the Peace Movement.' The Society met fortnightly and prominent among its members were A.V. Iredale, J.W. Beal and J. Wardropper.Two of these were to become very prominent in York during the war.
24. *Ibid* 16 January 1914
25. *Ibid* 20 February 1914
26. *Ibid* 11 February and 3 March 1914
27. *Ibid* 30 January 1914
28. *Ibid* 11 February 1914
29. *Ibid* 5 May 1914
30. See eg *Ibid* 28 April and 1 May 1914
31. *Ibid* 10 March, and 7 April 1914. Hartley said the Mansion House was too expensive and that the Corporation should create a small parlour for the Lord Mayor in its stead.
32. *Ibid* 14 and 16 May 1914
33. *Ibid* 1 June 1914
34. *Ibid* 17 June 1914. A survey of postal workers wages at this time was the subject of some controversy, but it showed that five per cent of postmen working in the North East received wages of less than £1 a week. *Ibid* 13 February 1914.
35. *Ibid* 25 March 1914
36. *Ibid*
37. *Ibid* 20 April 1914
38. *Ibid* 16 January 1914
39. *Ibid* 27 June 1914
40. *Ibid* 1 May 1914, The new rates were to commence in August for the joiners and on 1 January for the others.
41. *Ibid* 6 June 1914. There were prolonged and acrimonious strikes at this time also among the musicians employed at the Theatre Royal and the Opera House.The dispute at the former started during a visit of the Carl Rosa Company. For a note on the eventual settlement see eg *Ibid* 30 March 1914. For the start of the troubles see *Ibid* 23 January 1914.
42. *Ibid* 16 February 1914. On the leafleting of the Theatre Royal see *Ibid* 20 May 1914.
43. *Ibid* 29 April 1914
44. At one stage it was said there would be three candidates for the Guildhall seat. The third was to be Thomas Curran, a member of the Board of Guardians.
45. On the elections see *Ibid* 7 and 21 July 1914.
46. *Ibid* 24 July 1914
47. *Ibid* 10 January 1914
48. *Ibid* 10 and 17 January 1914
49. *Ibid* 16 January 1914
50. *Ibid* 27 June 1914
51. This was Colonel Innes-Ware. There is a tape recording of his reminiscences contained in the oral history collection mentioned several times before held at Churchill College, Cambridge.

About the Author

Katie Wismer writes books with a little blood and a little spice (sometimes contemporary, sometimes paranormal...and sometimes even poetry.)

Be the first to know about upcoming projects, exclusive content, and more by signing up for her newsletter at katiewismer.com. Signed books are also available on her website, and she posts monthly bonus content on her Patreon.

When she's not reading, writing, or wrangling her two perfect cats, you can find her on her YouTube, Instagram, or TikTok.

tiktok.com/authorkatiewismer

patreon.com/katiewismer

instagram.com/katesbookdate

youtube.com/katesbookdate

goodreads.com/katesbookdate

amazon.com/author/katiewismer

facebook.com/authorkatiewismer

bookbub.com/authors/katie-wismer

CPSIA information can be obtained
at www.ICGtesting.com
Printed in the USA
BVHW072211310123
657545BV00002B/25